Hidden in Plain Sight

McMaster Divinity College Press
McMaster General Studies Series, Volume 15

Hidden in Plain Sight

Sam Goudie and the Ontario Mennonite Brethren in Christ

JAMES CLARE FULLER

Foreword by Thomas E. Dow

◕PICKWICK *Publications* · Eugene, Oregon

HIDDEN IN PLAIN SIGHT
Sam Goudie and the Ontario Mennonite Brethren in Christ

McMaster General Studies Series, Volume 15
McMaster Divinity College Press

Copyright © 2024 James Clare Fuller. All rights reserved. Except for brief quotations in critical publications or reviews, no part of this book may be reproduced in any manner without prior written permission from the publisher. Write: Permissions, Wipf and Stock Publishers, 199 W. 8th Ave., Suite 3, Eugene, OR 97401.

Pickwick Publications
An Imprint of Wipf and Stock Publishers
199 W. 8th Ave., Suite 3
Eugene, OR 97401

McMaster Divinity College Press
1280 Main Street West
Hamilton, ON, Canada L8S 4K1

www.wipfandstock.com

ISSN 2564-4408 (PRINT)
ISSN 2564-4416 (EBOOK)

PAPERBACK ISBN: 979-8-3852-2938-3
HARDCOVER ISBN: 979-8-3852-2939-0
EBOOK ISBN: 979-8-3852-2940-6

Cataloguing-in-Publication data:

Names: Fuller, James Clare.

Title: Hidden in Plain Sight : Sam Goudie and the Ontario Mennonite Brethren in Christ / James Clare Fuller.

Description: Eugene, OR: Pickwick Publications, 2024 | Series: McMaster General Studies Series | Includes bibliographical references and index.

Identifiers: ISBN 979-8-3852-2938-3 (paperback) | ISBN 979-8-3852-2939-0 (hardcover) | ISBN 979-8-3852-2940-6 (ebook)

Subjects: LCSH: Mennonites—Ontario—History.

Classification: BX8118.6.O6 F95 2024 (paperback) | BX8118.6.O (ebook)

11/15/24

Contents

Foreword by Thomas E. Dow | vii
Preface | xi
List of Abbreviations | xv

Introduction | 1

1. The Goudie Family Gets Established in Ontario | 13
2. New Mennonites and Other Revivalist Mennonites in Ontario | 24
3. The Young Sam Goudie 1866–1885 | 35
4. Elder Sam Goudie: Probationer and Pastor 1885–1897 | 51
5. The Maturing Goudie 1897–1905 | 100
6. Presiding Elder Sam Goudie 1905–1907 | 136
7. The Pentecostal Crisis 1907–1908 | 153
8. Who Left? Who Stayed? | 178
9. Meanwhile Back in Ontario: Picking Up the Pieces 1908–1912 | 208
10. The Great War of 1914–1918 | 228
11. A History and a Mission | 241
12. Friendly Visitors, Mennonite Unions, Holiness Affairs | 256
13. Conference Matters 1924–1933 | 264
14. Return to the Pastorate 1933–1940 | 284
15. Family and Last Things 1940–1951, 1957 | 297

Contents

Appendix A | 323
Appendix B | 325
Appendix C | 329
Bibliography | 335
Names Index | 349
Subject Index | 361

Foreword

JAMES CLARE FULLER HAS presented us with a very well-written, very well-documented account of the early history of what has become the Evangelical Missionary Church of Canada. Other denominational histories have been produced, but none in such rich detail and none dealing specifically with the life of one of the earliest founders and leaders, Samuel Goudie. Goudie made a tremendous contribution to the ongoing life of the church through the final years of the nineteenth and several decades of the twentieth centuries, but I venture to guess that almost no one today has ever heard of this man, much less knows of his significance. In these pages, Fuller has admirably addressed this problem and given us a biography to make us grateful for the service Goudie has rendered to this small Christian denomination and to the larger Kingdom of God.

I have been associated with and intimately involved in the life of the EMCC for over seventy years. I have been a pastor, missionary, Bible College professor, and president; I have given my life to God and to the church. I confess that much of the material in Fuller's book has come as new information to me. I have gained a great deal of factual information, which has renewed my appreciation for the church and the many men and women who steadfastly laboured to give the world a small but excellent denomination.

Several aspects of church life treated in detail I have found particularly interesting and personally edifying. One such aspect is in Fuller's treatment of camp meetings. Camp meetings were a part of the history of many denominations in the Christian world westward across North America. The MBiC certainly made good use of them. Fuller describes how they were organized in several areas of rural Ontario and describes how important and vital they were to the life and growth of the church. The book summarizes what went on in these meetings, and describes one camp in considerable detail, which I found most interesting. This was the Elmwood camp held in 1896. The thing that struck me as particularly interesting was the number of sermons preached during the period of the camp. Fifteen preachers are listed. In all 23 sermons were preached in the 8–9 days of the camp. What an opportunity for church members to get to know and hear the preachers of the district. Two of these fifteen preachers were women! And what grand fellowship for the people attending from various congregations.

I am glad old fashioned camp meetings were still in vogue when I was a young Christian. I remember Kitchener Camp meetings in the 1940s—large and small tents, the "Tabernacle" with sawdust floor, some shouts of "glory," some waving of handkerchiefs, good singing, powerful preaching, holiness emphasis. Later as I was asked to be Camp Evangelist on several occasions in Stayner, Mishewah, and Kitchener. What an honour. But instead of 15 preachers there were just 2 of us for one Camp at Stayner, Mark Bolender and I. I preached 18 times in 17 days, Mark the same! Camping is still an important ingredient in the life of the EMCC.

Another aspect of church life described in the book was the Protracted Meetings. These were days set aside each year for services every night of a week on the strong emphasis on revival and holiness preaching. If results were positive and interest did not flag, further nights would be added. Here was another opportunity for church members to receive biblical teaching and exhortation. In some churches today this has dwindled down to an hour on Sunday morning. Again I appreciated reading about the meetings because I became a Christian in one such campaign held in Sarnia in 1954. A visiting evangelist, special musicians, an emotionally charged atmosphere, and I bowed at an altar and said yes to Christ! Not many years later, I was asked to be the evangelist in several churches for their annual "week of special meetings." Nowadays few churches could count on sufficient numbers to make such meetings viable.

I could mention the section on the beginnings of a missionary society by the denomination, stories of the City Mission Workers involved in founding churches, beginnings of the movement toward providing education for pastors and leaders and then to the other topics so interestingly detailed. But, dear reader, reading the book is before you!

From earliest years women had a large place in the life and leadership of the church. They preached at annual conferences, in camp meetings, in local churches, and missions. There was little formal recognition by way

Foreword

of credentialing them, but they were not demeaned nor ignored. I recall district conference sessions when ordination of women was under discussion and extremely disparaging things were said about women preachers. Undoubtedly these individuals expressing such sentiments would have profited had they been aware of the female preachers in Clare Fuller's book.

Here then is a fine biography of a faithful and long-serving leader, Sam Goudie. A good story of where we have come from and the many we have to thank for our good heritage.

—*Thomas E. Dow*

Preface

WHILE RESEARCHING FOR THIS book, I was confronted with an impossibility. I laboured to recover the identities of dozens of otherwise faceless personnel recorded only as "L. Homes" or "a certain Mr. Bedingfield." However, when roaming through graveyard after graveyard, scrolling through genealogical websites or searching census pages to determine which "Mary Davidson" might be the one I am looking for (out of 148 others living in Ontario in 1891!), I have been impressed that there will still be multitudes of ordinary people I will never notice or find. The census missed them. Or they barely made it into ecclesiastical or municipal records, sometimes not even their births, deaths, or marriages. Mary Ann Wilson, first wife of New Mennonite preacher Peter Geiger, has no parents named in her marriage record, a bit like Melchizedek. These unnoticed people formed the bulk of church memberships, pouring the tea at congregational events and re-shingling the church building roof.[1]

Our age has been proud to attempt to recover these thousands of otherwise anonymous lives, which is all to the good. So while this "life and context" study focuses on an ecclesiastical leader, Samuel Goudie and his world, there is an unavoidable bias toward ministers and congregational officers. I do not like the categories "clergy and laity" because they suggest unbiblical distinctions. Nevertheless, the experiences of "full-time workers"

---

1. In a similar way, Katz, "People," 300, estimates that 95 percent of the citizens of Hamilton, Ontario appeared only in census, church records, or street directories in 1851. Even then, numerous people were missed by the census, and were "caught" only in some other random way, suggesting that still others passed through living in Hamilton without leaving a trace. Made in God's image, and the subject of God's redemption, they too are "precious in his sight." Similar are participants with our congregations. The various Canada census results, while marvellous helps for a book like this, also miss people I know were in Canada at those times, but somehow were missed by the returns.

draw them together, and their exploits naturally receive more attention in the documents of the organization. Someday someone needs to look at the lives of the regular members of the denomination: the Levi and Fannie (Raymer) Raymers, the Jacob B. and Catharine (Hipple) Shantzes, the Isaac and Nancy (Bowman) Pikes, just as has been done for Jacob Yost Shantz and his three successive wives, Barbara Biehn, Nancy Brubacher, and Sarah Sherk.[2] I am sure such studies would greatly qualify the impressions about the Mennonite Brethren in Christ Church one could get from this study. I deliberately fill the pages with information about people and places that are otherwise obscure. It may make following Goudie's story more difficult. Think of this book as a contribution to an *Encyclopedia* of the Mennonite Brethren in Christ Church, and therefore, of the Evangelical Missionary Church of Canada and the Missionary Church, Inc. of the USA. The maps are important as well: place matters at this scale.

As an abbreviation, I use "MBiC" throughout, even though the denomination used "MBC" in its literature. I do this for two reasons. One, in Mennonite studies currently, "MBC" is often interpreted as standing for the Mennonite Brethren Church, which is a fine church, but not the one I am writing about. Secondly, "MBiC" associates the church in a friendly way, I hope, with the Brethren in Christ ("BiC" or "BIC") and the Church of the United Brethren in Christ ("UB" or "UBiC"), some of the EMCC's nearest ecclesiastical brothers and sisters. In Canada, this latter church is now called the United Brethren Church in Canada. All churches using "Brethren" in their names are under pressure to drop it because it is now taken as excluding women, whereas, of course, in their earlier context it was intended to be inclusive, unifying, family-oriented and, they believed, biblical.[3] For various reasons the MBiC dropped their name in 1947 to become the United Missionary Church (UMC), and after a merger in 1969, became simply the Missionary Church and in Canada, the Missionary Church of Canada (MCoC). Currently, the Canadian branch of the denominational family is called the Evangelical Missionary Church of Canada (EMCC).

---

2. See Steiner's beautifully researched and written *Vicarious Pioneer*. Jacob Y. Shantz was a founding member of the MBiC. Jacob B. was one of J. Y. Shantz's sons. Farm diaries by Fannie Raymer exist for most of the years 1893–1907 (Raymer Family Collection). Her diaries can be put in the context of other nineteenth-century Ontario women's diaries by Hoffman and Taylor, *Much To Be Done*. The Pikes have extensive genealogies online.

3. Even in the course of my writing, the Brethren in Christ in Canada have changed their name to "Be in Christ Church of Canada."

Preface

There are numerous people to thank for their encouragement, memories, documents, and photographs, not all of which find a place here, but may in some future study. I certainly have forgotten some; please forgive me. Thank you all: Carol Blake, Kevin Blowers (archivist, Missionary Church Inc. Archives, Mishawaka, IN), Eleanor Bunker and her son Tom Bunker, Caleb Courtney, David Doherty, Tom and Lois Dow, Timothy Erdel, Kevin Flatt, Harvey Fretz, Charles Gingerich, Mildred James, Jim McDowell, Ed Oke, Donna Preston, John Quanz, Hugh Rendle, Ruth Scott, and Allen Stouffer. Several people who helped in research done some years ago have since died: Flora Barkey, Ella Chester, Glenn Gibson, Doris Hoover, Eileen Lageer, Ellis Lageer, Earl Pannabecker and Ward M. Shantz. I am thankful for the work of the late Hugh Hill, former classmate and EBC librarian for collecting and preserving the core of the Missionary Church Historical Trust materials, and the common delight we shared in the history of the Church. I gratefully acknowledge the permission of the trustees of the MCHT to use documents and photographs from its collection in this work. Other thanks are due to archivist Laureen Harder-Gissing and staff of the Mennonite Archives of Ontario at Conrad Grebel University College, for their expertise, equipment, and kindness in helping me use their vast holdings. Thanks also to Dan Schmalz of the City of Cambridge for help in finding Sam Goudie's brief school record in the Brewster Collection, the reference staff of the Kitchener Public Library for help in the Grace Schmidt Room of Local History, and Jim Craig, archivist of the Pentecostal Assemblies of Canada, Mississauga. Did not my heart burn within as we talked over the urgency and joy of caring for the records of Canadian church history?

A special thanks to Samuel J. Steiner for showing the way in so many lines of research and interpretation, and recognizing that the Mennonite Brethren in Christ Church existed when many pass by on the other side! Although uninvolved directly in this research I wish to add my appreciation to the late Dr. Ian S. Rennie and to Dr. C. Mark Steinacher, who taught Canadian Church History at Tyndale (then Ontario Theological Seminary) and McMaster Divinity College, respectively. My errors and lapses in using interpretive tools they taught me are not their fault. Thanks to Rev. Dr. Thomas E. Dow, PhD, DD, for supplying the Foreword. His energy in teaching Church History at Emmanuel Bible College was infectious, and not just to me. Finally, thanks to my wife and children for enduring the years I have been engrossed in this research and writing, snatching time from busy family life and dragging them to many cemeteries.

Preface

It is also necessary to accept that despite all the help of patient advisers and correctors, all errors of interpretation and fact are mine. I would appreciate hearing from those who know better on any matter herein. The life of Sam Goudie and his times has been surprisingly detailed and complex. Just as Susan Fisher Miller noticed about her study of American Mennonite evangelist John S. Coffman, Goudie "supplies leads to every subject" involving the Mennonite Brethren in Christ Church of his day.[4] I hope that by leaving traces of my sources all over the place, other investigators will follow and revise or if necessary, rebuild the reconstruction, correct the guesses and extend the reach of what they find here. I wish we could generate a whole school of Evangelical Missionary Church of Canada history studies from the 1830s on up.

Of all the wonderful history teachers I have had over the years, none matches my mother, Isabel Katharine (Oliver) Fuller, one hundred and one years old as I write this. Her memories of growing up on a farm at Maple in Vaughan Township, York County, and of the Anglicans, Methodists, and United Church of Canada congregants there, her work at the Anglican Mission at Moose Factory, courtship and life with our father, Ralph Fuller, and with him leading us to be grafted into the United Missionary Church in the 1960s, have enriched my life as well as that of my brothers and sisters, and now my children, too. I dedicate the work to her.

—James Clare Fuller
Kitchener, ON, Canada

---

4. Miller, "Coffman," 93.

List of Abbreviations

AEM	African Evangelistic Mission
AGC	Associated Gospel Churches
AIM	Africa Industrial Mission (now SIM)
AoG	Assemblies of God
b.	born
BD	Bachelor of Divinity
BiC	Brethren in Christ Church/ Be in Christ Church
BTh	Bachelor of Theology
Can NW	Canada Northwest Conference
C&MA	Christian and Missionary Alliance
CBC	Canadian Broadcasting Corporation
CCCC	Congregational Christian Churches in Canada
CMWS	City Mission Workers Society (Ontario)
CWC	Christian Workers Churches
d.	died
DD	Doctor of Divinity
Discipline	The Doctrines and Disciplines of the MBiC Church (various editions)
DMin	Doctor of Ministry
EBS/EBC	Emmanuel Bible School/College

List of Abbreviations

EMCC	Evangelical Missionary Church of Canada
EUB	Evangelical United Brethren
EUM	Evangelical United Mennonite Church
EvA	Evangelical Association
EvC	Evangelical Church
FM	Free Methodist Church
GAMEO	Global Anabaptist Mennonite Encyclopedia Online
GB	*Gospel Banner*
GC	General Conference
HFMA	Hephzibah Foreign Missionary Association
HMC	Holiness Movement Church
HRA	Heavenly Recruits Association
I&O	Indiana & Ohio Conference
IMA	International Missionary Alliance (later the C&MA)
KGT	Kitchener Gospel Temple
MAO	Mennonite Archives of Ontario, Waterloo, ON
MBiC	Mennonite Brethren in Christ Church
MBiC FMSGB	MBiC Foreign Missionary Society General Board
MCA	Missionary Church Association
MCHT	Missionary Church Historical Trust
MCI	Missionary Church, Inc.
MCoC	Missionary Church of Canada
MTh	Master of Theology
NM	New Mennonite Church of Canada West and Ohio
NRRO	Non-Resistant Relief Organization
NWT	Northwest Territories
PAOC	Pentecostal Assemblies of Canada
PE	Presiding Elder
PHC	Pentecostal Holiness Church

List of Abbreviations

QM	Quarterly Meetings
SIM	Sudan Interior Mission/Serving in Mission
TB	Tuberculosis
TBTS/ TBC	Toronto Bible Training School/ Toronto Bible College
ThM	Master of Theology
UB/UBiC	United Brethren (in Christ)
UCC	United Church of Canada
UM	United Mennonite Church
UMC	United Missionary Church
UMS	United Missionary Society
UOMB	United Orphanage and Mission Board
WCC	World Council of Churches
WCTU	Woman's Christian Temperance Union
WMS	Women's Missionary Society
YMCA	Young Men's Christian Association
YWCA	Young Women's Christian Association

Introduction

THIS BOOK HAD TO be written. I believe God did something through a *small society* of Christians, as Sam Goudie often called it, that is overlooked by Canadian church historians and largely forgotten by her own ecclesiastical children.¹ To God be the glory for all that is good recorded here. A scholar of the binational church, Jasper Abraham Huffman, admitted the church was "small . . . and unpopular."² True, we are talking about numbers of people in Canada that, in relation to its larger denominations (Methodists, United Church, Anglicans, Presbyterians, Lutherans, Baptists, and Roman Catholics) will seem minuscule—a population the size of a small town, scattered across the Dominion. No wonder many historians haven't bothered to say anything more than list it among Canada's denominations; the small ones are many and unmemorable, apparently. This

---

1. Some fine books on Christianity in Canada the reader may find useful include Walsh, *Christian Church in Canada*; Grant, *Church in the Canadian Era*; Rawlyk, eds., *Canadian Protestant Experience*; Murphy and Perin, eds., *Concise History*; Handy, *History*; Noll, *Christianity*. Note that most of them barely mention Mennonite or Holiness churches, and certainly not a small group such as the Evangelical Missionary Church in particular. According to the studies of Christianity in Ontario by Grant, *Profusion of Spires*; Westfall, *Two Worlds*; Gauvreau, *Evangelical Century*; or Mann, *Sect*, the situation is scarcely better in western Canada. Grant (*Profusion of Spires*, 212) notes the Mennonite Brethren in Christ (United Missionary Church) in Ontario, but he is unaware of the 1969 name change. Mann (*Sect*) names the MBiC once but seems unaware they were the pioneering group at Didsbury, Alberta.

2. Huffman, *Seventy Years*, 23.

book is about Sam Goudie but also about the Ontario Conference of the Mennonite Brethren in Christ that he served.

Some recent histories of Canada barely recognize religion as a category of history of the peoples of Canada, not to mention denominations.[3] This is a bias and a blindness of our times in Canada, justified by a worldview which despises "organized religion." Beginning as a branch of the Anabaptist movement of the Protestant Reformation, the church and members I am writing about were grandly uninvolved in the politics of their day, and they were overwhelmingly rural, during the period when Canada was moving from a rural to an urban population.[4] While locally they might show an entrepreneurial spirit in business,[5] in church life on public issues they only pronounced against alcohol and tobacco, saloons, gambling and dance halls. They left no opinion about Sir John A. McDonald or Sir Wilfrid Laurier or Reciprocity, suffragettes or CanLit. They did not often join anything remotely military or climb to the leadership of Canadian cultural organizations or power. I avoid arguing, however, that this church contributed "far beyond its size," or that members influenced Canadian society for good in hitherto unrecognized massive ways. Maybe they did, maybe they didn't. Jesus did not judge by size alone (Luke 21:1–4), though he was concerned for numbers in that he desired the "harvest" be preserved, not wasted. (Matt 9:37; 20:1–12).[6] Elder Sam Goudie's life and works and the church he served then, can be a probe to investigate the works and spiritual life of

---

3. Look through the index of, say, Bumsted, *Peoples of Canada*. "Roman Catholic Church" has five references, all to the church and social issues. "Anglican Church" has two pages out of 640 of text. Bumsted has written on religious history, but this major text bypasses it as part of the history of *peoples*, surely a decision that misleads students.

4. There were exceptions. Beniah Bowman (1886–1941) was at one time a MBiC preacher and at another, member of the Ontario Legislature for Manitoulin and later Member of Parliament for Algoma East. Rural population changed as follows: 84 percent (1861), 75 percent (1881), 63 percent (1901), 51 percent (1921), 46 percent (1941), and 30 percent (1961). In contrast, in 1966, Missionary Church of Canada membership was still 75 percent rural according to Motz, ed., *Reclaiming a Nation*, 57 (quoted in Gibson ["Urbanization," 3]). I have reservations about the reliability of Canada census statistics of many small Canadian denominations which Motz uses and have raised them with Canada census employees in specific cases. See the questions raised in Hiemstra, "Evangelicals."

5. For example, Jacob Y. Shantz in Berlin, the McNally brothers and Samuel Bowman in Blair, or Samuel Bricker in Port Elgin.

6. Those curious about influences on my writing will recognize a basic aim of Donald McGavran's "harvest theology." Some denominational statistics are reviewed in Appendix A.

Introduction

some evangelicals in Canada—were they faithful to the mission God gave them? This is not a concern of sociologists, political scientists or economic historians but a massively important question, nevertheless. They would have approved of John Wesley's instruction to his preachers, that their only business was to get people saved (adding "and sanctified"), whatever other good works they might do. We will see they did perform basic-level social ministries as we go along.[7]

The question comes to the churches, in particular, to the Missionary Church in the US, to the Evangelical Missionary Church of Canada and anyone in the evangelical traditions: How do we live faithfully to the Scriptures and to the Lord Jesus Christ today? How did they try to be faithful in the past? There are six or seven official versions of the histories of components of the Missionary Church tradition scattered through the last century, but so much has yet to be told and interpreted.[8] I will flag untold stories as we go along and make suggestions for further study. Understanding Goudie's context—the people and circumstances around him—should enrich our understanding of God's work in our times, too. Any account of their testimony should include an attempt to understand what they were trying to do.

In addition, where historians of other church traditions have touched on the Missionary Church tradition in Canada or the US, its mix of evangelical, Wesleyan holiness, Pietist, Keswickian, Mennonite, Pentecostal, and now charismatic traditions,[9] their efforts are appreciated. However, as stated

---

7. Although the MBiC opened city missions in the end of the nineteenth century, the church did not join the theological discussions of alleviating poverty and integration of immigrants of the major Canadian denominations (see Allen, *Social Passion*).

8. For histories of the binational denomination, see Huffman, ed., *History*; Storms, *History of the United Missionary Church*; Lageer, *Merging Streams*. For histories of the merging denominations, see Lugibihl and Gerig, *Missionary Church Association*; Jesske, *Pioneers*. The current Canadian church history is discussed in Lageer, *Common Bonds*.

9. The writings of Timothy Paul Erdel are of prime importance here (esp. "Evangelical Tradition" on the "Five Traditions" [i.e., Anabaptism, Pietism, Wesleyanism, Keswickianism, and Evangelicalism]). The MBiC section of the Evangelical Missionary Church of Canada viewed the Deeper Life/Keswick movement theology from a distance and even criticized it at times. The Missionary Church Association was more influenced by the Christian and Missionary Alliance version of Holiness which, at a risk of oversimplifying, taught victory over sin as a *counteraction* of the flesh, rather than *cleansing* of the heart's motives and restoration of the image of God stressed by Wesley and the Methodist Holiness movement. A. B. Simpson, founder of the C&MA (Christian & Missionary Alliance), thought he had a better, third way to holiness in the Christian life—suppression or eradication being the Keswickian or supposedly Wesleyan paths—which

3

in the introduction to the biography of Alexander W. Banfield,[10] there are enough errors of fact and sheer ignorance in others' accounts concerning this story that suggest we should not leave the history and interpretation of the Missionary Churches to them alone.[11] In several chapters this book will offer corrections to some accounts of the origins of Canadian Pentecostalism, for example. It is hard enough for those inside the denomination to get their own facts straight.[12] Some people reading the official histories think that they have come to a church that has never known splits. The truth is more complicated than that. Goudie was witness to two partings of the ways in his own lifetime in 1908 and in 1947.[13]

In the novel *The Go-Between*, the author Leslie Poles Hartley says, "the past is a foreign country." The analogy is accurate. The past has its uses, but first it must be understood for its own time. The past has led to us today, but it is possible the path had twists and turns that the ancestors in the denomination would not recognize as directions they intended. The teachings and activities of the Christians of that day who are our spiritual ancestors look familiar and strange at the same time. We might experience culture shock if we look closely. We must go on to understand them and their time, learn

---

could be called "habitation in Christ" (Sawin, "Fourfold Gospel," 21).

10. Fuller, *Banfield*, 7.

11. For example, both the Missionary Church and the Evangelical Church are invisible in Stackhouse, *Canadian Evangelicalism*. He is sampling, not surveying, Canadian Evangelicals. Mackey's entertaining and shrewd observations (*These Evangelical Churches*, 204–5) are a survey and at least note the two churches and the merged EMCC and manage only two inaccuracies. Note the judicious, brief, but already at press time, out-of-date comments of Hobbs and Hobbs, "Holiness Churches." Burkholder (*Brief History*, 188–96) makes a kind and conscientious attempt to be fair about the separation of the MBiC from the Mennonite Conferences. The two books by Epp, *Mennonites in Canada, 1786–1920* and *Mennonites in Canada, 1920–1940*, dismiss the United Missionary Church after its shift from the Mennonite fold. Miller (*Canadian Pentecostals*) makes no use of Missionary Church materials when commenting on history involving the MBiC church, as all Pentecostal accounts in Canada do until Stephenson, "Choosing the Right Metaphor."

12. This book notes a number of problems with the profiles of Ontario MBiC elders in Huffman's history of the church, uncorrected as far as I know since 1920. Timothy Erdel has reflected on other difficulties of writing institutional histories, especially official denominational histories (see "Pedagogy").

13. This book examines the 1908 schism in Ontario in detail. The Evangelical Association had its own split in 1891.

their language and culture as cross-cultural missionaries would, instead of automatically reinterpreting them to seem like ourselves.

I believe this biography will demonstrate that Sam Goudie's convictions and practice were fully within the Mennonite orbit. He promoted following Jesus, non-resistance and non-conformity. I expect to show also he was a convinced Wesleyan holiness preacher: he wanted to see people convinced to submit to God's Holy Spirit for a heart-cleansing experience received and maintained by faith. His evangelical concerns prove that the desired conversion experiences, and that full conviction of the truth of the Scriptures and that joyful obedience to them was normal for a follower of Jesus. He believed Jesus provided a full atonement for sin by his death on the cross. As a Wesleyan evangelical he was Arminian with respect to God's self-knowledge as primary over God's will, so in preaching his appeal was to the will and feelings of the sinner. He expected God's Spirit to be preveniently preparing hearts to be ready to respond to the grace of God in Christ. He was convinced that the Christian can have assurance of salvation. We will see he had further convictions accepted by his developing community.

Sam Goudie is an almost forgotten leader in the history of the church. Yet he was a presiding elder (often abbreviated as PE) of the Canada/Ontario Conference of the Mennonite Brethren in Christ Church from 1905 to 1933, a founding member, secretary, President or vice-president of missionary societies from 1905 until 1945, and chairman of the General Conference Executive Committee from 1912 to 1943.[14] He represented his church in inter-Mennonite consultations and organizations—in one of them from 1917 to 1944—sometimes as the chair. He was involved in almost every endeavour of his Conference and many in the binational denomination over many decades of the first half of the twentieth century.

Goudie can also be practically invisible in the local history level. Many local heroes are mentioned in Jean Barkey's *Stouffville 1877–1977*,[15] even those who left the town and made a name for themselves elsewhere, but while Sam and Eliza's sons Allan and Fletcher are named and appear in photographs, the parents who lived in Stouffville most of the years from 1907 to 1951 and 1957 are not mentioned. Sam was a denominational church

---

14. Following my plan to use period language generally, I hope no one will be offended if the gendered nouns show up in the sources. I do expand names wherever I can, whereas the records normally use initials and surnames only.

15. Barkey, ed., *Stouffville*.

leader for years, but while ministers who served a year in one church or another are named, Sam Goudie, never a pastor in Stouffville, though he frequently preached there, is not.[16] Similarly, this is true of references to the MBiC, United Missionary Church and the EMCC in local histories to the present. At times, it seems ignorance everywhere reigns.

THE MODERN CONTEXT

At the same time, I feel there has developed a debilitating ignorance of the theology, community, spiritual disciplines and testimony of the Church of those days in its own membership now. As one of Canada's Christian denominations, and practically a home-grown one at that, the Evangelical Missionary Church of Canada suffers from obvious handicaps. Many of these difficulties are not unique to the EMCC; they are shared with many small sister denominations, but they are real. These difficulties include the following:

1. They are relatively small and geographically thinly spread. Small groups in a mobile society always suffer from the dispersion of their members, even if they are zealous. Erosion occurs because when members moved for marriage or in search of economic advancement, in most of the country they found no congregations of the denomination to join. I call this "leakage."
2. Confusion and shame over the identification of the denomination. As one sign of this, even though the denominations have been recognized in the Canadian census since 1981 (as the Missionary Church and the Evangelical Church; from 2001, as the Evangelical Missionary Church), the crudeness of the census in recording the church name produces bizarre results. Self-identification by the one who fills out the census long form means that the church is improperly accorded hundreds of adherents even in provinces where they never have had any churches. Migrant populations do not account for all this strange count. Similarly, in areas where they had numerous adherents, the denominational name was avoided by many. Denominational identification has negative implications for a growing number of Christians.

---

16. Sam Goudie's brother Henry was named as the Presiding Elder, and he helped dedicate the 1903 MBiC Stouffville church building (Barkey, eds., *Stouffville*, 146; Sam is visible in the photograph spread across pages 146–47, showing the Canada Conference delegates and visitors to the Annual Conference held in Stouffville in March 1905, but he is not named).

Because they feel ambivalent about denominational identification, they use broader terms such as "Christian," "evangelical" or maybe the neologism "Christ-follower."

3. They feel intimidated and bewildered by Canada's cultural shift from a once dominant orientation which favored Christian religiosity (in 1901, 97 percent of Ontarians said they were Christians) to indifference or even hostility to public expressions of religion of any kind. As any other minority, they often wish they could just fit in and often achieve it at the expense of Christian witness.

4. As a small denomination with arguably high membership standards,[17] such churches have constantly seen the erosion of their membership gains. Partly this was because members could not satisfy the legalistic tendencies of, in this case, Mennonite and holiness practices and left. In addition, children were embarrassed by the odd practices of the parents such as washing the saints' feet and declined to identify by membership. In the present, it is possible that devalued standards have the same effect. Who cares enough to identify when there is no gain to be in or loss to be out?

5. Alongside this is an appalling ignorance of, or indifference to, the churches' histories. In this way, we fail to love brothers and sisters in Christ of the past. The result often is members make heroes of temporarily visible popular leaders from TV, radio, magazines and on-line. They champion the theology of musicians, media preachers, devotional writers and new movements not known in the community. Not that there could not be any good in them, but that they displace those with wisdom in the weakening community.[18]

6. The evangelical tradition (which pretends to despise tradition) has tended to despise theology. What we have reaped is inability to resist

---

17. Schaller, *Middle Sized Church*, 138. Schaller calls such churches "high-demand" churches.

18. In the EMCC, for example, numerous congregations fail to report their annual statistics to the national office, which was rare in earlier generations. EMCC national men's and women's organizations have collapsed in recent years; congregations often do not know their nearby fellow congregations; congregational financial support for denominational budgets continues to decline as a percentage of their local budgets and missions giving to missionaries outside the EMCC World Partners recognition system is increasing. Fewer pastors who are hired by local congregations have studied at denominational colleges. A smaller percentage of members attend the summer camps than was once the case.

incompatible teachings brought in and enthusiastically promoted which we once thought non-biblical, or at best, the choices of others, but not ours. Some denominations can barely self-theologize, having the thinnest of a theological training system in place. It has been nice to be an experience-oriented, warm-hearted community, but the cost will be that heads, and then "hearts" as well, evaporate.

7. As cultural assimilation grinds down the EMCC's biblical connectional Mennonite and Methodist tradition, they approximate a bland generic Christianity with an individualistic spirituality in a congregationalist church life.[19] And some want it that way. They are in danger of fulfilling Jesus' sentence on salt without taste.

8. As Canadian culture blasts us all with doubts about evangelism ("don't shove it down my throat," and "cultural genocide"), Jesus' call to repent and believe is set aside.

For a couple of generations, EMCC leaders have promoted several approaches to restore vision and vigor to the church, such as boosting Sunday schools (thank God the Baby Boom worked for them), assuming that God works best by consecrated men, or by mass evangelism, or by mass mobilization campaigns (for example, "Key 73" in 1973), summarizing the purpose of the church in tag lines ("Keep the Main Thing, the Main Thing" that is, evangelism), following church growth prescriptions, promoting natural church growth, prescribing for a healthy church, tagging anything with the word "missional," leading by coaching/mentoring or simplifying the denominational structure (for example, eliminating the districts and their superintendency). These may be doing good, even much good. Yet the Church experience currently is two steps forward and two steps back in terms of adding congregations to the EMCC community.

Historical studies on their own do not produce revival, but I propose to contribute what I have to denominational renewal, by way of historical recollection and reflection. A final step might be proposing bold biblical remedies, perhaps even re-appropriation in some instances.

---

19. Cressman, "Developing Confidence and Competencies," 42. Cressman describes the EMCC without discussion as "predominantly congregationalist." This is probably true, but in the beginning, it was not so. The shift has been driven by cultural assimilation and possibly by economic rationalization or personal disposition, rather than by communal and agreed-upon biblical and theological reflection.

Introduction

THE EMCC IS NOT ALONE

Besides maintaining membership in the Evangelical Fellowship of Canada which in 2023 included 46 member denominations, the EMCC is a part of the World Partners International, a fellowship in 2020 of about nineteen national movements and denominations.[20] The EMCC has several roots; in this book I will recall the Evangelical Church in Canada, begun in 1836; and the Missionary Church of Canada, which had organizational origins back to at least 1852. Both took root first in Ontario.[21] The Evangelical Association (itself nearly forgotten), a German-language Methodist denomination based in the United States that was organized in the early 1800s, sent missionary preachers to Ontario when it was still called Upper Canada. The New Mennonite Church formed after 1842, when Ontario was called Canada West. Although the churches have not merged, I will note the large role of the Church of the United Brethren in Christ in Canada (now called the "United Brethren Church in Canada") in shaping the MBiC. Interestingly, in 2005, there was a union attempt on the part of the United Brethren in the US with the Missionary Church. Perhaps it is to be regretted that the attempt fell short by a few percentage points.

Although I write mostly of the Canadian church, I can't forget that most of the EMCC's history to date has been part of what I learned from Mennonite archivist Samuel J. Steiner to call a "binational" church. The United Missionary Church tried to bring Conferences in Nigeria, Brazil and India into the North American fold ("World Headquarters" was on the building in Elkhart, Indiana) in the manner of the Free Methodists and other General Conference-style churches, but world trends ended that attempt at centralizing. Still, "How good and pleasant it is when brothers live together in unity!" (Ps 133:1). Nothing I write here is meant to drive away the brothers and sisters in the United States. Some years ago, I thought I saw a delightfully incongruous statement in a former Missionary Church *Constitution* about "fraternal" relations between "sister" churches and the "parent body." It is for that kind of exuberant family spirit that I write.

---

20. Brazil, Canada, Colombia, Cuba, Dominican Republic, Ecuador, Ethiopia, Haiti, India, Jamaica, Kenya, Malawi, Mexico, Nepal, Nigeria, Sierra Leone, United States, Venezuela, and Zambia. There are some shifting memberships, and some are associate members.

21. A useful visual aid on the EMCC streams is the chart by Brown, Brander, and Kuykendall, "Connecting through History."

Samuel Goudie joined the Mennonite Brethren in Christ (MBiC) church in 1885. He lived in and served that church all his life. During his last four years he saw the name changed to the United Missionary Church and the large Pennsylvania Conference taking its leave (formalized one year after his death), but apart from that, the denomination was stable. During his 66-year membership from 1885 to 1951, its binational membership grew from around 2,100 to 13,300. Year by year the increases did not seem much in the several Conferences making up the MBiC, and in truth many denominations grew far faster in the same period. Meanwhile, during Goudie's membership the Canada Conference, or Ontario Conference as it was known after 1907, grew from about 950 to 2,300 adult members, remembering that Ontario donated about 700 members along the way to start Conferences in Michigan and the Canada Northwest.[22] That is not sustained vigorous growth, as Glenn Gibson pointed out.[23] We will also reflect on that, seeking to add to thoughts from Everek Storms, Eileen Lageer, Glenn Gibson, Timothy Erdel, Charles Gingerich, James McDowell, and others.

Generally, I will use the terminology of the time I write about, not updating to the twenty-first century; for example, not speaking of district or region when "Conference" is the language which members in the nineteenth century and first half of the twentieth century used; "presiding elder" (PE), instead of "district superintendent" or "regional minister;" "protracted meeting" or "revival" as the self-description, not "crusade." It will take some getting used to and will sometimes be repetitious as I try to connect old and new. The risk is that some readers will find the past only puzzling, but mine is a deliberate exercise to retrieve the past on its own terms first. The past *is* a foreign country before it is a familiar country.

NOTES ON SOURCES

Samuel Goudie's public life and labors are recorded. Goudie's life was so bound with the working of the Mennonite Brethren in Christ Church, that the proceedings of the various Conferences—General Conferences as well as the Canada/ Ontario Conferences—outline his life work. The pages of the denominational magazine, the *Gospel Banner*, peppered the year with

---

22. Gingerich ("Experiment") is an excellent study of the Canada/Ontario Conference which rightly includes the New Mennonite Church (1849–1875). As we will see, the Evangelical Association/Church and the Mennonite Brethren in Christ/MCoC touched in numerous informal ways.

23. Gibson, "Methods," 7.

INTRODUCTION

Goudie's reports and articles. This church paper, a typical small denominational magazine, is a treasury of information about the people, activities, opinions and teaching of the Church from 1878 to 1969. Issues of the *Gospel Banner* are now best preserved though incompletely on microfilm (accessible, for example, in Ontario at Conrad Grebel University College in the Mennonite Archives of Ontario) and in paper collections in Indiana at Bethel College, Mishawaka, and in Ontario in Elmira, ON. Some early years in paper are complete in the David Sapelak Fonds in the MAO.

Basic data about pastoral assignments ("stationing") must be collected from the *Conference Journals* of the Annual Conferences, originally published in the *Gospel Banner*, but from 1898 published as separate journals. Ordinarily, I do not footnote this basic and public information of who went where when.[24] The Missionary Church Historical Trust preserves the "Minutes of the Ministerial Conventions of the MBC Church, 1917–1948," according to which Goudie presented essays ten times and commented on others' essays frequently, though the content of his comments were rarely recorded.[25] The Everek R. Storms Collection at the Missionary Church Archives, Mishawaka, Indiana, contains some correspondence by or to Sam Goudie in his various official capacities. The Mennonite Archives of Ontario at the Milton Good Library (Conrad Grebel University College, Waterloo, ON) has records which connect with Samuel Goudie or his brother Henry, but especially in the archives of the Non-Resistant Relief Organization (1918–1965) with which Goudie was closely related for twenty-six years. Yet these are not all: some of Goudie's own pastoral records and pastoral diaries for some years were preserved by Goudie's granddaughter Eleanor (Goudie) Bunker which tally the visits and conversations of a minister's career.[26] Her son Tom Bunker has fleshed out Goudie family genealogies

24. Some of this data was organized mainly for the years 1920 onward by Lageer in an unpublished project given various names. He did not include probationers and helpers, nor the city mission workers' stationing and concentrates 1920 to 2005.

25. If there were earlier minute books, they are lost or destroyed. Activities of the Ministerial Convention before 1917 were reported to some extent in the newspaper *Gospel Banner*. After the second World War, the character of the conferences changed radically; it became like talks by professional communicators, not self-education of the licensed workers. The conferences then ceased altogether. The UMC/MCoC/EMCC has been trying to recreate this kind of forum ever since.

26. Eleanor Bunker Family Collection (the Pastor's Diaries cover 1902, 1903, 1904, 1907, 1908, and January to June of 1912. The Pastor's Year Books cover 1886–1894, 1893–94, 1894–1895, 1895–1896, 1897–1898, 1898–1899, 1900–1901, 1901–1902, 1902–1903, 1904–1905, and 1915–1923; the years 1896–1897 and 1903–1904 are missing or never produced).

immensely by his research, a copy of which is kept at the Grace Schmidt Local History Room at the Kitchener Public Library Central Branch. Mrs. Bunker has also helped by her book of *Memories* written for her family, which includes memories of her grandparents, especially helpful to add at least something to our impressions of the elusive Eliza Jane (Smith) Goudie. Lastly, publications of the Waterloo Historical Society and Elizabeth Bloomfield's series of Waterloo County history studies provide some context for the Goudie family's life in Waterloo County, even though rarely noting the family by name.

Genealogical sites on the internet have been extremely helpful in tracking down the Goudie relations and colleagues, though errors lurk there. I have turned to Canada census returns online from Library and Archives Canada over and over. Local histories and church histories have been frustrating in their tantalizing awareness of people, times and places that only local knowledge preserves, at the same time displaying ignorance of the significance of that knowledge to the wider picture of history.

1

The Goudie Family Gets Established in Ontario

IN 1951, THE YEAR of Samuel Goudie's death in Stouffville, York County, ON, McClelland and Stewart sold a novel called *High Bright Buggy Wheels* by Luella Creighton on the streets of Toronto.[1] Luella (Bruce) Creighton was born in Stouffville and raised there and in Winnipeg, MB. Her stepmother, a Stouffer of Stouffville, was a woman who, according to Luella's daughter Cynthia, "stood at the harsh end of the Mennonite spectrum,"[2] who decided Luella's easy-going Methodist ways were ungodly and apparently sought to transform her stepdaughter into her idea of a moral young woman. The attempt was extremely distressing to the girl. In her first novel, over thirty years later, Luella Creighton imagined a Mennonite girl called Tillie Shantz growing up in a fictional surrogate Stouffville called Kinsail and being torn between the strict ways of the Mennonite life and the freer ways of "the city." Tillie was equally torn between a sober Mennonite boy, Simon, and a city friend with interests in music and horse racing called George Bingham. George wins out, but his Tillie never quite drops all the Mennonite ways.

"Shantz" was the fifth most common Mennonite surname in Waterloo County, though rare in Stouffville. For her young Mennonite suitor, Luella Creighton strangely chose a surname that was actually Scottish, and borne by only *one* Mennonite family in the real Stouffville: "Goudie." Why Luella chose this name for Simon, Tillie's extreme "sinner-hating sectarian" suitor,

1. Flood, "Introduction," iii.
2. Flood, "Introduction," iv.

may never be known. It certainly doesn't speak well for the one family that she might have known in the years she actually lived in Stouffville as a teenager, and maybe of some members with whom she went to high school. There were several kinds of Mennonites in the Markham and Stouffville area, but the Goudies belonged to the Mennonite Brethren in Christ Church. This chapter explores the background of this Goudie family, but it does not take place in Stouffville at all. The Canadian public liked Creighton's story; the CBC even turned it into a Stage 52 radio play. Reviewers at the time thought Luella Creighton was fair and appreciative of her fictional Mennonites. Samuel J. Steiner recently said however that Creighton's portrayal of Mennonites "[d]escribes no discernible group in Ontario."[3]

This first chapter introduces the real family of David and Nancy Goudie, Samuel Goudie's parents, and how they settled in Waterloo Township, Waterloo County, Canada West (Ontario). Although the Goudies from Scotland were Presbyterians, David Goudie led his family into a major immigrant community in Waterloo, the German-speaking Anabaptists (Mennonites and Tunkers) from Pennsylvania.

IMMIGRATIONS

With the British conquest of New France in 1759–1760, a vast new territory was potentially opened to British colonization, but many steps remained before Europeans in any numbers appeared in this colder and less accessible land than in the thirteen southern colonies. The American War of Independence encouraged many loyal subjects of the British Crown to go north, and when the area which became Upper Canada was separated administratively from Lower Canada or Quebec in 1791, settlers saw the area as desirable. The Crown attempted to extinguish native control over traditional lands with an appearance of lawful treaties, freeing lands for grants and surveys for legal titles in some kind of orderly manner.[4] The

---

3. Steiner, "Review." Interestingly, two copies of Creighton's book were left behind in Nigeria by Canadian missionaries of the MBiC, surviving now in college libraries of the UMC of Africa. The story must have held significance for some readers in the mission. "Mennonite" officials named in the novel included such names familiar in the MBiC as Bricker and Reesor.

4. I use the term "appearance" because, in practice, the administrators and courts of Canada trampled on the rights and humanity of the First Nations (see Steiner, *In Search of Promised Lands*, 64–66; Flanagan, "Aboriginal Title"). The ill treatment of First Nations by Canada is finally getting needed attention.

relation of these Mennonites to Canada's First Nations and their lands is just beginning to be explored.[5]

The Swiss-South German Mennonite settlement of Ontario (a portion of the "Pennsylvania Dutch") has been told frequently and in great detail,[6] and colonization by various communities of American-born migrants, plus English, Irish, Scots, Germans (including Lutherans, Roman Catholics, Amish and later "Russian" Mennonites) and others has also been well described. It is somewhat bizarre that the Goudies were not German; actually the Goudie story concerns a *Scottish* Mennonite family.

DAVID GOUDIE MARRIES: SARAH FATHERS

What brought together in holy matrimony an eighteen-year old young woman living probably about 100 kilometers south of Waterloo County, and a twenty-five-year old Scottish-born man from Wellington County on June 17, 1841? These things happen all the time, but they are still amazingly random in appearance. Sarah Fathers—English in origin simply to guess by her name, as were others with the "Fathers" name in Haldimand County—may have expected nothing but the strenuous life of a settler's wife, as many teenage wives did in the first half of the nineteenth century in Upper Canada. According to Tom Bunker's genealogical work, "Sarah was one of eight children born at Marcham, Berkshire, England to stone mason Joseph Fathers (1792–1874) and Elizabeth Copas (1792–1861) and immigrated to Canada with her family in the early 1830s."[7]

Perhaps Sarah's husband, David Goudie, first met her while he was a farm laborer, or she a domestic on a farm, or perhaps they met at a wedding at a third location. He spoke as would a Scotsman born at Ballantrae, Ayrshire (May 28, 1816), having come to Canada with his family in 1828 at twelve years old, she as an English-born girl (October 16, 1822) with whatever accent her community west of London gave her. Apart from that

---

5. Steiner, *In Search of Promised Lands*, 64–73. Steiner notes that E. Reginald Good has been writing about Mennonite relations with Canada's First Nations.

6. See, for example, Reamon, *Trail*; for the Pennsylvania Germans, see Eby, Weber, and Snyder, *Biographical History*; Burkholder, *Brief History*; Epp, *Mennonites in Canada, 1786–1920*, Steiner, *In Search of Promised Lands*; see also Reid, ed., *Scottish Tradition*; Bassler, "German Canadians"; Akenson, *Irish in Ontario*; Dunae and Woodcock, "English Canadians."

7. Bunker, *Hugh Goudie (Gouldie) Family*, 5–6. Since 1974, Marcham has been part of Oxfordshire.

there seems to be no other news about her except the following, which is about a loss.

The Goudies may have had a family history stretching back through 400 years in Ayrshire, Scotland as Irvin Bricker claimed.[8] David's parents, Hugh Goudie and Jane Ayre (or Aird), were married in 1811, in Scotland. Hugh, it is claimed, was born in Ayrshire, a region, like an Ontario county, on the southwest coast of Scotland. Hugh and Jane may have thought cheap land in Canada sounded better by 1828 and made the move to Upper Canada.[9] They settled just to the east of what became the city of Guelph, Ontario, the year after its "first tree was cut." By 1830 he had one acre cleared, forty-nine acres wild, "with four males and two females in the household."[10] Bunker found that five of Hugh and Jane Goudie's relatives/ daughters at marriage settled near Galt (a place with many Scottish settlers south of Waterloo). The fact that rent payments on half of the Guelph farm ceased about 1833, and the rest in 1843, and others took up the land, is evidence that the older Goudie couple perhaps moved to the Galt area after a few years. That could also account for the farm work David did in Waterloo and the later connection with the Wanner family, northwest of Hespeler. To make Goudie household ends meet, young David, one of seven children, went to work on Mennonite farms in Waterloo Township starting with three and a half years for Jacob "Yoch" Schneider, a Mennonite patriarch in Waterloo County, near Bloomingdale (now part of Woolwich Township).[11] Jacob Schneider had bought 3,000 acres of land from the Beasley Tract and sold off to other Pennsylvania Mennonites who followed him. Later David worked for a Mr. Vance,[12] and finally John Groh (a Tunker) near Hespeler. In other words, he spent years of his adolescence working with "Pennsylvania

---

8. Bricker, "History," 20–37.

9. He was born on June 12, 1792, likely in Renfrewshire, according to Tom Bunker, and died in 1874 on his son David's farm in Waterloo, ON, when Sam Goudie was seven or eight. Jane was born in 1792 and died in 1855, also on the farm, before Sam was born. Bunker gives their wedding date as August 24, 1811, at Eastwood, Renfrew, Scotland, but differs in some details with Bricker's account.

10. Bricker, "History," 31. According to Bunker (*Hugh Goudie [Gouldie] Family*, 114), Hugh Goudie first leased part of Lot 1, Concession 3, Division C of Guelph Township from the Canada Company; that is, he was the first European on the land in 1829.

11. All of the former Waterloo Township in Waterloo County has been annexed to the city of Kitchener.

12. It was possibly John Vance whose son Archibald and wife are buried at Wanner Mennonite Cemetery.

Dutch" Mennonites in Waterloo Township and doubtless learned to speak German from them.[13]

Where the couple David and Sarah first settled, I do not know. On May 18, 1842 however, Sarah, now just nineteen, gave birth to Emaline (Emily) Goudie. By August, Sarah was a dead young wife at Cayuga, Haldimand County, a too common occurrence, and still common in majority world lands. I have visited dozens of cemeteries over the years, looking for relatives or subjects of research. It can be sad to walk in Ontario pioneer cemeteries. Here and there, a row of young children lie buried near their parents' gravestones. All too frequently, you see young first wives buried with dates sometimes close to the date of the death of a child.[14]

DAVID GOUDIE MARRIES AGAIN: NANCY WANNER

David did what many a grieving young farmer husband with young children did in nineteenth-century Ontario, he found another woman to marry after a fitting mourning period. The woman he chose was another eighteen-year old, Nancy Strycher Wanner (born February 27, 1825), from a Mennonite family with at least seven girls, just north of Hespeler in Waterloo County. They were married on December 18, 1843, in the same year Nancy's older sister Catharine married David Pannabecker, from a farm just east in Puslinch Township in Wellington County. Two years later, Nancy's father Tobias died, at fifty-four. He had been injured in a tree cutting accident and walked with a wooden leg he had carved himself. Tobias had also been a teacher for a while at the Doon Log School, one of the first five teachers in Waterloo County.[15] Two years after his death, part of the farm was split up and the two sons-in-law rented, and later bought from the Tobias Wanner estate, lands on the east side of the large farm, both touching the Speed River.[16] Nancy's uncle John continued to work a large farm to the west, which enclosed the Wanner Meeting House just south of Fisher's Mill. In 1861, David Goudie's farm was 90 acres and Pannabecker's

---

13. Eby, Snyder, and Weber, *Biographical History*, 714.

14. People bearing the "Fathers" surname in nineteenth-century Ontario lived in Haldimand County, but a generation later than Sarah. Several children of Owen and Elizabeth Fathers are buried at the South Cayuga Cemetery in Haldimand County. Owen was born in 1826, a younger brother of Sarah, according to genealogical work of Tom Bunker.

15. "Schedule 'B.'"

16. Panabaker, *Barefoot Farm Boy*, 9. Pannabecker descendants spelled their name in various ways. This Cornelius was a son of David Pannabecker.

was 77 (later increased to 170).[17] All these farms were just north of the village of Hespeler, in the southeast corner of Waterloo Township. The Goudie farm was somewhat hilly, underlain by dry whitish dolomite rock, which in the Pannabecker section at least, formed cliffs along the Speed River and even some overhangs that could be called caves. David Pannabecker had a farmhouse built of stone in the 1860s. At some point (around 1856), a railway from Guelph cut along the west side of the river down to Hespeler, Preston and Galt. These farms are covered with suburban housing now, and the one-and-a-half-story Pannabecker House, a Heritage building, is surrounded by new architecturally alien houses. The original wooden Goudie farmhouse has not survived, and the stone one burned in the 1960s.[18]

Nancy Wanner's family is well documented compared to Sarah Fathers', thanks to the extensive genealogical work and ethnic consciousness of the Mennonite settlers of Waterloo County. Ezra E. Eby in particular inquired with diligence into the Pennsylvania-Dutch ("Deutsch," that is, German) families who so extensively settled Waterloo County and published in Berlin a treasury of genealogy called *A Biographical History of Waterloo Township and other Townships* in 1895 and 1896.[19] Supplements in 1931 by Joseph B. Snyder and in 1971 by Eldon D. Weber extended the value of this collection of family lore. When combined with all the tools of census, land registry and newspaper notes, many of them now online, nineteenth-century Waterloo has good coverage for Mennonite genealogy.

Nancy's parents were both born in Pennsylvania. Tobias W. Wanner was born in Lancaster County (b. March 16, 1790; d. January 28, 1845); her mother Catharine Strycker, in Cumberland County (b. March 17, 1798; d. May 21, 1882). The families had immigrated to Canada together in 1810, and their farms were, at least in 1861, kitty-corner to each other in Waterloo Township. Tobias' father Henry Wanner, and Catharine's father Arnold Stricker, had bought their acreage in 1810 straight from Richard Beasley, the notorious land holder whose mortgage problems had held up Mennonite settlement in Waterloo for some years.[20]

17. Heritage status was designated in 1987 (see "Schedule 'B'"). Bloomfield and Foster, *Families and Communities*.

18. Bunker, *Hugh Goudie (Gouldie) Family*, 58. Bunker invited Goudie descendants for a reunion in 2016 at Cambridge, ON; Hill, "Goudie's Descendants." Judging by the photographs, the limestone and fieldstone Pannabecker and Goudie buildings were practically identical, typical Pennsylvania Mennonite Georgian houses.

19. Eby, Snyder, and Weber, *Biographical History*.

20. Bricker, "History of Waterloo Township."

In common with numerous first-and second-generation young farm wives in nineteenth-century Ontario, Nancy bore many children—in her case, ten sons, without any daughters. Sarah Fathers' Emily grew up on the farm, and married a Wanner neighbor, Samuel (though he spelled his surname "Warner"), son of George M. Wanner.[21] Emily married Samuel on January 10, 1865 in Waterloo. In the 1890s they were farming in Colbourne Township in Huron County and had two boys by then, David and George, according to Ezra Eby. There was also a daughter who reached adulthood, and three children dying as infants.[22] Samuel Goudie visited them when he was the pastor at nearby Port Elgin in the 1890s.[23] Emily died in 1909, and Samuel in 1929.[24]

Two of Nancy's sons died early, too, including her firstborn, a boy named Benjamin (b. October 9, 1844) who lived nearly two years, and Tobias, born on April 19, 1858, living only 23 days. All the rest reached adulthood, married and raised families, though none of them with as many children as their parents.

THE RELIGION OF THE GOUDIE SONS

The Wanner and Goudie families could attend "Wanner's meeting house," a building erected on land donated by Uncle Henry Wanner Jr., a brother of Tobias. On the Sundays when no meeting was scheduled for Wanner's, they might travel to Cressman's meeting house north at Breslau, Schneider's at Bloomingdale beyond that if they started in good time, or Hagey's, about five kilometers south toward Preston. Did David become a Mennonite on marrying Nancy? How did they meet, after all? David's years working for Waterloo Township Mennonites probably gave him an opportunity to know the Wanner family. In the 1851 census of Waterloo Township, David and family are listed as Mennonites, but his parents, Hugh and Jane, retired but living on David's farm, continued to report themselves as "F. Presbyterians," that is Free Presbyterians, who dissented from the establishment policies of the Kirk of Scotland in 1843. John Goudie, a thirty-eight-year-old sailor noted in the same census as part of the household, was also

---

21. Samuel's mother, as Emily's, had died soon, two months after giving birth. So, Samuel was raised by his aunt and uncle, Frances (Fanny or Veronica Wanner) and Henry Strycher.

22. Bunker, *Hugh Goudie (Gouldie) Family*, 48.

23. Eleanor Bunker Family Collection (see the 1893 yearbook).

24. Bunker, *Hugh Goudie (Gouldie) Family*, 146–48.

counted as a Presbyterian (cf. 1851 census of Waterloo Township).[25] The first Presbyterian church in Hespeler, St. Andrews, was not organized until 1855, so David's parents would have to be patient or travel farther afield for Presbyterian services in English when they could.[26]

The Mennonite orientation of the David Goudie family is told by the marriages the young men formed; however, the Mennonite identity was not fixed in stone:

1. Second-born John (b. September 30, 1846) married Margaret Cober on August 9, 1870 and joined her church, the Tunkers, known in Ontario as the Brethren in Christ after 1933, a German-speaking Anabaptist group. The Waterloo Tunkers, though organized in 1833 as a congregation, erected no building for themselves for worship until 1901–1902 at Rosebank, southwest of Berlin in Wilmot Township. However, Tunkers in the Waterloo/Puslinch town line area helped construct and share a Union Church building in Puslinch with Mennonites, the MBiC, and German Baptists from 1875.[27] John and Margaret moved to and farmed at Burnside, Lapeer County, Michigan, some time in the 1890s.

2. David W. (b. September 12, 1848) married Maria Holm (1851–1893) from a nearby Tunker farm family the same day John married Margaret. David was ordained a deacon in the Mennonite Brethren in Christ in Toronto in 1909 where he had lived since at least the early 1890s. His second wife, Martha (Pike) Reesor, (b. 1841) was a Markham MBiC widow, whom he married on December 26, 1894 in Markham.

3. Henry (b. January 16, 1851) was converted in the Mennonite Church during special meetings under Daniel Wismer in 1870 (more of this later), but baptized by Daniel Hoch of the New Mennonite Church about 1871 somewhere around Hespeler. His first wife Sarah Wildfong, whom he married on October 24, 1872, came from a neighboring Mennonite farm family. Henry, who became a minister in the MBiC, could preach in English or German.

---

25. David had a brother John. The census seems to have confused the age of John with his twenty-three-year-old wife Sarah Ann.

26. Ambrose, *Waterloo County Churches*, 54. A Presbyterian church in Guelph began about in 1835. A closer Presbyterian congregation was begun 1852 at Doon across the Grand River. Tunkers (Brethren in Christ) in the area met in homes of members until 1875 when the Union building at Puslinch was built.

27. Chester, "History of the Puslinch Community Brethren."

4. Isaac (b. June 26, 1853), identifying himself as a Methodist, married Susannah Witmer on May 16, 1883, from another Hespeler-area farm and they worshipped at first with the Tunkers (occasionally called Dunkards).[28] Susannah's father, Joseph Witmer, was a locally respected cabinet maker, and her parents retired to Isaac and Susannah's home in Hespeler in later years.[29] Isaac became a salesman and with his son Arthur R. Goudie developed a grocery and then a department store in Kitchener that lasted for two generations on King St. (1925–1988).

5. Abraham (b. February 1856), also identifying himself as a Methodist, first married Lydia Snyder from a Freeport United Brethren in Christ family on April 11, 1879 and worshipped with the UBiC church (a German Methodist, that is, a revivalist group) when living in Berlin. They farmed at Verona Mills, Michigan, in the 1890s. They returned to Ontario in 1905, with Lydia not well, and she died on March 21. By 1911, remarried after Lydia's death to a widow named Frances Benson on December 31, 1907,[30] he continued living in Toronto and the family identified itself as "Methodist" in the 1911 Canada census.

6. James (b. May 22, 1860) married Lydia Snyder's sister Caroline "Carrie" Helena Snyder (1859–1909) as Mennonites on August 3, 1881. They identified as United Brethren in 1891 and though he is buried at Wanner Mennonite burial ground, he and his children's religion in 1911 was also "Methodist." He had farmed much of his life near Chicopee, Waterloo Township.

7. Jacob (b. September 17, 1863) married Rebecca Hembling, the daughter of a Mennonite deacon from Woolwich Township who supported the Reforming Mennonite movement in the 1870s. Jacob followed his parents to near Breslau (where the international airport is now) when they moved there about December 1879. In the census of 1891 Rebecca was a "domestic" on the farm next to where the Goudies were living, and interestingly, Jacob and Rebecca got married the next year and settled in his parent's house. In 1911 they were still living there

---

28. Canadian laws about military exemptions used the term "Tunker" for the Brethren in Christ. So, it was important for the BiCs to make use of the term. Outsiders to the BiC in Ontario sometimes called them Dunkers or Dunkards, which was a name for members of the Church of the Brethren, which did not organize in Ontario.

29. Good, "Joseph Witmer."

30. Eleanor Bunker Family Collection (see the January 1 entry of his 1908 diary).

with their three children. They continued to list "Mennonite" as their religion, possibly attending the Breslau MBiC.

It was a trend of many Mennonite children in Waterloo in the nineteenth century, except for Old Order Mennonites, to leave the church of their ancestors. Of course, this habit is not confined to nineteenth-century Mennonites. One reason is, as South African Pentecostal David DuPlessis said, God has no grandchildren. Others went to the English-language revivalist churches (the Methodists especially) or to the German Methodist groups (the Evangelical Association or the United Brethren in Christ). It was also a custom for the youngest son to inherit the family farm, and for the older sons to move on to new farms or occupations. This is contrary to the impression I had growing up, assuming succession was as in the English monarchy, or in the Bible, where the eldest received two shares of the inheritance and probably the family lands. Daughters either married nearby or an unmarried daughter cared for the parents. Emily, of course was long since married, and there were no other daughters. Elizabeth Bloomfield tracked this wandering habit in her book *Waterloo Township through Two Centuries*.[31] The elder Goudies left the Hespeler farm in 1879 when Jacob and Sam were only 16 and 13. In 1890, five of the brothers were noted in a Farmers Almanac as farming in Waterloo Township, two (Abram, Isaac) and father David, on "ub [Upper Block] lot 116" near Breslau, and Henry and James on "bf [Broken Front] lot 1" near Preston.[32] Soon afterward, David W. moved to Toronto and Abram to Michigan. David Sr. died in 1896. Sam, the youngest son and his wife Eliza were caring for his blind mother briefly in 1901. Sam Goudie's diaries show that their mother was in Jacob and Rebecca's house from later in 1901 to her death in 1906.

As for the Goudie brothers' religious pilgrimages, a factor for them might be that, though married into Mennonite and Tunker families, the fact remains that they were "Scotch" as they usually reported on the census returns. One wonders why none of them returned to the Presbyterian Church. The boys may not have felt accepted in the Wanner church. They may have felt more accepted in the churches of their wives or were assimilating to English-language Methodism. David W., Henry and Sam all had definite conversion experiences which took them to the MBiC, and so their affiliation was more secure. There is another curious fact that many

---

31. Bloomfield, *Waterloo Township*, 220–24. A wider view of Canadian settler mobility is presented in Bumsted, *Peoples of Canada*, 108–11.

32. Newcombe, "Among the Farmers."

of the numerous Waterloo Wanners counted in one census (1881) reported themselves as having "No Religion." Some Wanners in Waterloo Township were Roman Catholics, perhaps not related to Henry and Catherine Wanner from Pennsylvania.

Finally, on August 11, 1866, a year after big sister Emily was married and a year before the Confederation of three colonies of British North America (Canada consisting of Upper and Lower provinces, New Brunswick and Nova Scotia), David and Nancy Goudie had one more baby, the subject of this book. Samuel Goudie was born.

2

New Mennonites and Other Revivalist Mennonites in Ontario

IN THIS CHAPTER, WE will get acquainted with some of the diversity in the Mennonite "house" of Ontario and indicate how the Goudie brothers fit into the story.

The Mennonite world of Ontario in the nineteenth century was not a sealed-off church community as some think of Old Order Mennonites now.[1] Oddly there were, strictly, no "Old Order Mennonites" until a division in the final decade of the nineteenth century. Every generation faces the call of God and responds in varieties of faith or in many shades of disbelief from indifference, distraction, an evil heart or the cares of life. Many voices preached the gospel or alternatives in Ontario, but church growth studies demonstrate that people, on the whole, consider a message seriously if they can understand it (in their language) from credible witnesses (living what they profess), and answering to some extent the aims of their worldview (addressing felt needs). In Christian theology, God is our great need, felt or unfelt (there is that famous Augustinian "God-made restlessness"). God uses all these avenues. Mennonites in Ontario spoke German, but some were beginning to be fluent in English. The majority would not be attracted to a Scottish Presbyterian church life, even if that church were experiencing revival in a Presbyterian way. The majority would suspect a church life that was linked to military participation or florid ("proud")

---

1. For histories of Anabaptists and Mennonites, see Dyck, *Introduction*.

ceremony as in establishment Anglicanism. German Lutheran neighbors might succeed in intermarrying with Mennonite families if a Mennonite's desire to marry surpassed loyalty to the community. There were numerous German Catholics in Waterloo County. However, Roman Catholicism in German, Irish or Francophone form would be unthinkable to the average Anabaptist home that read the *Martyr's Mirror* or identified the statuary of the parish churches as idols and the Pope as antichrist. In many localities, the attraction of German-language revival Methodist groups such as the United Brethren in Christ and the Evangelical Association, who held their preaching services every Sunday, often morning and evening, proved especially powerful to some young Mennonites.[2] This was especially attractive at Bloomingdale and Freeport in Waterloo Township to young Bowmans and Sherks. An Erb found the Evangelicals attractive in the Lexington area of Waterloo which led to Waterloo County's first camp meeting in 1839. Similarly, Freys, Hochs and a Bishop Gross found help from the Evangelicals in the Lincoln County settlement around the Twenty Mile Creek.[3] During the 1840s, some young Mennonites switched to the German revival churches, or where English use was increasing fast, as in the Niagara peninsula and York County,[4] to some branch of English-language Methodism, Wesleyan or Episcopal being the main types in York. Episcopal Methodists in particular might have been known in the US, where most of the Canadian Mennonites came from until European Amish started arriving after 1825. Evangelist Noah Detwiler's mother was a Kennedy from Inverness, Scotland. New Mennonite preacher Peter Geiger from Waterloo married an eighteen-year-old Mary Ann Wilson in isolated Hay Township in Huron County about 1858.[5] Nancy Schantz from southwest of New Dundee

---

2. Steiner, *In Search of Promised Lands*, 143. David B. Schneider's diary, as quoted in Horst, *Close Ups*, 101–2, mentions visiting Latchars' meeting house (Mannheim Mennonite), a Methodist church, a "Dutch Methodist," an English Methodist service, and the UBiC camp-meeting at Winterbourne from January 2 to September 11, 1859. David Bergey, according to his own diary of January 1 to July 28, 1866, visited UBiC prayer meetings and Ben Eby's (First Mennonite, Berlin) (see Horst, *Close Ups*, 103–4).

3. The fascinating question of "Mennonite identity" is a continuing discussion among Anabaptists. But it is mainly tangential to the scope of this book. For a review of the vast literature dealing with the issue, one could start with Sawatsky, *History and Identity*.

4. Nigh, "Lost Tribes." English was used by John Zavitz of the Black Creek Mennonites, but that did not stop losses to other churches in Black Creek. Nigh noted switches by Tunkers of the peninsula to Baptists and Disciples as the nineteenth century moved on.

5. In the provincial marriage register, Mary Ann with the English name "Wilson" has no parents listed. Perhaps she was an orphan.

toward Woodstock, though she never married, joined the almost totally English-speaking Free Methodists. She became a FM preacher-pastor when Michigan FM elder Charles Sage toured Ontario looking for evangelistic openings after the Canadian Methodist merger of 1874.[6]

In many cases, an isolated Mennonite family, wishing to worship God on the Sabbath, had to make do with whatever Christian congregation had built a place of worship nearest to them. In time, they might become members. This happened all over Ontario with other denominations, of course.

In all three of the main settlements of Mennonites in Ontario (Niagara, York, and Waterloo), and in the secondary settlements (for example, Norfolk, Oxford, Perth, Huron, Bruce, and Simcoe Counties), the pull of the revival message was felt.[7] Some went right over, but some wanted to remain Mennonite, just adding some favored practice or doctrine from the evangelical and pietist movements the individual or family were encountering. Preacher Daniel Hoch desired to add practices such as testimony prayer meetings with the accompanying call for definite individual conversions and assurance of salvation. He clashed with his fellow ministers at the Twenty Mennonite community in Lincoln County and Clinton Township. The conflict led to the first organizational break in the Ontario Mennonite community toward Methodist-like revivalism.[8] But he wanted to remain Mennonite.[9] Within three years after he was silenced by the Waterloo bishop Benjamin Eby in 1849, Hoch was ordaining ministers and organizing small alternative Mennonite groups in Niagara and Waterloo. He made visits to other scattered interested families in Welland, Norfolk, Huron and Simcoe Counties. By 1855, Hoch was contacting York County revivalist Mennonites such as Christian Troyer and Abraham Raymer and their followers. He was aware of and in contact with similar people in Pennsylvania, especially Jacob Oberholtzer, who encouraged him by visiting and

---

6. Sigsworth, *Battle*, 193–94. For the re-organizing of Canadian Methodism and the role of Free Methodists, see Kleinsteuber, *More Than a Memory*, 81–85.

7. Doherty, "Emergence."

8. Unless you count the Reformed Mennonite Church ("Herrites"), which took a limited number of practices from the revivalists (see Steiner, *In Search of Promised Lands*, 46–47). Informally, all the revivalist Mennonites were called "new Mennonites," no matter what they were called organizationally. One reason would be the frequent name changes they went through. The Hoch division is recounted fictionally in Coffman, "Samuel Fry."

9. Besides the full account of Hoch's movement (see Steiner, *In Search of Promised Lands*, 91, 95, 97–99, 108–17; see also Steiner, "Hoch, Daniel").

publishing reports in Oberholtzer's newspapers. Some conferences were initiated that gave some international status to Hoch and friends. The resulting General Conference Mennonite movement had to be restarted in Ontario later on when the majority of the revivalist Mennonites (the New Mennonite Church) joined a still newer revivalist Mennonite network, the Reforming or Reformed Mennonite Society of 1874.

New Mennonites in Waterloo County were not numerous but known in Roseville and Blair, led by John McNally in North Dumfries Township; at Doon (Waterloo Township) by Abraham Z. Detwiler; around New Dundee (Wilmot Township) led by Samuel Schlichter; toward Bright in Blenheim Township, Oxford County, helped by deacon Jacob Huber; around Mannheim in Wilmot, where John Rickert was a representative.[10] The New Mennonites probably had sympathizers in Ulrich Geiger (in Wilmot) and his nephew Peter Geiger (Hay Township, in Huron County), in John Baer/Bear, Sr., at Wanner's,[11] and Deacon William Hembling at Floradale in Woolwich Township. A Huber family and a few others had migrated to Bosanquet Township, Lambton County (near Sarnia, Ontario), and maintained a New Mennonite testimony.[12]

THE GOUDIE BROTHERS GET CONVERTED

Thus, it is no surprise that Mennonite preacher Daniel Wismer and Moses Erb were of those preaching what was basically a revivalist message in early 1870 in Bloomingdale and members' homes in Waterloo Township. It is no surprise that young people such as Henry Goudie from near Hespeler and others in Berlin itself, attending Wismer's testimony prayer meetings, became converted in the revivalist style. Henry was nineteen. Sam, his youngest brother, was just five.

---

10. The evidence from the Bloomingdale (Snyder's Meeting house) which led many to support their ministers Moses Erb and Daniel Wismer in revivalist practices points only to 1870 and later. Menno and Susannah Bowman, who worshipped at Snyder's, showed some United Brethren-like tendencies (Steiner, "Effects," 30), in wanting to be baptized by immersion in 1863 (Horst, *Close Ups*, 109). But Bowman rebuilt the meeting house in 1872 as a member, not as a New Mennonite.

11. John Bear (Baer) was briefly standing with Daniel Hoch in 1848. But he renounced the movement at the time.

12. Elias Eby's diary for August 5, 1872 (quoted in Horst, *Close Ups*, 112) mentions a Christian S. Huber as follows: "He has much to boast of his piety and great conversion. This may be so, but we have only his word for it."

In the 1930s, Lewis J. Burkholder, a Mennonite Conference preacher from Markham, interviewed the elderly Henry Goudie about his conversion experience in preparation for the book Burkholder was writing about the history of Mennonites in Ontario. Henry recalled that he and some others were prepared for baptism and therefore membership in the Mennonite Conference by classes conducted by Daniel Wismer. Wismer used the 1632 Dordrecht Confession, a standard Mennonite teaching tool in North America consisting of eighteen articles of faith agreed as a basis of union to settle disputes among Mennonites in Holland. The articles are recognizably evangelical. Except for an article on the use of a disciplinary practice called "the ban,"[13] there was nothing doctrinally unusual, and the EMCC could use it today.

When Henry and his fellow converts were presented to the area bishops Abraham Martin and Joseph Hagey (spelled "Hege" in some accounts) of Breslau, Hagey questioned them on the basics of the Christian faith and found their profession acceptable. However, Hagey asked a question that was not typical of the day, which touched on their participation in the contentious measure many Mennonite Conference members found leading to disorder and pride. This was the testimony prayer meeting, where men and women of various denominations spoke, and people who were not ordained preachers or deacons prayed. "Are you willing to come as all other candidates and forsake the evening prayer meetings?" All fifteen candidates said they could not promise that, since the meetings were the channel through which they had been converted. Henry Goudie thought that Hagey was forced by other Waterloo Mennonites to ask this question; perhaps he thought Hagey himself might have passed the issue in silence. But the question was asked, and Hagey announced that he could not therefore baptize the candidates. Henry Goudie could not remember whether this interview was conducted in 1870 or 1871. In his case, he turned to Daniel Hoch of the New Mennonite Church for baptism, which occurred

---

13. "The ban" refers to disassociation by members from those members who fall into wayward behavior that deserved public correction (sometimes called "shunning") (see Steiner, *In Search of Promised Lands*, 758). As a practice implementing a belief about the purity of the congregation, upheld by Menno Simons himself (attempting to embody Scripture such as Matt 18:17 or 2 John 10), the ban unfortunately has often disturbed Mennonite Conferences when leaders try to enforce it. The ban attracts legalistic interpretations which frustrate the intended use, which has been to discipline members in love so they will be led to restoration to the congregation. See comments by Gingerich, *Amish of Canada*, 50, on the disruptive results of the use of the ban.

in 1872 somewhere around Hespeler.[14] Other candidates obtained their baptism from bishop John Lapp of Clarence Center, New York State. Lapp was himself in a delicate situation. Steiner believes he was not in fellowship with the Waterloo Mennonites for many years, rather, he was closer to the New Mennonites.[15] Nevertheless, those he baptized seem to have initially been accepted by the Waterloo Mennonite community. Hoch's baptisms, however, were outside the Conference's regulation. Henry was a New Mennonite now.

Henry married Sarah Wildfong (Daughter of Eli [Elijah] Wildfong/Wildfang and Nancy Mosser) of the Hespeler area in Waterloo Township, at the end of 1872 while the controversy over the revivalist measures led now by Solomon Eby of Port Elgin, Bruce County, and Daniel Wismer in Waterloo was growing. Sometime in 1872, Henry preached his first sermon "from a Waterloo pulpit."[16] I wish we knew where exactly and who encouraged him, whether Wismer, John Bear[17] of Wanner's meeting house, or someone from a New Mennonite meeting location.

THE REFORMING MENNONITE SOCIETY OF 1874–1875

Solomon Eby broke Mennonite discipline and injured the community by baptizing people and holding communion services himself instead of waiting for his bishop. The diarist Elias Eby's words cut deep: "Here is truly a great disobedience. Now this young man stands up in his own justification, in our meeting houses, and tells us much about his conversion, and that out of love he would give his life for his Lord. If he were to resign his own will and his obstinacy, I might possibly believe the above."[18]

Later, he criticized revivalist Daniel Brenneman (who was on a visit from Indiana)[19] and Wismer the same way:

---

14. Horst, *Close Ups*, 107–08.

15. Steiner, *In Search of Promised Lands*, 112.

16. This comes from a newspaper interview (March 22, 1938). The source is unidentified newspaper clipping, probably the *Kitchener Daily Record* in Box 2500, "Henry Goudie" file, MCHT.

17. "Johannes Bear" (1804–1894) married Anna Pannabecker (1812–1875) (Huffman, *History*, 223). She was an aunt to David Pannabecker. Bear is the subject of "Uncle Hannes and Levi" (see "Uncle Hannes and Levi").

18. Horst quotes Elias Eby's diary for November 24, 1872 (*Close Ups*, 112–13).

19. Daniel Brenneman (1834–1919), from the Yellow Creek Church in Elkhart County, Indiana, became a major American leader of the MBiC (Huffman, *History*, 74–76).

> We visited Joseph Hagey today. The willful brethren cause the old bishop much sorrow and unrest. Too bad that peace has been lost ... Too bad that such men, who united and pledged themselves by the precious covenant of baptism, under these firmly established rules ... gained the confidence of the church ... Now they have gone so far astray that they associate with those who look on our nonresistant faith and regulations with scorn.[20]

On the other hand, Solomon Eby's haste is understandable from an evangelical standpoint. The apostle Peter once said that no one could forbid baptism, when the Holy Spirit had been received (Acts 10:47). To the "revived," seeking and promoting repentance and forgiveness of the unconverted were urgent God-ordained activities. Truly, the judgment in Huffman's book, transmitting S. Floyd Pannabecker's sentiments, often quoted, that if only people had exercised "a little more tolerance and patience ... on both sides at the time, the division might perhaps have been avoided," sounds correct.[21] Yes, but some theological shifting had been going on. The Reforming Mennonites were not merely adding Sunday Schools and four-part harmony, testimony meetings and preaching in English. For the Mennonite mainstream, fellowship was so important that disturbances to fellowship were against the body of Christ. Steiner pictures the difference as a difference of pieties, hence, of theologies of faith and obedience to God.[22] And I think he has moved closer to the truth.

Steiner now has the best account of the stages and conferences held to promote or check the movement.[23] When Eby and Wismer were finally disciplined by the Canada Conference in early 1874, they and others responded by organizing a new society at Christian Eby's meetinghouse (Berlin) on May 15 and followed this up by an initial semi-annual conference at the Mennonite Church at Port Elgin in September.[24] Henry, and presumably his wife Sarah also, became "charter members" of the new Mennonite society.[25] Hugh Goudie, Henry and Sam Goudie's grandfather, the

---

20. Elias Eby's diary for February 26, 1874 (Horst, *Close Ups*, 113–14).

21. Huffman, *History*, 37.

22. Steiner, *In Search of Promised Lands*, 127. Gingerich looks briefly at the new pieties in "Pietistic and Wesleyan Influences." An extended review is in Erdel, "Holiness."

23. Steiner, *In Search of Promised Lands*, 91–156.

24. Huffman, *History*, 52.

25. Huffman, *History*, 87n9.

Ayrshire-born Presbyterian Scotsman, died that year on the Goudie farm. Sam Goudie would have been eight years old by summertime.

Canada experienced an economic depression which started in the United States in 1873 and lasted the rest of the decade and beyond.[26] It is worth asking if the depression, in effect a social disturbance, was a factor in the rise of Mennonites looking for a better experience in their religion, as some sociologists theorize.[27] Although insulated somewhat from provincial affairs by self-sufficiency on many farms, ethnicity and a minority religion, Mennonites were heavily rural and farm prices affected the whole community as it would their Anglo (Irish, English, and Scots) farm neighbors. It could be argued that the earlier depression of the 1840s in Canada[28] also pre-disposed some people such as Daniel Hoch, Christian Troyer and Abraham Raymer to seek new meaning of current events. Solomon Eby and Daniel Brenneman, however, were turned to revivalist religion before the depression (1869 and 1850s respectively). Unless testimony is found that some Ontario Mennonites were distressed by their economic or social condition as a result of economic depression to seek help from their faith in new earnestness, it is too early for this sociological argument to carry weight.

Another organization, formed in 1874, in Owen Sound, Ontario, was to become a province-wide movement of reform: the Woman's Christian Temperance Union. Imported to some extent from the US, the WCTU had the sympathies of the revivalist Mennonites but rarely official support in the nineteenth century. Goudie's Conference supported resolutions against the evils of drink and tobacco nearly every year for a long period, but it did not encourage members to join temperance organizations.

In 1878, Henry Goudie became a probationer preacher in the United Mennonite Church, Canada Conference. He was immediately stationed at Port Elgin, Solomon Eby's church, while Eby, Presiding Elder since 1874, was released for roaming the province full-time as a superintendent-type of leader.

---

26. Macdonald, *Canada Immigration*, 112–13. Macdonald mentions that, as a result, exports "such as timber, wheat and fish" experienced a sharp drop in shipments. The price of wheat and the market for wheat would be a major concern of Mennonite farmers. Others see the depression continuing to 1893.

27. Westfall, *Two Worlds*, 174–75.

28. Macdonald, *Canada Immigration*, 54.

THE BINATIONAL CHURCH BUILDS UP

The Reforming Mennonites in Ontario were not alone. Solomon Eby had met Daniel Brenneman in Indiana on a visit in 1872. Indiana and Michigan preacher John Krupp (1840–1911) and Daniel Brenneman visited Ontario in 1873 to witness the activities of the Port Elgin and Waterloo Mennonite revival meetings. Brenneman visited Ontario again in 1874, preaching in services with Daniel Wismer.[29] Krupp and Brenneman were impressed. When they pushed for acceptance of the new measures, they were told "not yet." Events in Indiana led to the disfellowshipping of Krupp, and then Daniel Brenneman of the Yellow Creek Mennonite Church in Indiana in 1874, when he supported Krupp.[30] It did not take these preachers long to set up a new organization, though they considered joining other existing groups, as many revivalist Mennonites had been doing. In a letter to C. Henry Smith, Brenneman outlined his thinking on why they did not join the Evangelical Association, the Church of the United Brethren in Christ, the Free Methodist Church, or other churches, some of whom had expressed great sympathy for their expulsion, had offered them the use of their meeting places and with whom they had actually co-operated on some activities such as a Union Sunday School in Elkhart, Indiana.[31] As one might expect, the Methodist practice of baptizing babies rather than believers, and their willingness to fight in wars, discouraged the revivalist Mennonites from joining them. In addition, both the Evangelicals and the United Brethren were in turmoil over disputes about modernism, accepting secret society (lodge) members into the church and the powers of bishops, which led to bitter divisions in both churches a short time later. Brenneman and his associates were certain that membership in oath-bound societies were forbidden by Jesus Christ in the Sermon on the Mount and the letter of James (if only because of the instruction "Let your Yes be Yes, and your No be No"), and so disqualified those otherwise admirable churches as acceptable for uniting with. Brenneman, at least, wanted to remain Mennonite in doctrine.

29. Elias Eby's diary for February 26, 1874 (Horst, *Close Ups*, 114). Though part of the 1875 union with the New Mennonites at Bloomingdale, Daniel Wismer was not willing to have open communion as Solomon Eby desired (Storms, *History of the United Missionary Church*, 37–38).

30. Sam Goudie met this veteran preacher in Berlin in 1902, and immediately asked him to preach (Eleanor Bunker Family Collection [see the July 12–13 entry of his 1902 diary]). Krupp was serving another denomination in Arkansas at the time.

31. Wenger, "Documents," 48–56. A longer version is printed in Brenneman, "Letter." Brenneman wrote about 1908 or 1909 (not 1918), according to editor James Stump.

Looking ahead for a moment, the United Brethren in Christ divided in 1884 into the Radical (Old Constitution) and the Liberal (New Constitution) groups. In 1906, the New Constitution UBiC in Canada merged with the Canadian Congregationalists and disappeared from Canadian church life. At the 1925 United Church union, all the Congregationalists joined the union, and the Congregationalists disappeared from Canadian church life.[32] The remaining "Radical" UBiC churches, about a dozen, mostly in Waterloo, Welland and York County areas, continued on into the twenty-first century. Their Canadian Evangelical Association cousins avoided the split that occurred in the US, which became the Evangelical *church* after a reunion of the two parts in 1922. Canadian Evangelicals changed their name to the Evangelical United Brethren in 1946 when the New Constitution UBiC in the US merged with the EvC. Thus when the Canada Conference of the EUB joined the United Church of Canada in 1968, there were *no* formerly UBiC congregations involved, contrary to the impression you get reading Ambrose and others, since all the Canadian EUB were *only* formerly Evangelical Association congregations. And so, with a very big exception in the Canadian west, the Evangelical Church also disappeared from Canadian Church life, a group to which the MBiC/EMCC owes so much for sparking Mennonite revivalist piety in the middle decades of the nineteenth century.

Until 1876 there were no Free Methodist congregations in Canada, when FM Elder Charles H. Sage from northern Michigan was sent to follow up members who had moved to Ontario. The Free Methodists themselves were founded only in 1860 in New York State, splitting off from the American Methodist Episcopal Church. More importantly, according to Ralph Kleinsteuber, Sage responded to requests from Ontario Methodists who were not happy with the trends in Canadian Methodism which led to the first merger of 1874 (Wesleyan Methodist Churches and New Connexion Methodists) which seemed to discard the Methodists' revivalist tradition in favor of an urban value of "respectability." Desire for worldly "respectability" emerges again and again in the criticism by holiness groups against the large Methodist churches.[33] Although there are definitely a cultural clash and a rural/urban division involved, a component of a spiritual shift is mixed in as well. United Church historian Phyllis Airhart has traced the

---

32. The Congregational Christian Churches in Canada took the name "Congregational" later.

33. "Respectability" is a theme studied in Marks, *Revivals* (see, for example, 12–13, 61).

decline of revivalist piety in Canadian Methodist churches through the nineteenth century, which agrees in some ways with Kleinsteuber's analysis. C. Mark Steinacher also studied the changes in Methodist pieties in Ontario in the nineteenth century.[34] Thus the FM Church was organizing in Ontario among Anglo-Canadians at precisely the time the United Mennonites were doing so among German-Canadians. Their geographical areas of membership hardly overlapped, however.

---

34. Airhart, "Eclipse"; Westfall, *Two Worlds*, 50–81; Steinacher, "Homogenization of Methodism."

3

The Young Sam Goudie 1866–1885

SAM GOUDIE'S FAMILY WAS part of the Wanner Mennonite meeting house community (Or possibly Cressman's),[1] but events of the first decade of his life were to loosen the family connection in several directions, and in his second decade, to set Sam on a career of service in a newly-formed denomination.

While the Reforming Mennonite Society/Reformed Mennonite Church, and the New Mennonite Church and their successors by merger (United Mennonite Church in 1875, Evangelical United Mennonite Church in 1879 and then the Mennonite Brethren in Christ, December 1883) were organizing and growing,[2] Sam Goudie was growing up on the family farm north of Hespeler. Until 1879 he attended School Section 26 public school in Hespeler, across the Speed River, where his brothers attended before him.[3] Being the youngest Goudie, he inherited some of his brothers' textbooks. At his death, he still had his brother Jacob's school atlas, and a science book of David W.'s.[4] The rural children met with the children in the

---

1. Storms and Steiner, "Goudie, Henry (1851–1942)."

2. There are useful charts in Steiner, *In Search of Promised Lands*, 114, concerning the MBiC's merging antecedent churches.

3. For a description of changes the school went through, see Bloomfield and Foster, *Waterloo Township Schools*. Jacob and Samuel are recorded as in the fifth and fourth classes in 1879, respectively, in the "Hespeler Public School Register" (1878–1880) according to the City of Cambridge Archives, Brewster Collection.

4. As of 2023, it was still in the possession of the family of Eleanor (Goudie) Bunker,

village in a Union school for Township and Village with three classrooms. In the 1840s and 1850s, New Hope was a growing village expanding with businesses, becoming a small industrial town under the enterprises of the Wurttemberg Lutheran, Jacob Hespeler, which took his name when incorporated in 1859.[5] By 1861, a larger than average number of households were headed by people of first-generation Scottish (8.3 percent) and Irish (7 percent) origin than elsewhere in Waterloo Township, though by then "Canadian-born" citizens heavily predominated (54.3 percent) whatever their parents' ethnicity.[6] The churches were represented by the Methodist New Connexion (organized 1837), Evangelical Association (about 1840), Presbyterian (1855), Roman Catholic (1857), and Lutheran (1860) congregations. Later, Anglicans organized in 1882, the Salvation Army in 1886, and the Baptists in 1889.[7] Of 41 households in School Section 26 in 1861 however, there were 15 Lutherans; 4 "Dunkard" (that is, Tunkers); the Mennonites, Evangelicals and Methodists all had three each; Presbyterians: 2; Anglicans: 1. Ten families did not respond to the religion question, including Jacob Hespeler, yet he was a known Lutheran. Only eleven of the 41 households were farmers on their own land. Wanners, Goudies and Pannabeckers accounted for the Mennonites. Sam Goudie could have started school about 1872. Since it was a village rather than a purely rural school, it is an interesting question how this boyhood environment shaped the young man and prepared him for other than farming.

In 1879, the Goudie family for some reason moved from their first farm. Presumably, Sam finished his grade school in Breslau. In an autobiographical note at the front of his 1886 "Pastor's Book," Sam recorded his origins (unique punctuation and all):

> Samuel Goudie, son of David Goudie Sr. born near Hespeler, Waterloo Co. Ontario in the year of our Lord and Savior Jesus Christ, one thousand, eight hundred and sixty-six, lived there with his parents until about May 1st 1879 when they moved to Berlin for six months from there they went to where they now

---

Sam's granddaughter.

5. On Jacob Hespeler, see Bloomfield, *Waterloo Township*, 85.

6. Bloomfield, *Waterloo Township*, 215. Bloomfield indicates that, although villages with 750 inhabitants were allowed to incorporate, in fact, in 1861, only 438 were counted in New Hope. Fortunately for New Hope's aspirations, Jacob Hespeler was also the Census Commissioner when he was the first reeve of New Hope, which took the name "Hespeler," in recognition of his efforts.

7. Ambrose, *Waterloo County Churches*, 48–56.

live near Breslau (of course they took their son Samuel along as he is their baby). They gave him about 8 years common schooling after which he preferred farming to any other trade having tried clerking for a short time and while engaged by J. B. Hagey on the farm was led to Christ through the instrumentality of the S. Army June 15th 1884 and about a year after was convicted that he should preach the Gospel though realizing his weakness, consented and began Sept 8 of 1885, being then only 19 years 28 days old, willing to spend or be spent for God.[8]

After grade 8, Sam Goudie's classroom education stopped. He wrote the entrance exams for high school and took "continuation courses."[9] He also read and was examined in the probationers' reading courses when he joined the MBiC ministerial fellowship, of which more later. This experience was similar to most of his generation of MBiC preachers.

Sam attended Sunday School somewhere as well. In another autobiographical passage, Goudie mentioned the influence of his teachers:

> How well we remember when quite young and small what an influence the Sabbath School had on us, what an impression for good was made on our young minds such as we will never forget; often times when we were about to do or say something wrong how we would be checked by a verse we had learned, or something our teacher had told us while attending Sunday School, though this may have occurred years after . . .[10]

Meanwhile, Sam's big brother Henry and his wife Sarah were transferred to the Breslau field in 1881, where he served for three years, the maximum time under the MBiC General Conference *Discipline*. In Breslau Henry could have been his parents' pastor. The field[11] in 1881 included

---

8. Eleanor Bunker Family Collection (see the 1886–1894 yearbook). In this book, Samuel Goudie used a form of his name "S. W. Goudie" in the part of the book where he kept tallies of meetings he attended as a probationer of the fields. "W" would have stood for "Wanner," a middle name system frequently used by nineteenth-century Mennonites and was used by David Wanner Goudie ("Jnr.") to distinguish him from his Scottish-born father, David Goudie. Apart from this record book, I have never seen Sam make use of a middle name.

9. Huffman, *History*, 238.

10. Goudie, "Influence," 4. Could this have been in Wanner Mennonite Church since he was already 13 on the move to Breslau? Sunday Schools were a touchy issue in Waterloo Mennonite circles after the Reforming Mennonite schism. But they were gradually re-introduced. It would be instructive to know.

11. MBiC generally officially named their appointment groups "fields" rather than

meeting points at West Montrose, Conestogo, Bloomingdale, Breslau itself in a hall at the corner of Mader Lane and Woolwich St., nearly opposite their current site (their meeting house was not built until 1882), and the Union meeting house in Puslinch Township, in Wellington County, shared with the Tunkers and others. Blair in North Dumfries Township was added for one year in 1882. Samuel Pannabecker (a first cousin of David Pannabecker) was the helper in 1881,[12] Elias Shantz and young Henry Schlichter Hallman were in 1882. Samuel Pannabecker later went to Michigan and became an MBiC preacher there. Elias Shantz continued as a helper into 1883. He was a prominent Breslau member, frequently assigned to Conference committees whenever he was a delegate to the annual Conference before he migrated to Alberta. H. S. Hallman was beginning a career as a prominent pastor, editor and conference official. The official history of Breslau Missionary Church more or less starts at the construction of the 1882 building, during Henry's time, which is still the core of the structure today.[13] However, as we will keep reminding the reader, the construction of a building is rarely the true start of a congregation.

The Mennonite community east of Berlin was scattered all over Woolwich and Waterloo Townships and services were held in their meeting houses on alternate Sundays or even every three or four weeks, giving the opportunity for everyone within a reasonable buggy ride distance to meet for worship every Sunday. Evangelical Association and United Brethren preaching and revivals had been conducted in the area, the east side of Waterloo, however, and congregations formed, many members coming from the Mennonite community. The Evangelicals had appointments at St. Jacobs (1848), Conestogo (not recorded, but about 1860) and Bridgeport (from 1876).[14] There were UB congregations in Bloomingdale (started about 1860), West Montrose (from about 1861), Breslau (about 1866 to 1893), and Bridgeport (about 1871 to about 1884).[15] Thus there were many

---

the Methodist term "circuit." I will use both words interchangeably for stylistic purposes since Goudie and even the MBiC interchanged them.

12. "Helper" was someone officially approved by the Conference to assist the "minister in charge" of a field. This was distinct from "local help" who were qualified and available when called upon, from and for the field alone.

13. The history booklet admits, "Some type of fellowship was forming by 1872" (Losch et al., *Breslau Missionary Church*, 5). The booklet mentions that nine persons were baptized and 8 joined in church membership on May 16, 1880.

14. Ambrose, *Waterloo County Churches*, 41, 235, 218.

15. Ambrose, *Waterloo County Churches*, 36, 39, 43, 239.

who were attracted to revivalism in the area for some time. The Huffman profile reports Menno Bowman's conversion when he was 28, four years before the Port Elgin revival of 1869.[16] He was a leader in accepting Eby's and Wismer's revivalism in the Bloomingdale Mennonite church, and so many others agreed that the building was used mainly by the Reformed/United Mennonite group from 1874 until the Mennonite Conference reasserted control with a new deed surfacing in 1879.[17] The MBiC Breslau circuit therefore really began about 1874.

In the March 1884 Annual Conference of the MBiC Canada Conference in Markham, the first Conference under the new name "Mennonite Brethren in Christ," Sam's brother Henry was assigned by the stationing committee[18] to take charge of the "Bethel" field centered on New Dundee, southwest of Berlin.

The youngest Goudie was in the town of Galt in June 1884, when he was confronted with the gospel message by a newly arrived evangelistic organization. He was working on the farm of the family who were to remain long-time friends, J. B. Hagey.[19] What he was doing in Galt has not been recorded, whether visiting his Goudie aunts or being curious about the Salvation Army. Converting to Christ may seem a natural step for the youngest son of a religiously active family, but the day God met that son, it changed his life's direction. Despite his Mennonite family, Sam credited his conversion on June 15, a Sunday, not to his family, or his brother Henry, or any other MBiC activity such as a camp-meeting or protracted meeting, but as we saw in his autobiographical note, to the "instrumentality" (wonderful word! were they literally playing their instruments?) of the Salvation Army.

Three months earlier, the Salvation Army had "stormed the town" of Galt under Captain Fred Galletly, twenty-six, who had just come from

---

16. Huffman, *History*, 226.

17. Steiner, "Effects" (cf. Sauder, *Trail's End*, 10).

18. The MBiC's *The Doctrines and Disciplines of the MBiC* (hereafter called the *Discipline*) allowed Annual Conferences to constitute this pivotal Conference function in their own way. In the first years, ordained leaders formed the stationing committee, but in later years, normally it included the Presiding Elder or Elders and the delegates from the fields, *not* the elders and probationers. In the Canada/Ontario Conference, they were not elected except occasionally a Presiding Elder leaving office might be included for a year to provide wisdom and continuity.

19. Probably a son of the same Bishop Joseph Hagey who had refused to baptize Henry Goudie in 1870.

England.[20] In the Army, the Captain was "affectionately referred to as 'Lightning Fred.'"[21] Fred and his team may have noted the Mennonite teenager, but in another of those oddities of life, the boy was to become Captain Fred's "captain" (Presiding Elder) decades later. Of course, Sam's family and church connection informed his response to the gospel. Goudie spoke of his conversion and call many years later at a minister's conference, but unfortunately, no record of what he said survives. The secretary merely wrote, "He commenced his remarks by saying that he was sorry so many were in the ministry just because they chose to be. He briefly related his own experience."[22] In a letter to the editor of the *Gospel Banner* in 1949, Sam said he was sanctified in May 1885.[23] That is the only reference to the time of his sanctification, though the assurance ruled his life. Goudie was not one who often referred to his own inner life, a problem we will meet as we study his life. Sam did not join the Salvation Army, but they show up at various points in the Canada/ Ontario Conference story, as we shall see.

CAMP-MEETINGS IN BRESLAU 1881–1885

During Henry's time at Breslau, the Evangelical United Mennonites conducted their first camp-meetings in Ontario in Moses Burkholder's bush, flat land by the Grand River, west of the village, in September of 1881.[24] This land is visible (as of 2024) from Highway 7/ Victoria St. through the railway bridge. Immense crowds visited the camp on Sunday, some newspaper reports estimating three to four thousand people attending. The Evangelicals and the United Brethren in Christ had conducted camp-meetings in the area for some years especially at Winterbourne a few kilometers to the north, probably teaching the EUM people how to do it. I cannot account for the huge numbers of Sunday visitors.[25] Most could not have been Evangeli-

---

20. Moyles, *Blood and Fire*, 271. Ambrose, *Waterloo County Churches*, 20. The Salvation Army opened in Hespeler in 1886.

21. Ambrose, *Waterloo County Churches*, 20.

22. Missionary Church Historical Trust (see Minutes of September 26, 1921, Stouffville, Ontario). Goudie's remarks were somewhat impromptu because William Brown, the minister originally assigned the topic, "The Divine Call to the Ministry and How to Distinguish between the call to the Home and Foreign Missionary Work," was unable to be present.

23. Goudie, "Testimonies," 6.

24. Lambert, "[Report]," 7. The first camp meeting in the whole EUM took place at Fetter's Grove, Indiana, in August 1880 (see Weeks, "Legacy"; Huffman, *History*, 51).

25. Horst (*Close Ups*, 106) quotes Samuel Moyer who said the UB camp meetings

cal United Mennonites. But they must have known what to expect. People with wheeled vehicles had to ford the river as there was no road bridge as yet, just the railway bridge. About one hundred families pitched tents in the Burkholder bush for the weekday meetings, representing anywhere from four to six hundred campers. Since the Goudie family's move to just south of Breslau in 1879, they had every chance to attend. Sam would have been fifteen years old.

In 1884, reports on the camp-meeting in July, a month after Sam was led to Christ, show the MBiC were still pulling crowds to Breslau. This report also shows that though relations between some parts of the MBiC and the Salvation Army were cooler later for a while, they had begun well: "The Camp-meeting has been continued during the week, and on Tuesday twenty-six converts were baptized in the Grand River. A troop of the Salvation Army lent some assistance at times during the services. The attendance on Sunday is said to have reached five or six thousand..."[26]

BIG BROTHER'S ASSIGNMENT: BETHEL, 1883–1886

The rural Bethel field in 1883 consisted of five preaching appointments: (1) at the Bethel meeting house, constructed in 1878, northwest of New Dundee, on a corner lot donated by H. S. Hallman's father, Tunker preacher Wendell Hallman; (2) Mannheim just outside the southwest corner of Waterloo Township; (3) the Union Meeting House west of Roseville in North Dumfries Township, constructed by the New Mennonites and the Evangelical Association in 1853;[27] (4) Bright in Blenheim Township, Oxford County, and a short-lived appointment at (5) Innerkip also in Oxford, southwest of Bright in East Zorra Township. So many preaching points required a group of helpers who could share the preaching duties, though not necessarily would all the points be served every Sunday. Henry in 1884 to 1886 was assisted by Jacob Hunsberger, and for one year, Daniel Hagey, who had started as a helper on the field at Bright in 1881. Hagey was last mentioned by name in 1903, still as "local help." ("Local help" was an official position, often a retired preacher or a preacher with a Quarterly Conference license living in the area of the field). Jacob Hunsberger is first mentioned as a

---

were held all day Sundays at Breslau. This Samuel Moyer (1849–1941), who was quite a character, married a daughter of Daniel Wismer (Moyer, "Abraham's Children").

26. "Fields of Labor," 1.

27. Ambrose, *Waterloo County Churches*, 21. It was no longer used by 1900. No trace of this building remains visible above ground as of 2024.

helper to Conrad Bolender on the "Woolwich mission" in 1880, and apart from two years assigned as a conference evangelist, generally he served as a helper on the Bethel field (1884–1889), and a local preacher after that (1891–1897).

The Bethel field developed from the New Mennonite community of Waterloo County in Wilmot Township, encouraged by Daniel Hoch's push to incorporate revivalist piety in the Mennonite Conference. Mennonite-ordained preacher Samuel Schlichter (1821–1873) was probably the most visible leader around whom the rest depended locally.

The year 1884 was a momentous one in Canadian church life. It was the year of the big Methodist Church union, when the Methodist Church of Canada and the Bible Christians and Primitive Methodists joined to form the 190,000+ member Methodist Church (Canada, Newfoundland, Bermuda).[28] In contrast, all the MBiC Conferences counted 1,647 believing members in 1883.[29] The MBiC licensed its first female preacher in 1884, in fact the first Mennonite woman preacher in North America, in the person of Janet (Douglas) Hall.

The MBiC so highly valued evangelism that within two years, the MBiC General Conference accepted women as preachers, encouraged by their success as evangelists and through association with female Wesleyan and holiness teachers. The most influential was Lura (or Laura) Mains of the Free Will Baptists, but Hattie Bates of the Free Methodists in Michigan, and the Salvation Army women springing up all over North America, were also visible role models.[30] As early as 1887, women were even recognized in pastoral roles in the MBiC (the same Janet Douglas, assigned to Kilsyth and Dornoch,[31] in fact, she was the church planter of the two sites through evangelistic meetings). However, the denomination never achieved a stable theological understanding of their position. Social prejudice toward women's leadership in the denomination as it assimilated to Canadian culture and the percolation of fundamentalist (mainly Reformed) attitudes by 1940 effectively closed off for a period women's pastoral leadership in congregations. This decline occurred even though in the *Discipline/ Constitution*

28. Semple, *Lord's Dominion*, 5–7.

29. Canada Conference (909); Indiana, Michigan, and Ohio Conference (452); and Pennsylvania Conference (286). The BiC (Swankite) union in December 1883 added about 250 members (Huffman, *History*, 80, 92).

30. Methodist women such as Katherine Booth and Pheobe Palmer wrote books demonstrating a biblical case for women preachers.

31. Sullivan Township, Grey County, due south of Owen Sound, Ontario.

women were to follow the same path to public ministry as men, except for ordination.[32]

Henry probably involved his little brother Sam in the church life of New Dundee: in 1885, Sam was baptized in the Nith River near New Dundee on May 10. In the 1978 centennial congregational history of Bethel (New Dundee), Sam Goudie is remembered as "from" their church.[33] We don't know who did the baptism; it could have been his brother Henry. During tabernacle (tent) evangelistic meetings near New Dundee that fall, Sam preached his first sermon, 8 September. When Sam Goudie spoke at the opening of the newly constructed New Dundee building in 1921, he mentioned he participated in a "grand revival" during his brother's second year there. "It was one of the best I ever witnessed, and it was my privilege (sic) to be present during the last four weeks of the revival."[34] Sam also became a member of the Mennonite Brethren in Christ that year, May 24, but through what field, it is not recorded. The most likely circuits were the Breslau field, which was nearest the Goudie home after 1879, or more likely the Bethel field where his brother was serving.[35] Local Conference membership, license and recommendation were necessary for anyone in the new MBiC system to be accepted as a probationer in the Annual Conference, which Sam applied for in April 1886. He was nineteen, which is about as young a probationer as I have ever noticed in the ranks of the Canada/ Ontario Conference.

---

32. Swartz, "Woman." Core denominations in fundamentalism were Reformed in theology (Christian Brethren, most Baptist, and Presbyterian [see Marsden, *Fundamentalism*, 46]), which, for example, did not interpret New Testament prophecy as continuing past the age of the apostles (i.e., a *cessationist* view). Hence the phrase "your young women will prophesy" (Acts 2:18) would not be interpreted as in the Wesleyan tradition which renders it to mean that a preaching/evangelistic ministry continues to be available through the Spirit to women today.

33. Hoover, *History*, 60.

34. Missionary Church Historical Trust (see Sam Goudie's "History of the Bethel Circuit Compiled and Read Nov. 6th 1921 at the Dedication Services of the New Church by S. Goudie in Charge").

35. The earliest records of the Breslau MBiC community are lost, having been stolen with the safe in which they were kept, in the twentieth century (personal conversation with Carol [Sherk] Blake, January 10, 2018, in Breslau, ON). These records, which had not been inventoried, may have gone back to the 1874 Reforming Mennonite Society. In any case, a great loss to the story of the Bloomingdale/ Breslau branch and the whole Conference/ District. The baptism date is reported in Brunner, "[Samuel Goudie], 10.

THE STRUCTURE OF THE MENNONITE BRETHREN IN CHRIST CHURCH

We need to refresh our familiarity with the organizational language used by the MBiC. First for readers in the twenty-first century, we need to re-orient ourselves to the more collectivist culture of the nineteenth-century churches, which was shared not only by Mennonites or Methodists. Many see the post-modern habit of mind to be individualistic and where a local church is valued, our thinking by default is congregationalist. Controversies over personalities, money, liberal theologies, holiness, faith healing, tongues-speaking and stages of the last days and so on bred a habit in some Christians of dismissing denominational organization, connectional ties, membership and heeding authority. One cannot say all individualism is wrong or that denominational authority is always anointed. Membership separated from baptism and denominations are cultural expressions of our theology, and so are always open to sinful use and graceful amendment. But connectional identity and faithfulness is foreign to many Canadian Christians today, EMCC adherents and members included. The existence of a committee that could post a member of the Conference's unconditional ministers anywhere annually would seem chillingly autocratic to most of us today.

Second, there are the words chosen to organize the MBiC. Instead of a "Constitution," language mainly coming out of the American political experience, the MBiC chose to be ruled by a "Discipline," which was a word inherited from John Wesley's Methodists. The top authority in the church was the "General Conference," which in a large geographical area such as North America was divided into "Annual Conferences" (obviously meeting every year). After the 1969 merger these units of the church began to be called "districts," following the language of the Missionary Church Association. Preachers recognized by the Conference and ordained were known by the biblical term "elder" rather than the culturally supplied honorific "Reverend." "Presiding Elders" were renamed "superintendents" as early as 1946, but the "Conference" terminology remained at least in Ontario until 1969. "Presiding" was built on the action of the half-brother of Jesus in Acts 15, where James *presided* over the conference in Jerusalem.[36] MBiC Conferences could subdivide into "districts," so the language wasn't all that new.

---

36. As is well known, Greek *episkopos* means "overseer" or "superintendent." The monarchial *bishop* ruling in a diocese—a system foreign to the New Testament—developed later in church history. MBiC fields also had deacons, understood as servants of the

Under Annual Conferences came the "Quarterly Conferences" which represented the local organizations, the "fields," whether one congregation (a "station"), a self-supporting "circuit" (several locations served by preachers traveling around on a schedule), or a "mission" which did not yet have the resources to erect their own meeting places or support a pastor of their own. They met for business and reports every three months, that is quarterly, under a chairman, the Presiding Elder.

The MBiC *Discipline* gave licensing and ordination authority to the Annual Conference, not the denomination. This practice differed in at least two ways from the Mennonites. For one, MBiC ordination was not supervised by a congregation or the community of believers directly, but by ministers and delegates "in conference." Second, from the 1875 resolutions onwards, individual members had the option to offer themselves to the conference as ministers to be approved, rather than selected by the congregation (by lot or some other electing process), though they still needed recommendation from their local "class."

Allotting ordination to the Annual Conferences was an arrangement both practical and political. The Pennsylvania Conference, though initially small, had existed as a denomination since 1858, as had the New Mennonite Church in Ontario since 1852, and they had done their own ordaining. The Swankites in Ohio had been a self-governing group since 1860. The Mennonite practice, in which these groups were nurtured, had ordained at a regional level, and besides, the Evangelical Association *Discipline*, which the MBiC were copying, had ordained at the Annual Conference level. Getting together as a General Conference was an expensive affair, hence the plan to meet every three years (later, every four years). The process of authorizing the personnel of a vigorously evangelizing Conference could not wait for four years. From the 1879 merger onward there had only been three Conferences: "Pennsylvania," "Indiana and Ohio" which included parts of Michigan and a few isolated sites much farther afield, and "Canada" but others were soon to be added.

An applicant such as Sam Goudie in Canada went through a series of committee interviews and examinations on the way to becoming a probationer and finally approved for ordination. The first was, as mentioned, that the candidate had to establish membership in at least an organized "class,"

---

congregations, not as a step toward *priesthood* in a hierarchy. Deacons were ordained for life, as in the Mennonite Conferences, until at least the 1940s. The fields also had *stewards* to collect money—another biblical term for someone managing resources.

the basic unit of an MBiC field.[37] A class or a few classes held Quarterly Conferences, at which class officers, pastors, deacons, stewards and Sunday School superintendents would report and have to be "Passed," that is, accepted by vote by the class as having conscientiously attempted to fulfill the assignment given to them. The Presiding Elders or their designates had to be present, normally as the chair, and they also conducted the quarterly Communion service, and led in the Washing of the Saints' Feet ordinance. Baptisms, contrary to usual Mennonite practice, but established by Solomon Eby's urgency, could be conducted by the ministers in charge of a field at any time.

At the Annual Conference, the candidate would first be interviewed or reported to have passed an exam, showing that the person knew the MBiC *Discipline*. In later years Sam Goudie specialized in preparing candidates for this step. He spoke often of submitting to the *Discipline*, in whatever form it took as it evolved through the decades. I have never seen him dissent from it, though he urged people with contrary views to attempt to revise it, which happened fairly often in the first generation.[38] The "Articles of Faith" in the *Discipline* did not change during the years Goudie was chair of the denominational executive (1912 to 1943), although many procedures were changed.

The next step, taken during the Conference itself, was to examine the candidate on morals. There was, as in Wesley's practice, a series of questions into the spiritual devotions and habits of the candidate. If they passed that step, the candidate went to a doctrinal committee that checked the would-be probationer for doctrinal compatibility with the denomination. Finally, the candidate could be recommended to the Conference as a probationer, or a delay could be recommended. Sometimes if a candidate was just not ready even after several years, they could be "referred back to their Quarterly Conference," to preach at home when called on.

If the new probationers were considered ready, they might be assigned as "helpers" on a field for a year or two, before being assigned to circuits as the minister in charge. Women were treated slightly differently in the years before 1902. There were a number of variations on this pattern tried over the years. If the probationer served well (and at each Annual Conference,

---

37. The class was instituted by John Wesley. For more on the position of class leader in Methodism, see, for example, Atkinson, *Class Leader*. This was a book adapted from an American text. On the origin of the class and leaders, see Watson, "Methodist Spirituality," 230–33.

38. Noted in "Minutes of the Ministerial Convention" 81–82.

the Quarterly Conference minutes were produced to see if the minister had been "passed" each time!) there was a further committee to recommend people for ordination. Since the authority was from the Annual Conference, the Annual Conference often concluded with an ordination ceremony, then and there. The shift to local ordinations (though still approved at the annual District Conference), as in my own case at Evangel Community (EMCC) Church in Kitchener in 1998, reflects the growing power of the local church in the denomination at the expense of the district or national connection.

Running parallel to the Annual Conference committees were examinations, conducted by Annual Conference appointees, to test the candidates' pastoral preparation through a Reading Course. The first mention of a reading course was a list of books in the 1882 EUM *Discipline*, for German or English readers, to be studied in a three-year cycle. The MBiC community in Ontario, coming from rural Mennonites, rarely had members with more than "common school" education, as it was called officially in Ontario. This was eight grades of what we would call elementary school. Gradually, MBiC members started to attend high schools, but still not many until well into the twentieth century. Undergraduate education (BTh, BA) came only with Bible schools upgrading to Colleges in the 1950s. This path to ministry was rather different from the majority denominations which relied on undergraduate first degrees and graduate seminary (BD or MDiv) stages of preparation.[39]

Sam Goudie finished the common school, and he wrote and passed the exams for high school, but never went. He did some "continuation work."[40] He wrote frequently for the *Gospel Banner* and his writings show average fluency with English, improving with time.

CONDITIONAL AND UNCONDITIONAL: A FORGOTTEN MISSIONARY STRUCTURE

Sam Goudie declared himself, as was expected of someone who wanted to be a Conference member, to be "unconditional." This language came from

---

39. In passing, I think it also explains why the MBiC did not participate directly in the fundamentalist/modernist controversies of, say, the Presbyterian Church of Canada or the Baptist Convention of Ontario and Quebec. The MBiC observed and cheered the fundamentalists but did not have anybody in higher educational institutions (except Huffman) directly exposed to the allure of modernist theology, nor did they share all of the core (often Reformed) doctrinal commitments of fundamentalist groups. It would be wrong to say they did not pick up fundamentalist attitudes and theology at all.

40. Huffman, *History*, 237–38.

a distinction in the *Discipline*. Since the time of Wesley, ministers in his society were expected to be available for any assignment the Conference chose for them. This allowed for maximum flexibility in deploying workers, and is ideal for evangelistic church planting organizations. Roman Catholic missionary orders have always had the same kind of mobility, since their members promised obedience, were unmarried and owned little or no personal property. The organization can respond swiftly to any opening for its advantage. As congregations age, they look inward and can't see the reason why they can't keep a pastor they like for a longer period. Longer pastoral stays are, so the research suggests, generally good for a settled congregation. You can see this growing incomprehension in the *Conference Journals*: motions to remove limits on the length of time pastors stay with a field, and in anniversary booklets of Ontario District congregations in which they can't explain why they had so many pastors in the early years, preachers who never stayed more than three years. The past is a foreign country.

Protestants took some time to recreate anything like the Catholic missionary orders. Luther had undercut the whole theology of religious orders, but failed to think through the need for a new structure to fulfill the mission of the church. Both he and John Calvin (see Calvin's commentary on a harmony of the gospels) thought that the instructions of Jesus in Matthew 28 were addressed to the twelve apostles and were fulfilled by them and so the instruction didn't apply to the Church until Jesus returns. Protestants were stuck in the geographical parish pattern of European church life. Even before William Carey, others pointed out this blunder, and proposed solutions. William Carey was not the first to suggest the usefulness of the "Society" structure for missionary work, but the Baptist Missionary Society and the fulfillment of the model in India with distinction by Carey and his colleagues stirred others to copy it. By the twentieth century, the ecumenical movement was questioning this pattern of mission societies as untheologically parachurch, and tried, eventually successfully at the World Council of Churches New Delhi Assembly of 1962, to integrate the International Missionary Council into WCC (churchly) structures. Some mission societies involved considered the result, for evangelistic and missionary purposes, a disaster.[41] Some evangelical churches were convinced about

---

41. See Stephen Neill's confidence in the WCC theology in Neill and Chadwick, *History*, 410–13, yet their caution about implementation. Anglican Max Warren, leader of the Church Missionary Society for many years, opposed the integration, believing that it would blunt the activity of missions, as his study of history convinced him would happen (Dillistone, "Max Warren," 620–21). Winter ("Two Structures") sees the settled church

fifty years later by the same theology they had rejected earlier, under the flag of "the missional church," to bring evangelistic/ mission structures into denominational structures with unproven results so far.[42] My own studies suggest domestic issues *always* eventually swamp missionary concerns, unless the missionary structure is allowed some independence to flourish.

As Glenn Gibson demonstrated, in the first period of MBiC church planting in Ontario, there was a supply of zealous young preachers ready and willing to go wherever the conference sent them.[43] This helped the MBiC Conferences take advantage of opportunities to organize classes among scattered Mennonites as revivalist piety spread over Mennonite Conferences in the nineteenth century. You see this evangelistic flexibility working in the stationing of the similarly structured Methodists of a generation before, or the MBiC's contemporaries, the Free Methodists, and the Salvation Army. It is still functioning in the Nigerian United Missionary Church of Africa, but is also tested by large congregations in Nigeria as in Canada, that like their pastors and feel less need for the denomination's structures.

There were always some who felt they had to be conditional: workers who were worn out by long hours, long distances and low pay, or who had relatives to care for. The death of a wife was devastating to several MBiC preachers, such as New Mennonite Peter Geiger when his first wife Mary Ann died in 1873, or David Hartin of Brown Hill, when his wife Rebecca died in 1899. As time went on, congregations might get annoyed by the failures of the ministers sent to them, or the ministers annoyed by the fields, who each had their preferences. "Anyone but Elder So-and so!" "Anywhere but Circuit X!" In the beginning of the United Mennonites, most of the older ministers from the New Mennonites had big farms and big families and found it extremely hard to pick up and move under the new itinerant arrangement, consequently many of them became "conditional" and had to be assigned as local preachers or helpers, often under younger men. While they were alive, they gave excellent and mature stability to the old New Mennonite circuits of Sherkston, the Vaughan/ Markham/ Dickson Hill cluster, New Dundee/ Bright/ Blenheim and Blair/Hespeler.

---

and the mobile mission band as two expressions of the church. Lois K. Fuller agrees with Winter in her textbook for Africa, *Biblical Theology of Missions*, 129.

42. As far as I can see, this was the theology in "EMCC."
43. Gibson, "Methods," 9.

Sam Goudie was definitely from the new generation. He joined the Conference even before he was married, never bought a farm, and his family's size was far smaller than the generation before him. He was mobile. He was practically always "unconditional," regretting one time when he was not. Later in life, he criticized some who were conditional.[44] The issue of declaring oneself conditional or unconditional became more and more a burden to ministers as the decades passed, and I think when the distinction was abolished in the twentieth century, few mourned its passing. The denomination had shifted from an evangelistic mindset to a more professional clergy mindset. Congregations and pastors expected more facilities: parsonages, sizable meeting halls, and Sunday school space, and they expected a different set of pastoral skills. Sam had made up his mind to submit to the Conference early in life and did not feel the problems some of his colleagues did. As a long-serving Presiding Elder, one of whose major jobs annually was to supply preachers to the ever-shifting needs of the fields, of course he wanted a supply of willing preachers. Satisfying all the conditions some preachers stated made his committee's job harder.[45] In September 1912, Sam reflected on his career to that point:

> Say for 26 years I have been an unconditional preacher, except one year and I have repented bitterly that I ever made any conditions even for that one year for I have always been a happier and more useful man when unconditional . . . as long as our church continues with the system of church government that we have we owe it to one another and the church to be unconditional at least as long as we are able.[46]

---

44. Sam Goudie, "Visit," 12. On the visit, Goudie was impressed that all the ministers said they were "unconditional." Goudie wrote, "I am heartily sick and tired of men saying, 'I can't go here or there; or do this or that.' Be unconditional!"

45. The job of the Stationing committees was made difficult by "conditional" preachers; Goudie, "Unconditional," 10.

46. Goudie, "Unconditional," 1.

4

Elder Sam Goudie

Probationer and Pastor 1885–1897

IN THIS AND THE next chapter, the story follows Sam Goudie to his pastoral assignments, first as a probationer assisting others at Nottawasaga, Greenwood (in Michigan) and Sherkston, and then as an ordained elder at Port Elgin, Maryboro, Berlin and Toronto West. As he became involved in significant institutions of the Mennonite Brethren in Christ Church, we take time to examine the institution.

NOTTAWASAGA MISSION: GLENCAIRN, SIXTH LINE, SECOND LINE, SUNNIDALE STATION, EBENEZER, AND OTHER PLACES

The first location Sam was appointed to as a probationer in 1886 had a familiar face: when he was appointed to the Nottawasaga mission in Simcoe County, his brother Henry had just been appointed there too!

Mennonite and Tunker migration from Markham to the area south of Georgian Bay had been well underway when the United Mennonite Church was formed in 1875. I have not seen references to New Mennonite appointments in Simcoe County before the 1878 United Mennonite Annual Conference that met in Nottawasaga, but UM Church people were apparently quite familiar with the settlement. A membership record of the Nottawasaga field identifies its earliest members joining in 1876 such as

John Powers and his wife.[1] Levi and Fannie Raymer were another pioneer couple who settled in Sunnidale Township from Markham after 1871. They had been New Mennonite members since at least 1863.[2] They were notable but also typical among the steadfast MBiC members in the district. Sam often stayed with them later on his Presiding Elder's rounds.

Henry Goudie was assigned the help of two local men along with his brother Sam: August Baker and Jared Beeshy. The Nottawasaga field needed a number of local preachers because the members were scattered over a couple of rural townships. Sam reached the Nottawasaga field in time to start preaching Sunday in the "forenoon" of April 25. Sam Goudie's preaching and sermon text record begins on this day in a little notebook he kept for many years, now in the Eleanor Bunker Collection.[3] His brother apparently drew up a roster for himself and the other preachers, because Sam's record spreads his preaching over no less than six appointments, three (6th Line, Sunnidale Station and Ebenezer) with about twenty sermons each in the year Sam was with them, and seven sermons each at the Grange Hall,[4] Stayner and Glencairn. The first sermon, from 1 Pet 1:3–4, a salvation text, he preached in the Sixth Line Church. In the evening, he took his text from Matt 5:6, from the Beatitudes, on hungering and thirsting for righteousness, another passage which could easily encourage seeking salvation—or sanctification. Very early on Sam preached at a funeral at the Tunker 2nd Line Church,[5] text taken from Ps 90:2. Four other sermons were given at homes (two) and the others at local halls, one called the Hemlock Temple, and the other at Orr Lake, for a total of 88 speaking engagements in the Conference year. From the record, he balanced his preaching texts fairly typically for many Protestants, 63 times from the New Testament and 25

---

1. Missionary Church Historical Trust (see "Ebenezer Class Book" [Box 1008]).

2. The 1861 census of Canada West listed Levi's father John as a tavern keeper and his mother Sarah the "land lady" and apparently Church of England adherents. Levi claimed his parents became members of the New Mennonites in 1863 (Huffman, *History*, 39), which suggests the evangelistic efforts of Christian Troyer or Abraham Raymer. Levi Raymer was a frequent representative of the Sunnidale field in MBiC Annual Conferences.

3. Eleanor Bunker Family Collection (see Sam Goudie's "Preaching Diar" [1886–1894]).

4. This Grange Hall was apparently on the 2nd Line, Nottawasaga, beside the Tunker meeting hall (Sider, *Be in Christ*, 27) and later became known as the "2nd Line" appointment, just as did the BiC building.

5. This building, still standing but a private dwelling, was merely metres away from the MBiC 2nd Line building (now just a foundation) sharing a cemetery, still used, behind both sites.

from the Old, from a total of 55 texts. As with many preachers, he reused sermons in other locations, especially on the same day, to save preparation time. And if it were a good sermon, why not use it again? In this first year of his probation, he was only nineteen and then twenty years old. Someone could examine the preaching records of Sam Goudie throughout his career from all kinds of angles. I will not do that here; I give this as a sample.

After the 1887 Annual Conference, Henry stayed at Nottawasaga until 1889, but Sam was sent to Michigan to assist Elder William J. Hilts. Hilts came over from Canadian Methodism to join the United Mennonite eldership in 1878 as a probationer.[6]

ST. CLAIR COUNTY, MICHIGAN

By the 1880s, the best and cheapest land in southern Ontario was nearly all bought up, and young men who wanted fresh land were looking elsewhere. The Canadian Pacific Railway was completed to the Pacific coast in 1885 (just in time to rush troops to Saskatchewan to meet Louis Riel and Gabriel Dumont's Metis uprising), and settlement was starting to fill the west, but many from Ontario and elsewhere were crossing Lake Huron to Michigan's closer central counties. New Mennonites had settled as long ago as the 1850s in Kent County near what became Grand Rapids, but the region of the "thumb," covering many counties, was equally attractive, especially to Mennonites by the 1880s.[7] The young Canadian Amish Joseph Eicher Ramseyer (1869–1945), later of the Missionary Church Association, grew up on a farm near New Hamburg, in Waterloo County and followed his family first to Zurich in Huron County, Ontario (1881), before his family packed up and settled in 1890 around Elkton, Michigan. There, they identified with the Defenseless Mennonites, a group of Amish origin started in Berne, Indiana, in 1865, which they had heard of already in Waterloo.[8]

Canada Conference Presiding Elder Menno Bowman was especially interested in following up settlers. He visited them in his Presiding Elder

---

6. *GB* (June 1878) 6; see Appendix C for a select list of Goudie's writings in the Gospel Banner. Some early Hilts families were members of the Markham Tunkers (Sider, *Be in Christ*, 14).

7. An almost parallel account of Ontario Tunkers settling in eastern Michigan is given in Sider, *Be in Christ*, 42–45.

8. Ramseyer, *Joseph E. Ramseyer*, 20, 24. The Defenceless Mennonites, after several name changes are now the Fellowship of Evangelical Churches.

rounds.⁹ Hilts and Goudie were not the first assigned to visit scattered settlements in Michigan for the MBiC. The Indiana and Ohio Conference had actually served some locations, mostly in southern Michigan near the Indiana boundary, with Peter Cober, Samuel Sherk (ordained by the New Mennonite Church in 1860), Jacob Schlichter and David U. Lambert.¹⁰ The first three men were all from Ontario. In 1884, the Canada Conference sent Bernhard Kreutziger as their first missionary to Michigan, and in 1885, he was assigned Wesley Schlichter from New Dundee as a helper around Deansville (Brown City). Goudie may have known Schlichter before he made that trip, perhaps even in the period when Sam was around the New Dundee field in the 1880s, for he kept up a friendship with Wesley with letters and occasional visits, especially when Wesley was back in Michigan living in Yale.¹¹

The Michigan mission was not easy, even compared to the rougher places in Ontario. The preachers spoke to scattered small groups in homes and schoolhouses. One man slept in a barn until accommodation was prepared. There was minimal local organization, and as a generation before in southwestern Ontario, there were few completed roads. Mennonites of any kind were not well known. Other groups were touring the state as well, but all Christian workers were few. This year probationer Sam made his first report to the *Gospel Banner*:

> Dear Editor. Grace be to you and peace from God the Father and from our Lord Jesus Christ. Amen.
>
> I will write a few lines for the *Banner* to inform the brethren and sisters in Christ a little about Michigan. I came out here a few weeks ago, and met with a good many Canadian people with whom I was acquainted and also such that I never seen before; but, best of all, I met some real Holy Ghost Christians ...
>
> I spent two Sundays in Greenwood since I am here and both of them proved to be times of refreshing to my soul, especially yesterday. We had two meetings, one in the forenoon, and the other in the evening ... There seems to be a great opening here in Greenwood for our people ... There would be plenty of work to station a man at this place, as there are so many openings where people

---

9. For example, Bowman, "Report," 9, reporting on a Quarterly Meeting at Geneva, Gladwin Township, Gladwin County, Michigan.

10. Huffman, *History*, 251. Three have profiles in Huffman, *History* (i.e., Cober [229]; Sherk [266]; Lambert [251]). See also Storms, "Cober."

11. Eleanor Bunker Family Collection (see the January 11 entry of his 1902 diary).

want us to come and hold meetings. We will, by the grace of God, do the best we can. More cannot be expected from anyone.

As far as my own personal experience is concerned I can say with the Psalmist: "The Lord is my portion, in Him will I trust." My courage is good to serve the Lord with full purpose of heart, and cleave unto Him; hoping, dear reader, if you know the value of prayer, that you will remember to pray for me, that I may be kept humble at the feet of Jesus, there to learn of Him . . ."[12]

This long quotation not only gives a taste of the expression of the young Sam Goudie, but also illustrates the typical rhetoric of testimony in the MBiC. He used phrases that multiple members did in writing to the denominational magazine. "Real Holy Ghost Christians," "refreshing to my soul," "do the best we can," "my courage is good," "humble at the feet of Jesus," these are words he could have heard frequently in the testimony meetings of his church. Of course they could become empty cliches. This is the language of solidarity and re-enforced to the people back home that he was OK!

William Hilts continued in Michigan in 1888, now assisted by Jacob Schlichter, a brother of Wesley, and a preacher transferred from the Free Baptists of Michigan called Peter Upper (born in Welland, Ontario, however). Among the many places at which Sam preached in Michigan, one became the Lamotte Missionary Church, in Sanilac County, which he and Samuel S. Stauffer opened, according to local memory.[13] Sam left Michigan after one year, but a significant connection was made.

Sam met a schoolteacher, Eliza Jane Smith in Greenwood, St. Clair County, Michigan, in the course of the year, and two years later he went back to marry her.

The Smiths of Greenwood, Michigan

Eliza Smith's family is an example of the mobility of farming families in Ontario in the nineteenth century. Those that stayed on a family farm obviously maintain a presence in a community, giving an illusion of stability and feudal-like continuity. Those are the people who show up in community and Women's Institute Tweedsmuir histories and on century farms,

---

12. Goudie, "Michigan," 10.

13. Personal notes by Eleanor (Goudie) Bunker (March 2011), with help from Evelyn (Gooding) Milsted, who visited the Lamotte church about 1990. Evelyn boarded for some years at the Goudie home on Mill Street in Stouffville before marrying.

but as we have seen, many, perhaps a majority members of farm families—especially large families—roamed the continent, looking for land or work. Eliza's father, Orrin Smith, a farmer, was the second-born in what became a large family in South Norwich, Oxford County, Canada West (Ontario). He was born on January 24, 1832 (or 1833). His parents, William W. and Mary Smith, were born in New York State, but all their children were born in Upper Canada or Canada West as it became in 1842. Eliza's mother, Margaret E. Weaver, was also born in Ontario on May 6, 1842, in Norwich.[14] Orrin and Margaret were married in 1860 in Norwich (Margaret was about eighteen), and they farmed in North Norwich, Oxford County. Three children were born to this couple: William Edwin ("Edd") (born in Canada, 1861), Eliza Jane, and Clara Amelia (1870). Margaret died at age thirty-three on December 22, 1875, of that nineteenth-century plague, which Henry Goudie called the "dreadful disease consumption," tuberculosis.[15] Eliza Jane was born on July 3, 1868, in the Greenwood area, St. Clair County, in Michigan, after the family had moved to Michigan in 1864. A baby named "Fanny" was noted in the US Federal Census in Michigan of 1870 but appears to be a nickname of Clara as a baby.[16] With young children at home, Orrin married a second time, in 1879, to English-born Elizabeth A. Pritchett (November 5, 1839–February 3, 1904). She had arrived in Michigan only in 1876.

In Canada in 1851, Orrin Smith's parents were enumerated as Baptists, but the religion of the children, on the following page in the census book, is given as "Not known," which is contrary to the usual custom of enumerators in the nineteenth century. Usually, the children were recorded with the same religion as their parents. As a couple in 1861, Orrin and Margaret gave "E. Methodist" as their religion, meaning probably, Episcopal Methodist. In the US, where "Congress shall make no law establishing religion," no religious information is given about individuals.[17] There the Smiths were in 1887 when the MBiC probationer came to the Brown City/Deansville field which included Greenwood. Sam was able to make at least

---

14. This is based on Canada Census 1851. Margaret's parents were Peter Nelson Weaver (1810–1884) of Norwich, ON, and Phoebe D. Miller (1815–1884) according to the research of Tom Bunker.

15. Goudie, "Detwiler," 15. Comment in his obituary for Louisa Jane Detwiler who died at 30 years, 9 months, and 9 days after a long period of suffering. Henry preached in English, Henry S. Hallman in German.

16. "Smith."

17. Rosen, "Brief History." The US census did ask religious leaders questions about their organizations from the 1850s to 1946, but not about individuals.

one trip back to Greenwood, chronicled by preaching on July 9, 1888, in the Greenwood church. There must have been some courting correspondence, too, but so far as I know, none has survived. The wedding took place on March 20, 1889, just after the Canada Annual Conference at Mt. Joy (Markham).

Henry Goudie was assigned to the Markham field at that Annual Conference, which meant, after his pastorate at Breslau and New Dundee, he had now been assigned to all the "big" churches except for Berlin. Clearly Henry was judged to be a trustworthy, competent minister. Samuel was to be treated the same way.

THE TWENTY, SHERKSTON, CAYUGA (LINCOLN, WELLAND AND HALDIMAND COUNTIES)

The MBiC Canada Conference of 1888 assigned probationer Sam Goudie to "The Twenty" mission, in the Niagara area of Ontario. He would serve first under David Stauffer Shantz, and work alongside fellow helper John Abram Sider, who was from the Sherkston site. "The Twenty" refers to the Twenty Mile Creek that flows into Lake Ontario, twenty miles (thirty-two km) west from the mouth of the Niagara River.

Sherkston, in Bertie Township, Welland County, had a long history with Mennonite and Tunker families, back to 1788 at least. A Mennonite congregation, never very large, existed there long before 1828, when land was deeded for a building by a Samuel Sherk, to 1931, when their third building on the site was sold to the Tunkers (Brethren in Christ).[18] Sherkston is located inland north from Lake Erie, but these days the beaches east of Port Colborne are promoted as the "Sherkston Shores" tourist area. Preacher Daniel Hoch, from The Twenty Mennonite community (Jordan, Lincoln County), visited this community in the 1850s promoting a revival message, after he was silenced by the Mennonites of Waterloo in 1849.[19] At one time the Mennonite Brethren in Christ counted six different Mennonite denominations trying to survive in the Sherkston area![20] When

---

18. Fretz and Epp, "Sherkston Mennonite Church." This Samuel Sherk is different from the New Mennonite preacher.

19. On the contest in the leadership of *The Twenty* community whether to have prayer and testimony meetings that were considered too Methodist (Evangelical Association, in particular) (Steiner, *In Search of Promised Lands*, 108–13).

20. "From thence [*The Twenty*] we went to Sherkston where we have a small mission. Bro. Samuel Goudie is preacher in charge. The pilgrims there are encouraged to fight on

Goudie was assigned to the mission, the center of the field's membership was already shifting to The Twenty, but he was resident in Sherkston.

As long as Daniel Hoch was alive, the United Mennonites had stayed away from The Twenty. Hoch did not approve of open communion; Solomon Eby's group accepted it from the start. Hoch wanted the New Mennonites to keep in the General Conference Mennonite communion with Jacob Oberholtzer. But the majority of the New Mennonites had tried to keep friendly ties with both Oberholtzer and William Gehman's Evangelical Mennonite faction in Pennsylvania.[21] When Hoch died in 1878, The Twenty congregation associated with him was apparently just a handful of people. The United Mennonites moved to fill the vacuum around 1879. Menno Bowman organized a class of twelve people who met at the Union Church in Jordan, "across from the old Jordan School by the cemetery" until they built a meeting place of their own, dedicated on June 12, 1881.[22] A strong congregation developed in the area. In 1879, the United Mennonites merged with the Evangelical Mennonites of Pennsylvania and the new group drifted from associations with the General Conference Mennonites. The EUM did support General Conference Mennonite missionaries to the Arapaho Indians for some years, however.[23]

South Cayuga was a settlement still further west along the Lake Erie shore, in South Cayuga Township, Haldimand County, where a Mennonite congregation also convened from 1835 to 1966. Hoch had also traveled here, so there were some families who welcomed the revival message of the MBiC. The numbers never rose high enough to attain stability, and by 1901 the appointment ceased.

The usual *Gospel Banner* record of where Goudie was assigned from March 1889–March 1891 is missing. The Canada Conference decided to publish its proceedings in pamphlet form those years instead of in the *Gospel Banner*, and the leaflets may not have survived. The report from Presiding Elder Menno Bowman which placed Sam Goudie in Sherkston in early 1891 demonstrates that Goudie remained in Sherkston throughout these years. We can also reconstruct his work from the same preaching diaries he kept, noted earlier when he was at Nottawasaga and in Michigan.

---

in spite of many difficulties, there are six different kinds of Mennonites in that place, the Dunkards included" (Bowman, "Report," 9).

21. Steiner, *In Search of Promised Lands*, 115.
22. Gillham, ed., *Church on the Hill*, 6.
23. Kaufman, *Development*, 259 (cf. Huffman, *History*, 186).

Eliza's brother Edd married Martha A. Gillam sometime early in 1890 in Michigan, and just before the 1891 Annual Conference, Eliza's sister Clara Amelia was married to Josiah H. Reichard, on March 30 in Greenwood or Port Huron. Reichard was born into a Tunker family in Wilmot Township, Waterloo County,[24] though the family probably emigrated to Michigan when he was young. Thus, the three Smiths were all married in the space of three years, and all had most of their children born in the decade of the 1890s, except for Clara's youngest in 1901.[25] The Goudies probably traveled to Greenwood for both of Eliza's siblings' weddings.

PORT ELGIN FIELD: PORT ELGIN, CHIPPAWA HILL, SANG'S SCHOOL HOUSE, PINE TREE, AND OTHER PLACES

At the 1891 Canada Annual Conference, Sam Goudie had finally completed all the examinations of a probationer, and he passed the ordination interview at the Conference held in Berlin. He was ordained at Berlin. As had become a custom in the Conference, a new minister was posted to one of the safe small congregations. It was a stable and manageable group for a beginner. Port Elgin, the Conference's second birthplace (the first I propose should be The Twenty, Lincoln County, Daniel Hoch's congregation) was one of these. The Scott "field" in Scott and East Gwillimbury Townships became another circuit for newer ministers, such as O. B. Schneider for his first assignment, 1888–1890. In fact, the stationing committee had announced Goudie would go to Nottawasaga again under David Shantz, but after the Conference, the two Presiding Elders, Solomon Eby and Menno Bowman, altered the assignment to send him to Port Elgin. Silas Cressman, who was soon to become one of Sam's closest friends and colleagues, a newer man, went to help on the Simcoe County field instead.[26] This was an unusual act of the Presiding Elders, if one goes by the published record. In practice, they exercised their discretion frequently in other matters so that Mennonites observed wryly that MBiC leaders who had chafed under Mennonite bishops, ended up in fact giving their Presiding Elders more power than the bishops ever had.[27]

---

24. Canada census 1871 spelled the family name as "Richard." They do not appear in the 1881 census. Other Tunker Reichards are mentioned in Sider, *Be in Christ*.
25. Genealogical information from Bunker, *Hugh Goudie (Gouldie) Family*.
26. "Proceedings," 3.
27. Epp, *Mennonites in Canada, 1786–1920*, 153.

That April, Henry Goudie was posted to the sprawling Markham field, with its seven preaching points and two helpers. That year, "Markham" mostly in York County consisted of Mt. Joy, 3rd Line [that is, Gormley], Dickson Hill, all in Markham, Bethesda in Whitchurch Township, Altona in Pickering Township (Ontario County—now called Durham Region), Vaughan (at Edgeley) in Vaughan Township, and Lincolnville, just north of Stouffville on the Tenth Line in Whitchurch. John H. Steckley and Daniel Barkey were local help. "Dickson Hill" is spelled various ways, "Dixon's Hill" and "Dickson's Hill" being common.[28]

Solomon Eby managed to visit Port Elgin after the April Conference before Sam moved, but after the previous pastor, Amos Eby, left.

> Dear Bro. Hallman: I will by the help of the Lord inform readers of our beloved BANNER that I have started out on my old mission as Presiding Elder. I commenced my 1st round [of Quarterly Meetings] in Port Elgin. Here we had precious time Saturday afternoon, on a great shout Sunday morning. It was glorious. This is my old home where I lived nearly thirty years, of which time I preached 25 years. Bro. Samuel Goudie had not yet arrived, but they expected him the following week. May he have great courage. The pilgrims were waiting on him with bright anticipations of satisfaction, and hope that he is the right man in the right place . . .[29]

Those could be daunting words for a young (twenty-four years old) newly ordained man to fulfill, unless Eby judged Goudie up to it. The whole MBiC eldership was exhorted to have "great courage" for some reason; it was a frequent, favorite expression in the "battle again sin."

Port Elgin is on Lake Huron, in Saugeen Township, Bruce County.[30] Port Elgin had come into existence only after 1852 when the government allowed land to be bought in the area. As elsewhere, title to First Nations' land had to be cleared by treaty and purchase, however callously. By 1854, Mennonites from Waterloo County were among the first to buy lots. In 1858, the Mennonite community chose a minister and a deacon: Solomon Eby was the minister, and his father, Martin W. Eby, was selected as the

---

28. Missionary Church Historical Trust (see the note by Kenneth Wideman in "Dickson Hill" [Box 1010]).

29. Eby, "Report," 10.

30. Saugeen amalgamated with Southampton and Port Elgin and they are now called Saugeen Shores.

deacon. Solomon was just twenty-four.[31] The story is told in earlier histories of the stages of how Eby was troubled about his responsibility as a pastor, and how he responded to the revivalist urgency encouraging the new birth experience.[32] The revival in the Evangelical Association congregation at Port Elgin 1868–1873 disturbed him more.

Some years ago, in an unpublished essay, I speculated on the origin of the revival, guessing some members must have gone to the first National Association for the Promotion of Holiness camp-meetings in New Jersey, USA, which happened in 1869. It is still conceivable, as Evangelical Association people did attend, but unlikely people from Port Elgin did. New light has appeared recently with the translation of personal letters in German by the Evangelical pastor at Port Elgin, Elder Jacob Anthes, exactly in the years 1868–1873. These letters had been in the historical collection at the University of Waterloo but tied up with ribbon and unread for about one hundred years. Anthes refers to events and people in the revival that broke out in his church and nearby.[33] The Port Elgin Evangelical congregation constructed their first brick building in 1868. Solomon Eby had helped move stone for their building with his team of horses. Perhaps people were aware of the National Holiness camp-meetings, but Anthes does not mention them. Intriguingly, he mentions turning to Eby to preach three times for him when he was sick in January or February of 1869, nearly a year *before* December, the date Eby gave as the time of his conversion. Anthes said that some Mennonites were converted as a result of Eby's work! The implication is that Anthes must have appreciated Eby's spiritual experience enough already to hand over preaching like that. The men were close in age as well: Eby thirty-four and Anthes thirty-two in the winter of 1869. The United Mennonites constructed a new church building in 1875 in town, which still serves as part of their facility, leaving the old building for the remaining Mennonite community on Ben Shantz' farm two km out

---

31. The profile in Huffman, *History*, 233, reports the wrong parents; they were Martin and Catharine (Weber) Eby. Storms and Theissen ("Eby, Solomon") has it right.

32. Steiner, *In Search of Promised Lands*, 129–34; Storms, *History of United Missionary Church*, 35–38, 45–48; Huffman, *History*, 41–45, 51–52; Horst, *Close Ups*, 106–21. Martin Eby's obituary suggests that his conversion was in about 1871, that is, after he had been a Mennonite deacon about fifteen years, relativizing his older Mennonite experience as at best preparation for assurance of salvation.

33. Carrick Township (now part of the Municipality of South Bruce); Bentinck Township (now part of the Municipality of West Grey); and Howick Township (Bruce County).

in the countryside, built in 1861.³⁴ The Mennonite congregation survived the division until 1902. Interestingly, a Ben Shantz hosted an MBiC prayer meeting when Goudie was in Port Elgin.

Six churches had congregations in Port Elgin in the time Sam and Eliza were there: the United Brethren in Christ, the Evangelical Association, the MBiC, and New Jerusalem (Swedenborgian), which were all ethnic-German based, plus the Methodists and Presbyterians.³⁵

In later years many new MBiC ministers were assigned to Port Elgin after their probationer's period. Henry Goudie had started here in 1878 when he was a probationer, when the United Mennonites were expanding faster than they had ordained ministers to supply.³⁶ Port Elgin was Amos Eby's first assignment as a pastor in charge after years as a helper. Solomon Eby's father, the deacon Martin Eby (b. 1808), was living on the field, but he died in June 1891. Henry Goudie and others had as their helper, though, another experienced probationer/ deacon Amos Bauman/Bowman (1844–1891) a farmer who had been ordained to the Mennonite ministry as a deacon in 1873 while the church was under a cloud but not quite separated from the Mennonite Conference of Canada.

Goudie probably met Amos Bowman in May 1891 before Amos' death on 17 November, hopefully in time to learn some useful things about the community. Nobody was sent to be Sam's helper.

Goudie's charge at first included the following: (1) Chippawa Hill (northeast about twelve km from Port Elgin across the road from the Saugeen Reserve). During his three years, other rural appointments were

---

34. Epp, "Port Elgin Mennonite Church." See Horst, "Mennonite Settlement." Horst, in a semi-fictionalized account of the Mennonites in Saugeen, pictures Ben as an unstable church member (*Up the Conestogo*, 179).

35. Robertson, *History*, 23. It is curious that a Methodist preacher Joseph Hilts—who, as far as I can tell, has no relation to the MBiC William J. Hilts, though their names are German in origin—served a large circuit called "Invermay" that included Saugeen 1864–1865. From 1870 to 1874, Joseph Hilts was the Presiding Elder for the Huron District of the Methodist Episcopal Church based in Meaford on Georgian Bay. In all, he spent about twenty-one years in Grey and Bruce Counties up to 1883. His experiences paralleled the German-based revival churches (revivals, camp meetings, conversions, and building construction) except once in Elmwood, ON, in Grey County. There he met an Evangelical Association leader, and their paths rarely crossed, at least in his memoirs. The ethnic divide was still too large. He met Daniel Burkholder at Caistor in the Niagara area at one point, who was an assimilated Mennonite, supporter of a Methodist Church at the time (Hilts, *Experiences*, 34, 116–17).

36. Missionary Church Historical Trust (see Storms, "A Short History of the Port Elgin Missionary Church" [Box 1204]).

added to the field; (2) Elsinore (on the Arran-Amabel Township; boundary about eighteen km from Port Elgin on what is now Highway 21); (3) Sang's School House (along Concession B Side Road in Arran south of Chippawa Hill); and (4) Pine Tree. Not all the new work was Goudie's. The Pine Tree, Lindsay Township, appointment was the result of William Schroeder's evangelistic work on the Bruce Peninsula from 1885.[37] Now usually known as Pine Tree Harbour, it was more than halfway up the Peninsula's west coast, about sixty or seventy km as the crow flies.[38] Goudie actually visited Pine Tree before it was listed in the stationing report. Arriving at Port Elgin about May 1891, he was already at Pine Tree in June, as a letter from Letitia Ann Holmes (June 4, 1892) shows: "Last June 1891 when brother S. Gawdie came up to see us he anointed me with oil and praise the Lord! He healed all my diseases." Mrs. Holmes had complained of kidney and heart problems, pains and 15 years' soreness.[39]

Reports spoke of the effort it took to reach Pine Tree—the roads were bad and slow.[40] Actually, Pine Tree was just one of a collection of tiny settlements on the Peninsula (Holmes's settlement, Saddler's, Cape Chin, Pike Bay, Miller Lake, Ferndale, and others) that come and go in the MBiC literature over time. Goudie visited again in 1892. With Presiding Elder Menno Bowman, they were hosted by Mr. and Mrs. Joseph Shell at Pike Bay where he anointed Mrs. Suter and her little (eight years old) nephew. They preached in the Presbyterian church building at Pike Bay. In 1893, he was again with the Pine Tree class and reported good meetings there.[41]

Sam Goudie's "Pastor's Year Book" for 1893 and a number of other years survive in the Eleanor Bunker Collection[42] with records a pastor in the MBiC needed to make his or her annual reports: membership lists, membership changes, baptisms, visits and donations in money or produce for his family and Conference projects, such as support for the Presiding Elder. On the Port Elgin field, Goudie also recorded the homes where the

---

37. Storms (*History of the United Missionary Church*, 87, 122) summarizes William Schroeder's evangelistic career; see also Gingerich, *Peninsula Pilgrims*, 11–20.

38. Gingerich, *Peninsula Pilgrims*, 15, 23.

39. Holmes, "Letter," 10. Holmes wrote again about a healing (this time from breast cancer), again after anointing by Goudie "two years ago," 11.

40. Gingerich, *Peninsula Pilgrims*, 22–23. Goudie, "Trip," 10. See Hallman, "Editorial," 8. "Travelling is not so difficult there as it was a few years ago, the roads being considerably improved."

41. Hallman, "Editorial," 8.

42. Those surviving are for 1893–1895, 1897–1899, 1900–1902, 1904, and 1915–1923.

prayer meetings were held and sometimes a note about attendance ("larger than usual," "good") and even his internal dialogue about the meeting ("small and rather dry," "no one there but I & bro. [August] Meuser's family and the Holy Trinity." It was apparently the custom on the Port Elgin field and others in the Conference; nearly all of the households with members hosted the prayer meetings. Sometimes Goudie attended more than one a week, perhaps he did not get to them all. From a pastoral side it is interesting that although Solomon Eby had suspended Michael Haug's local preacher's license for an unstated reason, and the Annual Conference had confirmed the suspension in 1892, a prayer meeting was held in the home of Haug four times in 1893. He seems to have been a member in good standing locally. Goudie was still visiting him nineteen years later in Elmwood: "Went to M Haug's for tea & spent evening there had a good visit."[43]

Prayer meetings were held in the Krauth family's house as well. Goudie notes a Gottlieb Krauth family were members in the field, and that the oldest son, Charles F. Krauth, was a helper. Although no helper was named by the Annual Conference for Port Elgin, apparently Charles, perhaps with a Quarterly Conference license or more (*Conference Journals* reported him as entering the ministry in 1892), was beginning to exercise his gifts as a pastor. In 1891 the Canada census enumerator counted German-born Gottlieb's Krauth's blended family of twelve children[44] as Evangelical Association supporters in Port Elgin. Charles in 1893 would be about twenty. For some reason, the Krauths and Charlie had joined the MBiC and he may have felt encouraged by the example of the young MBiC pastor Sam Goudie.[45] Leaders talk a lot about coaching and mentoring these days and in his years as a pastor, Goudie had opportunity to bring along young men and women into public ministry. I have not found Goudie talking or writing about grooming or developing others. Nevertheless, when he returned to the pastorate after many years as a Presiding Elder, again his church was soon recommending someone to be a probationer. Possibly Goudie's

---

43. Eleanor Bunker Family Collection (see his 1912 diary).

44. Five or six children were from Gottlieb's side and four from Fanny's, with at least two more born since the marriage of widower German-born Gottlieb and Ontario-born widow Fanny Schroen (or Schran) Krauth around 1888. Genealogical websites suggest Charles's mother (Gottlieb's first wife) was Susanna (Susan) Sommer, also born in Germany. She and several other Krauth family members are buried in Sanctuary Park Cemetery, Port Elgin. Gottlieb and Fanny are buried at First Mennonite Church Cemetery in Kitchener, along with Charles and Lavina (Baker) Krauth.

45. See Appendix B.

hopeful attitude as a pastor translated into hopefulness about others in their calling, but he was not noted for being as active as his brother Henry in encouraging young preachers.

Still another set of prayer meetings were held in the home of a Conrad Steuernagle or Steuernagel family in the Chippawa Hill area, another family from Germany with Evangelical and Mennonite connections we will meet again.[46] A nine-year old boy of that family at the time Goudie moved on from Port Elgin grew up to become a valued leader in the Pentecostal Assemblies of Canada (PAOC) decades later, Reuben Eby Sternall.

During Goudie's three years at Port Elgin, the congregation hosted a camp-meeting. The first camp-meeting at Port Elgin in 1886 was held under the leadership of Presiding Elder Menno Bowman and reportedly had thousands attend the Sunday service, including about fifty Chippewa (Ojibwe) Indians from the nearby Reserve.[47] This opening with First Nations people continued even up to 1912, when as a Presiding Elder, Sam Goudie preached at Chippawa Hill, and he reported "a nice turn out, quite a few Indians."[48]

But first there were the protracted meetings. Port Elgin was Sam Goudie's first charge as an ordained elder with Eliza, and his reports sound excited and full of hope for good things to come (he was always sounding hopeful in his reports, even of events that were not in themselves so great to tell about). After five weeks of revival meetings in January–February 1892, he wrote to the *Gospel Banner*:

> I wish to write a few lines to inform you of what God has been and is doing for us here in Port Elgin. We closed our meetings Feb 14th, having continued them about five weeks, the Lord being with us, in awakening, converting, and sanctifying power. To him be all the Glory forever.
>
> There were twenty seven converted, ten sanctified and four healed, (three of LaGrippe and one of heart diseased [his word].) Thirteen

---

46. In 1891, the Evangelical Association was disrupted by a bitter dispute over the authority of her bishops. Although the majority in Ontario sided with Bishops J. J. Esher and T. Bowman, a minority may have been upset with the treatment given to Bishop N. Dubs and the minority members (Stapleton, *Annals*, 557–73). Some Evangelical members may have left the EvA (Evangelical Association) at that time in disappointment.

47. Missionary Church Historical Trust (see Storms, "A Short History of the Port Elgin Missionary Church" [Box 1204]).

48. Eleanor Bunker Family Collection (see the May 27 entry of his 1912 diary).

have given in their names as class-members and there are others that will follow shortly.

Brother S. Eby, our worthy PE was with us two weeks and did excellent service. We were sorry he could not remain with us to the close of the meetings. Bro. D. [David H.] Moyer was with us the last week and labored very acceptably in his usual energetic manner . . .

Bro. Hallman I think if you were up here now you would be like old brother Barnabas when he went down to Antioch among young converts, you could *see* the grace of God. Oh! I am so glad that men and women can be so changed that we can see it . . .[49]

The 1892 Conference sent Henry Goudie to Berlin, completing his introduction to all the "big" stations and fields. He stayed there until 1895.

In June 1892, Greenwood, Michigan, had a camp-meeting that Goudie (and I imagine Eliza, too) attended. Twelve ministers were present, including H. S. Hallman, the *Gospel Banner* editor. Another elder, Ebenezer Anthony, later to be a missionary to Nigeria and a Presiding Elder in the Michigan Conference, made a visit from Brown City, Michigan, to Ontario to his home area at Kilsyth, south west of Owen Sound, just before the camp, and also stopped in at Port Elgin to see the Goudies: "We found him with good courage to push the battle on that field."[50] Rain forced the Greenwood camp to set up the tabernacle in a new spot, but later the weather was beautiful, Hallman said. "Attendance was fair . . ."[51] Their camp-meeting closed with a circle and a handshake. The custom of closing a camp with a "circle" will be further described in the next account.

Port Elgin Camp-Meeting of 1893

The camp-meeting for Port Elgin was fixed by the April 1893 Annual Conference, and the *Gospel Banner* turned on the publicity. Sam Goudie was listed on a Conference committee that year, a minor routine one with a delegate H. C. Green and Elder Peter Cober, which decided how to pay the expenses of ministers and delegates to the Conference from levies on

---

49. Goudie, "Port Elgin," 12–13 (emphasis original).

50. Anthony, "Letter," 10. "While out here, I visited the farm where I spent my childhood days, saw the hall where I was converted [under Janet Douglas], also the place in the woods where I first felt powerfully the call from God to preach the Gospel. This was while the conference was in session at Maryboro in 1887."

51. Hallman, "Editorial," 8.

the fields. This was perhaps the first of hundreds of short- and long-term committees Sam was to experience during his career. Amazingly he never showed signs of being weary of committees. Goudie seemed to shine in committee work.

In the early decades of the MBiC, although the major centers of membership were regularly favored, there were definite attempts to take the benefits of camp-meetings to less central locations, such as Port Elgin, on the western edge of southern Ontario, and even Manitoulin Island. Perhaps Solomon Eby had seen a need for the congregation to get a "boost," for in his Quarterly report in May, he thought the QM (Quarterly Meeting) was "not so largely attended as on former times." He attributed this in part to the Evangelical Association in Port Elgin also holding their quarterly meetings at the same time.[52] But why would MBiC members go to the Evangelicals, and not vice versa? Something was not the best. Sam's own report on the winter protracted meetings was a bit subdued: "A number were converted, and others reclaimed . . . not what we desired . . . the difficulties I think will soon disappear . . . Bro. [William] Schroeder labored with us three weeks and did good service. Yours in Christ, Samuel Goudie."[53]

In any case, Solomon Eby gave a warm recommendation for the camp-meeting location:

> The camp-meeting in Port Elgin will commence (D.V.) on the 22nd of June. This is one of the most beautiful spots in Ontario. It is situated on the eastern shore of Lake Huron. The grounds are close to the railroad and about one hundred rods [half a kilometer] from the station, with all other conveniences that can be wished for. Come pilgrims, bring your tents and blankets, with faith for a God honoring and soul-stirring time. We wish to give a hearty invitation to the pilgrims of the eastern and western districts [Canada Conference], Pennsylvania, Ohio and Indiana, to attend this camp. Come to do good and to get good. Ministers from different parts of the States will be there.[54]

In the 20 June issue, William Brunner Musselman, a Presiding Elder from the Pennsylvania Conference, wrote that he was in Berlin, on his way to the camp, and later he reported visits to other MBiC fields on the

---

52. Eby, "Report," 8.
53. Goudie, "Port Elgin," 12.
54. Eby, "[notice]" 8.

way.[55] Likewise, the veteran New Mennonite preacher John H. Steckley from Bethesda (Markham), traveled through Ontario to the camp, enjoying stops at a series of country churches: Glencairn (Sunnidale Township. in Simcoe), Shrigley (Melancthon Township. in Dufferin County), Allan Park, Elmwood, and Dobbinton, all on the Elmwood field near Hanover. The first two were in Grey County, the third in Bruce.[56]

Sam Goudie was the local pastor and heavily involved in arrangements. The local committee consisted of Goudie, the Sunday School superintendent Peter Eby, and David Devitt. The Presiding Elder was expected to give the report. Musselman said, "The Port Elgin camp-meeting was a great feast to our souls . . . Truly God was here in power . . ." Steckley agreed, "This tabernacling together proved to be a season of enjoyment in the presence of the 'God of all grace by Christ Jesus'. We need not say more as to the grand success of the camp-meeting since Eld. Eby has already given a satisfactory report . . ."

Henry Hallman had visited the camp by a weekend train excursion ($2.20 only, round trip!) and said the Sunday meetings were glorious,[57] but left Eby to say the final word:

> Dear Bro. Hallman. With your permission I will inform your readers of the Lord's doings in the Port Elgin Camp-meeting. The Lord was with us, and sometimes in great power, from beginning to end. Quite a few were saved, and many were sanctified. The Word of God was preached in its purity and power and was listened to with good attention. This is a credit to Port Elgin. We can say of Port Elgin what Paul said of the Bereans, "They were more noble than those in Thessalonica." And I doubt not but what they "searched the Scriptures" to see if what was preached was true. The general expenses were small, Mr. Chambers, the owner of the grove gave us the use of the grove and the wood that was needed free of charge which we enjoyed with many thanks. Twelve or fourteen of our ministering brethren were there. Six were baptized. On Thursday evening we closed by forming a ring to bid farewell to all the pilgrims. To God be all the praise.[58]

From this I take it that some meetings were better than others, some non-MBiC people from the village came ("Bereans") to check them out,

55. Hallman, "Editorial," 8, and Musselman, "Trip," 9.
56. Steckley, "Letter," 9.
57. Hallman, "Editorial," 8.
58. Eby, "Port Elgin" *GB* 8.

and a good number but not a majority of ministers showed up (twelve to fourteen). They did not know how many were really saved or sanctified, but definitely six were baptized, and they closed with a "ring" of fellowship, a custom I can guess at, since the charismatic movement in Ontario at least closed some meetings this way in my own experience, seventy years later. People simply stood in a circle at the camp site, maybe holding hands or elbow to elbow, visible to everyone and seeing everyone. Probably they sang the best-loved songs, a great symbol of unity.[59] A reference to this practice is reported by Leamon Hunking. At the Dufferin County Maple Valley MBiC camp-meeting of 1890 the many worshippers made their final circle around the tent that could seat five hundred people. This story seems to be from a contemporary newspaper clipping. That report estimated seven hundred attended on the last Sunday.[60]

I think people in Port Elgin enjoyed themselves, but it was not thousands, or even many hundreds attending. They were on the edge of Ontario, as I said. I would judge it to have been a notable camp-meeting. Well done, Sam and church.

Once more, in January 1894, Port Elgin held a series of protracted meetings, assisted by Elder Peter Cober for two weeks, and after he left because of sickness in his family, Silas Cressman came and filled nearly a week of meetings. Once again Goudie reported the church in general had been revived, though not completely, nor as he hoped. They had some "real good meetings . . . some backsliders were reclaimed" and "a few sanctified . . . My all is on the altar . . . yours in the field of battle, Samuel Goudie."[61]

A further milestone for the Goudie family at Port Elgin, was the birth of their first child, Pearl Elizabeth, on March 20, 1892, the Goudie's third wedding anniversary.

Goudie as a Thinker

During these three years at Port Elgin, Sam also contributed theologically to the life of his church. His writings were not especially profound, and they were short. His main avenues of expression, apart from sermons, were brief essays contributed to the Annual Conference Ministerial meetings held on a day before the Annual Conference, articles directly written for the *Gospel*

---

59. Also mentioned in Anthony, "Cass River," 12–13.
60. Hunking, *Home Spun Flashbacks*, 15.
61. Goudie, "Report," 12.

Banner or talks given to the Sunday School Conventions of the Conference.⁶² Some of the essays were selected for publication in the *Banner* by a committee of ministers from the Ministerial Convention.

The first essay by Sam Goudie of which we have a record was from the Ministerial Association of the Canada Conference of 1889, held at Mt. Joy, Markham, on March 12, days before his wedding. His essay was called "Non-Conformity to the World."⁶³ This was one of the core values of the MBiC, as we would call it now, then called a conviction, announced in the masthead of the *Gospel Banner* since 1878. Non-conformity would be manifest in plain clothing styles, rejection of membership in secret societies, political parties, unions and participation in patriotic events, rejection of fund-raising by teas and rummage sales, of choirs and musical instruments in worship, non-attendance at "worldly" entertainments, plain speech and simple church buildings, temperance and non-use of tobacco. The MBiC did not use national flags in their meeting halls, or later use the "Christian" flag, as akin to it.

The second essay we have record of by Sam Goudie was one referred to above, "The Influence of the Sabbath School," read before the Ministerial Convention of 1892 in Breslau. He included cautions that the schools needed the right teachers, because there was the danger of having a "formal professor" as a teacher, that is someone who knows the doctrine, but does not know by experience (in the Methodist sense) of salvation and sanctification. It is as I often heard in Nigeria, "You can't give what you don't have," that is, giving by leading people into a living experience with God. Goudie also mentioned the problem of curriculum. The *Gospel Banner* for decades included Sunday School lessons written mostly by MBiC writers (mostly pastors) using the International Sunday School Lessons uniform outlines. There should have been no unwelcome theology. Perhaps there were congregations, as now, that ignored the main theological stream of the denomination and held to their favorite school or writer from another stream. One year in Port Elgin, Goudie reported their Sunday School used a Free Methodist curriculum in English and an Evangelical Association curriculum in German.⁶⁴

---

62. The first Conference Sunday School Convention in the MBiC was held at Breslau in 1889. Storms says it was the first one of any Mennonite group in Canada as well (*History of the United Missionary Church*, 182; Steiner, *In Search of Promised Lands*, 182).

63. Goudie, "Non-Conformity," 14.

64. Missionary Church Historical Trust (see "Annual Sunday School Report" [Box 1204]).

Holiness (or was it Mennonite?) concerns led Goudie to warn about worldly habits of teachers in dress, shaving (!), and talk.[65] The MBiC emphasized plain or moderate dress, especially for women, never prescribing precisely what was to be worn, as the Mennonite Conference of Ontario eventually did, but worldliness in *shaving* is a little hard to identify today.[66] Goudie himself never showed a beard of any kind in any photograph of himself from youth to old age, yet the majority of ministers in the MBiC up until about the first World War, wore a variety of beard styles. They either manifested the full beard with shaven upper lip (such as Solomon Eby) which was supposed to contrast with the military style of the rest of society or the full facial sported by men like Daniel Brenneman—and like Sam's own brother Henry. In a newspaper interview in 1938, Henry seems to be teasing somebody (the reporter?): "Remarked the octogenarian, with a smile: 'I also think all men should let their beards grow, as nature intended.'"[67] A Goudie family photograph from 1893 shows all the eight brothers, their parents and Emily, their half-sister. The men have about six beard and moustache styles among them, from clean-shaven (2), a big chest-covering beard (1), a handle-bar moustache (1), full face (2), and the upper lip shaven (2). One brother had something approaching a goatee. I suppose it is possible to be worldly in any mode imaginable. The past is a foreign country!

A more central concern of the MBiC than beards was addressed by Sam in an essay published in the *Gospel Banner* in 1893. Titled simply "Holiness," Goudie used 1 Peter 1:16 ("Be holy as I am holy,") as his text to introduce his subject:

> To be holy means to be restored to the moral image and likeness of God; a perfect separation from sin and the world in all its forms; and a perfect cleansing from every "root of bitterness," or the remains of the old carnal nature, and to have on the new man (Christ Jesus), which after God is created in righteousness and true holiness . . . To be holy means to be one with God.[68]

65. Goudie, "Influence," 4.

66. When I let my beard grow when I was seventeen—this was the late 1960s, when it was sometimes a sign of rebellion, I suppose—my pastor just looked at me, shook his head, and said, "Clare, Clare."

67. Missionary Church Historical Trust (see "'Let Your Beards Grow': Church Head's Advice." *Kitchener Daily Record* (March 22, 1938). Clipping in Henry Goudie File [Box 2500]).

68. Goudie, "Holiness," 6.

Goudie is describing holiness as John Wesley did many times in his sermons: "restored to the moral image and likeness of God."[69] He develops his theme by asking and briefly answering five questions: (1) What do we understand by being holy? (2) Why are we to be holy? (3) When are we to be holy? Answer: "Now"—he shared Wesley's optimism of grace, interpreted by a hundred years of American revivalism, especially the confidence that one could be sanctified instantaneously by simply asking God for it; (4) How do we become holy? Basically, by renouncing sin, resolving to receive holiness. Curiously, he does not say, "By faith," which was Wesley's constant reminder; and (5) The fruits of holiness.

His contribution is brief, simple, not engaging in the fine questions of debate, nor qualified by long pastoral experience yet. He denies Holiness provides infallibility, freedom from errors of judgment, backsliding, or temptation. But it is attainable. He declared himself in accord with the denominational distinctive.

In the 22 March 1893 Ministerial Convention at Mannheim, Wilmot Township, Sam was asked to address a pastoral question, the question of organizing young people's societies. (His brother Henry wrote on "The Peace Question and Our Relation to It"). A Conference-directed Young People's Society was developed in the 1920s, but in 1893, Goudie was against youth groups. The main examples he had in mind were the Methodist Epworth Leagues (founded in Canada in 1889) and the non-denominational Christian Endeavour groups (founded in 1880–1801) that were multiplying in the main Protestant churches. His essay was published on April 25 in the *Gospel Banner*. He said the objects of the League and Endeavour were good, but the results were not. He thought they were "machinery for getting young people to be in the church."[70] From what he had seen, spirituality had "leaked out" of them, especially with their acceptance of social events. He and Lucy Maude Montgomery would not have agreed,[71] but had he

---

69. Dunning, *Reflecting the Divine Image*, 43. It is not clear whether Goudie ever read Wesley's works directly. There is little evidence he was an owner of many books or read widely. Charles Wesley's hymns were no doubt a source of his worship language.

70. Goudie, "Christian Endeavour," 2.

71. The famous non-orthodox author of the *Anne of Green Gables* books wrote, "church is a social function and the only regular one we have. We get out, see our friends and are seen of them, and air our best clothes" (Marks, *Revivals*, 23). Henry Alline's conversion from popular youth social activities is detailed in his autobiography, Beverley and Moody, eds., *Journal*. Alline (1748–1784) was the New Light revivalist whose activities led to the dominant Maritime Baptist tradition.

known of Henry Alline, Goudie would have agreed with Nova Scotia's New Light revivalist on the worldliness of church youth "frolics."[72]

Sam contributed one more time to the *Gospel Banner* from Port Elgin on a pastoral issue of great importance to the young denomination influenced by Methodist models of piety: the personal testimony. Goudie began by noting that there seemed to be a lack of teaching about it. His first question then was, "Is it necessary that Christians testify?" In his answer (Yes), he gave two reasons for doing so. First, the Word of God commands it—from Isa 43:10; Rom 10:10–11; Joel 2:28–29; Acts 2:17; Rev 12:11, which he claimed were a "few out of many" references. Next, he said that testifying to our experience was "essential to our faith." In support of this he made a long quote from a favorite contemporary of the MBiC, a holiness writer from the Methodist Episcopal Church in the US, George D. Watson DD (1845–1924), from his book *Love Abounding*, chapter 14. Goudie concluded that "unless we testify to what we believe and have experienced our faith is not perfect and we will loose [sic] our experience."[73] A quote from other than the Bible is rare in Goudie's writings.

"Experimental," now called experiential, was a big word with the Methodists and its daughter, the holiness movement, and the whole evangelical revivalist emphasis. It connects to the pietist concern for a current, moment-by-moment living faith/ trust in God. Most revival movements are conscious of the difference between a "professor" of religion and one who depends daily on God in Christ for forgiveness, peace and wisdom. At the first conference of the Reforming Mennonites in May 1874, all those who believed in a "*present* salvation" (my emphasis) were invited to join.[74] The Reformed doctrine of the perseverance of the saints is not what they were aiming to correct by this phrase. Regarding the question of "once saved, always saved?" they were Arminian, as were the Methodists and many Mennonites.[75] As the English Puritan John Bunyan, a member of an evangelical revival movement, they had learned the difference between talk and believing faith. Recall Bunyan's character "Talkative," among others in *Pilgrim's Progress*.

Goudie's second question then was "To what shall we testify?" He gave a two-part answer to this. Positively, we testify "To all we personally enjoy of

---

72. Goudie, "Christian Endeavour."
73. Watson (*Love Abounding*) was a new book (published in 1891).
74. Huffman, *History*, 52.
75. Wenger, *Introduction*, 306.

the grace of God, no more, no less." Negatively, this Christian testimony was not to explain scripture, or comment on what a leader has said, or try to "say something that to them sounds great," or tell about someone else's experience. In addition, he urged that the Christian testify as often as opportunity is given, thus not confining testifying to a church testimony meeting. This led him to his third and final question, "How shall we testify?" He listed four ways: reverently; humbly; clearly; and by our lives, lips, and pens.[76] These exhortations would have, to some extent, answered Elias Eby's scoffing about Solomon Eby's and Daniel Wismer's testimonies in the 1870s.

In 1893, some younger Goudie relatives were starting to write to the *Gospel Banner*. Mina Ada Goudie, a daughter of David W. and Maria Goudie, wrote from Toronto of her conversion the previous fall. Matilda Goudie, another daughter, wrote of her salvation experienced in February 1887, and signed herself, "Your sister saved and sanctified and kept by the power of God."[77]

David's wife Maria (Holm) Goudie died on 15 December 1893 at forty-two. She had been converted nineteen years before (1874) and left eight children. Her death brought the Goudie family together and allowed them to make the photograph which begins this book—the one of David and Nancy (Wanner) Goudie, their sons, and David's first child, Emily (Goudie) Warner. This photograph was taken in Berlin 18 December in the studio of Henry A. Huber.[78]

Sam and Eliza's three years at Port Elgin were up and the Annual Conference of 1894 stationed the couple to the Maryborough mission. Port Elgin was given Christian Martin Shantz (1856–1940), an older probationer, who was in his third year of the Reading Course. He was the youngest child of Henry Shantz, a bishop of the Mennonite Conference of Ontario at the

---

76. Goudie, "Testimony," 14. In an announcement of topics to be included in the upcoming Canada Conference Sunday School Convention scheduled for December 26–27 at Stayner, Goudie was listed to address the topic, "How to Make the Sunday School Interesting." But the talk was not selected for publication.

77. Mina Ada Goudie, "Letter," *GB* (14 March 1893) 10; Matilda Goudie, "Letter," *GB* (20 June 1893) 10. Mina Ada (1877–1951) married MBiC Elder Wilhelm Oscar Mendell (1871–1941) in Greenwood, Michigan, in 1899; Bunker, *Hugh Goudie Family*, 71. Matilda later married MBiC Elder J. Norman Kitching, his first wife. She died in 1903 in Brown City, Michigan. Maria's obituary: *GB* (19 December 1893) 16. David W. Goudie remarried a year later to widow Martha (Pike) Reesor of Markham.

78. Henry Albert Huber (b. 1867 in New Hamburg) was a grandson of New Mennonite preacher Samuel Schlichter and was counted as a "New Mennonite" in 1881.

Detweiler congregation of Roseville, Waterloo County.[79] Shantz was given as helper, C. F. "Charlie" Krauth.

"MARYBORO" MISSION: MARYBOROUGH, WALLACE, GLENALLEN (WELLINGTON AND PERTH COUNTIES)

At Maryboro, an inland field, Goudie was following Henry S. Wismer, who was ordained just that year and was sent to Markham. Maryborough Township was in northwest Wellington County, and the circuit was due north of Waterloo County.[80] The preaching appointments here were based on Waterloo Mennonites who had migrated north looking for cheaper land. A Mennonite congregation formed in 1864 and built their first building in 1871 at Wallace, a hamlet south of Palmerston, northeast of Listowel, in Wallace Township, Perth County. So, it was a field as old as the United Mennonite merger, if not slightly older. Glenallen (now called Glen Allan), on other hand, was in Peel Township of Wellington County. Some African-Canadians had settled here. If any were part of the MBiC, Goudie did not note them in particular, in fact many of his references to Glenallen were to using German.

The first Wallace church building was constructed on land donated by a farmer, later a postmaster, with the wonderful name of Montezuma Brothers. Starting about 1871, the Brotherston Mennonite congregation was strongly moved by the revival of the early 1870s and there was a division in the congregation. Marlene Epp says although the two groups were about equal in numbers, and shared the building for a while, the newer group obtained the building at Wallace, even before the official expulsion of Solomon Eby and Daniel Wismer.[81] The Mennonite Conference members rebuilt at Kurtzville about 1879.

As before, Sam Goudie was not given a helper for the three-point charge. There seems to have been an assumption Sam was competent to handle the responsibility. He plunged into the round of prayer meetings in homes, pastoral visits, and of course, preaching. A feature of his sermon records is that he noted when he preached in German—twenty-one times in the first eight months, for example. At the home of Isaac Stauffer at Glenallen, he always

---

79. See njshantz.ca/myproject.

80. In 1999 Maryborough Township was joined to Peel Township to make the Township of Mapleton. MBiC writers generally used "Maryboro" when referring the field, not the township, which we will try to copy here.

81. Epp, "Wallace," *GAMEO*; see Steiner, *Promised Lands*, 133.

preached in German. That year, Daniel Hostetler at the Maryboro appointment was the deacon. When he took his family off the farm and moved to Berlin, Isaac Stauffer replaced him as the deacon in 1896.

Sam's first comment to the *Gospel Banner* was a report of two baptisms on 17 September, one of a woman converted at a camp-meeting (probably the one in Berlin) and another converted in a home prayer meeting (Mrs. Joe Ernest, Glenallen, and Mrs. Robert (Sarah) Cherry, Maryborough). They went to the Conestogo River at Glenallen for the baptisms.[82] Later he reported on a Thanksgiving service: "Bro. Hallman did not come, but the Lord came and stayed all day."[83] Not a bad substitution!

Sam Goudie, or the MBiC generally, seem to have had a habit of planning revival meetings early in the new year on their fields. He reported still another series at Wallace in mid-January 1895 "with Bro. and Sis. Good of Berlin."[84]

Cyrus Nathaniel Good and his first wife Lovina Schneider/Snyder (1873–1899) were married only about ten months at the time of the revival meetings, and he was only a probationer, but already C. N. Good, as he was generally known, was becoming a pulpit regular. As with Silas Cressman, Good was soon to become a steady colleague and friend of the Goudies. Goudie had reported four people converted, and some restored. In his second report, they added three more had found peace in Christ. "Had a glorious meeting to wind up with."[85]

Unhappily, meetings with Good at another site of the three-part field had "but little results, a number have been reclaimed and the pilgrims revived, the attendance most of the time [four weeks] was good . . . let all the *Banner* readers pray for this place."[86] Sam was not one to whitewash a disappointment. Imagine if these things were said of your congregation by your leaders to all the denomination today!

In the summer of 1895, however, Eliza and Sam had the joy of welcoming another Goudie into the world at the birth of a son, Fletcher Smith Goudie, on 24 July.

In the fall of 1895 Goudie's field received attention from the Presiding Elder of his district (Peter Cober) and MBiC evangelist Noah Detwiler. In a

---

82. Sam Goudie, "From Maryborough, Ont.," *GB* (25 September 1894) 12.
83. Sam Goudie, "Maryboro, Ont., *GB* (27 November 1894) 12.
84. Sam Goudie, "Wallace, Ont.," *GB* (22 January 1895) 12.
85. Sam Goudie, "Wallace, Ont.," *GB* (5 February 1895) 12.
86. Sam Goudie, "Maraborough [typographical error]," *GB* (18 March 1895) 12.

report of 21 September, Cober, visiting all his district fields for their Quarterly Conferences noted that at Wallace on the Maryboro charge:

> While real spirituality on the whole is not running at so high a tide on this field as may be desired, yet there are quite a number here who have a deep interest in the work of the Lord. The congregations were rather small through the week, but on Sunday morning there was a fair attendance ... in the afternoon the children's missionary meeting ... In the evening we preached in Maryboro to an attentive congregation. Bro. Goudie, their pastor, is doing what he can to forward the work ... Bro. Detwiler with his band of workers ... [is] at Glenallen.[87]

Detwiler, a little more energetic in reporting, said that he started

> a week ago last night and opened fire on the enemy the same night ... our congregations are large ... On Sunday night the tent was full and fully as many outside ... four have been gloriously converted ... The Methodist minister, Mr. Bowlby, preached for us last evening. Bro. S. Goudie is ... greatly encouraged ... Bro. S[amuel] S. Stauffer and family came here Tuesday night ... My wife [Fanny (Busch)] came about a week ago ... Our sister workers, sisters [Maude] Chatham and Gardner are happy. God is using them ...[88]

In March 1896, another protracted meeting was going on the Maryborough field, though at which of the three locations the report does not specify. Cober had been visiting Henry Goudie's circuit of Elmwood and Allan Park, both near Hanover, and followed that by a visit to Sam Goudie's circuit, 80 km south of Hanover.

> In Maryboro a protracted meeting was in progress ... so of course we joined in and helped ... congregation very small through the week—three or four claimed to have been sanctified. Quarterly Meeting—peaceable and quiet. There was none of the outbursts of glory manifested that broke upon us at some of the previous ones ... Bro. Goudie ... manifests a good deal of stick-to-itiveness.[89]

---

87. Peter Cober, "PE's Report," *GB* (1 October 1895) 12–13.

88. Noah Detwiler, "Ontario Tabernacle Work," *GB* (1 October 1895) 12. I have not been able to learn more about "Sister Gardner." She does not appear in any list of MBiC evangelists from the period. Possibly she is the Mennonite domestic, 34, of German ancestry, who was working on the Jacob and Mary Miller farm in Wilmot Township, Waterloo County, in 1901. She is probably the "Sis. Katie Gortner" mentioned in *GB* (24 April 1899) giving assistance at St. Thomas. Variant spellings appear in the *Gospel Banner*.

89. Peter Cober, "PE's Report," *GB* (17 March 1896) 12.

Cober's remark suggests that Presiding Elders watched the mood of young ministers for signs of discouragement and hints of dropping out, which happens regularly in many walks of life, not just from the high expectations of the MBiC for pastors. Goudie normally seemed to have impressed his contemporaries with an optimistic attitude and determination, a characteristic that supported his presiding eldership later.

Also in 1896, David Goudie, Sam's Scottish-born father, died at home in Breslau on Christmas Day. No comment from Sam, David W. or Henry in the *Gospel Banner*, just the bare obituary saying he left a wife and nine children. "80 yrs, 6 months, 27 d."[90]

Apart from a few weddings and burials, Goudie reported little more until another camp-meeting was held on his brother's field in the fall at Elmwood, when Sam Goudie's cup of joy overflowed.

The Elmwood camp-meeting of 96

Sam Goudie wrote the report of the Elmwood camp-meeting for the *Gospel Banner*. Goudie was so excited by this camp that he supplied the magazine with a long-detailed report which took two issues to print, which was not the usual editorial practice. Guidelines for the *Gospel Banner* later specified much shorter camp-meeting reports. Nor was the display of emotion on the part of Samuel Goudie his usual form. Almost his first words were, "Wonderful! Wonderful!"[91] "The preaching was on the Holy Ghost line." As headline news, Goudie reported fifteen or sixteen were converted and twenty to thirty reclaimed and sanctified.

We will examine Goudie's report in some detail, partly because it is so long. It gives us an example of a camp-meeting at this time from the ministry side. It shows what Goudie, Hallman, and presumably the MBiC in general would have hoped to see in their camp-meetings. Goudie reported every preacher and every text in each session, but also characterized the response of those attending to many of the sermons, except to his own. These remarks show what he saw as significant at this point in his career, ten years into public ministry and in his thirty-first year of life. These expressions of faith will seem radical or wild or ordinary to the reader today, depending on your own church experience and beliefs. They certainly show that neither Pentecostals nor charismatics have been the only ones

---

90. "Goudie," *GB* (5 January 1897) 16.

91. Sam Goudie, "Elmwood Camp-Meeting," *GB* (29 September 1896) 8, and (6 October 1896) 8.

to display "Holy Ghost fire." Canadian Brethren in Christ Bishop Ernie J. Swalm commented about the demonstrative MBiC he knew in the Stayner area: while his BiCs overreacted to the MBiC's "emotional extravagances," in the direction of restraint, he still liked their "more vital life style," and he thought their "freedom was wholesale and genuine."[92] Mennonite observer Lewis J. Burkholder of Markham writing in 1935, said that the MBiC began with a lot of uncontrolled emotionalism, but that wise leaders by his day had directed the church into saner manners of expression. Sam Goudie was the chief MBiC leader Burkholder would have known over many years, almost neighbors in the Markham-Stouffville area. I wonder if Goudie was chiefly on his mind. Whether Burkholder was right, good people will differ in judgment.[93]

The camp began on September 7 with an evening meeting led by the Vice-Presiding Elder of the district, who was none other than Henry Goudie that year. The preachers were all MBiC except a certain "Brother Bedingfield."[94] Many were young: August F. Stoltz (age 30), Charles Krauth (24), Jesse S. Guy (34), and Euphemia Guy, his wife (37), Alex Bell (33), Ephraim Sievenpiper (26), Joshua Schell (19), Silas Cressman (33), Maude Chatham (26), and Sam Goudie himself (30). Henry Goudie (44), the host pastor of the camp location, preached only on the last day, with Presiding Elder Peter Cober (43) and Henry S. Hallman (38), the *Gospel Banner* editor, adding to the roster of preachers.

August Stoltz started off the preaching with a message from 2 Pet 1:10–11 with a slight tilt of this passage toward the holiness emphasis: ". . . those only are elected who yield fully to God." Next morning, Sam Goudie had his first chance at preaching, taking Ps 45:7 as his text, but how he developed it he did not say, nor anything about response. On Peter Cober preaching on Acts 4:33 (Thursday afternoon), Goudie commented, "The Lord helped him and graciously owned and blessed the word." The scripture would have been appropriate at the start of a camp-meeting where testifying to the work of God could be very important for the progress of conversion and the excitement of the congregations. In the evening ". . . after a real good fellowship meeting, where shouts of glory were in order,

---

92. Swalm, *Nottawa District*, chapter 4 [not paginated].

93. Burkholder, *Mennonites in Ontario*, 195.

94. Probably Charles Bedingfield, a local preacher on the Methodist Stayner circuit about 1898. www.ucstayner.ca. Entry for January 29, 2006.

Bro. Alex. Bell preached on consecration from I Chron. 29:5."[95] Although the text could lend itself to asking for big offerings, the MBiC was interested in personal dedication to the service of the Lord.

In the Friday morning service, "some danced, some walked, and others shouted."[96] "Bro. Krauth preached in German from Rom. 6:12, 13." This scripture warns of sin's tyranny, but also exhorts to present oneself to God. This was followed by the usual invitation to come to the front (the "altar") for response in prayer: for salvation, reclamation of backsliders, and sanctification. On Friday afternoon, Jesse Guy preached "with supernatural strength from 1 Peter 5:10 on grace from and for glory [underlining original]," and somehow, he found sin and hell from this text as well. Brother Bedingfield followed the fellowship service with a message from Ps 40:1–3, just before the altar service.

Ephraim Sievenpiper preached Saturday morning on Matt 3:11, the scripture where the baptism of fire (of the Holy Spirit) was promised. Joshua Schell preached "with liberty and power" from Ps 25:14 that while justification is a great secret, sanctification was a greater one. "While we as a church are opposed to secret societies, yet we belong to one. We are initiated into it in our conversion."[97]

Also, Saturday afternoon, Jesse Guy preached on "feetwashing," the observance obeying Jesus as recorded in John 13. Typically, the Canada Conference observed this ordinance after communion at Quarterly Conferences, but Goudie's report suggests they conducted the washing of the saints' feet that afternoon. Goudie summarized the message, "It is the shadow of a substance which embodies the plan of salvation." He continued, "Many obeyed and got blessed. The fellowship meeting in this meeting and in the evening are indescribable. God wonderfully displayed his power. Dancing, laughing, walking and running were in order." Jesse Guy was already sick with the TB that was to take his life in March of the next year at Stayner where he was the pastor with fellow preacher Euphemia (Pool) Guy, his wife. I confess I do not know exactly what Goudie and others meant by the expression "... were in order." He doesn't mean the activity named was orderly, but seems to mean, "was appropriate to the occasion."

---

95. Alexander Bell died in 1900.

96. Free Methodist Church camp-meetings of the time matched this repertoire as well: "leaping, weeping, shouting, laughter." Sigsworth, *Free Methodist Church*, 23–24.

97. Joshua Schell was to die of pneumonia from the rigors of pioneer pastoral work at Didsbury, Alberta, in 1901.

Goudie reported a children's meeting Sunday at 2 pm addressed by Alex Bell, Sister J. S. Guy and Henry S. Hallman, during which some children expressed a desire to become Christians. Then Stoltz preached, and Hallman again.

Monday morning, after the usual 5 a.m. prayer service, the camp continued with Silas Cressman preaching from 1 Pet 1:16 on holiness, ". . . the central truth of God's Word." More altar services led to notable conversions. The fellowship meeting lasted nearly all afternoon. "It was something wonderful. Great conviction came upon the unsaved and a most gracious altar service followed. One young man threw his tobacco, gold chain, tie and big cuffs away while seeking."

In the evening, Maude Chatham, who was to serve nineteen years in western Canada including starting several institutions in Edmonton,[98] preached from Acts 8:21, with another altar service afterward. Next morning, Euphemia Guy preached from 1 Cor 1:27–29 on God's frequent choice of the weak. Goudie recorded several details about the sermon which he did not do for other sermons, listing some of her illustrations (taking Jericho, feeding 5,000 with a few loaves and fish, story of a girl used in the conversion of her father). "Then there is the foolishness of testimony. They say women are weak things, but God often chooses them and uses them." An altar service followed, basically, another time of invitation to respond publicly to the message.

Tuesday morning Euphemia's husband Jesse Guy preached again (Exod 33:16) on the MBiC insistence on separation from the world and plainness (in clothing). Here is where the legalistic tendency in holiness interpretation often showed up in churches like the MBiC. Lacking a theology of culture, they found themselves in long struggles with accommodation to prevailing culture, with lines drawn and redrawn, and each acceptance of a new style suffered as a defeat caused by the world. I do not know what specific items of clothing Jesse found worldly, but going by the comments of MBiC women preachers themselves in the *Gospel Banner*: Lucy (Bingeman) Rosenberger, Mary Ann (Hallman) Simmons, Sarah Pool, Euphemia (Pool) Guy and such, I am sure he found plenty to denounce. The next generation remembered evangelists going down aisles at camp-meetings snipping feathers from women's hats.

---

98. Beulah Mission included a shelter for homeless men, a home for unwed mothers (Beulah Home) and Edmonton Bible Institute. See her profile in Fuller, "Chatham."

In the evening Sam Goudie preached again, on Col 1:12, a straightforward salvation text. On Wednesday, Bedingfield preached again and in the evening, the Presiding Elder Peter Cober preached on baptism, in anticipation of the need to baptize the converts, from the Great Commission verses of Matt 28:19–20. Finally, on Thursday, Sam's older brother Henry Goudie got his turn to preach, then August Stoltz (from Rom 8:14 on the Spirit-led life) and Presiding Elder Peter Cober again, from the great description of the Spirit-filled church life of the Jerusalem congregation (Acts 2:42).

This camp, too, closed with the ring-fellowship activity we noted before. The progress of the messages seems too orderly to have been coincidental. Either the organizers of the camp encouraged the preachers to follow a pattern of preaching suitable to the stages of conversion, sanctification and exhortation to persevere, or the pattern was sufficiently well understood that most speakers knew what was expected of them. Goudie was certainly right that the messages were "on the Holy Ghost line." Although the sources in the Bible were nicely varied from Old and New Testaments, the variety of speakers could have lifted the similarity of the themes (conversion and holiness) from being unduly repetitive. The general youthfulness of the preachers may have given energy to the messages, and since many attenders were members of the fields the preachers served, their personal connections may have given additional interest. We remember, too, that preachers stayed on circuits no more than three years, so the pool of preachers was widely known, much more so than would be the case today in the EMCC. Like them or not, the camp-meeting goers knew these preachers. Camp-meeting reports frequently noted the relative numbers of attenders compared to other camps. Since Goudie does not remark on that, attendance may have been typical of the times.

By a later custom at camp-meetings, for which Goudie and the Conference executive were responsible, selected professional evangelists supplied the main preaching activity. Was either custom (preachers from the Conference eldership or professional evangelists) more effective in producing converts and sanctifications? A conclusion is not obvious. I seem to have heard more older members reporting they were converted under the preaching of the church's own preachers and evangelists than under the professional evangelists of related, but different, church affiliations. More study would be needed to identify any trends. Camp-meeting activities in the EMCC now do not correspond to the pattern in Goudie's day, so that comparison cannot be made. The past is that foreign land to us now.[99]

The MBiC certainly went on holding camp-meetings annually in every Conference. The Canada Conference often held two, one for each district, for a while called the North and South Districts. Later the Conference re-named the divisions the East District, centered on Markham/ Stouffville, and the West District, centered on Berlin (Kitchener). You can read more about the camps and daily life on the campgrounds in the official histories and in the booklet by Lloyd Brubacher and others. It is also instructive to read about other denominations' camp-meetings, such as the Methodists of Ontario in earlier decades[100] or references in Sigsworth's history of Canadian Free Methodism. They sound so similar, yet the denominations did not interact much except at some annual conferences in Ontario. Canadian FM Charles V. Fairbairn recounts eight annual camp-meetings (1917–1924) under his chairmanship, of the Godfrey Holiness Association in eastern Ontario (Frontenac County) which were deliberately across holiness denominational lines—C. N. Good was even invited in 1920 though unable to attend—which suggests informal fellowship was possible.[101] The editors of the *Gospel Banner* received copies of a couple of dozen similar magazines and regularly quoted doctrinal articles, but rarely news items, from them. Anecdotes suggest that some people attended other denominations' camp-meetings because they supported the activity and holiness teaching whole-heartedly, not necessarily the denomination as such.

Holiness—Wesleyan and Otherwise

"Holiness" as a doctrinal emphasis in the MBiC was also mentioned in the masthead of the denominational paper, the *Gospel Banner*. We have mentioned holiness many times without reflection. Neither the New Mennonites of Ontario nor the Evangelical Mennonites of Pennsylvania were

---

99. I would have mixed reactions to some of the demonstrations Goudie reported, which I could take as a cross-cultural experience, but less easily as daily fare for myself and a family. The practices were not that unusual historically in revival situations.

100. See Steinacher, "Homogenization of Methodism," 131–165; also Airhart, "Eclipse." Airhart's work is also accessible in Westfall, *Two Worlds*, chapter 3: "The Tempering of Revivalism and the Transformation of Experience," 50–81.

101. Fairbairn, *Remembrance*, chapter 34 "Eight Seasons of Grace," 150–54. Fairbairn reports preachers from the Wesleyan Connexion, Holiness Movement Church, Standard Church, Wesleyan Methodist, Methodist (Canadian or American he does not specify), Gospel Workers Church, Pilgrim Holiness Church and of course, Free Methodist Church.

Wesleyan holiness revivalists. They practised a Methodist revival style in the UBiC and EvA way,[102] as the doctrine was not a specific issue in Methodist churches until the American Civil War period. The doctrine was developing new terminology and practices, borrowed from the general revivalist/ camp-meeting set of doctrines and practices after they started. The latter half of the nineteenth century was a period of separations, siftings and shiftings in the Methodist churches of Britain and North America concerning holiness.[103]

The MBiC came into the orbit of the holiness movement just when advocates were starting to be discouraged by Methodist leaders from emphasizing "second blessing" teaching. In response, associations were springing up to promote the doctrine and experiences believed to be essential.[104] Eventually a call to "come out" from the "apostatizing" churches were listened to by an increasing number of holiness promoters. Associations transformed into proto-denominations and eventually into outright holiness denominations. The largest in the United States were to become the Church of the Nazarene and the Church of God (Restoration Movement, also designated by "Anderson, Indiana"), but there were dozens more. In Canada, the main denominational expressions of holiness teaching were rather smaller: the Free Methodists (organizing after 1876), the Salvation Army (early 1880s), the Reformed Baptists in New Brunswick and Nova Scotia from 1888, (split from the Free Christian Baptists, an Arminian group now part of the Wesleyan Church, not related to Calvinistic Reformed Baptist Churches in the region today), the Wesleyan Methodist Church of America (in eastern Ontario, from 1889) and the Holiness Movement Church organized by Ralph Horner (1897). Still others were the tiny Holiness (later "Gospel") Workers Church around Georgian Bay, ON (from 1902), the Church of the Nazarene (in western Canada from 1902, 1920 in Ontario), the Brethren in Christ (adopted the doctrine in 1910) and other small groups.[105] Many in the MBiC worked to move the MBiC to a thoroughly second work of grace Wesleyan holiness position from 1883 to 1947, but the stance of the

---

102. Steiner, *Promised Lands*, 108, says the New Mennonite Church explicitly rejected some typical holiness elements and Evangelical Association polity.

103. A good study of this development in North America is Peters, *American Methodism*. See also Failing, "Developments in Holiness Theology," 14–31.

104. Another account of these changes is given in Synan, *Holiness-Pentecostal Movement*, 44–50.

105. Documented in fascinating detail in Jones, *Wesleyan Holiness Movement*. See also Hobbs and Hobbs, "Holiness Churches."

Pennsylvania Conference forced frequent doctrinal compromises and accommodations in the Articles of Faith and tensions over holiness teaching in the *Gospel Banner*. At the individual Conference and camp-meeting level outside Pennsylvania, there were fewer compromises, and Wesleyan holiness was freely promoted. By 1947, forces were at work that eventually diminished the holiness witness in parts of the United Missionary Church, just when it finally seemed to triumph. But that is another story.[106]

Any attempt to rediscover the doctrine of sanctification for understanding the Mennonite Brethren in Christ's theology, just as in pursuing its Anabaptist historical and theological roots, should be learned from the basic works. For Wesley, some books would be *A Plain Account of Christian Perfection* first of all, his *Standard Sermons*,[107] *Explanatory Notes upon the New Testament*, the *Journals*, his brother Charles' hymns, studies of John Wesley's life and theology, and that of his circle in the eighteenth century. Writings by holiness authors of the nineteenth and twentieth centuries must be considered, especially those chosen for the reading course: Thomas K. Doty, Milton L. Haney and T. Wilson Hogue. The MBiC read quite a range of writers, given the evidence of books which survive owned by various leaders, such as Noah Detwiler,[108] Sam Goudie,[109] and Alvin Traub.[110] One finds such authors as John A. Wood, Randolph Foster, George D. Watson, and Daniel Steele of the American Methodist Episcopal Church, Martin Wells Knapp and S. B. Shaw (independents), Samuel Logan Brengle (Salvation Army), Albert Sims (Free Methodist) and many other writers.

John and Charles Wesley and the Holy Club at Oxford, England in the eighteenth century, with George Whitefield and others shared the assumption of the Church for ages that God was in many ways the ruler of the universe, a great monarch, King of kings and Lord of lords. God therefore ruled in the manner of a king, by his will, that is, his word and by extension,

---

106. For an overview of doctrinal shifts including Arminian Wesleyan evangelicalism in the EMCC see Oke, "Theological History," 362–73.

107. In a marvelous edition with comments by a Canadian Methodist theologian: Nathanael Burwash, *Wesley's Sermons*. My first copy, bought in Kingston, Ontario, was lost in a doctor's office in Toronto, with all my personal notes and especially, additional index material I had developed over the course of the years it took to read all the sermons slowly.

108. James A. Wood, *Purity and Maturity*, author's collection.

109. Joseph H Smith, *Pauline Perfection*, Box 6016, MCHT.

110. Seth Cook Rees, Benjamin T Roberts, Albert Sims and Martin Wells Knapp, author's collection.

his law. I would judge that our generation typically rejects this category (law) of God's relation to us; whether we are justified in that is another question. John Wesley lived in the long period when monarchy was the nearly universal experience of European Christianity, and kings decreed and ruled through laws. Wesley had great respect for the law of God. He saw the will of God expressed through law plainly taught in Scriptures and wanted to fulfill it in his life. It took him until his Aldersgate experience (May 24, 1738) to finally trust God for his salvation by faith, (which some take as the time of his salvation, but others take as his assurance of salvation),[111] but that never changed his desire to conform his life to the will of God revealed in the Bible. "[W]ithout holiness no one will see the Lord" (Heb 12:14) would be an assumption throughout his ministry as an Anglican minister. Regeneration (the new birth) was the work of God in beginning to recreate humans fully into the image of God. This coordinated with justification, the declaration by God, on the basis of Christ's freely provided atonement, received by faith, that sinners were right in God's sight when they submitted to God's righteousness. Wesley was not content with a mere declaration of being right with God, he longed for what he believed to be the proper ultimate business of the Christian, to somehow be conformed to righteousness, God's will, in heart (being) and action (doing). "Offer your bodies as a living sacrifice, holy and pleasing to God . . ." (Rom 12:1–2) became an important program text for both the Deeper Life and Wesleyan holiness movements.

A question Wesley asked was, when would a believer be pure in God's sight, complete in heart-holiness? The Reformed said it would only happen at "glorification," at death. The Roman Catholics said some saints would be holy now (in this life), some at death but most of us after a purging period after death. Wesley leaned to the Catholic answer, except he rejected the purgatory doctrine. Wesley further asked, what is stopping us attaining holiness now? God was not weak or reluctant or powerless, it must be only from our side that "perfect love" (Wesley's preferred scriptural term from 1 John 4:18) does not occur. He deduced that we must seek perfect love, and receive it by faith, and that it is an event in our experience of salvation that could be received concurrent with regeneration/ justification, but typically subsequently. If believers neglect to pursue holiness or are ignorant of their privilege, he expected that as with the Reformed, God would grant entire sanctification (a Wesleyan holiness term not common with Wesley) only

---

111. Job, *Wesley's Heart*, 13.

at death, though as through fire. As many writers have pointed out, James Packer included, Wesley published others' testimonies of experiences of perfect love, but in his writings, including his journals, never claimed the complete experience himself.[112]

John Wesley used a logical argument from 1 John 1:7 and 9 to support his case: if the blood of Jesus Christ cleanses us from *all* sin, how much sin is left uncleansed or unforgiven? He thought it was unanswerable that any sin, any morally significant non-conformity to the will of God, was left over for Christ to cleanse. He allowed that a Christian in perfect love could be in error due to ignorance and fall short of intended action; what he claimed was that the thoughts and intentions of the heart were freed from sin. Growth of the believer in many areas was still to be expected, but "confessable" sin was reduced to zero while the believer lived in daily faith in the sustaining power of God. On the idea of confessing all known sins, William E. Sangster, an English Methodist who believed and preached holiness as the Christian aim, found in psychology's "discovery" of the unconscious what he considered to be the unknown flaw in Wesley's argument. We can't confess all our sin because we can hardly ever be aware of all the motives of our hearts. Thus, we are ever in an interim state. Sangster's analysis could leave us very close to the Reformed view, but by a different (extra-biblical) route.[113]

Wesley also argued, in Enlightenment fashion some would say, that we cannot be charged as sinners for any unknown "sinfulness of being" with which the Reformed charge us all. If you confess anything you are aware of, what more can God ask of us? He thought living in a state of "saved but still a sinning sinner" was to go back to the condition of Luther in the confessional booth, dragging up any scrap of doubt about his standing before God, and assuming there was more to be confessed. The Lutheran and Reformed argument is that 1 John 1:8 and 10 are simultaneously true with vv. 7 and 9, that though cleansed, we are still "not without sin," and that, if we say (present tense) we are (now) without sin, we are lying. Wesley had no problem with v. 10, because it is past tense: "If we claim we have not sinned . . ." and he said v. 10 explains the application of v. 8.[114] When I read Wesley's

---

112. For example, Packer, *Keep in Step*, 118. Not surprisingly, holiness writers have rejected this interpretation: Failing, "Developments in Holiness Theology," 13.

113. Sangster, *Path to Perfection*, 72–76, 119–23.

114. Sangster, *Path to Perfection*, 49.

A Plain Account of Christian Perfection, I was troubled by the tense of verse 8 and so I was unconvinced, though Wesley's logic seemed true as well.[115]

Jean Guilliame de la Flechere (John William Fletcher) (1729–1785), a godly Swiss-born Christian who in England became an Anglican minister along with the Wesleys, who John Wesley hoped would continue leadership in the movement, died before Wesley did. In several theological works Fletcher developed defenses of Arminian Methodist preaching.[116] He also saw in the Baptism with the Spirit which the 120 in the upper room received at Pentecost (Acts 2), the very heart-cleansing work of God, and therefore that event which was the second stage of God's work the Methodist movement longed for. This "pentecostal" language was picked up by holiness promoters in the nineteenth century, though Wesley did not emphasize the baptism imagery himself. In the Conference Sermon for 1930 which was also an ordination sermon for Russell Pike on Acts 1:8, Sam Goudie continued to identify perfect love and the Baptism of the Holy Ghost, promised by Jesus as the Power received at Pentecost.[117]

John Stott's short book called *Baptism and Fullness* made a good case that Baptism with the Spirit is an initiatory event, one of the many acts of God applied to the one who believes the gospel at the time of justification.[118] In other words, it is not subsequent. In his interpretation, "fullness" is the scriptural term for any subsequent renewing of our hearts into conformity with God, and that these re-fillings could happen frequently with great power, *or not*, in our experience of being saved, that is, the Christian life. I think he left it an open question whether this fullness was an on-going experience or not, though as a moderate Calvinist, Stott leaned toward the expectation that this was never a completed work in this life. James Packer, a fellow Reformed Anglican, wrote that the reason total heart-cleansing in this life is not to be expected is that God never promised it, that this life is a continuing development (some would say "struggle") toward conformity to

---

115. By a trick of memory, I later thought 1 John 1:7–10 was the major passage on which Wesley founded his reflections in the *Plain Account*, but in fact he had about 30 texts he used over the course of his long ministry; Sangster, *Path to Perfection*, 37–52. Wesley, *Christian Perfection*, 25. I decided that in any instance of temptation, we *need not sin* was the moment-by-moment holiness God was calling us to.

116. Mostly in his series against antinomianism. For Fletcher's life, there is Joseph Benson's *Life*, but there are many others.

117. Outlined in *Ontario Conference Journal 1930*, 42.

118. Stott, *Baptism and Fulness*. Enlarged and published as *The Baptism and Fullness of the Holy Spirit*, Chicago: InterVarsity, 1975, in the US.

God's will and that *progress* in maturity is God's will. "Who will rescue me from this body of death?" (Rom 7:24). Jesus *will*, but not yet, is the implied answer, Packer says.[119]

What can we say then about the heavy emphasis in the MBiC on sanctification as subsequent to salvation? In practice, the MBiC pastors accepted as Christians people with less than perfect practice of Christian faith. They confronted this common phenomenon with frequent special services: (1) protracted meetings . . . though the term died out; (2) revivals . . . though there was misplaced trust in Finney's formulas for almost mechanically producing what strictly only God sovereignly grants; and (3) holiness conventions. It was good that the leaders of the MBiC did whatever was in their power to lift the level of Christian practice from mere profession to a daily lively faith in the Lord Jesus Christ. By song, preaching, prayer and testimony, they were hopeful of better things, of an abundant life available for the children of God, of realizing increasing or—why not?—full release from bondage to sin and living in victory over sin. Nevertheless, the second blessing doctrine has some drawbacks for church life.

The Eastern Orthodox Churches think that they evangelize chiefly by conducting their liturgy. Roman Catholics preach belief but have historically been satisfied if someone assented to the instruction or authority of a priest. Anabaptist practice has been to demand the on-going following of Christ in community, marked by certain discipleship stages (very close to the Pietist and holiness stances). Occasionally, Protestants have been content with submission to creeds or cultural forms, but a person who merely professes is described as "nominal" by evangelicals of any type, Puritans, Pietists, Methodists in Wesley's societies, Baptists, Pentecostals and charismatics, the revived of any tradition who pursue Jesus with a whole heart.[120] It is unhealthy for a church to suppose and be content with two classes of Christians, whether they are named the masses and the religious, lay or clerical, ordinary and initiates, psychical or spiritual, merely born-again or entirely sanctified. These distinctions seem gnostic-like, that there are the Christian elite and the common masses who know nothing much. Christians are better classified as backsliding, static, or progressing and maturing. Some need to confess sins, others to humble themselves to the Lord,

---

119. Packer, *Keep in Step*, 107.

120. For a beginning definition of "nominals," Mandryk, *Operation World*, 22: those who "know nothing of a personal faith, true repentance from sin and working out their salvation in relationship with the living God."

to "see if there is any offensive way" in them (Ps 139:24). All need to call on the Lord to fill us with his Spirit again whenever we are made aware of sins and deficiencies as in Eph 5:18. The verb in "be filled with the Spirit" is a present tense, implying a continuous operation. Because it involves real-time experience, the feeling of filling is subject to ups and downs.[121]

The Mennonite Brethren in Christ of Sam Goudie's day, and Goudie himself, were convinced of the second work of grace doctrine and experience. They expended a lot of energy to maintain a feeling, perhaps more than living a life of faith.[122]

The Fourth General Conference, Coopersburg, Pennsylvania, 1896.

Shortly after the successful Elmwood camp-meeting, Henry Goudie and others from the Canada Conference met in Coopersburg, near Allentown in eastern Pennsylvania, for the MBiC General Conference (GC). Henry was an official delegate elected by the Canada Conference. There were only nineteen members in total at this GC, but the Canada Conference had a large delegation because of its relatively large membership. We have met many of these delegates: the three district Presiding Elders, Menno Bowman, Peter Cober and Ebenezer Anthony (who was representing the proto-Conference of Michigan, which the Canada Conference had been preparing for full Conference-status for some years and was ready to release at this GC). With them traveled Solomon Eby, Henry Goudie, Jesse S. Guy, Oliver B. Snyder, August F. Stoltz, William Graybiel, and Henry S. Hallman. Unfortunately, Menno Bowman had sickness in his family, so Henry S. Wismer went as his alternate. By the time Sam Goudie was elected a Presiding Elder in 1905, most of these men from Ontario were gone from leadership, but many issues they worked on were still those he met: for example, difficulties with the *Gospel Banner*, doctrine in the *Discipline*, texts for the Reading course, revision of the hymnbook, and the stance of the Pennsylvania Conference to the rest of the Church. The question of foreign missions was asked but not resolved to the satisfaction of all, as several

---

121. Stott, *Baptism and Fulness*, 32–33.

122. A reader, notes on a draft, to the author, June 2018, wondered if the sanctification practices of North American holiness churches were, sociologically speaking, "gentrification" tendencies applied to frontier spirituality, an interesting suggestion to pursue. The MBiC, in other words, faced with urbanization in society away from pioneer farming, de-emphasized conversion and water-baptism discipleship (catechetical instruction) in favor of meeting-based invitations for salvation, sanctification experiences, and patching the lapses of backsliders.

young members were joining a variety of mission societies. Goudie was to give decisive leadership in favor of a denominational mission, but it would take decades yet.

Peter Cober was elected chair of this General Conference. Almost for the last time, the German language was accepted for use in the deliberations: "German members shall have the privilege to speak in German." C. H. Brunner was elected the interpreter.[123] Despite this attention, the German language edition of the *Gospel Banner*, the *Evangeliums Panier*, ceased publication later in 1896.

Most of the Conference was taken up with further revisions of the MBiC *Discipline* which had likewise occupied earlier General Conferences. There was also preparation for a GC Constitution, which in the end did not get approved.[124] The Reading Course for probationers was frequently a source of dissatisfaction from the various Conferences. Only the General Conference had authority to change the course and it proved difficult for individual Conferences to persuade others of the wisdom of their preferences and change came slowly. Early on it became apparent that Pennsylvania Conference had a different theological shade than the others, and by the 1890s often tried to get Keswick-style or Christian and Missionary Alliance (C&MA) textbooks approved. "A short treatise on Christ's Coming shall be added by the Committee," marks the growing consensus in the MBiC that the premillennial doctrine was correct, adding to the simpler four-fold Mennonite/classic consensus of resurrection, return of Christ, judgment and final state of new heaven and earth.[125] The *Gospel Banner* editor gave his report and his re-appointment was confirmed. Michigan Missionary Conference was approved as a new full Conference of the Church. Canada Conference handed over 571 members to it.

Conference leaders gave brief reports and submitted statistical summaries of the quadrennium. Briefly, the MBiC had 61 ordained ministers with 32 probationers, 61 deacons, with 27 more on probation. The

---

123. "General Conference Proceedings," *GB* (27 October 1896) 3–5, 15.

124. The vote happened in the summer of 1897, with 2,152 approving, 213 voting against, with 1,514 not voting, and thus a 2/3 majority of the whole membership (3,879) did not give consent, according to the rules of the denomination at the time. The proposal to have a Constitution was thus defeated, which situation continued until the 1950s. H. S. Hallman, "No Constitution," *GB* (13 July 1897) 8.

125. For example, the 1632 Dordrecht Confession, Article XVIII, "Of the Resurrection of the Dead and the Last Judgment." Jesus' coming again is mentioned in Article IV; in Wenger, *Doctrines*, Appendix 2.

Conferences reported 2,679 baptisms but 2,271 new members, against 1,118 losses in various categories over the 4 years since the last General Conference. These were all young adult or adult members, of course, as they maintained the Anabaptist conviction that only believers were called to be baptized and members. They now claimed to have 3,879 members in Canada and the US. Preaching was going on at 178 locations at all stages of organization. Church buildings owned by the MBiC were reported to be 78 and 1/2! They also reported preaching 33,872 sermons, though I am not sure what use would be made of that statistic. If all the sermons were delivered by the 93 licensed and ordained people, the average number of sermons per preacher would be about 364. So much teaching!

The institution of deacon was undergoing ups and downs in the MBiC. In 1896, there were almost as many as the elders. Storms noted that the position of deacon died out in the Pennsylvania Conference,[126] and it has continued to oscillate in frequency as the descendent American and Canadian denominations sway between business or biblical terms for church governance.

One last item of business: an MBiC hymnal which was compiled by a committee established by the 1892 GC was commended for use in all the regular English church services. This book may have been an edition of *Choice Collection of Spiritual Songs*, originally prepared in 1881 by Daniel Brenneman, Solomon Eby, and Benjamin Bowman, and the "Executive Committee" was given "authority to order a new edition of our Church Hymnal if necessary."[127] The *Gospel Banner* editor Hallman, himself the compiler of a song and chorus book (*Songs of Glad Tidings for the Worship of God* which went through many editions) advertised in the very next issue, may have hinted at the reason for the hymnal issue.[128] Some hymns in use in the churches did not support descriptions of the spiritual life of the sanctified in the manner a holiness church would desire. Hallman explained

---

126. Storms, *United Missionary Church*, 72. Deacons were ordained in the Mennonite Conference of Ontario and the MBiC, and the MBiC collected statistics on the number of deacons, but gradually the visibility of deacons has declined. In the congregationally individualistic EMCC, does anybody know how this arguably biblical office fares across the church? We live in another country.

127. See Steiner, *Promised Lands*, 160. The 1881 hymnbook, printed in Elkhart, Indiana, had words only, not even acknowledgement of authors of texts, the lack of which could have infringed copyright laws in the United States. The 1889 edition, printed in Berlin, ON, could have done the same in Canada.

128. Henry S. Hallman, "[Hymns]," *GB* (10 November 1896) 4.

that the MBiC understood Rom 7 as the experience of an unsanctified, struggling believer, a persona which Paul adopts temporarily before emerging into the Spirit-led life of victory in Rom 8, *not* the typical experience of a normal believer assumed now by many evangelicals, not just Reformed-leaning church members who reject second work of grace sanctification. Perhaps Missionary Church/ EMCC believers today in the US and Canada would not agree with Hallman because increasingly the generic or default evangelical theology of many members has been persuaded by Reformed theology in Anglican, Baptist, Presbyterian or non-denominational forms, or perhaps defeat by sin is too common an experience.

The Executive Committee was the only link of continuing authority at a General Conference level between General Conferences. Most of the time their work was solving the frequent difficulties with the finances of the *Gospel Banner* or its editors and policies. Since the MBiC was a collection of Conferences without a hierarchy, (foreign to our notions of leadership by CEO presidents), the denomination's Executive Committee had very few administrative tasks and did not decide theological questions. The Keswick theology-leaning Pennsylvania Conference, as it grew in size and wealth, liked to have the freedom to pursue its own policies. Everek Storms, writing after the parting of the Pennsylvania Conference and the other Conferences, begun in 1947 and finalized in 1952, sounded relieved that at last the United Missionary Church was unified under a General Superintendent. He thought there was evidence centralized programs were beginning to benefit the mission of the denomination.[129]

That same 10 November 1896 issue of the magazine contained the program of the next Sunday School Convention for the Canada Conference—set to take place on the Maryboro field over the New Year, with a welcome address to be given by Sam Goudie.[130] A. F. Stoltz was on the planning committee, but around December, he resigned from the MBiC, citing difficulties agreeing with MBiC doctrine of justification and sanctification. By coincidence, a George Lambert also resigned from the Indiana and Ohio Conference. Lambert was from a prominent MBiC family which had two others in the ministry, and a niece would soon become a missionary

---

129. Storms, *United Missionary Church*, 76–81. The earlier history edited by J. A. Huffman, *Mennonite Brethren in Christ*, could not speak openly about the differing approaches to the unifying/ centralizing issue, though heated words sometimes were used in General Conferences.

130. [H. S. Hallman], "Programme of Canada Conference Sunday School Convention," *GB* (10 November 1896) 8.

to Armenia. He joined a Mennonite congregation in Elkhart, while Stoltz joined a United Brethren in Christ church in Waterloo County. The Mennonite magazine *Herald of Truth* took note of the resignations and implied things were not well in the MBiC, a judgment which Hallman of the *Gospel Banner*, who had been on the planning committee with Stoltz, disputed.[131]

The Beginning of MBiC Missions outside North America

In 1895, the *Gospel Banner* started reporting news from the Ottoman Empire of fighting between the Turks and Armenians. Since the first story was of Armenians suffering from government reprisals for violent Armenian protests, the editor (Hallman) could not resist pointing out the accurate observation of Jesus that all who draw the sword will die by the sword. (Matt 26:52). The editorial did not note that the Armenians were known as Christians or that the Turks were Muslims.[132] By coincidence, this same issue reported that a certain "Sister Gerber, Deaconess, of Cleveland" was visiting Waterloo County churches for help with an orphanage in Cleveland, Ohio, founded by the enterprise of John A. Sprunger of Berne, Indiana, and his Light and Hope Missionary Society. A series of letters and appeals started to show up in the *Gospel Banner* from Gerber. She seems to have been an effective fund raiser. In barely three years' time, Swiss-born Anna Maria Gerber with Rose Lambert would be heading for Armenian Turkey to start another orphanage, this time for Armenian orphans newly made so by massacres in 1896–1897. In 1896, an orphanage in Berlin for Waterloo County was announced to commence, to be operated by Elder August F. Stoltz and his wife, Caroline (Rickert/Reichert) Stoltz, then still part of the MBiC.[133] The project was not an MBiC project as such, nor even

---

131. This resignation of George Lambert stung somewhat: Daniel Brenneman wrote in the (15 Dec 1896) issue: 8–9, of the reasons for the resignation, especially since George's brother Sidney and father-in-law were members of the Indiana and Ohio Conference eldership. George Lambert had just returned from a tour of Asian countries, India and Turkey in particular, and had written a book about his experiences of famine and massacre. Henry S. Hallman, "Editorial," *GB* (5 January 1897) 8–9. In *GB* (19 January 1897), 8, Hallman also disputed a *Herald of Truth* report about the MBiC 1896 General Conference. Andrew Good, veteran MBiC evangelist, commented, *GB* (26 January 1897) 2, that perhaps the radical action which the *Herald of Truth* editor did not like was a resolution against tobacco use.

132. Henry S. Hallman, "Editorial," *GB* (15 October 1895) 8–9.

133. Gerber's initial appeals reported in Henry S. Hallman, *GB*, (29 October 1895) 8, *GB* (5 November 1895) 8; Anna Maria Gerber's letters appeared in *GB* (5 November 1895) 2; (10 December 1895) 4–5; Orphanage: *GB* (5 November 1895) 8, (7 April 1896) 4; (12 May 1896) 8.

a Mennonite one, and quickly became a civic one. Orphanages seem to have been one of the "ministries of the day," though totally out of fashion in Canada since the 1960s.[134]

More Armenian massacre news appeared in the magazine[135] and the MBiC started collecting relief funds. Sam Goudie does not refer to the Armenians at this time, but soon other MBiC members started to go as missionaries to Turkey, some from Ontario. Although the New Mennonites and the MBiC had fund-raising mission societies quite early, they had no missionary-sending structures until 1905. The church's well-known story of Eusebius Hershey from the Pennsylvania Conference had him in retirement at sixty-seven years old heading to Liberia in 1890 as the "first" Mennonite foreign missionary. His letters, testimony and death there moved some church youth to take action.[136] A portion of MBiC leaders preferred sending missionaries by what became the Christian and Missionary Alliance, others admired American Methodist Episcopal missionary bishop William Taylor's self-sufficient mission strategy. A few at this time wanted to have a denominational mission.[137] Some time in the 1890s, perhaps on the death of Eusebius Hershey as it was for several MBiC youth, Sam Goudie began to give his attention to the need of the MBiC to form their own mission board. Menno Bowman, his Presiding Elder, may have been an influence here, who with H. S. Hallman and J. B. Detwiler were a committee of the 1893 Canada Conference at Mannheim, instructing pastors to preach at least once each July on the demands of foreign missions and

---

134. John Joseph Kelso, the Children's Aid Society promoter, had addressed a "Berlin audience" in December 1894 concerning the need for child welfare reform; Hayes, *Waterloo County*, 89. In 1907, MBiC member Peter Shupe was the president of the board, Menno C. Cressman, a member of First Mennonite, the 1st vice-president and for twenty-five years the treasurer; 2nd vice-president was Abraham S. Hallman, a Mennonite-turned-Methodist. The orphanage was located then at 203 King St. W. between Francis St. and what was then Wilmot St. (now roughly Victoria St.) on the south side. *Twin City Directory and Official Guide to the Towns of Berlin and Waterloo 1907*, 39.

135. *GB* (10 March 1896) 8–9; (21 April 1896) 3; (5 May 1896) 4. According to *GB* (5 May 1896), 8, the MBiC was starting to collect relief funds for Armenians.

136. The most detailed account on Eusebius Hershey is the unpublished paper by Ziegler, "Eusebius Hershey," in the Everek Storms Collection, Missionary Church Inc. Archives in Mishawaka, Indiana.

137. This question is explored more in Fuller, "Nigeria," chapter 3 (esp. 45–54). The 1896 Canada Conference actually recommended that all foreign missionaries go through the IMA and attend the Missionary Training Institute in New York, *GB* (7 April 1896) 14.

take up an offering for it.[138] This conviction remained with Goudie until the United Missionary Society finally was created, and beyond. As a Conference leader, Goudie did not put himself on or get elected to some of the many Conference administrative committees, but as long as his health permitted, he did always get elected to the five-member Conference Foreign Mission Board and the three-member Home Mission Board. These positions suggest some of his central interests.

Some MBiC missionary beginnings should also be noted here. After three years training at the C&MA school in New York, Breslau convert William Shantz went to China in 1895. After the Coopersburg General Conference, Sarah Pool from the Markham field went on to New York to be interviewed by the International Missionary Alliance council (as it was then called), took a few weeks training and she too was appointed to China. Pennsylvania Conference member Calvin F. Snyder also headed for China in 1897, with the Alliance. As the Church's histories note, because Shantz was approved and officially supported by the Canada Conference, Shantz became the first "official" MBiC foreign missionary ever.[139]

Maryboro Special Meetings

Meanwhile, Sam Goudie was pushing on with special meetings on his field, at Wallace,

> This time I will give you a short account . . . and under the special favor and blessing of God and powerful working of the Holy Ghost, [the meetings] have proved to be a marked success and general victory . . . Four were converted, and a number were sanctified, and the light is shining on many others . . . Sister Chatham was with us these five weeks and labored very hard. From here she goes to Bright to assist Bro. Miller . . .[140]

When protracted meetings were shifted to Maryborough in February 1897, there was not a big response: the meetings were small, with one seeker. Goudie referred to "discouraging circumstances owing principally to

---

138. "Proceedings of the Canada Conference of the MBiC," *GB* (4 April 1893) 2–3. Bowman had read his essay on this topic at the Ministerial Convention just before the Annual Conference, reported in *GB* (11 April 1893) 4.

139. *GAMEO* articles exist for two of the three: Fuller, "Shantz, William Albert;" Fuller, "Pool, Sarah Ann." A sketch of the life and work of Calvin F. Snyder and his wife Phoebe Brenneman, a daughter of Daniel, is in Storms, *What God Hath Wrought*, 24–26.

140. Sam Goudie, "Wallace, Ontario," *GB* (1 December 1896) 14.

sickness in the community."¹⁴¹ When he closed the meetings in early March, he wrote, "the visible results were not as great as the brethren would have desired though the meetings were good." His co-worker from Sherkston, David S. Shantz, had been with them for most of those weeks.¹⁴²

Holiness Conventions

My own remoteness from the "foreign country" of the Mennonite Brethren in Christ Church shows up in the lack of attention I have given to an institution that became common for more than a generation—the "holiness convention." I have been studying the MBiC for thirty or more years and have noted these meetings, but never researched their start, conduct, or reports in the *Gospel Banner*. In other words, I have been blind to them because they do not fit into my experience as do some other institutions of the MBiC. Huffman's 1920 history does not have an index, but his frank discussion in a chapter called "Practical and Doctrinal Developments," refers in one sentence to the commencement of holiness conventions, so named, as occurring "since 1900 or a little earlier," which is a little imprecise.¹⁴³ The index of Storms' 1958 history does not include them, because their character had changed and other terms were being used already in the 1950s, but he does give a brief history of their rise in the MBiC.¹⁴⁴ Storms thought that holiness conventions were first reported in November 1893 from the Pennsylvania Conference, quickly followed by one in Stayner, Ontario, in December. Actually, they were already being reported in 1891 *Gospel Banners*. Sam Goudie certainly at this stage of his life approved of all the Holy Ghost phenomena mentioned in a report from 1894 from the Indiana and Ohio Conference: "Wave after wave of His glory and power went over us, causing all kinds of demonstration, generally seen only in Holy Ghost meetings, such as weeping, laughing, shouting, leaping, and falling under the power. One sister lay for four hours and came out with the shine of Canaan on her face. Deep conviction was upon the whole congregation,

141. Sam Goudie, "Maryborough, Ont.," *GB* (23 February 1897) 5. He asked for people's prayers for revival, "... the Lord knows we need it."

142. H. S. Hallman paraphrasing Sam Goudie, [news], *GB* (9 March 1897) 8.

143. Huffman, *Mennonite Brethren in Christ*, 162. Menno Bowman sent a report to the *Gospel Banner* (17 January 1899) 12, about a holiness convention at St. Thomas involving "Susie Bowman, Katie Gortner [Gardner?], Lizzie Moyer and Livy Hallman." The event was not reported as new.

144. Storms, *United Missionary Church*, 224-25. Lageer's books, *Merging Streams*, and *Common Bonds*, do not mention their existence.

especially the last night [of three]."[145] While the pastor at Berlin and the West End Mission in Toronto, Goudie hosted several during 1902–1905, participating in others he could get to, such as one in Breslau which began 1 January 1903.[146] He and Noah Detwiler also joined in one in Newmarket in 1905, at which Sam, his brother Henry, and Peter Cober preached.[147] Even as a busy Presiding Elder, Goudie could conduct a holiness convention, as he did in Vineland, in January 1910.[148] Others, he visited, such as the one at Ferndale on the Bruce Peninsula in 1912. He went with members from the Wiarton mission just for the day.[149]

The basic plan of a Holiness Convention seems to have been a series of messages all dedicated to explaining and encouraging the congregations to understand and desire to receive God's offer of a clean heart by faith, and giving people opportunity to seek the blessing in extended prayer times. The conventions seem to have lasted about three to five days each. They were still advertised in some Conferences until at least 1935.

Another Writing by Goudie

Goudie has one essay recorded from his days in the Maryboro field, written for the Ministerial Convention of 1897. This was a pastoral topic, "What Should the Members Expect from their Pastor?" His advice was straightforward: The members should expect to be led, fed, reproved. They should see their pastor acting loyally to the church, giving sound doctrine, showing impartiality, punctuality and caution, leading, not driving. The pastor

---

145. *GB* (13 October 1894) 8, as quoted in Storms, *United Missionary Church*, 225.

146. For this one in Breslau, Goudie listed ministers who participated as John A. Sider, Moses Weber, Solomon Haug, Milton Bricker, W. Stadelbauer (from Michigan), Solomon Eby, Amos Detwiler, Menno Bowman, C. N. Good and later Mary Ann (Hallman) Simmons (also from Michigan, originally from Mannheim, ON), plus himself, Sam Goudie, "Diary 1903," 1 January. This Amos Detwiler is treated as a minister in Goudie's diary, but he is not recorded in Canada/Ontario Conference records. He could be Amos S. Detweiler (b. 1859), son of Deacon John Z. Detweiler, (and nephew to Abraham Z. Detweiler, a New Mennonite preacher from Doon, ON) who had moved to Brown City, Michigan, and was farming there by 1896. The Michigan Conference did license an Amos Detweiler in 1902 serving at Brown City. Although he withdrew in 1904, he was a congregational representative in later years. W. Stadelbauer was also licensed in 1902, and continued until 1907; Kevin Blowers, archivist of the Missionary Church Inc. Archives, Mishawaka, Indiana, e-mail to the author, 18 November 2018.

147. Sam Goudie, "Diary 1905," 6–7 February.

148. C. H. Brunner, "Announcement," *GB* (23 December 1909) 9.

149. Sam Goudie, "Diary 1912," 29 February.

should lead the members in practical and experimental religion (Wesley's language; we would talk of "experience"). It would be expected of pastors to study the wants of members and feed them accordingly with a variety of food.[150] This is all conventional wisdom, not shared by all pastors, nevertheless. It is interesting he included "caution" as a desirable trait in pastors.

The March Annual Canada Conference re-assigned the Goudies, their three years at Maryborough being up. Conference sent them to The Twenty Mission, re-named as Bethesda and Zion.[151]

---

150. "Report of the Ministerial Convention," *GB* (6 April 1897) 8.
151. "Report of Canada Conference," *GB* (6 April 1897) 2–3, 8.

5

The Maturing Goudie 1897–1905

THE TWENTY MISSION: BETHESDA AND ZION, 1897–1900

MUCH HAD HAPPENED ON the Sherkston/ Twenty field since Sam Goudie had served there as a probationer. By 1894, the Canada Conference had split Sherkston from The Twenty, with John A. Sider in charge or as a helper to those who were in charge, as Sam had been.[1] A small meeting place was added to Sherkston at Shisler's Point on the Lake Erie shore. Cayuga had been dropped by 1892, though Goudie did preach there once in 1898. Charlie Krauth was appointed to Sherkston in 1897, and Sider finally went off to be the pastor on the Maryboro field.

The Twenty had been served by Jesse Guy and more recently by Christian Raymer. We will meet him again in 1908. There had been no mention of a "Zion" or a "Bethesda" in the Conference record until 1897. A history of the Vineland congregation does however mention that as soon as the EUM group in The Twenty constructed their first building (1881), they named the place "Bethesda."[2] What was Zion? A smaller center with a building at Jordan with James Troupe as a member, according to local memory.

---

1. First to Franklin Wismer Moyer and Samuel A. Moyer, or Jesse and Euphemia Guy, or Sarah Pool for Sherkston itself.

2. Gillham, *Vineland*, 6. The "Vineland" name was chosen in 1894 when a new post office at the site needed a name. F. W. Moyer was the first postmaster, at the same time he was the preacher for the MBiC.

So, Sam Goudie knew the Vineland area, having lived at Sherkston. Eliza and Sam moved into the parsonage Bethesda and Zion provided, just south of the church building. The Vineland main church building is at the first crest of the hill climbing from the flatlands by Lake Ontario. For some reason the Niagara Escarpment is not a high sharp cliff at Vineland as elsewhere and the road, while maybe difficult for a horse, can go straight up the hill.

We don't hear much from Sam at first; he attended the Berlin camp-meeting in June, and in July the Quarterly Conference report from Presiding Elder Menno Bowman noted that the meetings at The Twenty and Sherkston were "well attended." At Sherkston, Goudie joined his younger colleague from Port Elgin, Charlie Krauth, with people from The Twenty and several former members, now from Buffalo, New York.[3] The Twenty had been picked to host a camp-meeting in September 1897, Goudie reminded people through the church magazine on August 24. Unfortunately, collections of the *Gospel Banner* are incomplete through the rest of 1897 and some of 1898, so we don't know the result of the camp-meeting.[4]

Goudie's preaching roster for The Twenty field from August to October 1897 survives and shows he shared the preaching with two other preachers: "F. Fretz," and "E. Chatham." There were many Fretz clans around Vineland. "F. Fretz" (probably Frank) does not show up in MBiC Conference records for long. In Goudie's 1898–1900 Pastor's Yearbooks, Frank is routinely named and identified as a trustee at Zion.

On June 23, 1898, Eliza gave birth to their third child, Howard Allen Goudie. The next we hear from Goudie is a notice in December 1898 that probationers in their second year of studies should be ready for their exams.[5] In other words, Sam Goudie had been appointed their examiner in the Canada Conference program of ministerial improvement. This program was going to involve Sam for decades to come, so it is a good time to look more closely at this.

The MBiC Probationers' Reading Course

When the Reforming/ Reformed Mennonite Society began in 1874, they were beginning a journey of denomination-building that Charles Gingerich

3. "Bro. and Sis. Menno Moyer, Bro. and Sis. Edwin Snyder, and Samuel Moyer." Menno Bowman, "PE Report," *GB* (27 July 1897) 12.

4. This camp-meeting location of 1897 is omitted from the helpful annual list of them in Brubacher and others, *Camp Meetings*, [12–13].

5. Sam Goudie, *GB* (24 December 1898) 8.

has examined for the Canada/ Ontario Conference.[6] They had only three or four ordained ministers, no bishops, and a few ordained deacons. Even when they joined with the New Mennonite Church in 1875, they still had a small number of leaders, and many of the New Mennonites were older men. At least one NM preacher, Abraham Z. Detwiler of Doon, never did join the merged group, and NM preachers Christian Troyer and Caspar Wideman in Markham soon dropped out. Yet the movement for a more "revivalistic piety," as Samuel J. Steiner calls it, seemed to unleash a small rush of Mennonite members in Ontario to the new group, creating small groups scattered around Ontario mainly centered in older Mennonite settlements. The movement had to become "aggressive"—respond quickly to follow up interested revival-leaning families, form nurturing groups (the "classes") and congregations, often without church buildings. The leaders, Solomon Eby and Daniel Brenneman especially, turned to the model they saw as effective, the German Methodist denomination, the Evangelical Association. Solomon Eby, Benjamin Bowman and John Steckley were made a committee in 1878 to come up with a church structure that would answer their need. When they brought their recommendation, the "Discipline" they proposed was clearly heavily dependent on the *Doctrines and Discipline* of the Evangelical Association (EvA).[7]

One aspect of the EvA plan was a reading course for ministers, partly inspired by John Wesley's recommended reading for his lay preachers in the English Methodist Society. By the later 1800s, the EvA was beginning to be well-supplied with colleges and seminaries, but the evangelistic movement model of educating ministers by a reading course for probationers was still in place.[8] The United Mennonites (1875–1879) and the Evangelical United Mennonite Church (1879–1883) needed some kind of ministerial education, but they were wary of colleges.[9] Of course few qualified for existing theological schools anyway, few having gone to high school. The first recommended reading course list was published by the EUM General

---

6. Gingerich, "Experiment in Denominationalism."

7. Storms's comment, *United Missionary Church*, 219, that the polity chosen was "somewhat modelled on that set up by John Wesley for the Methodist Church" can be made much more precisely: the model was exactly that of the Evangelical Association. An initial study of the Probationer's Reading Course by Clare Fuller is forthcoming.

8. The Evangelical Church still had a four-year reading plan for one for whom study at an Evangelical Church theological school was not possible or complete in 1939, *Doctrines and Discipline 1939*, 261–65.

9. Lageer, *Merging Streams*, 127–28.

Conference of 1882 and included works in both German and English. Sam Goudie was not involved in the selection of these works. He was only fifteen or sixteen and not yet converted to Christ. He was to become involved in discussions to modify the lists throughout his career.

A glance at the 1882 reading course lists shows some surprising features. First is that John Wesley's numerous works are missing. The EUM/MBiC knew holiness teaching in its nineteenth-century American holiness form.[10] John Fletcher's Arminian perfectionism is represented by his work on total depravity, not by Wesley's book, *Christian Perfection*. Second is that Mennonite works are represented only by Menno Simons's *Complete Works*, too much for any busy young minister to afford or read. The complete *Practical Works* of Richard Baxter, if that is what "Baxter's Works" meant, was published in twenty-three volumes, also too many for a useful study course. When examinations on the readings were introduced a few years later, such big collections were dropped. Baxter's single title, *The Reformed Pastor*, was selected.[11] None of Menno's works were retained. The Dordrecht Confession, the doctrinal basis of the 1875 union of the Reforming Mennonite Society and the New Mennonite Church, is also missing.

Even more remarkable is the breadth of denominational sources for the reading course: works picked from the Reformation to the nineteenth century by Reformed Puritan, Congregationalist and Presbyterian writers, and a Lutheran. It is not surprising to see several Wesleyan Methodists, and a book by the great evangelist of the early nineteenth century, Charles Finney. The thread joining most of these choices seems to be practical, not mainly doctrinal: these are works that would be useful to activist evangelizing holiness Mennonites.

From the 1882 list until 1965,[12] the denomination maintained a list of Bible sections and books to be read over a three-year cycle by probationers for the ministry. Gradually, the church's youth made increasing use of Bible college training, in or out of the denomination. The opportunities for formal studies in the denomination, at first in 1900–1904 in Indiana, from 1926 in the Canada Northwest Conference, 1940 in Ontario, and 1947 in

---

10. Some MBiC member even owned EvA editor Hezekiah J. Bowman's compilation of articles on sanctification, *Voices on Holiness*, from an Evangelical Association magazine, for it made its way by donation to a Bible college in Nigeria.

11. By "reformed," Baxter meant re-formed, parish ministry after a new pattern, not doctrinally Calvinist.

12. *Constitution and Manual 1965*, 80–81, published the last such list, effective until the next UMC General Conference, 1968.

Indiana, were not easily available, so youth went where they could find congenial schools. Eventually denominational colleges became the main sources of ministers and missionaries for a while. In the United States, many young people had chosen to go to Fort Wayne Bible Institute/ College in Fort Wayne, Indiana, the school of the Missionary Church Association with which the MBiC kept in touch since the MCA's founding in 1898 until merger in 1969. Fort Wayne Bible Institute was started in 1904. In the Ontario Conference, at least, the Conference began accepting college credits in place of parts of the Reading Course.

In the twenty-first century in North America, demographic shifts (for example, less youth as a percentage of the population, more so in Canada than the US), a general disconnect with denominations (switching churches is a frequent resort to find interesting programs or solve problems), and attraction to education which promises lucrative pay are discouraging Canadian Bible Colleges. Many schools have tried to stay alive by transforming themselves into university or liberal arts colleges, some with success and some not. Perhaps parents are also discouraging or silent about the value of a Bible or Christian College education. Whereas once a corporate culture was achieved by camp-meetings and circulation of the preachers in the Conference structure, and later on by the Bible Colleges, fewer experiences of denominational community fed looseness to the community. Like it or not, cohesion as a denomination has been weakened by the resulting lack of a church culture. The consumer pattern of wanting "choice" has encouraged the growing independence in congregational life and autonomy in individual choices. Leakage is inevitable as a movement grows. There are ways of strengthening the shared experiences and sustaining them for a time against erosion. Churches keep hoping and praying for revival, though frankly, the instances of revival in older movements are few. God does surprising things for those who hunger and thirst and ask, however.

Protracted meetings on The Twenty

In common with the methods of the Mennonite Brethren in Christ and other revivalist denominations, Sam Goudie planned regular protracted or revival meetings for his field. While Sam's field was busy with their meetings, Solomon Eby was reporting on six weeks of meetings at Roseville, North Dumfries Township. in Waterloo, assisted by Susie Bowman, Laura Moyer, A. Bowman, and Henry S. Cressman. Other pastors were active with protracted campaigns on their fields.

From November 27, 1898, meetings on the Vineland field at the Zion meeting place were assisted by a couple named Sprott of Collingwood, Ontario. As usual, Sam was frank about the results compared to his hopes, noting a few souls saved, not the number he thought there should have been.[13] Then on December 11, the Sprotts and others shifted to the Vineland (Bethesda) site for three weeks, spreading over the Christmas season. In this larger congregation, he reported backsliders reclaimed, three sanctified, and was certain others were under conviction of sin. "Bro. Miller [almost certainly Christian Roth Miller,] is with us and doing good service."[14]

One of the reasons for Sam Goudie's few reports to the *Gospel Banner* in this period may also be because, though he had a good physician, he had been down with a severe illness he called "catarrh of the stomach" from May to September 1898. For six weeks he lived on only milk and raw eggs. He felt ready to testify to his complete healing in January 1899 and an extended quote will give a better impression of Goudie's thinking than a summary:

> [A]t the Markham camp-meeting I obeyed the injunction of Jas. 5:14, 15 and thanks be to God I was healed instantaneously, never doubting my experience for a moment... though tested... I have the victory through our Lord Jesus Christ. This new experience has brought great blessing to my soul as well as my body. I have learned to trust Jesus as never before, and I feel I can recommend Jesus as a perfect Saviour. Jesus is my Saviour, Sanctifier, Healer and Coming King. Sometimes people wonder why there are not more cases of healing. Is it not, brethren in the ministry, because we fail to teach it as we ought. Faith cometh by hearing. Oh, let us not limit the Holy One, for all power is in his hand.[15]

The Christian and Missionary Alliance "Fourfold Gospel" slogan popularized by A. B. Simpson comes out clearly in Goudie's account. Simpson was just beginning to be well known as a teacher of healing through the atonement received by faith. The MBiC *Discipline* had added an article on "Divine Healing" in the General Conference of 1888. Goudie never lost this confidence in the healing power of Christ, referring to it even in a testimony in 1949.[16]

---

13. Probably Henry and Jane Sprott, Methodist friends from Nottawasaga, who reported themselves as Mennonites in the Canada census of 1901.

14. Sam Goudie, "Vineland, Ont.," *GB* (10 January 1899) 5, letter of 6 January.

15. Sam Goudie, "Testimony," *GB* (17 January 1899) 15.

16. Sam Goudie, "Testimonies," *GB* (14 April 1949) 6. On A. B. Simpson and healing, see, for example, Sawin, "Fourfold Gospel."

Goudie also reported two sad funerals on New Years Day 1899. The first was for a ten-month old baby, "Franklin Webster Storms," son of Richard and Fanny Storms at Vineland. Richard was a blacksmith. The two were the parents of Dorwin Storms who, with his wife Nancy (Good) Storms, was in Turkey assisting the mission for Armenian orphans 1912–1914.[17] Chris R. Miller assisted Goudie, while he preached from Rev 21:4 ("There shall be no more death," KJV). Infant mortality continues to be a source of family tragedy and a pastoral issue that tries the faith of many and their pastors.[18] The second funeral was of a twenty-six-year old man, Arthur J. Wismer, who fell, paralyzed, before dying at Campden, a village southwest of Vineland, where Goudie assisted the minister at the funeral, a "Rev. Mr. Yeager," the Evangelical Association pastor in Campden that year.[19]

Strange as it may seem, the *Gospel Banner* was full of death notices and reports of funerals with participation by MBiC ministers for members of other churches. Probably such funerals were for people who were close relations of MBiC members. Though the MBiC was confident they had a full gospel with full salvation, they did not shun other Protestant churches locally when they knew each other. Obviously, the Methodists in the nineteenth century, as we have seen, were the most widespread revivalist church in Canada, (though their revivalism was diminishing) and contact was more widespread than at funerals. Occasionally Methodists who appreciated the MBiC joined in camp-meetings. References to Brethren in Christ, United Brethren in Christ and Evangelical Association, even Church of the Brethren (in the US) members are common in the early decades of the *Gospel Banner*.

By the time of the *Gospel Banner* of February 7, Sam was able to report, happily from the tone of it, that when the meetings closed on January 22, they had recorded 23 reclaimed or converted and fifteen sanctified. There was good interest and large attendances; the church was cheered and the pastoral couple from Sherkston, the Millers, assisted for over two weeks.

---

17. Huffman, *Mennonite Brethren in Christ*, 267. Dorwin and Nancy were the parents of Everek and Paul Storms, editor of the *Gospel Banner* and *Emphasis* and prominent pastor in the MBiC/ UMC/ Missionary Church, respectively. Mrs. R. Storms wrote the *Gospel Banner* a letter published in (27 March 1900) 15. D. J. Storms was assigned as a helper to A. G. Warder on the Shrigley field later in 1911, where Goudie met him, Sam Goudie, "PE Report," *GB* (1 June 1911) 12.

18. See Dow, *When Storms Come*.

19. Probably W. J. Yager or Yeager, licensed 1887, d. 1938. Goudie records visiting him a time or two each year.

During the last five days they had their "venerable" and able worker, the Presiding Elder Menno Bowman to assist. It is a bit surprising that from all this, only three people actually joined the MBiC church in Vineland that occasion.[20] In his own report on the quarterly conferences at Vineland and Sherkston, Bowman mentioned again people from Buffalo, NY (Ed Snyder, M. Moyer), but also some from Bridgeburg (now a part of Buffalo), and George Webb, formerly of Toronto, a Congregational Union of Canada minister who had become a friend.[21] Webb met Goudie again in Toronto in September 1903, and preached for him.[22]

Goudie did not let up evangelistic activities in Vineland and Sherkston. Chris Miller reported that during tabernacle meetings at Sherkston in June 1899, that "The labours of Bro. S. Goudie and Sis. Guy were owned and blessed by the Lord." He also acknowledged the help of "Sis. Cora Sider and Daisy Young, and also Bro. S[ylvester] Fretz."[23] Goudie, as a vice-Presiding Elder, was asked by Bowman to act on his behalf at the June quarterly meetings at Sherkston, and he reported a time of blessing. He took the opportunity to comment a little on this former field of his:

> This is the place of many churches but in spite of it all, I do believe we as a people have a perfect right there for there is not another Society that takes the doctrine of "holiness" nor the "second coming" definitely but our own. Bro. and Sis. Miller have good courage to battle on . . . the tabernacle meeting was by no means a failure though visible results were not great.[24]

Given the growing emphasis on holiness in the Brethren in Christ in the latter decades of the nineteenth century, this is a bit of a strange assessment by Goudie, but he knew the local scene. As to the "second coming" it is true that other Mennonites had not committed to a pre-millennial teaching as had the MBiC from the 1880s.

The request by Menno Bowman for Goudie to deputize for him at Sherkston is another sign of the trust the MBiC was placing on Sam. Bowman wrote, concerning a Quarterly Meeting at Vineland in July, "Bro. Goudie has his conflicts (*strabatze*) with the devil, but he keeps on the

---

20. Sam Goudie, "Reports," *GB* (7 February 1899) 12.
21. Menno Bowman, "PE Report," *GB* (7 February 1899) 13.
22. Sam Goudie, "Diary 1903," 20 September.
23. Chris R. Miller, "Reports," *GB* (13 June 1899) 13.
24. Samuel Goudie, "Reports," *GB* (20 June 1899) 12.

top."[25] In the winter, it was announced that, among others, Sam Goudie would read a paper at the Canada Conference Ministerial Convention on March 22 on "The Model Presiding Elder."[26] That responsibility would not come to him until 1905, but it did fall to his brother Henry Goudie in March 1900. Henry Goudie had served the Berlin church 1892–1895, Elmwood/Hanover 1895–1898, and Shrigley in rural Melancthon Township, Dufferin County, 1898–1900.

Once again, as the Annual Conference of the Canada Conference approached in March 1900, the Goudies, Sam and Eliza, knew that they would be transferred again; where, they could not know until it was announced in the Conference.

The Canada Conference of 1900 must have been persuaded that the century change was a significant year and celebrated a little by issuing a first-time souvenir photo collection of the ministers of the Conference on a cardboard stock. The Missionary Church Historical Trust collection has received a number of copies of this studio souvenir in various states of wear, suggesting it was fairly popular with the membership. This photo collection is our only photographic source for some of the ministers.[27] The City Mission Workers (all women), organized just two years previously under a committee of three members of the Conference, also took a photo of themselves as a group outdoors on the snowy steps of a house in Berlin. This important photograph survives in the archives of the Missionary Church in Mishawaka, Indiana, and recently in a donation from the Chester/Hunking families to the MCHT in Ontario. It also is the only photographic record of several of these women in the collection.

BERLIN (BETHANY) STATION, 1900–1903

Sam and Eliza Goudie followed Christian and Christina Raymer again as the pastoral couple at the largest congregation in the Canada Conference, which reported 140 (adult) members around 1900.[28] With several retired

---

25. Menno Bowman, "PEs' Reports," *GB* (25 July 1899) 12.

26. Henry S. Hallman, "Editorial," *GB* (7 February 1899) 9.

27. A few of these men were dead within a few years or even a few months (for example, Alex Bell (b. 1863), 1900; Joshua Schell (b. 1877), 1901; William John Hilts (b. 1842), 1901; John Hoover Steckley (b. 1826), 1904.

28. Shantz, *Bethany*, 68, 66. Although the rural New Mennonite Church communities of Blair/ New Dundee and Markham/ Stouffville were older, large and influential themselves, only urban Bethany in Berlin was a stand alone "station" of the Canada

preachers in the Bethany community, and only one place to care for, no helper was assigned to the church. Under Sam Goudie, the congregation continued to grow steadily to about 175 members. Membership reached 200 by 1905 under Solomon Eby in his last years before he retired in Berlin to a house on Chapel Street.

The 1977 centennial history of Bethany Missionary (now Evangelical Missionary) Church had the fortunate circumstance of being written by a long-time member and denominational leader, a man of unusual historical insight, Ward Montford Shantz (1910–2009).[29] Many customs and institutions of the MBiC are described with understanding, as well as the local application of the *Discipline* in an important congregation. As is common in the Church's congregational histories, however, the book follows the practice of dating the forming of a congregation by the year a church *building* was constructed. The ability to finance and oversee construction of a building does give a measure of the functioning of a church community. To the worshippers, a building allows for shelter of course, but also stability, freedom of expression, and visible unity. The construction process often brings together members, especially the men, who can offer their practical skills which are valued by other men. All that being said and all being true, still, theologically, God said very little, if anything, about a New Testament congregation being defined by a building.

Ward Shantz knew this, but still commenced his narrative with a question about the Lancaster Street building at the corner of Chapel Street, constructed in 1877 for the United Mennonite Church in Berlin. In reality, a worshipping community was formed in Berlin out of the Mennonite membership centered in but not defined by the Benjamin/ Christian Eby Meeting House on King Street, Berlin.[30] A few weeks after their preachers Solomon Eby and Daniel Wismer were disfellowshipped in March 1874, supporters met in Eby's to form a new society, and they began meeting

---

Conference—self-supporting, and not included in a field in 1900.

29. Fuller, "Shantz."

30. Good, *First Mennonite*, 77–87, has an excellent chapter on the division of 1874 in Waterloo. Horst, *Great Awakening*, 40–121 contributes unique Old Order Mennonite perspectives on the New Mennonite and Eby schisms partly due to his translations of rare German manuscripts and documents. Steiner, *Promised Lands*, 125–34 builds on these and supersedes all previous versions including S. F. Pannabecker's research in Huffman, *Mennonite Brethren in Christ*, 32, 34–55, 60–61, Burkholder, *Mennonites in Ontario*, 188–196, and Storms, *United Missionary Church*, 30–50.

separately from the main Mennonite community in Waterloo. That, in practice, is the start of a congregation.

In addition, because it is organized around institutions of the church, Ward Shantz' book does not exactly tell the chronological story of the congregation, nor examine the activities of the church pastor-by-pastor. He had access to the congregational quarterly minutes and saw how decisions were made over time, separate from the presence of the ever-changing ministers.

The Fifth General Conference, Berlin, Ontario, October 1900

Sam Goudie was elected by the Canada Conference of March 1900 as an alternate ministerial representative to the quadrennial MBiC GC in October. This conference convened in Berlin, Waterloo County, Canada. Goudie was not needed as an alternate, though he did attend as an observer, since the GC was hosted by his congregation.

At this General Conference, a few Annual Conferences, including Canada, petitioned for a GC mission board, but this plan did not pass. Again, Canada, along with a few others, requested that the MBiC hymnbook be revised, but this too, was rejected. Some dissatisfaction surfaced over the theological textbook recommended for the probationer's reading course (the 1887 edition of English Methodist Benjamin Field's *The Student's Handbook of Christian Theology*).[31] Pennsylvania Conference in support said they wanted "more Bible . . . not more theology," Canada wanted the GC to "reconsider" the Reading Course without saying what they had in mind. Iowa and Nebraska Conference wanted to include "Finney on Masonry," and the Indiana and Ohio wanted to increase the pass mark for probationers on individual exams to 50 percent and need for an average of 60 percent on them all. None of these objectives (except Canada's which got debate at least!) was agreed to.[32]

Several other intriguing items came up in this GC especially in the recognition of advisory members. Daniel Brenneman often scouted for like-minded Mennonite/holiness bodies to approach for merging; that is how the Evangelical Mennonites of Pennsylvania in 1879 and the Swankite Brethren in Christ branch in 1883 were incorporated. Brenneman also had conversations with Daniel Warner, the leader of what became the

---

31. Interestingly, in 1923 Jasper A. Huffman was still promoting Field's *Theology*—he was selling it—with the blurb, "There is no better compendium of Divine truth as expounded by John Wesley, than this. 339 pages, cloth $2.00." *GB* (April 12 1923) 15.

32. *Fifth General Conference 1900*, 13.

"non-denominational" Restoration movement Church of God (Anderson, Indiana). The EUM had even published a book for Warner in 1882.[33]

Searching for More Partners

Before we look at those who were welcomed as advisory members, it would be good to note some relationships the MBiC had with similar groups in those days. After 1894, the Canada Conference spent several years holding Quarterly Conference meetings in Toronto in company with a band of Christian Workers Churches, many of which were led by ex-Salvation Army officers, such as Peter W. Philpott, Alfred W. Roffe, and George E. Fisher.[34] Some of these men emerged a generation later as leaders in the indigenous Canadian fundamentalist denomination, the Associated Gospel Churches. Some others were attracted to the denomination-in-formation, the Christian and Missionary Alliance in Canada.[35] Pastor Reuben J. Zimmerman with the Alliance in Peterborough and George Webb of a Congregationalist church in Toronto, along with Philpott, Fisher and another Christian Worker pastor called Robert McHardy even participated in an

---

33. Warner, Daniel S., *Bible Proofs of the Second Work of Grace* (Goshen, IN: Evangelical United Mennonite Publication Society, 1882). The talks with Warner failed when he began attacking denominations such as the MBiC.

34. Jesse Guy and Henry S. Wismer participated in a Christian Workers Church Annual Conference on 25 May 1894, Redinger, *A Tree Well Planted*, 20–21. The *Gospel Banner* began printing their reports as "Department of the Christian Workers," by Elder P. W. Philpott and Elder George E. Fisher, *GB* (18 September 1894) 606. Quarterly Conferences were reported being held at Fisher's CW Church on Dennison Avenue; for example, Maude Chatham, "Toronto Quarterly Conference," *GB* (25 April 1895) 12, named MBiC ministers present as Solomon Eby, John Steckley, Jesse Guy, Henry Wismer and herself "and many from Markham," plus Philpott, Fisher, Desson, Murray, Kerr and others from the CWC. Chatham also reported Baptists, Congregationalists and Methodists, one hundred ten attending in all, fifty being from Toronto itself. Menno Bowman attended Bethany Tabernacle where John Salmon of the Alliance was pastor and visited CWC churches, *GB* (4 June 1895) 12. See also a report, *GB* (17 September 1895) 13; (10 March 1896) 9, with the comment, "Our members that live in the city were all present that could possibly be"; (22 December 1896) 14; (18 May 1897) 9. Redinger's book does not mention the disagreement the Salvation Army men had with their church, that is noted in Moyles, *Blood and Fire*, 123–28. The *Gospel Banner* editorials expressed disapproval of Salvation Army fund-raising tactics at the time, in sympathy with the Christian Workers' complaints. Moyles says that the Army leaders were trying to rein in the heavy expenses of continually opening new corps across North America and seemed to some members to be abandoning evangelistic goals.

35. Reynolds, *Footprints*, 170–72. See also Moyles, *Blood and Fire*, 123–28.

MBiC camp-meeting in Markham in 1894.[36] The quarterly conferences in Toronto were held despite the MBiC having no congregations in the city. There was a small but increasing number of former rural members (from Markham and Berlin especially) living and working in Toronto who were probably attending Methodist churches for want of something better, such as Sam Goudie's own brother, David Wanner Goudie ("D. W." often in Sam's diaries). The *Gospel Banner* started printing the reports of the Christian Workers, until about 1896 or 1897, when Philpott moved to Hamilton and the MBiC decided to open up her own missions. Goudie kept Peter Philpott in mind, however, and invited him to preach at the Berlin Holiness Convention in 1902 and the family attended his church in Hamilton on a holiday trip to Vineland that July.[37] The push into Toronto was led by the veteran evangelist, Noah Detwiler, at two sites, one east and the other west of Yonge Street. Rapprochement with the Christian Workers Churches diminished about that time, but not completely. And as we have seen, Rev. Webb dropped in on the Vineland meetings while Sam Goudie was pastor.

Still another alliance being explored in the 1890s was with an evangelistic band in Pennsylvania called the "Heavenly Recruits Association" which included evangelist Christian Wismer Ruth, who had relatives in the Evangelical Association and the MBiC. Again, reports on the activities of the HRA were published in the *Gospel Banner* for some years. The HRA, part of which became the Holiness Christian Church with C. W. Ruth sometimes as a leader, eventually merged with the Pentecostal Church of the Nazarene in 1908 (now simply "The Church of the Nazarene"). Relations with the MBiC remained cordial, and Ruth was called on to be a camp-meeting evangelist for some years in the MBiC Conferences.

Thus, the presence of advisory members at the General Conference of 1900 from other organizations and denominations in these years was common but not routine. Some contacts might lead to mergers. The young Rowland Victor Bingham, "returned missionary from Africa" was present and spoke.[38] H. S. Hallman was to be elected a member on the Africa Industrial Mission board, as Bingham's council chose to call their mission.[39]

36. Euphemia (Pool) Guy, "Markham Camp-meeting," *GB* (18 September 1894) 12.
37. Sam Goudie, "Diary 1902," 21 January, 1 July.
38. *Fifth General Conference Journal 1900*, 10.
39. This corrects my speculation that the board member was Noah Detwiler, in Fuller, *Banfield*, 19. Later, when industrial missions fell out of favor among fundamentalist-influenced missions, the AIM went back to the earlier name, the Sudan Interior Mission.

William Egle represented the Light and Hope Association, Sprunger's organization based in Berne, Indiana, which was leaning heavily on MBiC personnel for their related mission to Armenian orphans. John A. Sprunger himself was made an advisory member later in the Conference.

S. D. Burley of the "Egly church" was also present, representing the Defenseless Mennonite Church from which Ramseyer's Missionary Church Association had split a few years before.

Rev. Mr. Jonathan S. Williamson of the Methodists represented a local Berlin congregation, as did Rev. Mr. Franz Friedrich for the (German) Baptist Church on Benton Street.[40]

Still later in the Conference, August F. Stoltz, now minister of the "Radical UB Church" (Church of the United Brethren in Christ [Old Constitution]) on Alma Street (now Charles St.) was welcomed as an adviser. Stoltz attended a few Canada Conference annual meetings, so apparently his resignation from the MBiC was, thankfully, not acrimonious.[41] His colleague the Rev. W. Backus joined later.

Rev. Samuel R. Knechtel of the Evangelical Association in Berlin showed up and last of all, Rev. Aaron Y. Haist, pastor of the 1200-member Zion EvA congregation a few blocks away.[42] Waterloo County had many groups of German origin, but the unusually large number of visitors to the MBiC GC suggests the good will the MBiC generated with its mixture of Mennonite, Pietist, evangelical and Wesleyan holiness affiliations.[43] As we move into Goudie's pastorates at Berlin and especially Toronto, we will see how broad (and narrow) his own affiliations could be.

A closer connection with the Missionary Church Association which had just been organized in 1898 was clearly in everybody's mind, as three delegates to their next conference were appointed: Menno Bowman, H. S. Hallman and Daniel Brenneman. These men were all senior elders of the MBiC, able to discuss merger possibilities. While Sam Goudie was not an

---

40. *Benton Street Baptist*, 2.

41. In return, Sam Goudie attended a part of a United Brethren Sunday School Convention in 1903, Sam Goudie, "Diary 1903," 19 June.

42. References to advisory members: *Fifth General Conference Journal 1900*, 10–21; H, *Zion Evangelical*, 59, 61.

43. See the *Reflections* issue on the five Missionary Church theological traditions (combined volumes 11–12, 2011/2012), and the work of Timothy Paul Erdel. I believe this recognition of fellow Christians goes against the church-sect typology used by Samuel D. Clark in his influential pioneering sociological study of Canadian Christianity; Clark, *Church and Sect*.

official member of the GC of 1900, he was to become a chief officer of the MBiC in Canada, and of many General Conferences to come.

Events at Bethany 1900–1903

Once again, unfortunately, preservation of the *Gospel Banner* for some of the early years of the twentieth century has been spotty, whole years being unavailable in microfilm for example (almost half of 1902, plus 1904, 1907 and 1908), although individual scattered issues exist. Goudie sent in reports from his congregation, wrote a few reports and essays for the annual ministerial convention (1900, 1903), reported on a visit to the mission in Woodstock, Ontario,[44] and deputized for the Presiding Elder at his former appointment at Wallace for a Quarterly Conference.[45] Thankfully we do have his pastoral Year Books 1900 to 1902 and diaries from 1901 to 1903, so certain matters are well covered.

In Woodstock, Goudie visited Henry and Lucinda (Miller) Wismer, and participated in an evangelistic meeting on the Sunday night. He was pleased to report one sister had her heart cleansed (sanctified).

At least three articles by Goudie appeared in the church magazine.[46] One, "Compromising to Gain Influence," warned against reducing standards of Christian behavior, a common theme in MBiC writings. Goudie's cautions would be interpreted as proof of legalism today: he complained, "You can go almost anywhere you wish and wear what you please and deal as you like in your business transactions and belong to any society you choose whether secret or open and it is all right as long as your *heart is right.*" [his emphasis][47] The MBiC, of course, frequently warned against any such license. Goudie also refers to preparing an essay on Fletcher's *Appeal* late in 1902 while visiting at Blair (with Robert Eltherington and the pastor Milton Bricker seeing John McNally and Angus H. McNally), but no mention of it appears in the index or microfilm record of the *Gospel Banner.*[48]

In 1900, the use of German in the Berlin church's services came up for discussion again. The young men's Sunday School class had already been using English since the 1880s and other classes gradually followed. The

---

44. Sam Goudie, "Visit to Woodstock," *GB* (11 October 1902) 8.
45. Sam Goudie, "Wallace Quarterly Meeting," *GB* (1 November 1902) 13.
46. "Our Individuality," *GB* (2 November 1901) 3; "Compromising to Gain Influence," *GB* (4 January 1902) 8; "Whoso Offereth Praise Glorifieth Me," *GB* (14 March 1903) 13.
47. Goudie, "Compromising to Gain Influence," *GB* (4 January 1902) 8.
48. Sam Goudie, "Diary 1902," 11 December.

main Sunday services used German, but in 1900 it was decided to retain German for every other Sunday morning service. Sam Goudie, of course, could preach in German when he needed to, so this was not an issue for him as it had been for John Steckley from Markham, pastor of Bethany in the 1880s. In Markham the transition to English had gone farther earlier than in Waterloo. Steckley asked for prayer because, as he said, "German preaching goes very hard for me."[49] In 1905, Solomon Eby, who had been posted to the church in 1903 before he retired in 1906, suggested the church drop German entirely, but it was another few years before that plan was accepted.[50]

During Goudie's years at Bethany, the church, which had been thinking about building a parsonage for her pastors, canvassed the members for donations from May 1901 and apparently had it constructed by the winter.[51] A small front porch, a vestibule for coats, was added to the blue Bethany building during Goudie's days "and a new platform was built incorporating an altar rail."[52]

From Shantz' book, it is not possible to say how much Sam Goudie influenced these various decisions of the church in its business sessions in the Quarterly meetings. Generally these meetings were moderated by the visiting Presiding Elder, and resolutions were moved and seconded by Bethany members, with implementing committees which did not often include the preacher. In the case of the "altar rail," the evangelistic use of that piece of liturgical furniture was derived from the revivalist pattern (said to be an innovation of Charles Finney) of using a "mourner's" or "penitent's bench" between the first pew and the pulpit, where those who responded to invitations for salvation, restoration of backsliders, or sanctification might kneel to "pray through" in the Wesleyan fashion of waiting (tarrying) in prayer until assurance of salvation (or restoration or holiness) was given. "Altar" in no way implied there was any sacrifice happening, as in the Roman Catholic mass, in this Mennonite meeting, rather, this was a place where the sinner was called to offer one's body as a living sacrifice to God, as in Rom 12:1–2.

49. Shantz, *Bethany*, 13.

50. Shantz, *Bethany*, 13. German use in some Berlin churches was an issue when the first World War commenced in 1914. Benton Street German Baptist Church switched only in March 1918. Zion Evangelical switched to English in its evening service in April 1896. Except for the Old Order groups, Ontario Mennonites had largely switched to English before the war, Steiner, *Promised Lands*, 159.

51. Shantz, *Bethany*, 17.

52. Shantz, *Bethany*, 7.

Sometime after David Goudie's death in 1896, maybe following the old Mennonite tradition of parents being taken care of by the youngest son, Samuel's mother Nancy (Wanner) Goudie, now blind, joined the household of Sam and Eliza briefly, probably when he became the pastor at Bethany. Certainly, she was with them in Berlin at the time of the census in 1901. Shortly afterward she moved back to the home of Jacob Goudie (second youngest son), living on the Goudie farm south of Breslau. Sam went to see her whenever he visited Jacob, which was often, even when he was transferred to Toronto. Since Eliza's own father Orrin Smith died in 1902 (in Michigan), and her stepmother, Elizabeth (Pritchett) Smith, followed in 1904, all of the Goudie children's grandparents were gone in the ten-year period 1896 to 1906. Eliza's own mother, Margaret (Weaver) Smith, the reader will recall, had died long before, in 1875.

Sam and Eliza had been following Orrin Smith's health: nearly every year since he met Eliza, Sam traveled to Michigan and preached in Greenwood, Port Huron or Brown City while they visited family. Then in January 1902 he received a letter from Mrs. Smith stating that Eliza's father was very ill.[53] When Sam was a fraternal delegate to the Michigan Conference in March, he was met by Clara at the station and he and his traveling companion stayed with Clara and Josiah Reichard. On the way home on 31 March, he stopped at Yale, saw Edd Smith and his father-in-law. Edd and Clara called for Eliza 23 April, and she went to Michigan and was able to talk with her father before he died. Sam joined her in Yale, Michigan, for the funeral on May 1. Sam reported sixty-nine teams of horses at the church.[54]

Elizabeth's declining health was the concern in the winter of 1904–1905. "No word from Michigan," he wrote on 8 January.[55] On January 19, Goudie went to Michigan, to Yale, where Edd Smith and his wife were caring for Elizabeth. During his eight days in Michigan Sam stopped in to see William Graybiel in Port Huron and Wesley Schlichter in Brown City, both formerly from Ontario, now elders committed to the Michigan Conference, and also his brother John Goudie, farming near Brown City. At the Smiths', Goudie often stayed up overnight with his mother-in-law, accompanied by other Smith family members. In the daytime he helped cut up firewood. A Pritchett relative, Thomas Pritchett, came for a few days and stayed with

---

53. Sam Goudie, "Diary 1902," 13 January.
54. Sam Goudie, "Diary 1902," 23 April, 1 May.
55. Sam Goudie, "Diary 1905," 5 January.

her overnight a few times. Goudie returned to Toronto on January 27, but soon after, on February 3, Mrs. Smith died.[56]

Berlin Days

While in Berlin, Sam Goudie had opportunity to widen his Christian experience and grow in his knowledge of world missions.

Some Sundays, Sam spoke at the YMCA institute and once he took in lectures by prominent Baptist Elmore Harris from Toronto on Philippians: "It was grand. [W]ish I knew my bible like he does."[57] He attended the Waterloo County Sunday School Convention in October 1902, an interdenominational organization, and confessed he learned some things.[58] Goudie attended a Lord's Day Alliance meeting on November 11 and the next day the Waterloo Temperance Convention at the YMCA. He got involved in the temperance campaign in the fall of 1902 to push for acceptance of the 1902 Liquor Act in an Ontario-wide referendum. Goudie attended temperance society meetings, allowing ministers Snider and Frederick to address audiences at Bethany, and did some canvassing to sign up scrutineers for the December 4 vote. At the end of day, with 199,749 votes cast in favor of the Act, he wrote, "This is a notable day in the history of Ontario. We were pleased with the numbers of votes cast in Ontario in favor of the Liquor Act of 1902. yet sorry that not enough to bring the act into force. 213,000 votes required. I was busy all day doing what I could."[59]

Goudie's involvement, as brief as it was, is also notable in the history of the MBiC at least in Ontario, for I have not seen any other MBiC personnel cooperate with societies with political agendas like this to that date.

Early in January 1902, Goudie mentioned he stopped in at the *Gospel Banner* Office to ask some questions about "our foreign missionary work." Editor H. S. Hallman received missionary newsletters and many mission society magazines, so his office was certainly a great place to go to. Goudie mentioned meeting at the Post Office "bro. [Garabed D.] Hagopian," an Armenian visiting Berlin for two months, communicating news of the persecutions Armenians were facing in Ottoman Turkey. He was not in Berlin at random: Hallman was president of the Armenian Orphan Relief

56. Sam Goudie, "Diary 1904," 19–27 January.
57. Sam Goudie, "Diary 1902," 19 January and 2 November (YMCA); 24–25 (Harris). Harris was President of the Toronto Bible Training School at the time.
58. Sam Goudie, "Diary 1902," 28 October.
59. Sam Goudie, "Diary 1902," 11, 12 November and 4 December.

Committee.⁶⁰ Just before departing in March, Hagopian spoke at Bethany.⁶¹ Anna Gerber who was the promoter of an orphanage in Cleveland six years before, spoke at Bethany in July 1902 about the Armenian mission and orphanages for which some Ontario people, Fredericka Honk, Ada (Moyer) and Ford Barker, were working.⁶² As mentioned, the *Gospel Banner* editor, Hallman, had become a member of the council of the African Industrial Mission. Goudie would certainly be aware in these years of the two MBiC members who joined the AIM based in Toronto headed by Rowland Bingham. One who joined was the colleague from Ontario but then the Presiding Elder of the Michigan Conference, Ebenezer Anthony, the other a young one-time Methodist who had come under the East End Mission (Toronto) led by Robert Eltherington by 1900, Alexander Woods Banfield. Anthony and Banfield sailed for northern Nigeria via Liverpool on 21 September of 1901.⁶³ Sam Goudie, William Graybiel, and H. S. Hallman accompanied Anthony to Toronto where with Banfield, the AIM held a farewell meeting for the two.⁶⁴ Goudie went to hear Bingham speak in Toronto, when he visited his brother D. W.⁶⁵ Sam mentions meeting a "bro. Zook and son" at the Berlin train station in September "and brought them to our place. [H]ad a meeting for them in the evening." This is probably John Zook, a Brethren in Christ mission leader from Iowa.⁶⁶ The Brethren in Christ had organized their denominational mission just six years before,

---

60. Max Haines, e-mail to the author 17 December 2019.

61. Sam Goudie, "Diary 1902," 7 January, 9 March. Hagopian was back in Berlin, 16 December.

62. Sam Goudie, "Diary 1902," 19–21 July. Fredericka Honk was sent off by Bethel circuit, supported from the Indiana and Ohio Conference in 1899. She died of typhoid fever in Alexandria, Egypt, 30 May 1909; Hoover, *Bethel*, 61; Storms, *What God Hath Wrought*, 85.

63. The story of the four-man "Patigi party" of the SIM has been retold in SIM literature, though, as is common in much mission literature, very little is said on the background of the two Baptist and two MBiC missionaries. On Anthony, see Huffman, *Mennonite Brethren in Christ*, 222; on Banfield, see Fuller, *Banfield*; Fuller, "Nigeria," 52–55; and Fuller, "Banfield."

64. Reprinted from 1901 in "Glimpses of the Past," *GB* (27 September 1951) 6.

65. Sam Goudie, "Diary 1902," 31 January, 1 Feb.

66. Sider, "Zook," Sam Goudie, "Diary 1902," 30 September. Pennsylvania Conference elder Menno P. Zook, who became a missionary to Chile in 1905, was not yet married to Anna Erskine, and thus not the person Goudie met, Storms, *What God Hath Wrought*, 138, see also 115–17.

something Goudie and others would try to do in 1904, so this could have been a formative encounter.

The annual *Canada Conference Journals* pick up some of the information lost from missing *Gospel Banners*, by telling us what Sam Goudie was doing in the Annual Conferences and throughout the years in Berlin. At the Conferences he was becoming a busy committee man: in 1902 alone, he was on at least six committees (1) to examine Conference minutes; (2) to examine third-year candidates for the ministry; (3) to prepare the schedule of Bible exams for probationers (since at least 1899); (4) "to station the Presiding Elders and apportion their salaries" (on which he had served at least as early as 1898); (5) to appropriate Home Mission funds; and (6) to frame resolutions summing up various affairs of the conference (since at least 1900). He was also re-elected to a board (Foreign Mission Board of the Canada Conference), elected conference assistant secretary to Berlin member John Troxel, and Vice-Presiding Elder for the South District. Vice-Presiding Elders had few duties—occasional Quarterly Meetings mostly—but gained experience in Conference affairs. He had been a vice-Presiding Elder since at least 1899. Not least, he was elected to be a fraternal delegate to the Michigan Conference which ensued that same month of March, which allowed him to see his father-in-law.[67] Sometimes Eliza could have used such official duties to also visit with family in Michigan.

In these committees, Sam worked closely with people at various stages of their careers, such as his friends and age-mates Silas Cressman and C. N. Good, his brother Henry (chair of the conference that year), the denominational editor Henry S. Hallman, and two veteran pastors, Solomon Eby and his cousin, Amos Eby.[68]

Just at the end of Goudie's pastorate at Bethany, the church commenced their winter special meetings on 1 February. H. S. Hallman, who had been elected City Mission Workers Society President in 1902, was the main speaker for the first three weeks, but in the normal way of things in the MBiC, others shared in the exhorting and preaching. Writing on 7 March 1903, Goudie reported results he could be happy about: that the congregation, holding meetings every night, had seen over 50 saved, reclaimed, sanctified, and some of them both saved and sanctified. Goudie acknowledged the help of Sister Cora Mae Rudy, a City Mission worker

---

67. *Canada Conference Journal 1902*, 62–103.

68. Huffman, *Mennonite Brethren in Christ*, 233. Amos's wife's maiden name should be Moyer, not Mayer, though spellings, as ever, were fluid.

from the Indiana and Ohio Conference in Canada helping at the *Gospel Banner* office. "The Waterloo Mission Workers sisters [Susie] Bowman and [Emma] Block were as busy as Bs could be, helping us." Sam Goudie seems to have enjoyed making puns. He expressed the regret that "we feel sorry to have to leave at so early a date [Annual Conference was coming]. Hope the Lord will send a better man in my place."[69] The one the Conference chose was Solomon Eby, no less.

TORONTO: BETHEL (WEST END) MISSION, 1903–1905

The 1903 Annual Conference of the Canada Conference had to send the Goudies somewhere new, according to the *Discipline*. The day of the Stationing Committee report, Goudie wrote, "All were on hand to hear our doom." The Committee decided to send Sam and Eliza and their three children to Toronto, to the western mission started by Noah Detwiler in 1897.[70] Goudie had his doubts: "I fear lest it be a mistake, but the will of the Lord be done. I telegraphed home to let Ma-ma know what was done."[71]

As we saw earlier, the Canada Conference had tried to interest some zealous groups in Toronto in their brand of holiness-Mennonite faith, but after Peter Philpott moved to Hamilton in 1896, the interest largely dried up. I believe this is one of the factors that led Menno Bowman and the Ontario MBiC to encourage their best evangelist, Noah Detwiler, to follow his desire and direct evangelism and church planting in Toronto.

The Toronto Bethel Mennonite Mission which Goudie served for two years is chronicled by an excellent congregational history which introduces Noah Detwiler's work in founding the congregation, and perceptively leads the reader through the oddness of the past.[72] Dr. Arthur Sherk's story follows the arc of the congregation though time, in which pastors sometimes are stray figures that come and go like animals in headlights because of the three-year rule the MBiC followed. A few pastors (for example, Milton Bricker) settled down in Toronto and their children come to life as they marry people who are remembered by the people Sherk is writing for. They participate in the life of the known church. In contrast, congregations in the

---

69. The Waterloo Mission was closed in 1904. Goudie preached in it occasionally and reported Berlin young people receiving victory at its services.

70. See Fuller, "Detweiler, Noah," and Huffman, *Mennonite Brethren in Christ*, 232.

71. Sam Goudie, "Diary 1903," 21 March.

72. Sherk, *Banfield Memorial*, 12–18. Banfield Memorial Church was renamed Wellspring Worship Centre about 2006.

biography of a preacher may seem like scenes along the roadside seen from a traveling car: pretty (or not), snapshots of moments, and then they recede into the past. In fact, a congregation's story grows and re-forms, withers and changes. So also the preachers'; they have back stories and futures that may or may not involve the congregation. I am trying to keep both tracks alive. Re-reading Shantz's *A History of Bethany Missionary Church* or Sherk's *Keeping Faith* after working through Sam Goudie's intense years as pastor of Bethany, Berlin, or Bethel, Toronto, as recorded in the diaries and the two years when the family lived in Toronto, but he was busy as a Presiding Elder makes for strange reading. I see family names of people Goudie worked with and notice gaps where people that he saw all the time no longer appear. People that are stalwarts of the congregation for decades afterward are unknown in his time. The next generation appears, where Goudie knew the parents. The past is a strange country to the present, we think we see the continuities (there are some), but the past refuses to be the present.

The Conference leaders knew that a significant number of members from the country churches were making their way into Toronto and were, in effect, being lost to the denomination. Many names in the membership list Goudie maintained in his two years at the West End Mission were recognizably families from the rural churches. But there were also significantly large numbers without German background. In time, Mennonite scholars such as Harold Bender, the editor of the *Mennonite Encyclopedia*, noticed this influx of Anglo/ non-German members.[73] Detwiler's strategy was simple: announce protracted tent meetings and start city missions east and west of Yonge Street. The MBiC devoted a number of personnel and held camp-meetings over the next few years in support of this project. Noah himself had the experienced John Bolwell as a helper from 1899 to 1901. One project flourished, the other nearly foundered, and a third never did get much off the ground (Toronto-Dundas Junction). Some key members led significant new ventures for the MBiC arising from these missions, and also introduced destabilizing new doctrines. Samuel Goudie was going to become involved with them all.

"City Missions" was a new thing for the overwhelmingly rural Mennonite denominations in the last part of the 1890s, but not new to the major churches of Britain and North America. A study of *Might's Toronto Street Directories* shows many missions run by Canadian denominations: Methodist, Presbyterian, Baptist, Brethren, the Alliance, Mennonites of

---

73. Bender, "Evangelism," 272–73.

two sorts, holiness, Pentecostal and independents in the years 1897–1911. Of course, the Christian Workers Churches and the Salvation Army were practically city missions. Into this welter of institutions, the Mennonite Brethren in Christ came as yet another in a well-known class.[74]

Goudie was not following Detwiler, who asked to be relieved of the west mission in 1901. Detwiler continued evangelizing in the Toronto Junction/ Dundas St. area for another year, but his health gave way, and he could not take an appointment after that until his death in 1914, but he did preach when he could, especially at the West End Mission. Instead, Goudie's comrade from Sherkston, John A. Sider, served the small mission which met at a couple of sites along Spadina Avenue from 1901 to 1903.

Again, the lack of most of the *Gospel Banner* issues for 1903 and 1904 hampers our record of Goudie's work in these two years. Two reports from Toronto, and one of a deputizing visit to a Quarterly Conference at Vineland survive. Thankfully, Goudie's pastoral diaries cover these eventful years as well.[75] Sam's first Sunday as pastor in Toronto was 12 April, but soon in a letter to the *Gospel Banner*, 8 May, Goudie recorded that a few attenders had been reclaimed and one sanctified.[76]

Sam Goudie's diaries tell us he went to hear Dr. G. D. Watson, the man whose instruction on testimonies had impressed Sam ten years before. In May 1903, Goudie attended a prayer meeting at Broadway Hall, a favorite venue for Christian conferences,[77] and went back with Eliza in the afternoon to hear Dr. Watson. "[I]t was grand," Goudie wrote, which was his top-level praise. Amazingly, Goudie and Mr. R. Robinson, a West End

---

74. The house at 651 Queen St. E. became famous as the Hebden's Pentecostal mission, but from 1900 to 1902, the buildings across the street at 658/60 were listed as a Baptist mission room, then as a "Pentecostal Mission" from 1903–1912 at least. The C&MA had a "home" at 564 Parliament Street sometimes called the "Four-fold Gospel Chapel" from 1897, led by a Mrs. Elizabeth Risdon (Reynolds, *Footprints*, 198). Risdon also wrote frequent devotionals for the *Gospel Banner*. She had some earlier relationship to the MBiC I have not been able to pin down. The Hebden's used 651 Queen St. E. from 1906 to 1910, after which it was listed as "vacant"; *Might's Toronto Street Directories 1897 to 1912* (in the Toronto Metropolitan Library). The Mennonite Conference of Canada (Mennonite Church of Ontario after 1909) started their first city mission in Toronto in March 1907, Steiner, *Promised Lands*, 172. In November 1907, the location was 461 King St. E., and from 1909, there was another started on Danforth Avenue.

75. *GB* (16 May 1903) 12; (22 August 1903) 13; (20 February 1904) 13.

76. Sam Goudie, "Letter," *GB* (16 May 1903) 12.

77. Possibly Broadway Methodist Tabernacle, Spadina Ave. and College St., demolished 1924.

Mission leader, decided they should cancel their meetings in favor of the Convention. Goudie was clearly delighted. "It was a feast," Goudie wrote of the Friday night meeting. He was impressed by Watson's associate's altar service, a Mr. Farnham. Saturday morning, Watson spoke on healing, also in the afternoon, and again Farnham in the evening. Sunday was the same to Sam: "[T]he A. M. sermon by G. D. Watson was just something extraordinary . . . God bless the dear old saint of God."[78]

The visit to Vineland in July, a former pastoral charge, reminded him of the peculiar temptations a fruit-growing area made on a congregation at harvest-time, but he could not resist another pun: it "would have been better if people had not been buried by berries and other fruit." Although the Sunday meetings were well attended, "the 'gossip devil' still has a strong claim at Vineland and surroundings," he claimed.[79] Sam was not alone in leadership criticizing faults of a circuit. One wonders how the congregations took the comments, which would probably be considered improper from a visiting church leader today. A holiness church was used to evaluations of behavior, however, and numerous letter writers to the *Gospel Banner* urged the leadership to maintain standards.

Sam and Eliza tried to make the Quarterly Meeting trip to Vineland in the height of the fruit season into another family holiday as they had done in 1902.[80] They crossed the lake by excursion boat. Eliza and the children stayed with friends while he did the preaching and visiting, but overall, this combination did not work. When they got back to Toronto, he wrote: "We all rejoiced to be at home & concluded that others are welcome to the P. Eldership only let us be at home."[81] Traveling on his own later, Goudie seemed to have no problem sleeping in different guest beds every night, but it was stressful for the children. Even so, Goudie was always glad to be back at home after the QM tours.

After a visit with the ailing missionary to Jews, David Fretz, Goudie traveled south to Sherkston with Archibald ("A. G.") Doner. He confessed his deep interest in the place, and prayed that a Spirit-filled worker might be stationed at Sherkston, so it would not be neglected. He affectionately

78. Sam Goudie, "Diary 1903," 21–24 May.

79. Sam Goudie, "Vineland, Ont.," *GB* (22 August 1903) 13.

80. Sam Goudie, "Diary 1902," 1–11 July. People visited were David Fretzs, Jacob Hunsbergers, Aunt Barbara Kratzs, Samuel A. Moyers (where they picked a crate of strawberries!) and in Hamilton on the way back, Franklin W. Moyer, now a local help, but obviously not out of the attention of Sam and Eliza Goudie.

81. Sam Goudie, "Diaries 1903," 1 August.

names the people whose families they visited.[82] Goudie also preached in the St. Catharines mission one evening. The workers that year were Sarah Pool and Martha Dunnington. The meeting moved him to exclaim, "God bless our City Missions and Mission Workers. I love the City Missions."[83]

The West Toronto Mission, as it was also known, itself had a visit by a deputy of the Presiding Elder as reported in the same issue of the church paper as Goudie's visit to Vineland. His friend C. N. Good, then a pastor at Breslau, saw both Toronto missions for Peter Cober in August. The East End was dedicating a new site along Parliament St. (Their former landlord did not appreciate the noise they made in their services, I believe). At the western site, Good attended a Monday evening prayer meeting, and it was not a "killing time," but rather lively, he said. He was up for an early morning prayer meeting on Sunday and led the communion service in the afternoon. It was an "old-fashioned time," Good wrote. "The spirit of testimony was upon the meeting so that we had no time to preach. We were not without a shout in the camp, either." And how did the pastor feel about this? "The work in this mission is encouraging. Their pastor, S. Goudie, feels quite at home and is enjoying city work."[84]

The MBiC was quite confident they had a biblical, powerful, saving and cleansing gospel to preach, but as a church based in the countryside, they were self-conscious about their presence in the city. Could they make it as a denomination in a city? In the Canada Northwest Conference, some felt they shied away from city work there, leaving women like Maude Chatham and her partners to struggle in Edmonton without much Conference encouragement.[85] A parallel mission in Calgary in 1920–1921 was closed because people were saying pastoral supply to the established country fields was suffering.[86] The Ontario Conference had even urged the Can NW to consolidate their rural churches before venturing into the cities, advice some regretted following. So, there was some hesitation across the whole Canadian part of the MBiC about "city work." Not until the 1960s would

---

82. George Traub, J. Shisler, Titus Sherk, Elman Zavitz and Mrs. Brillinger

83. Sam Goudie, "Vineland," *GB* (22 August 1903) 13.

84. C. N. Good, "Reports," *GB* (22 August 1903) 12.

85. Gibson, "Church Planting," [7]; Dr. Ed Oke, member of the EMCC National Historical Committee for western Canada, e-mail to the author, 28 April 2015, with notes from Donald Taylor, one time Mountain View Bible College president and a descendent of Beulah Home staff.

86. *Canada Northwest Conference Journal 1921*, 13. Reference brought to the author's attention by Dr. Ed Oke, e-mail, 3 March 2018.

The Maturing Goudie 1897–1905

the Ontario church catch up with the move of Ontario's population to the cities. From his diaries, Sam Goudie looked quite comfortable whipping about the city on a bicycle ("my wheel," he called it), tram cars and railways, visiting the sites, shops and parks, but adapting a rural church way of life to the urban character is another thing.

If all we had were *Gospel Banner* reports, Goudie's part in the development of the congregation's facilities would not be clear. They do not mention him at all. As early as July 1903, however, Goudie had looked around for a new meeting place, and again in September, "as the one we have is a poor one no light nor fresh air to be had."[87] Probably a hot summer spent in the hall on Spadina showed him its failings for the purposes of a Mission. And in October their Friday service was annoyed by a concert in the hall above theirs.

At the end of September, Goudie found a little building on Brunswick Avenue, four blocks east of Lippincott St. and suddenly the diary filled with references to it: on September 29, with Pearl and Fletcher, he went for a walk to look at it again, and by the next day he had tracked down the owner. Mr. Fell had to see someone he had promised to be allowed to buy first. On October 5, he took Peter Cober, his Presiding Elder, to see it. On October 11, Goudie finally got a hint from Mr. Fell that they might be able to buy the hall, and next day, at a meeting at Oliver Pannabecker's house, trustees (Geddes, Boswell and Hallman) were appointed with authority to buy. The following week, after a Sunday School Convention in Stayner, Goudie was again pressing Mr. Fell for an answer, who promised that on Monday, October 19, they would know. As soon as Mr. Fell told them so (a day later, however) the trustees met with Sam, and they had Fell sign an agreement the next day. Then came appointments with a lawyer, a Mr. Urquart, throughout October, and by November 2, the deed was turned over to the trustees. The first day of November was the last night in the old hall: "[S]ome were sad. I was glad," wrote Goudie.[88] The small building on Brunswick was the first permanent site of the MBiC in Toronto, and had full approval from the Presiding Elder Peter Cober.[89] The transition was so fast Sam and some church women were up to 10 pm the night of November

---

87. Sam Goudie, "Diary 1903," 16 July, 24 September.

88. Sam Goudie, "Diary 1903," throughout 28 September to 2 November. Strangely, "Geddes" does not show up on the membership list Goudie maintained; Boswell's name shows up in the diary. Simeon S. Hallman was in the membership list.

89. Peter Cober, "Presiding Elder's Report," *GB* (21 November 1903) as quoted in Sherk, *Banfield Memorial*, 18–19.

3, cleaning ("oh my wasn't it dirty.") Sam was still distributing notices about it the morning of the opening and they didn't even have time to paint the sign board until a week later.[90]

Goudie is not remembered as a "building" pastor. We have seen that what he wrote about was mostly meetings, conversions, reclamation of backsliders and sanctifications. The opening day of the new hall at 189 Brunswick Avenue[91] attracted notable visitors, including Rev. William Stewart of the Toronto Bible Training School (later Toronto Bible College, now Tyndale University), the mayor of Toronto, Thomas Urquhart, both of whom gave short addresses, and Solomon Eby, who also spoke. For such men to show interest in the MBiC is unusual and curious: who invited them? Cober? Detwiler? Eby? H. S. Hallman? Through Hallman, the MBiC had a connection with Bingham and the SIM which had close contact with the students and staff of TBTS. Some Toronto mayors, such as William Howland (mayor 1886–1887), were promoters of city missions. Urquhart, a Baptist from Walmer Road Baptist Church (itself a strong supporter of TBTS) was in his first year of three as mayor. There was a collection, ($46), but next day, Sam was at the Bible Training School to pick up Dr. Stewart's articles specially written for the Toronto newspapers, the *Globe*, and the *Mail and Empire*. Later in November, Rev. Elmore Harris added his own gift. From the diary, it would seem the main mover of the opening day, 4 November, must have been Sam Goudie himself. The opportunity to improve the mission's facilities stirred Goudie to this (for him) uncharacteristic real estate activity.

While all these activities were taking Sam Goudie's time, the regular round of services at the Mission continued without interruption: three meetings each Sunday, prayer meetings at member's houses, preaching services Monday, Wednesday, Friday and Saturday nights. There were visits to congregational members and the sick, hosting visitors and even sightseers to the city in the summer and the Toronto Exhibition in the fall. There were frequent visiting preachers. It is amazing to catalog them for six months alone, from April to October, Goudie had the services of, for

---

90. Sam Goudie, "Diary 1903," 3–13 November.

91. Numbered "161" in *Might's Toronto Street Directories* 1904–1908. From 1909 onward, the number was 189 Brunswick. In 1903 the building was used by "Disciples of Christ," but still called "Forester's Hall" in 1905. The Parliament Street mission was far less stable than the West End, occupying five places on Parliament plus one on Carlton St., 1899 to 1912, in contrast to the west's two or three. The difference probably reflected class differences in the respective areas of the city.

example, John N. Kitching, Peter Cober, William Graybiel, George Chambers, "Bro. Stewart" of Louisville, Kentucky, C. N. Good, a Bro. Wickware (a member of the mission),[92] Noah Detwiler (frequently), Andrew Good, Archibald G. Doner, George Webb, Rowland Bingham, Samuel A. Moyer, and a Mr. Chalmers of Pittsburg, PA. Later members of the City Mission Workers and other women preached; in 1903–1905, they were a Miss Baker, a Miss Lawson (missionary to India), Mary Anne White (later married to John S. Finlay) from Didsbury, Emma Block and Emma Hostetler from Waterloo, and Sarah Pool from Markham, serving in the city. This is typical, and I have not listed everybody. True, the West End Mission had seven preaching opportunities a week, and in the twenty-first century many pastors have about only one shot at preaching a week. Think about the effect this narrowing of preaching services has on Christian formation as we like to call it now.[93]

Sam Goudie enjoyed the institutional and interdenominational environment of Berlin but, even more so, of Toronto which was unavailable in Port Elgin. In practically his first week, he and Eliza tried to get into the funeral of Ontario's long-serving premier, Sir Oliver Mowat, at the government buildings, but the crowds were too much to get in (April 21). (Mowat would have been the premier [1872–1896] during most of Sam's adult life, so Sam, though a Mennonite, did notice government after all!) They frequently enjoyed shopping at Eaton's and Simpson's huge department stores. They explored the buildings at "the Queen's Park," City Dairy, Riverdale Park and Cemetery, and elsewhere. Goudie visited special events at other missions and churches: in 1903 alone, he went to Union Mission Hall for the farewell of "Bro. Smedley" (May 9); the farewell of missionaries going to Nigeria at the Bible Training School (May 13);[94] and a Christian and Missionary Alliance Convention (June 30 and July 1). Later with H. S. Hallman, he went to the Christian Workers' Mission (December 3) and

---

92. Possibly C. B. Wickware who in the 1901 census gave as his religion "Chr'n [W]ork[ers]" (second word not clear).

93. I remember revival days in the United Missionary Church in North Bay in the 1960s with a special meetings several nights in a row. Normally, even we only had two services a Sunday, and a Wednesday night prayer meeting. The level of activity at "the Mission" was duplicated at the East End Mission on Parliament, where Goudie often visited, and at most of the city mission sites that Goudie attended over the years. It is practically a foreign country to me and maybe some readers to see such frequent meetings. Not that they were all solidly attended! Rural appointments did not see this level of activity.

94. And did it again in 1904: Sam Goudie, "Diary 1904," 20 August.

tried the Evangelical Church on Arthur Street hoping to hear Bishop Sylvanus Charles Breyfogel, only to hear the Revs. Wagner, Litt and Comfort instead (December 7).[95] In 1904, Sam looked up the pastors of the Christian Workers Churches, Alfred Roffe and George Fisher, and made sure he heard Philpott preach at the Christian Workers meeting on Clinton St. in September.[96]

In Toronto, Sam showed he was interested in reclaiming or training young men for ministry, George Chambers being one. Another was Fred Carlton (b. 1877), who had served as a helper to Noah Detwiler in the third year of the Toronto mission (1899–1900), and who also assisted T. Ford Barker in the Guelph Mission 1900–1901. In 1901, he was absent from the Canada Conference proceedings.

However, Fred Carlton showed up at the new hall on Brunswick Ave., November 11, 1903. On November 25, he visited Sam at home and "opened his heart to me," Sam wrote. They had another appointment at the Ontario Parliament buildings, December 11, but something about Fred's story made him doubtful of its truthfulness. Goudie was trying to encourage him to get past some experience or failure. At a prayer meeting at the Goudie's, "F. Carlton made a fresh start. May the Lord help the poor boy." Nothing more was noted about Fred until he attended the mission on December 7, 1904. In the New Year 1905, on January 4, Goudie noted Fred was present and claimed a new salvation experience. On January 10, the diary records "L. Pipher and Fred called this eve. had quite a visit." What about, Sam did not say, but the story unfolded bit by bit: L. Pipher (sometimes Goudie wrote it "Pifer,") was a young woman from a Whitchurch Township. Mennonite farm family who was working in the city, a member of the West End Mission. Luella visited the Goudies on her own on January 14, and her mother on Monday, January 16, "relative to Luella's trouble."[97]

Sam had Fred go visiting with him, as Fred probably used to do with Detwiler and Barker, on January 18, and brought Fred to their house the next day. On January 20, Fred made a profession of being sanctified. Goudie sounded cautious: on February 14, he again met with Fred. Sam

---

95. Sam Goudie, "Diary 1904," 30 June 30, 1 July, 3, 7 December. The Evangelical ministers were probably Louis Henry Wagner and J. G. Litt. There was a Merritt I. Comfort, a United Brethren in Christ minister in the 1901 census in Berlin.

96. Sam Goudie, "Diary 1904," 4 February, 12 November and 26 September.

97. Sam Goudie, "Diary 1903," 11 and 25 November, 11 and 14 December. "Diary 1904," 7 December.

also called on Fred's parents, Irish Methodist immigrants in the city.[98] Mr. Robert Carlton was a foreman gardener, and Fred was following in his father's footsteps. The following Sunday, Goudie noted in his diary, "Rec'd N. H. Reichard and Fred into church fellowship." But Goudie's doubt had a reason—on March 4: "Called at Mr. Carlton's found Fred out. his mother said he was drinking poor fellow." Sam recorded looking for Fred "in Park" [which?] this A.M. [11 March] in vain."[99] And Fred passed out of Goudie's diaries. In mid-March, the Canada Conference assigned Sam Goudie a new job, and Henry his brother took over the West End Mission. The 1911 Canada census suggests a better outcome than this incident for the young man: Fred has married Mary Luella Pipher, they have two children (five and three), Fred was a "foreman contractor," and one of Luella's sisters was living with them, as well as one of her brothers, also another sister-in-law of Fred's. Fred's father was also with them, Fred's mother, Elizabeth, having died sometime since the last census. The family were listed as Methodists. And in the 1921 Canada census, Fred and wife listed themselves as Mennonites again![100] We will think the best of them.

The other feature of Goudie's diaries for Berlin and Toronto is the constant visiting going on between Sam and his brothers and their families. Except for Henry Goudie, who was a Conference official, none of his relatives are noted in the MBiC record and of course several were not members of the MBiC. Sam's brother D. W. lived down the street at 11 Lippincott St., so dropping in on him and Aunt Martha was easy, but there were also younger relatives coming to Toronto for work or school. In January 1904 Uncle Abram gave up his farm in Michigan and asked Sam to help him find work in Toronto. When Sam thought he had a job lined up, he telegraphed his brother and Abram took the train and got there that night. His wife Lydia came later. Abram got work at Massey Harris, the farm machinery company, within a week.

Whenever Sam was in Waterloo County, he would look up James and Jacob, Isaac, Uncle Dave Pannabecker and remoter relatives like the Dixons. Occasionally, the diaries mention going with a brother to visit graves: Wanner's to view their father's or the Berlin "East End Cemetery" (beside First Mennonite Church), where D. W.'s wife Maria was buried.[101]

98. Sam Goudie, "Diary 1905," 4, 10, 14, 16, 18, 19 January. Canada census 1901.
99. Sam Goudie, "Diary 1905," 14 and 18 February, 4 and 11 March.
100. Canada census 1911 and 1921.
101. For example, Sam Goudie, "Diary 1902," 5 November, "Diary 1908," 24 May.

When Sam went to the Berlin camp-meeting in June 1903, he mentioned several times how much he enjoyed seeing his Berlin friends. After the camp, he went to his brother Jacob's,

> where I met mother & [his half-sister] Emily [Warner] . . . I walked over to Jas' & got a horse and rig to meet Ma-ma & the children at Breslau [train station]. We went to Jas' for the night. Uncle Dixon came there too. [the next day:] This is Allie's Birth-day so I bought some strawberries for dinner. Elton [James' son] drove us to Mr. Hagey's just before supper where we stayed for the night.[102]

Not only did Sam and also Eliza visit family and church families, they did a lot of hosting of visitors—common enough for a minister's home, though it was sometimes hard on Eliza, according to Sam's diary. Many weeks they had people for "tea" and nearly as often for "dinner," (mid-day meal), less often at night ("supper,") but still frequent enough and noted by name in Goudie's diaries. Nevertheless, the level of hospitality equals the visits back and forth recorded in Fannie Raymer's farm diaries in Sunnidale. The Goudies seem to show as much hospitality as regular rural MBiC members.[103]

The Sixth General Conference, Nappanee, Indiana, October 1904

While he was in Toronto, Sam Goudie was chosen one of the Canada Conference's delegates to the MBiC GC in Nappanee, just south of Elkhart in northern Indiana. As before, the total membership of this GC was not large, not even thirty, men elected from their Conferences specifically for the Conference. The only paid staff member was the magazine editor, accountable to the General Conference. All the other functions were voluntary or *ex officio*. Decisions were by democratic procedures and by the *Discipline*. (Later guides such as *Robert's Rules of Order* were used.) The number of ministers and congregational delegates were proportional to Conference membership. Canada had seven.[104]

This is unfamiliar territory for the twenty-first-century Evangelical Missionary Church of Canada. The EMCC has paid national staff. It has an elected national board who develop "governance by policy" so that the

---

102. Sam Goudie, "Diary 1903," 22–23 June.

103. Hoffman and Taylor, *Much To Be Done*, "Visiting," 135–50, describes visiting from the women's point of view in both rural and urban settings. Sam and Eliza seem to have practised the rural version generally.

104. *Sixth General Conference 1904*, is reviewed in this section.

The Maturing Goudie 1897–1905

many members of the General Assembly seem to have very little to do except what is required by Canadian charity law. One system is not better than the other, they are both customs developed to work in cooperation, which is part of what anthropologists mean by culture, and as is mandated by scripture in Gen 1:28. I am saying the systems are strange to each other, each reflecting their times and understanding of the Bible, neither completely embodying it.

Goudie refers to one action at this conference in his brief history in 1928 of the formation of the United Missionary Society.[105] The Canada Conference delegates went very hopeful, he wrote, that they along with other Conferences would agree to a uniting of the foreign mission efforts of the individual Conferences into one denominational mission society. The motion was not met with encouragement or success. The fact is that the Pennsylvania Conference was quite satisfied with its mission program which supported missionaries (nine by 1905) under existing boards, chiefly the Christian and Missionary Alliance, and here, as in several other matters, they protected their independence. All the General Conference could agree to was to repeat a resolution of the 1896 General Conference (itself continuing a resolution as far back as 1885),[106] that any Conference could pursue foreign missions as they wished, or band with other like-minded conferences to do so. In 1905, three Conferences finally did just that: Canada, Michigan, and the Indiana and Ohio Conferences[107] agreed to form the "Mennonite Brethren in Christ Missionary Society, General Board" sometimes also called the MBiC (General) Foreign Missions Board. It was even called the African Board at times. Sam Goudie became a member of that Board, with Ebenezer Anthony as President, who served for five years. Anthony had missions experience, having recovered from illness after two years in Nigeria (1901–1903) under the Africa Industrial Mission (SIM). The Michigan Conference re-elected him as a Presiding Elder with O. B. Snyder in 1904.[108] Later, Goudie served as chair of this General Board until

---

105. Goudie, "Origin," 6–7.

106. Storms, *What God Hath Wrought*, 152. The intention of the 1885 resolution appears to have been to encourage missions preaching and giving, not entrench independent conference action.

107. Indiana and Ohio were separated only in 1942. Storms, *United Missionary Church*, writes anachronistically of the "Indiana and Ohio districts" as if they were separate Conferences all along, only partly clarifying the relationship on page 116. Fuller, *Banfield*, 37, also continued the error of supposing they were separate Conferences in 1905.

108. Storms, *What God Hath Wrought*, 31.

the United Missionary Society superseded it. The General Board was not a General Conference entity, and did not have to report to it, but which for the same reason did not have to be cared for by the GC. It had to be sustained by those zealous to carry it out, which, on its own is not actually that bad an idea, especially in the short term.

Goudie remarked that after a short time a conference, which he did not name, dropped out. In fact it was the Indiana and Ohio (I&O) Conference, and "in later years the Canadian Northwest Conference joined."[109] The I&O Conference did send out and support missionaries—at least seven by 1909, but their personnel were all under other boards. Pheobe Brenneman was under the C&MA in China, and the rest were with the United Orphanage and Mission Board in Armenian Turkey. Indiana and Ohio therefore had no stake in a denominational mission society until Joseph Ummel went to Nigeria under the UMS in 1923. Thus for a while only Ontario and those conferences formed from Ontario (Michigan, Canada Northwest) cooperated in a united mission effort on behalf of the MBiC. The 1904 permission for Conferences to individually band together was a step in the right direction, nevertheless, Sam Goudie wrote, "This did not measure up to the ideals that were formed in the minds of our most outstanding missionary people, both in the ministry and laity, whose vision took in a larger territory . . ."[110] Although Goudie was not alone in wishing to see a denominational mission, his leadership in this direction is plain. Probably his colleagues on the MBiC FMB or the Canada/Ontario Conference Foreign Mission Board were the main supporters of the desired missionary society plan—C. N. Good, H. S. Hallman, Silas Cressman, Peter Cober from Ontario, plus Ebenezer Anthony and Oliver B. Snyder from Michigan.[111] Abraham B. Yoder from Indiana, treasurer of the UOM Board and a Presiding Elder of the I&O Conference served from 1908 for a time as well. John N. Kitching who worked in both Michigan and Ontario and Benjamin A. Sherk of Michigan both joined at various times.[112] In 1916 the

---

109. Goudie, "Origin," 6.

110. Goudie, "Origin," 6.

111. In 1918, Jasper A. Huffman, the editor of the *Gospel Banner*, began promoting a denominational mission and support immediately came from smaller districts in the western US and Canada, and former missionaries. See Huffman, *Seventy Years*, 127–29. Apart from noting the Ontario Conference was the Conference most receptive to the idea of a General Conference Mission Board, Huffman does not credit Goudie's desire for or role in its formation nor that of the others with him. See Fuller, "Nigeria," 61.

112. See Hallman, *Report*, an 8-page illustrated leaflet which listed all the General

representation had to be renewed, because an invitation went out from the "African General Board" to the Michigan Conference and the Indiana and Ohio Conference to send representatives.[113]

From their writings, or lack of them, I do not see that any of these men introduced any innovations in missionary strategy that missiologists love to see. The MBiC leaders simply wanted to implement in their Mennonite church what they had watched happening in the evangelical world, as Gingerich noted.[114] That was their innovation. Although the MBiC were the first North American Mennonite body to send out foreign missionaries (Eusebius Hershey 1890; William Shantz 1895), they were not the first Mennonite body to organize a foreign mission sending agency.[115]

There have always been Christians and others who ignore or even disparage Christian organizations ("organized religion" has been a smear word for decades), but in fact no human endeavour has been without institutions, in the anthropological sense at least. Organizations serve and conserve some human goods since Genesis 1, as was mentioned in relation to MBiC polity. God's "mission" in Jesus blesses agencies and even those who speak against agencies ("Not a dollar goes to overhead..." is the naive boast of some). Such people form small institutions of their own inevitably, despite their criticism of agencies, and somebody pays for the lights.

In other GC action that Goudie was involved in, he was on the committee that introduced the recommendations or resolutions from the Conferences. I find especially interesting two areas: the request for a bishop, and revision of the Reading Course.

Canada Conference put their request cautiously; they simply requested discussion about the "advisability of having a Bishop." Whereas a

---

Board members. This publicity effort does not seem to have been repeated unfortunately. There may have been an edition in 1907 as well.

113. Sam Goudie, "Specials—Annual Meeting of the African General Board," *GB* (27 July 1916) 12.

114. The thesis of Charles Gingerich, "Experiment in Denominationalism," 58–59, is exactly that the MBiC, at least in Ontario, was trying to develop a church with a full suite of denominational institutions, including a missionary society. Gingerich's section on missions, 61–2, should be corrected by Fuller, "Nigeria," 45, 48, 50–1, 61.

115. The first world-wide was the Dutch Mennonite Church. Erdel, "I Wish," 8–9, has documented an African-American, George Liele, who went to Jamaica and organized a church with an Anabaptist constitution much earlier than Hershey. There were cross-cultural missionaries sent out by the General Conference Mennonites, which the MBiC supported, earlier than Hershey. Being first is a game that dies by qualification when you look into it. See Fuller, "Nigeria," 17, 35 n. 40.

similar motion in 1900 was refused without debate, this time there was a "lengthy discussion," and a motion was passed to have "no Bishop at this present time."

Several Conferences had suggestions about the Probationers' Reading Course. Nebraska and the Indiana and Ohio Conferences agreed that they wanted John Fletcher Hurst's *History of the Christian Church* (1901), instead of George Park Fisher's *History of the Christian Church* (1893). That seemed easy enough. Michigan simply said they wanted as good a theology text as the General Conference could get. Pennsylvania again had a protest about the theology books. They wanted to substitute some books on the deeper life in Christ instead of Thomas Doty's *Lessons in Holiness* that had been in use since the early 1880s which was a thoroughly *Wesleyan* holiness book, as opposed to the Keswick Conferences' or Simpson's more Reformed views. Both Indiana and Ohio Conference and Pennsylvania now wanted the pass mark to be dropped to 30 percent per course (I&O) or at least not so high (P). Pennsylvania also protested against "more books on theories, arts, etc."[116] There was strong prejudice against higher education for preachers in some parts of the MBiC at this time. A Bible Institute in Indiana and Ohio ended after just four years (1900–1904) partly because of objections to the school's mere existence. The pioneering western Conferences keenly felt the need for training before the eastern ones were able to address their educational needs permanently.

Events in Ontario

Sometime in 1903–1904, one of Sam's colleagues in the Canada Conference, Henry Wismer, a man he had worked with several times, found himself at odds with the MBiC and he did not show up for the 1904 Annual Conference. Somewhere I found a record that he had gone to Michigan. Oddly, maybe by an oversight, he was not recorded as being among "Ministers Absent" as he should have been. Another minister, Franklin Wismer Moyer (1845–1923), who was noted as being absent, had a complaint against him from his membership field (Vineland), as recorded in the Quarterly Conference minutes book. His case was dealt with by a committee which included his delegate, his pastor and three current or past Presiding Elders. The committee approved the Vineland Quarterly Conference's own approach to discipline him, and that report was received.

116. *Sixth General Conference 1904*, 13.

The Maturing Goudie 1897–1905

Something different was going on with Henry Wismer, though, because he was not present and did not report by letter, but no complaint is recorded. He was the man Goudie visited in Woodstock. Sometimes the Conference merely admonished the forgetful member (especially if they were retired or were known to be ill), but in Wismer's case, a high level committee was formed to investigate (Amos Eby, Solomon Eby, Peter Cober, Christian Raymer, Henry Goudie and New Dundee delegate Moses Bock).This suggests that many people knew what Wismer's problem was, but could not act until something official had come out, either by Wismer himself, or by Conference investigation. In fact, there was evidence of something between him and Peter Cober, but it only came out much later in the Conference. What exactly that was, was still not reported. The following year, Cober reported that Henry Wismer wrote him saying he (Wismer) could not be loyal to the church, so he asked for a letter of dismissal. The Conference granted that letter.[117]

---

117. *Ontario Conference Journal 1904*, throughout.

6

Presiding Elder Sam Goudie 1905–1907

AFTER SAM GOUDIE'S SECOND year in Toronto, the needs of the Conference and the new mission Conference centered in Alberta initiated big changes for both Goudie brothers, for in 1905, Sam Goudie was elected as a Presiding Elder for the Canada Conference and Henry was soon to go west. In his diary, Sam merely noted, "PEs were elected and many other important things were done."[1] He was succeeded for one year only at the Toronto West mission by his brother Henry (who was now appointed Sam's Vice-Presiding Elder!), before Henry was appointed to go to Didsbury as the organizing Presiding Elder of the new Canada Northwest Conference in 1906.[2] Early in Sam's years as a Presiding Elder the Ontario Conference was to be tested by a new movement coming out of Toronto and Los Angeles. After describing the work a Presiding Elder was expected to do, the following three chapters will examine the progress of the new movement through the Conference's personnel and congregations, Sam Goudie's response to it and assess some of the losses and gains for the Ontario Mennonite Brethren in Christ.

---

1. Sam Goudie, "Diary," 24 March.

2. J. B. Detwiler, in the west since 1894, had served a year as a "missionary Presiding Elder," 1905–1906; Fuller, "Detwiler, Jacob B.," *GAMEO*.

PRESIDING ELDER'S DUTIES: TRAVELS, QUARTERLY MEETINGS, VISITS AND CAMPS

At the March 1905 Canada Conference, Samuel Goudie was elected one of two Presiding Elders. The other, re-elected, was the veteran Peter Cober. Solomon Eby retired from the pastorate at the largest congregation in the Canada Conference after one more year in 1906, at Bethany in Berlin. He was seventy-two. Menno Bowman had moved into retirement already in 1900 and died in 1906 just short of his seventieth year. A generation change was underway.

Samuel Goudie was only thirty-nine, but he had been a pastor for twenty years, and had demonstrated steadiness and competence in leadership. The first generation of leaders (the Hochs, Troyers, Raymers, Schlichters and McNallys of the New Mennonites, the Ebys, Bowmans, Detwilers and Webers of the Reforming Mennonites) were charismatic, loud men who had come out of the older Mennonite body in Ontario. Sam Goudie was a product of that new movement. It is tempting to see him as an upholder of an inheritance, one to put into practice the innovations of others, an administrator of a system. And I think this is partly true, as I pointed out on his attitude to the MBiC *Discipline*. He saw plenty of alterations to the *Discipline* over his years, but never saw a reason to sweep it away. He was "unconditional" every year but one in his long career until 1941 when he was seventy-five.[3]

This is a good place to list the places and people involved in the "Canada/ Ontario Conference" of the MBiC in 1905 that Goudie was to help oversee. Many of these we have already met.

Peter Cober and Samuel Goudie were set over 22 circuits and Conference missions while the City Mission President was charged with the care of 9 City Missions. Six churches were single location churches, while 16 had multiple sites cared for by a pastor and local help and probationers, so that the Conference counted 52 "appointments" plus the 9 city missions, or 61 locations of worship. For better administration, normally the Conference was divided into two districts, each served by a Presiding Elder, who was not appointed to a field. The boundaries of the districts were adjusted from time to time, depending on the abilities or health of the Presiding Elders, or gradually changing memberships of the two. Normally, the districts were

---

3. *Ontario Conference Journal 1941*, 41.

kept roughly equal in size, with an eye to convenience of the traveling conditions within the districts.

Cober was elected by the Conference to have oversight of the 11 fields in West District:

Fields	# of Appt's	Names of Appt's	Membership	Pastor in Charge	Helpers, Probationers
Berlin	1	Bethany	199	Solomon Eby	local
Bethel	5	New Dundee, Bethel, Mannheim, Roseville, Bright	157	Ephraim Sievenpiper	Amos Geiger, and local
Breslau	3	Breslau, West Montrose, Conestogo	110	Harvey Frey	local
Hespeler	2	Hespeler, Blair	67	John Francis "Frank" Gugin	Solomon Haug, and local
Maryboro	2	Maryborough, Wallace	67	Christian Raymer	
Elmwood	3	Elmwood, Hanover, Allen Park	99	Charles F. Krauth	Harvey Stauffer
Port Elgin	2	Port Elgin, Sang's School House	36	Milton Bricker	Lorne Benner
Kilsyth	2	Kilsyth, Dornoch	24	Archibald G. Doner	Daniel C. Eby
Aylmer	1	[added in 1906: Orwell]	36	C. N. Good	
Bruce Peninsula	2	Miller Lake, Ferndale	30	Sylvester H. Fretz	
Manitoulin Island	2	Salem, Long Bay	17	R. J. McLaren	
Totals	25		842	11 active	5 itinerant

Table 1. Eleven Fields of the West District

Samuel Goudie was elected therefore to superintend the 11 fields of the East District:

Fields	# of Appt's	Names of Appt's	Membership	Pastor in Charge	Helpers, Probationers
Vineland	2	Vineland, Sherkston	82	Amos Eby	local
Toronto East	1	(On Parliament St.)	59	George Chambers	supervised by Henry Goudie
Toronto West	1	Bethel	67	Henry Goudie	Lewis P. Ramer
Markham	5	Mt. Joy, Dickson Hill, 3rd Line, Bethesda, Vaughan	180	Joshua E. Fidler	Local and Wilmot G. Barkey, Robert Bloye
Stouffville	3	Stouffville, Altona, 4th Line of Uxbridge	88	Robert Eltherington	Wilmot G. Barkey and Robert Bloye
Scott	2	Mt. Pleasant, 6th Line	22	William Brown	
Stayner	3	Stayner, 6th Line, 2nd Line	89	John Ball	local
Sunnidale	3	Ebenezer, 9th Line, Glencairn	80	Joseph Clark	Charles Isaac Sinden
Shrigley	3	Shrigley, Shiloh, Mt. Pleasant	64	Webster Irish	Albert Remington
Collingwood	1		25	David Brittain	
Didsbury	4		143	Samuel S. Stauffer	Maude Chatham
Totals	27		899	11 active	6 itinerant

Table 2. Eleven Fields of the East District

In addition to these stationed elders and probationers, there was one person assigned to roving evangelism: tabernacle worker C. R. "Chris" Miller. Locally recognized workers that Peter Cober and Sam Goudie could call on were (mostly retired preachers, but some who had other "conditions" such as sickness): John A. Sider, Noah Detwiler (Toronto), Moses Weber (Markham), Peter Geiger (Breslau), Menno Bowman (Breslau), David S. Shantz (Canada Northwest), Jacob B. Detwiler (Canada Northwest), T. W.

Brook (Toronto), David Fretz (Vineland), Henry S. Cressman (Canada NW), Christian Shantz (New Dundee), John McNally (Blair), David Hartin (Markham, Stouffville, and Scott), I. Wyant (Stayner area), Sister Euphemia Guy (Mt. Joy), Fred Galletly (Galt), and Samuel A. Moyer (Vineland). I have included where these people lived at the time, if known.

The City Mission Workers Society was separately directed by its President, Henry S. Hallman, who lived in Berlin, but there was a fair amount of interaction throughout the year as the women assisted evangelism in their assignment, or they had the help of the Conference evangelist or other pastors. You will notice that not all women were directed by the CMWS, in fact one (Maude Chatham) was enrolled in the circuits, and one was in the local help list (Mrs. Euphemia Guy). Both women were designated Approved Ministering Sisters in 1905. The roster of women, who were at this time mostly young, was constantly changing as they came for a few years' experience, got married, got sick (financial support was minimal at best) or left for other reasons. In 1905 they were:

City Mission	Membership	Pastor/ leader	Helper
Owen Sound "Beulah"	45	Susie Bowman	Ruby Reeve
Wiarton	3	Sarah McQuarrie	Carrie Loop
St. Thomas	12	Jennie Little	Mary Dresch
Ingersoll	2	Mary Dunnington	Diana Shantz
St. Catharines	9	Edith Evans	Frances Matheson
Newmarket	7	Mary White	Maud McClelland
Guelph	11	Emma Block	Emma Good
Winnipeg	-	Emma Hostetler	Mary Markle
Orwell	-	-	-
Berlin Toronto East End Nigeria		Cora M. Rudy, Sarah Pool, Mrs. Althea (Priest) Banfield	Assisting H. S. Hallman slum worker missionary
Totals	89	20 women in all: others entering 1904/1905: Rebecca Hostetler, Luella Swalm, Anna Srigley	

Table 3. Female Ministers

Presiding Elder Sam Goudie 1905–1907

The MBiC Canada Conference had several categories of workers, so it is a bit difficult to state how many people were in the ministry, but we could say there were 22 male pastors leading churches, with two Presiding Elders, one CMWS President, one evangelist, one ordained missionary (Alexander W. Banfield, whose ordained status was omitted from the 1905 *Journal*, but rectified the next year); 20 women workers in the CMWS, plus one conditional woman, plus one more in the circuits; 10 male probationers or stated helpers, plus 16 male retired or otherwise conditional men. Seventy-four credentialed workers (53 males and 21 females) for 22 circuits and nine city missions or 31 "parishes" to use an alien term. At least three women were entering the CMWS in this period but were not yet deployed. Two workers, Elder Alec and Mrs. Banfield, were that August to go to the British "Protectorate" of Northern Nigeria (annexed by declaration and violence 1900–1905), not yet amalgamated administratively with the southern Nigerian "Protectorate." In time nine of these women gained missionary experience outside Canada.

Sam Goudie and family remained in Toronto at 134 Lippincott St. as he started out his work as a Presiding Elder. The Toronto West Mission was his family's church, and they continued to attend. At least for 1905–1906, his brother Henry was his family's pastor, and their uncle David W. Goudie was their deacon. Goudie gave his "farewell" sermon the morning of Sunday 9 April, and Henry preached in the evening.[4] Uncle Abram his brother lived in the city with his wife and children, attending a Methodist church. Visits and teas in the parks (in summer), coming and going of relatives and friends fill the diary. A rare year of family closeness.

Goudie knew what was expected of a Presiding Elder and began a decades-long round of visiting the fields in his district every three months. Starting with eleven fields in 1905, he normally could make forty-four visits a year. He conducted their business meetings, moderated the "passing" of circuit officials (pastors, probationers and other local help, Sunday School superintendents, class leaders and stewards), conducted the communion and foot-washing duties of the Presiding Elder. He made steady reports to the *Gospel Banner*, eventually hundreds of them, which it would be tedious though instructive to review for trends and personal styles and choices for him alone, and in comparison, with other Presiding Elders. I will only make selections from these reports.

---

4. Sam Goudie, "Diary 1905," 9 April.

Presiding Elders announced, partly organized and led the camp-meetings, a much anticipated and energetic time in the Conference year. From 1888 until 1915, with a few exceptions, the custom was to conduct camp-meetings in each district each summer.[5] Thus in June 1905, Goudie announced a camp-meeting in Dundalk, Grey County, for his East District but he also announced a second one for Didsbury, Alberta, still in his district, but soon to be the center of a new Conference, and he exhorted members to make plans to attend.[6] Peter Cober announced a camp-meeting for the West District at Berlin. Meanwhile Sam launched into his first Quarterly Meetings: West End Mission, East End Mission, Vineland with a side trip to Sherkston in April; Stayner, Collingwood, Shrigley, in May. He reported on his first visits to the fields of Stouffville and Markham in York County, and Scott in East Gwillimbury Township, York County, and Scott Township, in Ontario County.[7] He made a journey to enjoy the Berlin camp-meeting, and since he had few duties there, he visited friends and relatives, such as his mother at Jacob's farm at Breslau. She was not well, but not changing fast. On 26 June he finally bought tickets for the west, boarding the train in Toronto for Alberta the next day. It was totally new territory for him. On the fourth day, his train reached Calgary and was met by J. B. Detwiler and David S. Shantz who took him for the night to another former Ontario man, L. C. (probably Levi) Snyder.[8]

Didsbury, District of Alberta, was a just a signboard on a telegraph pole early in 1894 when it was waiting for settlers from Ontario. They arrived that April and pioneered through all the typical hazards of the prairies.

---

5. Brubacher and others, *Camp Meetings*, [12–13].

6. *GB* (10 June 1905) 8. Dundalk since 2000 has been part of the Township of Southgate, incorporating Proton and Egremont Townships as well.

7. The rural Scott field consisted of two appointments, sometimes three. Some MBiC meetings had been held in the area from 1883 to 1888. Mt. Pleasant, in Scott Township in Ontario County (now part of the Town of Uxbridge, Durham Region), was the first to be organized in 1888 about the same time with an appointment at Brown Hill with Oliver B. Schneider (Snyder) assigned there by the Conference. Mt. Zion, the appointment in East Gwillimbury Township, York County, became permanent in 1890, with help from the congregation in Mt. Pleasant (Zephyr). Some of the people had Bible Christian backgrounds; Black and Weller, "The History," [11–13]. Scott field appeared in the stationing record for the first time in 1891 with Christian Raymer, but the stationing reports for 1889 and 1890 are not currently known. Mt Pleasant church records preserve the first Quarterly Conference records of Scott Mission of 17 May 1889. Other appointments were known as Cedarbrae and Maple Grove (5th of Scott), both in the 1930s.

8. Sam Goudie, "Diary 1905," for April, May and June, throughout.

Berlin entrepreneur Jacob Yost Shantz, who had helped settle thousands of Mennonites from Russia in western Canada, persuaded some of his fellow members of Bethany MBiC to set up in what was then still the Canadian Northwest Territories. Later others, including members of Markham, Ontario, and a few from Michigan also went west. The tale is told in several church histories.[9] Until 1906, the membership of the western fields were overseen by the MBiC Canada Conference, but preparations were underway to raise up another MBiC Conference. Migration and evangelism in the west had not been as heavy as what produced the Michigan district, or migration was more scattered. By 1896 the Brown City district had over 500 members when the Michigan Conference was created out of the Canadian one. Nevertheless, 188 members were in the Territories, mostly at Didsbury, and the Canada Conference appointed Jacob B. Detwiler, the respected elder from Roseville, Waterloo County, Ontario, (and a son-in-law of J. Y. Shantz), as the interim Presiding Elder for the western Missionary Conference (1904). He had accompanied the first group of settlers in 1894 and had served them faithfully.

WINNIPEG/ MANITOBA MISSIONS, 1905–1908

The Canada Conference had been exploring another area of the Canadian west. As early as 1884, Elder Michael Haug was sent by the Conference to the area of Niverville, Manitoba, just southeast of Winnipeg, as a colporteur of the Upper Canada Tract Society, which had some understanding with the MBiC Canada Conference. Haug returned to Ontario early, discouraged, however.[10] The matter did not end there.

As soon as Sam Goudie moved to Toronto in 1903, he started noticing people from his circle heading west. He was quite aware of the Bethany contingent that settled at Didsbury in 1894, and the smaller group from Markham that followed later, but now he saw the movement west firsthand. Even in Berlin he had seen "the N.-Westerners" off from the train station.[11] In May 1903, he went to Union Station, Toronto, to see off a Mrs. Abe Shantz and her mother, also "Sis. Hutchings" going to the District of Assiniboia,

---

9. Swalm and Swalm, *Canada Northwest District*; The account in Huffman, *Mennonite Brethren in Christ*, 125–32 was written by Daniel C. Eby. Read more about J. B. Detwiler in Fuller, "Detwiler, J. B.," and about Jacob Y. Shantz in Steiner, *Vicarious Pioneer*.

10. *GB* (March 1884) 2.

11. Sam Goudie, "Diary 1902," 8 April. See also entry for 15 July: "I took Lydia Shantz to the station she and her father and some others left for Didsbury."

now southern Saskatchewan. In July, it was Peter Cober and "others who were going to the north-west." In September, "Frank left for Winnipeg."[12] He mentioned in his diary saying farewell in early 1904 to two sisters and the husband of one from the West End Mission going to Manitoba.[13]

It was no wonder then that in 1905 H. S. Hallman sent two women to Winnipeg, Manitoba, to open a mission in that booming city.[14] After some decades of stagnation and slow growth of population in western Canada, in the later 1890s and the first decade of the twentieth century, immigration to Canada, and especially to the Canadian west increased dramatically. Winnipeg counted 25,639 inhabitants in the Census of 1891, added 16,701 to reach 42,340 by 1901, but more than tripled to 139,863 by 1911.[15] From a church growth viewpoint, it was an excellent time to begin church planting, or as they called it, correctly, missionary work. The women's immediate attention may have been to follow up MBiC adherents in the city who had gone west, but they also had experience in small town Ontario evangelizing Anglo-Canadians. The rural MBiC did not have much experience in meeting and evangelizing those from non-Anglo or non-German backgrounds, and so far had failed to see French Canadians as a mission field. The church as a whole was just emerging from its own German-speaking sub-culture.[16] Those who took up missionary work tended to be English-speaking young people who were comfortable in their identity as Americans or Canadians in addition to their evangelical holiness-Mennonite emphasis.

Many Ontario-based denominations were experiencing a flow of members west, from the mighty Methodist Church of Canada to the smaller Evangelical Association.[17] Since the EvA was a Methodist church and had a Germanic background in some ways similar to the MBiC, it would

---

12. Sam Goudie, "Diary 1903," 26 May, 4 July, 24 September. "Sister Hutchings" was Sam's own niece, Ida Almina Goudie, D. W. and Maria's daughter. I do not know who "Frank" is unless it is a young husband Frank Robson, who became a member of Bethel (Toronto) on 22 February, Sam Goudie, "Pastor's Year Book 1904," in which case he came back, based on Sam Goudie, "Diary 1903," 4 December.

13. Maggie and her sister Tillie Bushart; Sam Goudie, "Diary 1904," 25 March.

14. For a description of Winnipeg at the turn of the twentieth century, see especially the account by the Methodist James Shaver Woodsworth, *My Neighbor*.

15. Woodsworth, *My Neighbor*, 32.

16. I owe this suggestion to James McDowell, World Partners Canada Associate Director 2000–2007.

17. Jesske, *Evangelical Church*, 24–31.

be instructive to look at their work in western Canada as a comparison and contrast to that of the Ontario MBiC in the west at this stage.

COMPARISON: THE EVANGELICAL ASSOCIATION NORTHWEST CANADA MISSION

The EvA Canada Conference centered in Canada West (that is, Ontario) was organized in 1863 with about 6,000 members.[18] By 1901, the Canada census recorded 10,193 people across the land who reported themselves and their families as "Evangelical." The Northwest Canada Conference of the EvA was not separated from the Canada Conference until 1927, when 1,433 members, 18 ministers and 21 circuits were bound together. Many were still using German in their services. Theodore Jesske has an account of the steps that led to the creation of that western Conference.[19]

The Evangelical Association Canada Conference noted the need of missionaries to Manitoba as early as 1876, at the Annual Conference at their Lingelbach Church in Easthope Township, Perth County, Ontario, under the chair Bishop John J. Esher of Chicago. A committee of two was assigned to investigate, and reached Winnipeg, but brought back a discouraging report.[20] Later the American EvA Minnesota Conference expressed some interest, but the territory was eventually left for their Canada Conference to follow up. Some activity of the EvA Dakota Conference also followed up American EvA members in the Northwest Territories, occasionally sending out preachers, though no churches were planted, from 1884 to 1899.

In 1899, the EvA Canada Conference, meeting in Tavistock, Oxford County, Ontario, under the same J. J. Esher finally faced its obligations and appointed a startled Elder William E. Beese (1872–1957) to go west. He determined he could not go alone and married Barbara Miller ten days before arriving in Winnipeg by Canadian Pacific Railway.[21] Beese and his wife worked for five years, leaving Winnipeg and the groundwork of a

---

18. Albright, *Evangelical Church*, 413. They had about 50 ministers. The Canada census of 1871 was not sensitive to the Evangelical Association and recorded only 4,701 "Evangelical" adherents. The census did not even collect Evangelical statistics in 1881 or 1891. These numbers include children.

19. Statistics in 1927: Jesske, *Evangelical Church*, 36–37; language: Albright, *Evangelical Church*, 413; the whole story: Jesske, *Evangelical* Church, 24–42.

20. Mosquitoes, maybe, as Russian Mennonites noted near Winnipeg in 1873; Steiner, *Vicarious Pioneer*, 83. Access to Manitoba was still through the US in those days.

21. Jesske, *Evangelical Church*, 27.

growing district throughout the west. He was joined by Elder A. W. Sauer at Rosthern, District of Saskatchewan in 1900, and Elder C. G. Kaatz at Didsbury, District of Alberta, in 1902, for example. The Didsbury members were probably attracted by the successful MBiC settlement of 1894. These pastors were clearly following up EvA members from elsewhere, for by 1907, there were 7 preachers and 13 stations, and by the following year, 20 preaching places and 432 members in the west.[22]

The Ontario MBiC could not have been unaware of the sudden organizing of the Evangelical Association in the west, and perhaps Goudie and others thought it was time to take steps to conserve their western members and to be ready for growth as had been done ten years before for Michigan and Nebraska Conferences.[23]

DIDSBURY CAMP-MEETING, NWT, 1905

As a venture of faith, a first camp-meeting for the western district was planned for Didsbury to start on July 7, 1905. The new Presiding Elder Sam Goudie traveled west June 27 with Bethany song-leader Peter Shupe to inaugurate the camp.[24] In Didsbury on July 2, he preached in the morning at the Methodist church in town, but in the afternoon and evening he was in the MBiC church building. "I enjoyed myself much with the pilgrims." For the next few days, they went visiting and driving in the country, and by July 6 the leaders had decided where to set up the camp, a site where the district met until the 1950s at least. It became the site of Mountain View Bible College and has been converted to dwellings today.

Only the tabernacle top reached Didsbury by train on the morning of July 7, but they set to work erecting family tents and the tabernacle anyway,

---

22. Jesske, *Evangelical Church*, 31. Canada census of 1881 and 1921, though the 1921 census is in error recording Beese as sixty-nine rather than forty-nine years old.

23. The eastern Mennonite Conference of Ontario was also watching their migrants who went west in 1892 but mostly after 1901, organizing their people in the Northwest Mennonite Conference in 1903, starting with congregations near Didsbury and Carstairs, Alberta (organized 1893); Gingerich, Burkholder, Voegtlin, and Steiner, "Northwest Mennonite Conference." Andrew Weber from Berlin, who was in the 1894 party to Didsbury, was an early member in this Conference; remembered in both Huffman, *Mennonite Brethren in Christ*, 128, and in Tiessen, "Mennonite Novelist," 93, 96–98. Ephraim Weber, the novelist, was Andrew's son.

24. Sam was not the first Presiding Elder to visit in the west. His brother Henry had visited for several weeks in 1901, mentioned in a report, reprinted in "Glimpses of the Past," *GB* (16 August 1951) 6, and Peter Cober in 1903; Sam Goudie, "Diary 1903," 4 July.

opening the camp as planned in the evening. Goudie wrote that the interest was good, and at first, so was the weather. On July 10, with rain and strong winds, they shifted to the MBiC building. Because the trains passed through once a week, the sides of the tabernacle finally arrived only on July 14 (Sam noted, "thank God"), which was good because the days continued showery. The main camp-meeting preacher was the Ohio MBiC evangelist, Andrew Good, but other preachers were present: Mahlon J. Carmichael of the MBiC Washington Conference, Samuel S. Stauffer, the Didsbury pastor and the women preachers Maude Chatham, Luella Swalm, and Laura Morgan. Chatham and Swalm were credentialed first from Ontario, Morgan from the west. A Presbyterian Church minister, Mr. Moffatt, joined them as well. Goudie reported attendance was fair. He wrote:

> The Lord was with us in a special way from the very first meeting and as the meetings went on the tide of spirituality seemed to rise and conviction settled down upon those who were not right with God and some yielded while others refused to give up. A goodly number were reclaimed, saved or sanctified... Most of the church, I do believe, received a grand lift in the right direction.[25]

Seventeen tents were set up for families. On the closing day, Monday, July 17, nine people were baptized in the Rosebud River, which flows northwest to southeast through Didsbury, on the east side of the town, at the end of the eleven-day camp. There is a bend in the river by a wheat field that was convenient to use for baptisms for many years.[26]

As far as I know, Sam Goudie never journeyed west again, though his brother Henry spent about fourteen years there (1906–1919). Sam seems to have made the most of his chance, staying in the west until the end of August. At the close of the camp Sam got on the train and rode to Edmonton, hosted there by a Mr. Suder (or Suter), whose family was prominent in Edmonton MBiC circles later. They traveled around visiting many families until Goudie returned to Didsbury to conduct their Quarterly Meetings on

---

25. *GB* (5 August 1905) 12–13 and Sam Goudie, "Diary 1905," 3–14 July. J F "Frank" Gugin claimed that in 1910 Didsbury was the only holiness camp-meeting in western Canada; Huffman, *Mennonite Brethren in Christ*, 141. Storms said that Goudie was the camp evangelist, but Andrew Good seems to have served that position. Probably every preacher present took a turn or two. Why Goudie preached in the Methodist church and no notice is made of the Evangelical congregation is a mystery to me. After the 1993 merger the Evangelical and the Missionary congregations merged in 1995 and have got on well.

26. Dr. Ed Oke, e-mail to the author, 22 October 2018.

July 29. A Mr. Anderson, pastor of the Methodist Church, preached for the congregation that evening, which Goudie appreciated. The next day, the Sunday, Goudie preached in all three services, on the MBiC understanding of the Lord's Supper, baptism, and disciples enduring hardness for the sake of the kingdom. Finally, the congregation took down the tabernacle the last day of July because they wanted to use it in Calgary.[27]

In company with Samuel S. Stauffer and the "mission girls," Sam helped set up the tabernacle again somewhere in Calgary and the night of August 2 he opened the tabernacle meetings (no tenting this time) preaching to small numbers. On August 5, a Mr. Porter preached and on August 6, J. B. Detwiler, to improving audiences, with a little help from the Salvation Army.[28]

Leaving the Alberta people, Goudie began his slow return to Ontario on August 7. He stopped for several days at the farm of his niece Ida (Goudie) Hutchings, and her husband Charles, who lived near Forget, District of Assiniboia, southeast of Regina.[29] He did some duck hunting, shooting three, adding to Charles' eight for a meal of duck. Ida (b. 1885) died in 1906, unfortunately.

On August 11, Sam continued on to Winnipeg and interacted with some of the holiness community there as well as the MBiC mission. His hosts were a Mr. and Mrs. R. J. Scott, perhaps people he knew from Ontario.[30] Without mentioning how he knew them, he also recorded visiting a Mrs. Williams and family.[31] Even before seeing the MBiC City Mission Workers, Emma Hostetler and Mary Markle, he was preaching in the evening at the Main St. Mission,[32] which suggests he had his own contacts with

27. Sam Goudie, "Diary 1905," 17–31 July.

28. Sam Goudie, "Diary 1905," 1–6 August.

29. Bunker, *Hugh Goudie Family*, 74. "Forget" was named after Amédéé Forget, who was a Lieutenant General of the NWT and the first of Saskatchewan. The town name is pronounced as "For-jay."

30. Miller, *Canadian Pentecostals*, 71–72, probably refers to this R. J. Scott who in 1906 was an enthusiastic convert to Pentecostal teaching who moved to Los Angeles to get involved more deeply in the Azusa phenomena. Sam records meeting Mrs R. J. Scott on the streets of Owen Sound in 1908, Sam Goudie, "Diary 1908," 9 August.

31. Six years later, J. B. Detwiler married a widow of Winnipeg, an Elizabeth Williams, a little over two years after his first wife, Harriet Shantz, died in Didsbury in 1908; Fuller, "Detwiler, J B." *GAMEO*. Possible connection? Possible.

32. Possibly the Home and Foreign Mission of the C&MA, which was on Main St., Winnipeg. See article by C. M. Ward, *Pentecostal Testimony* (May 1956), and Kulbeck, *Pentecostal Assemblies*, 138.

some in the city, as something set up beforehand. The two women took him on Sunday, August 13, to the Holiness Movement mission, then a place called Bethel Mission, and in the afternoon, he preached in their own Beulah Mission. The next day he returned to the Main St. Mission, delivering another message. On August 15, after attending a Bible reading given by the Church Missionary Society missionary, the Anglican Archdeacon Robert Phair, who became involved in the Pentecostal movement a couple of years later,[33] Goudie again spoke at the Beulah Mission. The day he took the train for Ontario, they visited an institution called the "Home of the Friendless" that re-appears in this story.[34] Arriving in Toronto on August 18, he found everybody at home happy to see him again, as he normally recorded at the end of all his trips. He was happy, too.[35]

On September 1, Prime Minister Sir Wilfrid Laurier, the Governor General Earl Grey, and various dignitaries met in Edmonton to declare the creation of the new Province of Alberta. On 4 September, in Regina, they did the same to proclaim the inauguration of the Province of Saskatchewan.[36]

In Toronto on August 19, Goudie merely reported that the first day back, he was tired. Small wonder. On the second day, a Sunday, he was back to preaching, once, at the West End Mission with two "seekers" at the altar. The rest of the week was for family: on the Tuesday he took his sons Fletcher and Allen to the fruit market in downtown Toronto, where Uncle David worked. The next day the whole family went to High Park for a picnic, but the same day in the evening, he attended a funeral service for someone at the residence of Noah Detwiler.[37]

Within a week Goudie was off visiting for the eleven Quarterly Conferences. Peter Cober in the West District had a similar number.[38] Goudie was faithful in writing QM reports for the *Gospel Banner*. By the time he retired from the position in 1933, he was to write at least four hundred five. In the midst of this particular round, Sam met Peter Cober and they

---

33. Miller, *Canadian Pentecostals*, 71, 77.

34. For a summary of the institution for orphans and unwed mothers, started in 1900 by a Methodist woman from Louisville, Kansas, see "Memorable Manitobans: Laura Belle Shaw Crouch (1872–1937)." www.mhs.mb.ca/docs/people/crouch_lbs.shtml.

35. Sam Goudie, "Diary 1905," 9–18 August.

36. Tracy, *History of Canada*, 1070–71.

37. Sam Goudie, "Diary 1905," 19–23 August.

38. *GB* (15 July 1905) 16. H. S. Hallman also had eight visits scheduled at the city missions as City Mission Society President.

"talked matters over . . . re the NWT . . ."[39] They must have agreed their hopes for a new Conference were on track, for the plans moved ahead and the Alberta Conference was set up in 1906 and accepted by the 1908 GC as a full Conference of the Church.

During this particular tour (fall 1905), Fannie Raymer recorded an impression of Sam Goudie as a preacher at Sunnidale, the only such reference I have found so far. Sam arrived on the Friday evening. "Ebenezer" is the name of an appointment on the Sunnidale field, near Wasaga Beach. Mixing weather, farm and church notes side by side, for Saturday, October 4, and Sunday, October 5, she recorded:

> 4 Saturday fine to day Quarterly Meeting this afternoon Sam Goudie was here [the Raymers' house] had a good meeting going to build a shed Dick Atkinson is giving the timber Christina still here she went to day to Pickerings to stay overnight Richards came here from Eutoff [Uhthoff] overnight. /5 Sunday lovely day for this time of year had a good meeting Bro Goudie Preached with Power [C. R.] Miller here all day.[40]

The last time Fannie could have heard Sam Goudie preach might have been the year, 1886–1887, when he was a probationer on the Nottawasaga field, before it was split into Stayner and Sunnidale, or maybe at campmeetings. She still had the same to say about his preaching in the winter of 1906, though his first message didn't spark any comment, or she makes it seem part of the "nothing special":

> 19 Friday nothing special took place to day meeting at Ebenezar this evening S. Goudie preached / 20 Saturday got our old mare from McCourt Paid 45 dols for her her naime is Maud Saturday quarterly meeting at Ebene[zer]. We went up with slay [sleigh] Bro Balls and Elringtons [Eltheringtons] here for dinner it turned very warm snow most all away till evening we came home in the mud we had a good meeting / 21 Sunday quarterly meeting we had a good meet. Goudie preached a wonderfull sermon from 3 Philipines 20 & 21 . . .[41]

Judging by the entries in Sam's Yearbooks, a typical visit to a field for Goudie began with a train ride from Toronto, or after September 1907, Stouffville, to some junction town or central station such as Aurora or

---

39. Sam Goudie, "Diary 1905," 29 August.
40. Fannie Raymer, "Diaries 1905–1907," 4–5 October 1905.
41. Fannie Raymer, "Diaries 1905–1907," 19–21 January 1906.

downtown Toronto, then a trip to close to the field on a local line. He would be met at the station by someone, often the pastor. If the field was not served by a train, someone might take him by horse and buggy or later, by car to his lodging for the night. Depending on the time of day, Goudie liked to visit some of the members with the pastor in charge, and at night conduct some part of the Quarterly Conference, normally preaching or either chairing the business part or the ordinances. Goudie took his responsibility seriously: if the field had several appointments, he normally visited them all. He might preach more at the larger station, if there was one, but he usually preached at every site at least once and his visits to a circuit took a few days. In his diaries he mentions at whose house he dropped in for tea or spent the night, and it was not often in the pastor's house. He knew by experience the pastor's home was not wealthy, and he did not burden them. Since he had been pastor on many of these fields or had preached occasionally on them, he knew many of the families already. Normally, he would continue on to the next field nearby and repeat the pattern.

Goudie obviously liked the work, but he also enjoyed the return to his home. His children were glad to see him, and he them. He helped Eliza around the house, helped with the washing, chopping wood in the earlier years, going shopping in Toronto at Eaton's and places like that. In summer he worked on their garden. He preached in Stouffville a surprising number of times. He seemed to have favorite city missions, such as St. Catharines, as he often added a visit there from Vineland, or Wiarton, when he was in Port Elgin. Occasionally, Goudie had tussles to settle between pastors and congregations, such as between Henry Shantz and the congregation at Port Elgin in 1907. In one Quarterly Conference, all the field officials (deacons, stewards, Sunday School superintendents) were "passed," that is, voted as fulfilling their duties acceptably to the field membership, but the pastor was not. Goudie took his time to talk with both sides and usually he could report a satisfactory outcome.

MANITOBA MISSIONS IN 1906

Very little information has survived about the two MBiC missions in Manitoba because their lifespan was only about three years as we shall see. The first two women preachers appointed to Winnipeg were Emma Hostetler and Mary Markle.[42] In 1906, Hostetler and Markle continued church planting in Winnipeg, but during the year, Hostetler was accepted to the new mission in Nigeria and returned to Berlin to prepare. A new CMWS President, J. N. Kitching, acting in faith in 1907, sent two additional women to Manitoba. However, forces from outside the denomination, though definitely welcomed by some from the inside, confronted the Ontario Conference in 1907–1908. Sam Goudie faced the challenge and steered the Conference through to one vision of the future, leaving others with another vision to find their places outside. The Manitoba missions were to suffer from this disruption.

---

42. Some of the Hostetlers' story is told in a YouTube video by Bennett, Fuller and Fuller, "Hostetlers." Mary Ellen (Markle) Ward (1882–1961) was from Hanover, Ontario. Her life will be examined in more detail later in this chapter.

7

The Pentecostal Crisis 1907–1908

PENTECOSTAL EXPECTATIONS

SOME STUDIES HAVE INVESTIGATED the heightened rhetoric and desires of holiness leaders around the turn of the century which encouraged some holiness, Deeper Life and Keswick communities to project that God was restoring first _century Pentecostal phenomena through their movements. The Holiness Movement Church (founded 1897), based in eastern Ontario but spread across Canada, certainly thought so, and unwillingly supplied many workers to the early Pentecostal movement when the crisis came.[1] Charles Nienkirchen has studied the teaching of C&MA founder A. B. Simpson and called him a "precursor" of Pentecostalism because of his speculations about God's plans for restoring charismatic gifts to the church.[2] Simpson was not alone in his speculations. His associate John Salmon in Toronto had put into the constitution of Bethany Chapel (not to be confused with the MBiC congregation in Berlin) as early as 1891 the expectation that Pentecostal gifts would manifest, depending on the

---

1. Fuller, "Holiness People," in MCHT.
2. Nienkirchen, *A. B. Simpson*. See Dayton, *Roots of Pentecostalism*, especially ch 4, "The Triumph of the Doctrine of Pentecostal Spirit Baptism," 87–113, for the shift from Wesley's perfect love/ Christian perfection language to John Fletcher's (and Asa Mahan's and Phoebe Palmer's) Acts ch 2/ Pentecostal baptism with the Spirit theology. On Palmer's theology see White, *Phoebe Palmer*, 105–59.

spiritual condition of the members.³ The MBiC also were hopeful about the expansion of the work of the Holy Spirit through their Church. In Goudie's terms, they would appear to welcome anything along a "Holy Ghost line."

PENTECOSTALS AND CHURCH GROWTH IN CANADA AND THE MBIC

Missionary Church historians have not ignored the disturbance in the Ontario Conference over Pentecostalism in 1907–1912, but neither have they given much attention to its significance. To Pentecostal historians, on the other hand, the Berlin (Kitchener) "revival" of 1908 is told and retold as one of their earliest remarkable moves of the Holy Spirit. The sketch of the life of Solomon Eby in the earliest Church history notes the change in Eby's views with respect to the baptism with the Holy Spirit, and his switch to the young Pentecostal assembly in Berlin by 1916, but did not connect Pentecostalism to a loss of MBiC members and ministers.⁴ Everek Storms did note all these components in two paragraphs in partial explanation for the slow progress the Ontario Conference made in his "Middle Period (1908–1947)."⁵ It is interesting that he picked 1908 as a significant turning point year. In Glenn Gibson's judgment, the 1908 crisis had a "crushing effect" to the growth of the Conference.⁶

Years later another Missionary Church historian, Eileen Lageer, asked this writer if he thought the rejection of Pentecostalism in 1908 crippled the Church's evangelism and growth. She turned my attention to this question and after a fair amount of research, I still cannot say whether the rejection clearly diverted the Ontario Conference from greater usefulness in reaching Canada and the world compared to, say, the Canadian Pentecostal movement, which has reached to well over a thousand congregations. Clearly, the Missionary Church tradition has a smaller numerical imprint on the world than some other traditions.⁷ In the MBiC, the rural Ontario Conference grew much slower than the more urban Pennsylvania Conference, and the growth rate in Ontario did not change much in the immediate decade before and after the 1908 crisis.

3. Reynolds, *Footprints*, 289.
4. Huffman, *Mennonite Brethren in Christ*, 56–58.
5. Storms, *United Missionary Church*, 92.
6. Gibson, "Church Planting," 7.
7. It is not easy to get statistics after the recent focus on the "missional church," which uses other ways to measure the church's faithfulness. See Appendix A.

It may be that a generational effect toned down the "demonstrations of the Spirit" evident in the first decades of the MBiC, Holiness Movement Church, Free Methodists, Salvation Army, etc., as it did in Methodist Church piety through the nineteenth century.[8] What I mean is that the children of shouting, jumping, running, "revived" converts often cannot repeat the performance of their parents' generation. Although Pentecostalism expanded far beyond the growth of this "small society" of revivalist Mennonites, Pentecostals too, have met a soft wall to further rapid growth in Canada after a hundred years, though this has not yet happened in many parts of the two-thirds world. I suspect a similar change may happen as the charismatic movement moves past its fiftieth year in Canada.

The American Conferences of the MBiC also encountered the new Pentecostal movement, but the evidence I have is less abundant. Although the reaction of the Indiana and Ohio Conference to articles on tongues-speaking in 1908 suggests they were being agitated as well, so far I only know of the MBiC city mission in Dayton, Ohio, which exposed Pentecostalism to the denomination in the US. J. A. Huffman's memoir from many years later demonstrates that the encounter was not trivial.[9]

At the March 1907 Canada Conference, several unusual decisions were made. For one, the approval of the inauguration of the Canada Northwest Conference centered at Didsbury in 1906 required the renaming of the Canada Conference, which now became the Ontario Conference for the next sixty-two years. The beginning of the Conference year was changed from March to the early fall. This meant that the 1907–1908 Conference year would be practically eighteen months long. And for this long Conference year, the Ontario Conference chose to have only one Presiding Elder. I have seen no explanation given for the decision. In his diary, Goudie merely mentions that Conference made a "great change."[10] The Ontario Conference went with one PE in 1917–1918 (Goudie again), and also in 1941–1945, when first Milton Bricker (three years) and then Reginald Beech presided alone. Three of these periods occurred in war time, but the 1907–1908 period did not.[11] I suspect there was some financial rationale.

8. An American Methodist book reprinted by the HMC to commend the practice of "shouting": Henry, *Demonstrations*.

9. Huffman, *Profile*, 24–25.

10. Sam Goudie, "Diary 1907," 15 March.

11. Several times motions came from the Canada/Ontario Conference to ask the General Conference to discuss the advisability of having bishops, even the 1908 Conference had one. Each time the request was debated but not accepted. I do not know the

In 1907, the Ontario, Michigan and Canada Northwest Conferences published a hymnbook in Berlin for the MBiC with music and a dark cover containing 772 hymns and hundreds of tunes. The Ontario Conference had urged the General Conference to revise its earlier hymnal, but the only action was to permit the Annual Conferences to do so if they wished. A committee consisting of Ebenezer Anthony, Oliver B. Snyder from Michigan, Sam Goudie and Peter Cober from Ontario worked on it from 1906 and H. S. Hallman produced it by the summer of 1907. None of the four had extensive musical training, as far as I know.[12] Only one text was written by an MBiC contributor, Ella Rudy, but all were evangelical, holiness hymns and gospel songs. The MCHT collection has a number of copies of the hymnal, some of which were heavily used, but as a whole the effort did not encourage preparing any other for the church until the 1960s.[13]

---

sources of this request, or if Goudie was party to it. The nature of the episcopal office desired by these requests is not clear either, though the Evangelical Association had bishops as a higher level of leadership than Presiding Elder between their General Conferences. The powers of the episcopal office was exactly the center of dispute that split the Evangelical Association. The Brethren in Christ's bishops offered another nearby model. As chair, Goudie had influence in entertaining the motions. This is a topic for further study.

12. *Ontario Conference Journal 1907*, 48. One oddity is that very few of the hymns and gospel songs have credits for the authors of the words, though all of the tunes' composers are named. The 1881 hymnbook had no credits at all.

13. Ella N. Rudy was a sister of Cora Mae Rudy from the Indiana and Ohio Conference. The matter of the music used by the MBiC from the beginning is fascinating, but I am untrained in assessing it. There must have been vast regional differences, if a common hymnbook tradition never started or fell out of use. The Pennsylvania Conference produced its own hymnbook, *Rose of Sharon Hymns* in 1917. The MCHT has a marvelous collection of congregational hymnbooks and songbooks gathered by New Dundee song leader Eldon T. Sherk from about 1926 to the 1980s, which incorporated collections from still earlier song leaders, father and son Moses and Emerson Bock at New Dundee, Jesse Connor in Berlin and his Breslau-born wife, Amanda Zeller, with selections from still other musical members such as Hattie Shupe from Blenheim, and Sherk's second wife from the Cressman family, Boxes 6044-6046, MCHT. Some of the earliest were UBiC and Evangelical Association songbooks. This is also a topic for further study. The MCHT also has a collection made by Paul L. Storms, Box 6070. Other leads: Dan W. Raymer led singing at Markham for fifty-nine years, using a tuning fork, McDowell and others, *Markham*, 30; Noah Stouffer was song leader at Stouffville before 1931, Ratcliff, *Stouffville*, 5. More generally, one could start with Geissinger, "Hymnody," with its extensive bibliography, including Myron Leland Tweed's "A Study of the Function of Music Within the United Missionary Church Communion," PhD dissertation, 1970, University of Southern California. See Steiner, *Promised Lands*, 159-160, as another starting point. Geissinger at www.bfchistory.org/musicbfcgeissinger.pdf. Tweed was one of the editors of the 1963 UMC/BiC hymnbook, *Hymns for Worship*.

Sam Goudie would have seen the unifying power of common worship and wished for that help to that end, part of the "denomination-building" studied in Charles Gingerich's thesis.[14]

Sam and Eliza were house hunting most of the spring and summer in Toronto, and even put a down payment on a lot further west in Toronto. Suddenly in August 1907, a Mr. Albert Pugh of Stouffville in Whitchurch Township, York County, offered to rent them his house on Mill St., Stouffville, for $10 a month. Within days, Eliza and Sam inspected the place, liked it and accepted a rental agreement that Goudie kept in one of his pastor's Year Books.[15] They did not record it as an answer to prayer, but over one hundred ten years later, it looks like it to me. Imagine rental payments like that in Markham or Stouffville today, one of Canada's most expensive places to live in! The past is a different country in more than one way. The family moved 1 September, to live among one of the two main canters of the MBiC in Ontario, the Markham-Stouffville area, the other of course being in Waterloo County. The house on Mill St. was home for Sam and Eliza until his death in 1951 and her death in 1957. In 1918 they actually purchased it.[16] For many years the Conference voted the Presiding Elders a rental allowance on their houses. Many leaders of the Ontario MBiC retired to the Waterloo area, but not Goudie. Even after retiring from the Presiding Eldership when Sam returned to pastoral work for seven more years, the Goudies kept their house, allowing their son Fletcher and family to live in it.[17]

STOUFFVILLE—HOME FOR THE TRAVELER

Stouffville in York County, about fifty kilometers northeast of downtown Toronto, straddled the Markham and Whitchurch Townships' town-line, and started out between two Township north-south roads (called "Lines"), that is, between Ninth on the west and Tenth Line, now Reesor Road, on

14. Gingerich, "Experiment in Denominationalism," 94–96.

15. Dated 7 August 1907. In Eleanor Bunker Collection. Goudie's choice of Stouffville seems strategic for a leader to balance the heavy Waterloo County orientation of the Conference, but this remains a speculation for now.

16. T. Bunker, *Hugh Goudie Family*, 119.

17. Eleanor (Goudie) Bunker, telephone interview by the author, 24 February 2011, from Minden Hills, ON. The diaries speak of the house in Toronto at 134 Lippincott St. where the Goudies lived 1903–1907. Lippincott is nine blocks east of the major north-south street, Spadina Avenue, and parallel to it. John and Louisa Sider had lived there before the Goudies.

the east. Named after Abraham Stouffer who bought land at the site in 1805 after he and his brother-in-law Peter Reesor (who started Reesorville, now Markham village, a mere twelve km south and west of Stouffville) with their families and goods migrated from Pennsylvania the year before, the settlement grew around Stouffer's grist mills on creeks in the area. Although the farms were first settled by Mennonites, soon people of other lands, churches and no religion filled in the area and defined the character of the village, which had the usual mills, smithies, taverns, schools, shops, a post office and so on of a small Ontario town. So many immigrants to Ontario came from the British Isles—Irish, English, Scottish, Welsh, plus transfers from the American colonies—that very quickly the majority "others" were from everywhere else than the Germans from Pennsylvania. There was a uniformity in Ontario town and rural life suggested by Stephen Leacock's fictional Mariposa (Orillia, Simcoe County) in *Sunshine Sketches of a Little Town*, but also ably described by Kate Aitken of the real Beeton, Simcoe County.[18] By 1851 Stouffville had 350 inhabitants, by 1866 it had about 600, 950 by 1885, 1,223 in 1901, but 1,034 in 1911.[19] A railway line passed through the village in 1871, and a second started from it to Lake Simcoe in 1877. Already in 1866 there were five congregations (Congregational, two kinds of Methodists, Presbyterian, Disciples). Mennonites met in rurally situated meeting houses at places such as Edgeley in Vaughan Township, Bethesda, Dickson Hill, Cedar Grove, Hebron and the Wideman site in

---

18. Aitken, *Never a Day*, 5, beautifully remembers growing up in one such village: "Our village, Beeton, was not unique; its story could be duplicated almost anywhere across this Dominion." Beeton in Simcoe County, which was mainly home to settlers from the British Isles, did not have a rural Mennonite population, however. Creighton's 1951 *High Bright Buggy Wheels*, though fictional, is directly based on Stouffville and surrounding countryside of the 1910s with much local reference. Lynne Marks studied aspects of three nineteenth-century "Anglo-Celtic" small Ontario towns: Ingersoll in Middlesex County, Thorold in Welland County (now in the Regional Municipality of Niagara) and Campbellford in Northumberland County, between Belleville and Peterborough, introducing them for her purposes in Marks, *Revivals*, 16–19. The Ontario communities with Pennsylvania-German and German populations stand out as being atypical of the province's small towns and rural areas in some ways.

19. Barkey, *Stouffville*, 2, 9, 13, 56; Wikipedia, "Whitchurch-Stouffville." Whitchurch was organized as a township in 1851 with a reeve. Markham organized in the same year in response to Canada West legislation. Champion, *Markham*, 201. By 1877, Whitchurch had a population of four thousand, and Stouffville was separated as a village with its own reeve. The position became "mayor" only in 1971 when the town was set within redrawn boundaries to be firmly in the new Town of Stouffville-Whitchurch. The drop in population between 1901 and 1911 may represent migration to western Canada.

Markham, though two churches at Altona, just across the county boundary in Ontario County, now Durham Region, were the nearest to Stouffville. The Brethren in Christ met at Heise Hill in Whitchurch. Several other denominations were established by the time Sam and Eliza arrived: Baptists (1873), Anglicans (1879), Christians (1903).[20] A house to house survey by a Stouffville newspaper in 1907 claimed they found 317 Methodists, 151 Baptists, 147 Presbyterians, 134 Christians, 79 Mennonites, 65 Anglicans (number unclear in microfilm), 24 Disciples and 23 (again number unclear) of "other faiths," with a total of about 1,043 inhabitants in the town, which is very close to the 1911 population.[21]

In 1903, the Congregational congregation disbanded. The MBiC's Silas Cressman had held revival services in the fall and winter of 1902 and 1903 at Dickson Hill and Altona and then in the Congregational church building in Stouffville and had such encouraging local response in new converts and revived local members of the whole Markham field that there was a desire to set up a meeting point in the town. A bid was put in for the Congregational building, but it was acquired by the Christian Church members from the rural areas who were moving into town, and so the MBiC built a new place on Main St. The Markham field was divided at that time, and Stouffville was paired with Altona for many years and various other shorter-lived appointments such as "4th Line Uxbridge." The Stouffville church commences its official congregational histories from 1903, but it would be correct to affirm its origins in the New Mennonite Society of Markham going back to the 1850s.[22]

Stouffville MBiC became then the home church for Eliza and Sam Goudie and their children. Goudie frequently preached for the congregation; Eliza taught a Sunday School class of women. The family settled into a large community, a mixture of small-town and country people, much like the farms on the edge of towns that Sam Goudie knew growing up. The family could not have expected it, but for them, the itinerant life moving every three years with a Mennonite Brethren in Christ elder, was practically over.

20. Barkey, *Stouffville*, 144, 146.

21. *Markham Economist*, quoting a Stouffville paper (probably the *Tribune*) (May 2 1907).

22. The official minute book of the New Mennonite Society of York and Ontario Counties records a unified membership list beginning in 1863, but this formal record summarizes activity begun in the 1850s. Box 1010, MCHT. The congregation has moved to a large new building and uses the name EastRidge EM Church, meeting on Tenth Line, Whitchurch-Stouffville today.

By way of an aside, in Altona, just 3 km east and a little south of the Stouffville road, a meeting place was shared by the Christian Church and the MBiC for one hundred years, 1875 to 1975.[23] Expropriation for the proposed Pickering Airport in March 1973 ended the community of Altona and its churches. In town, the MBiC and the Stouffville Memorial Christian Church had buildings close together on Main St., sharing buildings when one was renovating, sometimes attending each other's meetings and camp-meetings. The Christian Church (and later Stouffville Baptist) did not have a large congregation. Eventually, the MBiC church cooperated with the large 2nd Line Markham Baptist Church, now called Springvale Baptist. After the second World War, the cooperation was through flourishing Youth for Christ activities.[24] Sam Goudie lived only to see the very beginning of such collaboration. Baptists are conspicuous by their relative absence in the history of the MBiC in Ontario. Though sharing a commitment to believer's baptism by immersion and an evangelical orthodoxy, most Baptists have supported Reformed theology. The MBiC had continued a connectional polity which Baptists rejected out of conviction, and Baptists generally accepted militarism.

PENTECOSTAL MOTIONS, 1906-1907

Another unusual circumstance occurred at the 1907 Ministerial Convention which immediately preceded the Annual Conference. Sarah Pool, the energetic slum worker in Toronto's East End, was asked to preach a kind of Conference sermon. Never as prominent a custom as it was among some denominations, say, the Canadian Presbyterians, the practice of a conference sermon has died out in the EMCC.[25] It is not clear what was happening in Sarah's life, but in the outcome, she was queried for expressing in her sermon "disloyalty to the doctrine of our church."[26] I have not seen this kind of happening recorded at any other Ministerial Convention, nor the

23. Byer, *Altona*.
24. Allen P. Stouffer, conversation with the author, 6 April 2017, in Kitchener, ON.
25. In my experience, limited to some of the years 1980–2002, District superintendents gave reports, sometimes with vigorous exhortation at annual conferences.
26. *Ontario Conference Journal 1907* 47. In August 1908, the *Gospel Banner* printed an address of hers to a Sunday School Convention from a few years earlier, but because of the incompleteness of the issues preserved 1903–1908, it is not necessarily her last while Hallman was editor. An earlier article of hers had criticized church leaders who in her opinion tried to suppress manifestations of the Holy Spirit. Whether these leaders included Sam Goudie, is not known.

response of the Annual Conference. Goudie did not mention it in his diary. I believe Pool and later her pastor at the East End (Parliament Street) Mission, George A. Chambers, were responding to the extraordinary claims coming from the nearby Queen St. E. mission of Helen and James Hebden. Begun as a holiness-style mission in May 1906, by the year end, the Hebdens's mission was reporting speaking in other languages, healings and manifestations of power that were interpreted as possible only by the Holy Spirit. Chambers, Pool and other members at Parliament St. felt jealous in contrast, or as Chambers put it, "desperately hungry for reality in God." C. N. Good was pastor of the West End MBiC mission, and he felt no such depression. He even took the funeral for a family that Chambers could not face, former members of the East End Mission, burned to death by a forest fire in northern Ontario.[27]

In the first part of 1907, Goudie was still living in Toronto and constantly in touch with the West End Mission and the East End Mission where he also preached, for example on the evening of 4 March. In the afternoon of 6 March 1907, in fact, Sam Goudie with "bro. Good" (C. N. Good or possibly another friend, J. R. Good) and a "bro. Shantz," visited "the Mission where they claim the gift of tongues. [W]e heard some speak in strange tongues and acted strangely, they all seemed to shake." This was certainly the Hebdens's mission. On 25 March, after the Canada Conference at Mt. Joy, he recorded that on his own he "went down to Queen St.," likely another reference to checking out the Hebdens's East End Mission. Goudie does not report any positive reaction to the Hebdens's meetings, the way he often did when visiting other church meetings. On March 10, for example, he had gone to Massey Hall to hear the Salvation Army's General Booth preach. The sermon was from Isa 55:11, and he said the General "preached well."[28]

Could Goudie have listened to the founder of the holiness Salvation Army and not reflect that the General's orders through a chain of command moved a band of recruits under "Lightning Fred" Galletly to storm Galt back in 1884? And that the presence of the Army that May led to the sealing of salvation in the heart of a seventeen-year-old Mennonite from Breslau? It is a wonder. Booth would never meet Goudie, nor know what

27. Chambers, *Fifty Years*, 11. This was in the summer of 1906. In the winter of 1908, he was in the same condition. Chambers' memoir, while valuable, has a few anachronisms, and errors of names and dates for the earliest years of his ministry. Use with a bit of caution; Thomas Miller, letter to the author, 1987.

28. Sam Goudie, "Diary 1907," 6, 10 and 25 March.

his organization had done for Sam. A series of teachings and preachings led to Sam Goudie's trust in the sanctifying power of God in 1885 at an MBiC tabernacle meeting on the Bethel field. There is no evidence he thought tongues-speaking was a required evidence of an experience of sanctification.

In 1906, Emma Hostetler began the year in Winnipeg, with Mary Markle as helper, but Hostetler was accepted to go to Nigeria by the MBiC Foreign Mission Board, for which Goudie was the secretary at the time. Hostetler returned to Ontario to prepare, and she went to Nigeria in May 1907. It seems that in her place, J. N. Kitching, Hallman's successor as President of the City Mission Workers, thought to send Susie Bowman, but in the end Martha M. Hisey went instead.[29] Hisey worked with Maude McClelland, while Mary Ann Dresch was sent to assist Mary Markle to open a city mission in Brandon, the next largest city in Manitoba. Sam and Eliza knew Dresch well, because although her family were from Elmwood, he had been the pastor of her, her sisters, and widowed mother in Berlin. In fact, Goudie baptized two of the sisters and brought them into membership in 1901. In his pastoral rounds, Goudie visited the family regularly. Mary Ann even spent ten days living with the Goudies in January 1902 after a sickness she suffered.[30]

In June 1907, Markle came back from Brandon and Goudie met her in Toronto on the 8th. The next day she had dinner with the Goudies and H. S. Hallman. She was preparing for her wedding, perhaps asking Goudie to conduct the wedding. Her fiancé, Alfred George ("A. G.") Ward (1881–1960),[31] arrived in Ontario, on June 13, in time for the camp-meeting at Berlin, which he attended.[32] Ward was a sometime Methodist preacher, and at the time had been the western Canadian agent for the C&MA. Later that June, a second camp-meeting was held at Hanover (June 25 to July 1). Goudie mentions that A. G. Ward and others joined the camp on June 29. The next day, the last Sunday, Goudie recorded as "a successful day all told." Back in Toronto, on July 3, Goudie stated "Had baptism and I took bro.

29. Goudie mentions seeing Martha Hisey off to Winnipeg, Sam Goudie, "Diary 1907," 27 March.

30. Sam Goudie, "Pastor's Year Book" for 1901–1902. Mary Ann at sixteen in 1901 was a domestic in a Berlin home at the time of the census in April. I have not yet traced the family of Maud McClelland (1880–ca 1952).

31. Not to be confused with Alfred George Warder (1876–1930), usually known as "A. G. Warder" in MBiC accounts.

32. Sam Goudie, "Diary 1907," 8, 9 and 13 June 8, 9.

Ward into the church." This is an unusual record by Goudie. He was not serving as a pastor, but he did on occasion baptized people in his Quarterly Conference rounds.[33] But what congregation would A. G. Ward be counted as a member of? Obviously, he must have resigned his appointment with the C&MA. Baptism is not a private affair and normally connects one to a congregation. As a former Methodist, Ward would have been christened as a baby, but the MBiC, as we know, accepted only believer's baptism, hence Goudie's action. As a Christian and Missionary Alliance agent in Winnipeg, Ward might not have been required to be baptized by immersion, although immersion as a believer was also the standard mode practised by the Canadian C&MA. Those were days of looser organization and the C&MA frequently denied that they were a denomination at all. It seems that Ward was preparing not merely to marry a Mennonite mission sister but was willing to join her church. On October 16, 1907, Sam Goudie recorded that he and Joshua Fidler (the Elmwood pastor) married Mary Markle and Alfred G. Ward in Elmwood, Ontario, in a little wedding in the evening.[34]

This wedding meant Mary Ward left the City Mission Workers Society. Records have not been found to show if Kitching replaced her or how the Manitoba mission was reorganized as a result from October 1907 to September 1908. Other events were arising that ended the whole Ontario MBiC mission in Manitoba until a totally different attempt at church planting under the Missionary Church in the 1980s.

The year 1906 was a notable one in North American Church history. The Azusa Street Mission in Los Angeles, California, was noticed in numerous Deeper-life and holiness circles. Although research has turned up many individuals and small movements before 1906 that practised speaking in tongues as a New Testament spiritual gift that God was restoring to the church, Azusa boosted a movement that spread throughout the world by the end of the twentieth century.[35] Well-publicized by the pastor Wil-

---

33. For example, three people at the Collingwood mission, (William Waldron, pastor); Sam Goudie, "PE's Report," *GB* (21 September 1911) 12.

34. Sam Goudie, "Diary 1907," 16 October. Ward, *C. M. Ward Story*, 15, says his mother Mary "was loved by the Mennonites, so they were married by a Mennonite elder [Goudie!] and enjoyed work in Eastern Canada as a young married Mennonite couple." The Goudies' affection for Mary Markle can certainly be taken as so from the diaries.

35. Evidence that James and Helen Hebden's mission at 561 Queen St. E., Toronto, also known as the "East End Mission" (do not confuse with the MBiC mission with the same name), witnessed tongues-speaking about the same time, independently from Azusa, is found in Miller, "Hebden Mission," 5–26.

liam Seymour, Frank Bartleman and others, people from many places in North America read about the phenomena experienced at Azusa St. and traveled to witness it first-hand. If possible, they would also "tarry" (pray for a long time, maybe over many days or weeks [see Luke 24:49]), for an experience of speaking in other languages. The histories are often told, and there is no need to repeat them here.

Of importance for Sam Goudie and the MBiC is that in the holiness movement prayer meetings that Markle, Dresch and Hisey joined in Winnipeg, also attended by Free Methodist, Christian and Missionary Alliance and Holiness Movement Church people, there were some very interested in the Azusa St. Mission reports.[36] A. G. Ward was one of those who wanted to get the evidence of being baptized with the Holy Spirit, and at some point early in 1907, he received what he wanted.

THE 1908 NEW YEAR REVIVAL MEETINGS AT BETHANY

When Charlie Krauth,[37] pastor of Bethany MBiC in Berlin, was thinking of a preacher for the New Year's revival meetings 1908, the former C&MA agent from Winnipeg, A. G. Ward, was recommended and the new husband of Mary Markle started preaching in the new year.

At first Ward impressed the congregation and the Conference officials. According to Chambers, Sam Goudie encouraged all the members of Conference to attend the meetings if they could.[38] However already by mid-January, Sam was in Berlin to listen and observe. He was in no hurry to condemn, but obviously was watching the process of events. In his regular rounds on Sunday, January 19, he was in Breslau in the morning speaking about Foreign Missions, and in the evening he was in the Berlin church to lead in the ordinances (Lord's Supper and Washing the Saint's Feet) with

---

36. Most of these people, writing long after the events of 1906–1908, neglect to mention their denominational affiliations at the time, perhaps because they had long since repudiated them. Most Pentecostal writers continue the tradition of ignoring their early workers' previous affiliations. An attempt to recover their affiliations is found in Fuller, "Holiness People." The writer believes he demonstrated what has long been asserted, with some evidence, for example, Miller, *Canadian Pentecostals*, 21–31, that at least in Canada, the vast majority of the earliest Canadian Pentecostals were formerly members of holiness churches in addition to some Methodists. Further research only strengthened that finding.

37. Spelled as "Krouth" in most Pentecostal histories. Some Krauth siblings anglicized their name. One brother, a minister, spelled his name "Crouth."

38. Chambers, *Fifty Years*, 12. Chambers avoids naming Goudie in his account.

a full house. The next morning, after staying with Peter Shupe, Bethany's song leader, "I . . . had a talk with bro. Ward. & went to C[hristian] Raymer's home for dinner. Made a few calls this P. M. & attended church this eve, I preached."[39] Christian Raymer had strong objections to the Pentecostal tongues teaching. The very next day (Tuesday), Goudie added, "We met in the church to consider the doctrine of this latter rain or tongue movement quite a number of preachers were present we had a good day. [l]ater had a good meeting this eve." On Wednesday, still in Berlin, he and Ephraim Sievenpiper attended the Mennonite Bible Conference and liked the experience.[40]

Goudie was back to Berlin at the end of a month of Quarterly Meetings from Owen Sound to Wallace and Maryboro in March 1908 for the Missionary Board meetings. Perhaps that was the time he suspended the special meetings at Bethany. Speaking in other tongues seemed to be everywhere that March. Sam and Eliza had close friends in Toronto originally from Breslau that they visited practically every week, Josiah ("J. R.") Good and his wife Esther (Trafelet) Good.[41] They moved to Toronto shortly after the Goudies were posted there in 1903. Returning from Berlin, Goudie called on his friend J. R. Good in Toronto before going on to Stouffville. Noah Detwiler was there, too. J. R. told Sam he "received this new experience & spoke in tongues." No other comment from Sam. What could he say? He had other colleagues and friends leaning to the Pentecostal experience.[42]

Pentecostal and Missionary Church sources disagree on the character of what happened next, though the outlines are clear. Though Ward doubtless preached the need for the work of the Holy Spirit in the believer's life, a familiar theme to the MBiC, soon he taught the new message of the *evidence* of the Baptism with the Holy Spirit, that is, the possibility and necessity of experiencing the accompanying phenomenon of speaking in other tongues (languages). George Chambers, who came from Toronto's East End Mission to Berlin with his wife Ida to attend the meetings in Bethany, says that when a few people, Bethany members and visitors, started speaking in tongues, the meetings began to take off: "This was like

---

39. Sam Goudie, "Diary 1908," 19, 20 January.

40. Sam Goudie, "Diary 1908," 21, 22 January.

41. The Goudies knew some Trafelet families on the Maryboro field, according to Sam's pastoral records.

42. Sam Goudie, "Diary 1908," 16, 17 March. J. R. and Esther were the parents of J. Henry Good (1900–1979), a pastor of the MBiC/ UMC from 1928 to 1972.

a bomb bursting. It set fire to the Convention and created a holy uproar . . . From this time on, people were saved, healed and filled with the Holy Ghost."[43] As we have seen those claims (except the speaking in tongues) were nothing new to the MBiC.

The congregation that arose from the Pentecostal movement remembered those who were first to speak in tongues as Chris R. Miller, Robert Barley (1883–1948), Aaron Shoemaker (1871–1928) and Charlie Schaaf (1878–1942), all men.[44] Miller was the ordained MBiC minister. Aaron Shoemaker had been licensed in 1906; Schaaf was still listed in the 1911 census as a "New Mennonite," that is, an MBiC adherent, as was English-born Robert Barley and family. In other words all four first tongues-speakers were MBiC members or adherents and two of them remained so at least for a few years. A prayer meeting for tarrying for the Pentecostal gift was opened at some point, first in the home of Bethany deacon Daniel and his wife Lydia (Shantz) Hostetler. MBiC editor H. S. Hallman's wife, Maria (nee Rosenberger), was also remembered as a participant in those prayer meetings, as was Esther ("Hettie") Eby, the wife of Amos Eby.[45]

Stanley Howard Frodsham and others such as Chambers, Ward and Robert E. McAlister,[46] assuming that all Pentecostal happenings could be described as sudden, unexpected, unmediated (that is not human-induced) and powerful manifestations of the Holy Spirit, described the manifestations positively, while MBiC preachers such as Christian Raymer could describe the events with the sarcastic title in his booklet of 1908, as *Latter Rain and Fog*. Jasper A. Huffman, while believing mistakenly as it turned out that tongues-speaking was a passing fad, also wrote about the errors and moral wreckage he thought he saw connected with the practice. He continued to affirm that what the MBiC/ UMC believed was true, and the

---

43. Chambers, *Fifty Years*, 12. By calling it a "convention," Chambers was using Pentecostal terminology. Notice also the replacement of the expected language of sanctifying favored by the MBiC, with "filled with the Holy Ghost."

44. Spaetzel, *Kitchener Gospel Temple*, 3.

45. Spaetzel, *Kitchener Gospel Temple*, 5. Full list on that page. Of the twenty-five or so names, which includes individuals who joined in 1911, at least ten were MBiC members. Fred Galletly, the one-time Salvationist, who later worked with the MBiC, is likely related to the Miss Galletly remembered in the Spaetzel list. Fred and his wife Sarah had two daughters, Christina (twenty-one in 1911), and Emma (thirteen in 1911, or ten in 1908). Christina, eighteen in 1908, would probably be the "Miss Galletly."

46. Miller, *Canadian Pentecostals*, 66–67.

Pentecostal teaching contained doctrinal errors, but recanted his blanket condemnation of Pentecostal people.[47]

Holiness/Deeper life churches around Toronto were visited by newly tongues-speaking people connected with the Hebdens including some of the Christian Workers Churches. John Salmon, pastor of the Christian and Missionary Alliance-related Bethany Chapel in Toronto spoke in tongues at an Alliance convention in Beulah Park, Ohio, and testified to the new experience.[48]

An American Episcopal Methodist missionary to Liberia, John M. L. Harrow, was in the congregation in Mt. Joy, when John Ball asked him to speak at the suggestion of some members. He had come from the Hebdens's mission in Toronto.[49] Euphemia (Pool) Guy and her sister Sarah Pool could have been excited by the missionary's message which was not about his work in Liberia but about the need for speaking in tongues, which he had learned from the Hebdens's mission. Apparently more than two dozen agreed and spoke in tongues during the three weeks he stayed at Markham, tarrying in prayer meetings in John and Maggie Ball's house.[50] Goudie heard Harrow speak at the Markham camp-meeting in June 1908.[51]

Thus, by the spring of 1908, MBiC members from Toronto and Markham in York County, Berlin in Waterloo, and soon several from Vineland in Niagara and the Squire (Dornoch) appointment south of Owen Sound, Grey County,[52] were impressed by the Pentecostal phenomena, embraced the doctrine and found biblical support for the experience. Nearly

---

47. Raymer, *Rain and Fog*; Huffman, *Speaking in Tongues*.

48. Reynolds, *Footprints*, 289.

49. Rudd, *Early Days*, 52-3. The account suggests some Markham members had visited the Hebdens Mission. John Ball replaced Joshua Fidler in April 1907. Emma Hostetler preached there and left for northern Nigeria 5 May. In August, a local paper reported Ball was sick with typhoid fever, which lasted until the end of October; *Markham Economist* for April, May, August and October 1906. Ball's daughter places the origin of this sickness at Stayner. The age she gives Ball, twenty-seven, agrees with his time at Markham, and this newspaper report. Reva J. (Ball) Irvine, Transcript of an Oral Interview with Jim Craig, PAOC Archives, Mississauga, Ontario. Typhoid fever, assuming the diagnosis was correct, can take a long recovery time.

50. Kulbeck, *Pentecostal Assemblies*, 110. This event was in 1908, not 1910, as Canada Conference Journals and these newspaper articles confirm. Parsonage tarrying: Ball, "Early Days," typescript from original manuscript.

51. Sam Goudie, "Diary 1908," 15 June.

52. Sam Goudie, "Diary 1908," 8 August: "Bro. Doner was not passed owing to his new theology."

all these people would have been individuals and families that Goudie knew personally as their pastor, worked with in meeting after meeting or at least as their Presiding Elder in Quarterly Conferences. As I have researched this story, it has impressed me that the conflict involved people who knew each other and evangelized, worshipped and prayed together, some for many years. The disruption would have been very distressing on all sides, like a family break down. Emotions were strong.

DIVISION GROWS

The tongues-message troubled people because of the accompanying teaching that no one could claim to be baptized with the Spirit, equated with being sanctified, without an episode of speaking in another language as the Spirit gave utterance. This automatically invalidated the testimony of the hundreds or thousands of MBiC members as to their sanctification/ filling/ baptism/ deeper life. The MBiC were not totally fixed in their language about these experiences subsequent to salvation partly due to the many terms used for the works of the Holy Spirit in the Bible, but also to the reluctance of the Pennsylvania Conference to commit to a fully Wesleyan holiness article for the *Discipline*. The implication was plain however: If you have never spoken in tongues, *you have never been baptized in the Spirit; you have never been sanctified; you are deluded.*

By February 1908, the leaders of the Indiana and Ohio Conference were writing to the *Gospel Banner* asking that Editor Hallman cease publishing articles about speaking in tongues. He refused. Already in 1907, the Mission in Dayton, Ohio, had been "wrecked" over the tongues issue, according to Jasper Huffman, who was sent to try to pick up the pieces.[53] Huffman says the tongues-speakers he knew devastated the Mission and then moved on. He claimed they acted in ways that were morally wrong.

In Stouffville Goudie recorded in his pastoral diaries a number of people coming to talk to him about the discord at Mt. Joy and the "new theology," as he called it. Retired Elder Moses and Tina Weber came to talk about the troubles. He welcomed their help. The next day a Mrs. Tobias Wideman

---

53. Huffman, *Profile*, 24–25. Under Huffman, the Dayton church recovered and went on to become a strong and large congregation. Report of the MBiC Executive Committee mentioning the petitioning from the I&O Conference, the Executive Committee granting the petition and Hallman's refusal are in *Seventh General Conference 1908*, 19. It would be helpful if there were memoirs from the people involved in Dayton from the Pentecostal side.

"gave me more light on the new theology."⁵⁴ He apparently pleaded with people not to rush into opposing camps, but to bring their views to the next Annual Conference, scheduled for September in Berlin.⁵⁵ A. G. Ward attended MBiC camp-meetings in Ontario in the summer of 1908; he even preached some days. Goudie recorded discord in the camps and finally an emotion about it: "Meetings were good in one sense & in another not so for the new theology sought prominence in a way that seemed repulsive."⁵⁶

SOME THEOLOGY: LANGUAGES AND STAGES

At this point in the Pentecostal movement, many tongues-speakers assumed that they were speaking in actual human languages—their papers are full of testimonies of missionaries or citizens of other lands claiming they recognized the tongues-speeches as languages they knew, and could give the meaning of the words the people with the evidence were saying.⁵⁷ There was a great expectation that a new era of missionary advance was dawning. In fact it did and did not. Pentecostal Christian communities were sown in an amazing number of countries in a short period. However, in just a few years, Pentecostal missionaries found that they had to learn other languages the hard way just as earlier non-Pentecostal missionaries—grammar and vocabulary, practice with native speakers and so on. Yet they were granted converts as were other traditions. Tongues was not the power it was thought to be. Many Pentecostals stopped expecting the new tongues to be actual human languages and some retreated to describing them as possibly "tongues of angels" or utterances that only the Holy Spirit could interpret. Some analysts of recorded tongues-speeches say the phrases exhibit no sign of human grammar and are often quite repetitious.⁵⁸

For people of holiness background, the first thought they had if they accepted the new teaching was to simply add it to their holiness theology, and so become "three-stage" Pentecostals. They recognized the work of God in justification/conversion, in sanctification, and now, in baptism with the Spirit with tongues-speaking. Obviously they could no longer identify

54. Sam Goudie, "Diary 1908," 15 September.
55. Chambers, *Fifty Years*, 13.
56. Sam Goudie, "Diary 1908," 13 June.
57. For example, articles in the Hebdens' *Pentecostal Testimony* (1907–1910) available in the PAOC Archives, Mississauga, ON, and Frodsham, *Signs Following*, 35, 39–40, 49.
58. Faupel, "Glossolalia," 95–109; Poythress, "Glossolalia," 130–35. That finding agrees with my own limited exposure to modern tongues-speaking in Canada and Nigeria.

sanctification with the baptism with the Spirit, as many deeper life preachers at the end of the nineteenth century had been doing.[59] Those who went this three-stage route tended to join groups like the Church of God (Cleveland, Tennessee), the Apostolic Faith Church or the Pentecostal Holiness Church (PHC), which is what happened at Markham, where a PHC congregation formed, not a two-stage PAOC-type assembly. The other prominent holders to this variant were people from the Holiness Movement Church, which had already experimented with teaching three stages, identified as justification, sanctification and the baptism of fire, which they found in passages such as Luke 3:16. Many HMC members who were attracted by the new teaching simply slipped tongues into an already rich experience set. John Salmon of Toronto C&MA followed this route as well, as mentioned earlier.[60] After a few years, the influence of people with Baptist/Reformed backgrounds, who had no commitment to an experience of sanctification as subsequent to justification, held the expected experiences to just two, as happened in the Assemblies of God (AoG) in the US and the PAOC.[61]

SAM GOUDIE RESPONDS

Goudie wasn't completely alone in Conference leadership, there was a Reference Committee, which in later decades was called the district Executive Committee. This group conducted Conference business between Conferences, mainly having to do with camp-meetings, but they also adjusted pastoral appointments and disciplined members of the Annual Conference.[62] In 1907 those elected to the Committee were S. Goudie, Peter Cober, H. S. Hallman, Silas Cressman, and C. N. Good. Nevertheless, Goudie was the leader who took the main steps to reduce harm, as he saw it.

As the months moved on, Goudie, as the only Presiding Elder in the Conference, had to take action to reduce the disharmony resulting from differing views on the tongues issue. On April 1, 1908, Goudie was present at the West End Mission (Bethel) where A. G. Ward preached, and Goudie took the "after service," the follow-up, urging people to respond to

---

59. Miller, *Canadian Pentecostals*, 30–31, quotes William Seymour at Los Angeles in September 1906 already making the necessary distinction between sanctification and baptism with the Spirit theology seemingly required by the new phenomena.

60. Reynolds, *Footprints*, 289.

61. See Dayton, *Roots of Pentecostalism*, 100–108.

62. Ordinarily, not the discipline of members of Quarterly Conferences or classes, those were local issues.

the message. This is puzzling, considering the story we have received from Pentecostal sources is that Goudie suspended the meetings at Bethany in mid-March, ostensibly over Ward's advocacy of tongues. In addition, C. N. Good was the pastor of the West End Mission and he was not a supporter of the teaching of tongues as evidence of Spirit Baptism. The next day Goudie heard George Chambers preach at the East End Mission. Goudie recorded, "I stayed at bro. Chambers' last night & had a little talk with him this morning." Probably Goudie was cautioning him about certain issues that had to do with the new theology, but Goudie does not mention in the diary whether he suspended Chambers. It seems possible to me that Goudie was giving Ward and Chambers a chance to explain their views in sermon form or time to reconsider.[63]

Goudie's first tactic, as we saw, was direct discussion among the preachers as early as January 1907. The next tactic, a common one for leadership facing a divisive issue, was to ask people who insisted on teaching the necessity of speaking in tongues to simply stop teaching it. To him it was clearly against the MBiC *Discipline*. As we have seen he participated in discussions to change procedures in the *Discipline*, and participated in doctrinal discussions, so in theory, he could accept doctrinal change, but it had to be by the agreed community rules, the *Discipline*. A statement found in the earliest version of the *Discipline* from 1878 right up to about 1924 said that wherever the *Discipline* was found not following the Bible, the Bible was to be followed. This is permission for dissent, in theory. Of course this situation was ironic in view of the objection the first generation of the Reforming Mennonites gave to the Mennonite Conference's insistence that decisions of the bishops and Conference be submitted to. Solomon Eby had set aside the will of the brethren, appealing to the Word of God as sufficient authority. Now the same appeal was used against the MBiC leadership of 1908 as mentioned in Chambers' memoir. Perhaps Chris Miller (conference evangelist that year) and John Ball at Markham, were among those who accepted this advice, for although they resigned later, they are not recorded as among those who were suspended.[64] However, there is evidence

---

63. Porter, "Missionary Identity," 42–47; Porter claims Chambers changed his theology of sanctification (dropping the holiness movement form) only after meeting A. G. Ward again in Berlin in 1908. Sam Goudie, "Diary 1908," 1–3, April.

64. Ball remembered being asked to stop his teaching (Miller, *Canadian Pentecostals*, 49) and he remembered toning down a little; Ball, "Early Days." As he had resigned in the September 1908 Annual Conference, and was replaced by C. N. Good, this "ultimatum" would have been before the Conference.

from Isaac Pike, secretary of the Markham field, that he (Pike) was briefly in charge of the circuit, perhaps a clue that Ball was in fact removed just before Conference.[65] Although injunctions like Goudie's might persuade people with new convictions to delay promoting them, sooner or later they will probably declare "we must obey God rather than men" (Acts 5:29), and disobey anyway.

Goudie's third action was to suspend preachers and if they were pastors, replace them. First, according to Pentecostal sources, he called an end to the meetings in Berlin with Alfred G. Ward. It was not until months later, however that Ward was suspended as a preacher: in his diary for September 1908, Goudie recorded that he suspended Ward, Sherk and Pike.[66] Ward's wife, the former City Mission Worker Mary Markle, was not strictly a member of the Conference, having married. The other two Goudie suspended were Jesse Ramer Sherk (1880–1953), a local preacher at Berlin, and William Raymer Pike (1888–1954), another local preacher in Markham. There is no record he suspended Aaron Shoemaker, a one time probationer who had served at Breslau as recently as 1906–1907, though he is reported as among the first to speak in tongues in Ward's meetings. George Chambers did not speak in tongues until a few years later, but he was convinced and would not agree to stop teaching the new doctrine in Toronto. He invited A. G. Ward to speak at the East End Mission before Goudie suspended him and before Goudie replaced Chambers with another.[67] While this tension was spreading, Conference leaders were supporting Goudie. At Hespeler on 1 August, Peter Cober conducted the Quarterly meeting for Goudie, and

---

65. Inferred from data "from the records of Mr. Isaac Pike" on inside cover of Gormley's 1973 centennial booklet, *Gormley*.

66. Sam Goudie, "Diary 1908," 8 September. Shantz, *Bethany*, 25, says A. G. Ward was a minister of the Ontario Conference. Shantz had access to Bethany's Quarterly Conference minutes: it is conceivable that Ward received a Quarterly Conference license which would show up in Bethany's documents only, or that he received one from the West End Mission in Toronto, where Goudie had baptized him. It is true that the Annual Conference "[r]esolved, we substantiate the action taken by the Presiding Elder in reference to suspending Bro. A. G. Ward." (*Ontario Conference Journal 1908*, 16). As I understand it, only Conference action could make him a Conference member. That could have happened only in March 1907 or September 1908. Perhaps the Presiding Elders had other authorities not plain to me.

67. The pastor who replaced Chambers is not named in Conference records, and Chambers, *Fifty Years*, 13, does not name him. Joshua E. Fidler (1868–1936), a relative newcomer (1904) to the Ontario Conference from Pennsylvania Conference was appointed to the East End Mission in the 1908 Conference. Fidler had been at the Elmwood field. Probably the helper at the mission (1907–1908), T. W. Brook, was asked to take over.

in his remarks, Cober said, "I am here by request, not by choice. We had good QM at Breslau. Our PE was quite an inspiration to us the Lord thus far has wonderfully helped our PE"[68]

John Norman Kitching, elected City Mission President in 1907 to replace Hallman, also had work to do. Some of his City Mission Workers, especially those from Manitoba, refused to stop teaching that tongues were the necessary evidence of the Baptism with the Spirit. He had to suspend Mary Dresch, Mary (Markle) Ward's helper in Brandon. Others would leave or resign later.

Shortly after the close of the meetings with Ward, Bethany Church began to tear down the old "Blue Chapel" that had served them since 1877. Just before the demolition, someone took a picture of the building with the pastor Charlie Krauth, looking lonely standing on the front steps. The wood frame structure was at the end of its life and too small for the congregation.[69] In May the congregation pitched a large tent along Chapel Street and used it all summer while the construction went on of the "unassuming" red brick building that was still the core of their facility at the corner of Chapel and Lancaster.[70]

Sam Goudie preached in the new building on the morning of the dedication, Sunday 20 September 1908. According to Sam Goudie's diary, the week was very hot.[71] The hall, estimated by the newspaper to hold seven hundred people, was packed. Krauth preached in the afternoon, and their former Ontario colleague, Ebenezer Anthony, the Presiding Elder from Michigan and a fraternal delegate to the Ontario Conference, in the evening. The Ontario MBiC Annual Conference, planned as long before as March 1907, was to start on Wednesday, after the Tuesday Ministerial Convention.

ONTARIO ANNUAL CONFERENCE, BERLIN, ONTARIO, SEPTEMBER 1908

The "Annual Conference" consisted of around thirty-three "elders" (we would call them "ordained or licensed ministers in charge of fields" today)

68. "Quarterly Conference Book—Blair Mission 1898" 95. Box 1007, MCHT.

69. Shantz, *Bethany*, decaying:19–22 and too small: 21.

70. Local newspaper quoted in Shantz, *Bethany*, 23. The MBiC *Discipline* required all buildings erected should be "kept plain . . . and with free seats." Lageer, *Common Bonds*, 303, called it "stately," nearly one hundred years later.

71. In fact it was hot every day except one for nearly three weeks. Samuel Goudie, "Diary 1908," 9–27 September.

and about twenty delegates from the circuits. These were all men, in the understanding and practice of the day. Goudie was the chair of the Conference. Goudie appointed, and the Conference elected, members to all the temporary committees of the Conference. Although these committees were not vital to the Pentecostal issue, it may not have escaped everyone's attention that Goudie appointed no one who was a supporter of the new theology. In two of the twelve sessions, Goudie stepped down from the chair, and Ephraim Sievenpiper conducted the business. In one, the suspensions of Robert Eltherington and George Chambers were considered, among other business, and in the second, votes to return to having two Presiding Elders and elections of other Conference leaders were conducted. H. S. Hallman chaired the part of the Seventh Session when the Presiding Elders were elected: Goudie and Sievenpiper.[72]

As usual at Annual Conferences, various people, men and women, were accepted as advisory members. Some of them stayed briefly, as did the two Presiding Elders from the Pennsylvania Conference, Harvey B. Musselman (b. 1868) and William George Gehman (b. 1874). Some stayed throughout, as did Oliver Bricker Snyder, a Berlin native, now representing Michigan Conference as another fraternal delegate. Some advisory members were women, such as Sister Anna Bowman from Michigan, Sister Thompson of the Salvation Army,[73] and Mary (Markle) Ward, and missionaries Ada (Moyer) Barker, and Althea (Priest) Banfield. Even A. G. Ward was accepted as an advisory member. At one point, as we will see, the issues of the Conference led to allowing all the mission workers (all women) and probationers to be advisory members in the private sessions that dealt with the *Discipline* and discussion of the doctrine of sanctification, especially as it related to Alfred G. Ward's suspension by Sam Goudie.[74]

The Pentecostal issue was not the only case dealt with by the Conference. Robert Eltherington's suspension by Goudie for "immoral conduct" in Toronto was upheld and the Conference expelled him when he did not appear to meet with a committee to discuss his behavior.[75] The Reference

---

72. *Ontario Conference Journal 1908*, 12–18.

73. Probably Hattie Thompson (1889–1958), who joined the MBiC city mission work in 1909, later married to Charles Dunlop.

74. *Ontario Conference Journal 1908* 9, 11, 16.

75. *Ontario Conference Journal 1908* 12, 24. Brother Robert (1857–1933) "Happy Bob," as he was once called, *GB* (27 June 1899), changed his mind later (1913) and reconciled with the Conference, returning to a productive pastoral career, *Ontario Conference Journal 1913* 13. Goudie preached at his memorial.

Committee reported that Brother [Webster] Irish (who had settled in western Canada by this time and was no longer a member of the Ontario Conference) still owed an apology to Peter Cober.[76]

Nevertheless, it is apparent that the tongues issue manifested at various points in the Conference, not merely in the matter of suspended individuals. In the normally routine "Report of Committee to Examine Ministers, Helpers, Local Preachers and Evangelists," it was recorded: "In one case a charge of sowing dissension was preferred, and in several cases, brethren were accused of teaching contrary to Discipline as interpreted by the Conference."[77] The committee consisted of Peter Cober, John N. Kitching, John A. Sider, Solomon Eby, and Samuel Goudie.

Normally, several Annual Conference sessions were devoted to private sessions when reports on conduct, probationers and ordinations were given. Often in earlier years at other sites, the Conference adjourned to another building for the private sessions. Bethany was a large and new building. An unusual number of private sessions were conducted during this Ontario Conference in the basement of Bethany. However, not all discussion took place there. The main floor auditorium witnessed an event that lived on in legend-like form, with Chambers reporting that Solomon Eby stood up to appeal for peace.[78]

THE PIGEONS STORY

During one stage of the discussion (during an opening hymn according to Chambers), the windows of the new church were open (because of the heat) and a pigeon (or two) flew in and landed on the balcony railing. Later it, or they, left. That is the basic event, I believe.

In one version of the story, George Chambers claimed there were two doves that came in and flew around, landed and then flew out the same window.[79] In Thomas Miller's retelling the two doves have become one pigeon (following the opinion of Gordon Atter, he says), adding that the bird stayed until a decision about tongues was made, upon which the bird flew

76. *Ontario Conference Journal 1908* 13.

77. The "D" on "Discipline" was printed in lower case, but in the manuscript minutes, it is clearly capital, "MBiC Ontario Conference Minutes 1898–1909," 327, Box 4121, MCHT.

78. Frodsham, *Signs Following*, 55, quoting G. A. Chambers. The 1941 edition shortens and rephrases the versions of 1926 and 1928 extensively.

79. Frodsham, *Signs Following*, 55.

out.⁸⁰ Paul Hawkes collected a version of this story from Reuben and Eva Mae (Hostetler) Sternall, in which the pigeons did not alight in the building. The Sternalls reported the belief that the withdrawal of the pigeons signified that the Holy Spirit did not find a place in the MBiC Ontario Conference.⁸¹ In still another variant, Kitchener Gospel Tabernacle pastor Richard Burton writes,

> A pair of doves flew in the church through an open window and after flying around the interior of the church, rested on the altar rail facing the congregation. *When the negative vote was announced* the doves flew around the interior of the church again, sat on the open windowsill, for a short period, inclining their heads to the people, and flew out. Elder Solomon Eby stood up and said "Brethren, see those doves, cannot we live in peace *and accept it?*"⁸²

This version appears to be built partly on the 1941 Frodsham version, ultimately from Chambers, but has unique details. Some of the added details, with a pro-Pentecostal slant, distinguish it from the next version.

I collected an MBiC version of the pigeons story in 1986, from a minister (b. 1910) with origins in Bethany, Kitchener, who said he heard this story "many times." In this version, there were two pigeons which "flew into the church, lit on the altar, and in a few minutes one flew out a window on one side of the church and the other flew out a window on the opposite side of the church. According to the story, the disenters [sic] took this to mean that the groups were to separate and thus the Pentecostal Church began."⁸³

Renovations in the building would make this double exit impossible today, but as originally constructed, not unimaginable. Bethany was the first MBiC building to be constructed with a balcony and the balcony railing is not far from the windows. This makes the main floor altar railing,

---

80. Miller, *Canadian Pentecostals*, 45–46, 67 also hints that Chambers' reporting style tended to "glowing accounts" compared to Ward and R. E. McAlister's more restrained versions. Ward's son, C. Morse Ward provided still another version which he said he substantiated many times, that a pure white dove flew into the auditorium where the presiding elder was giving a ruling about proper conduct concerning tongues, and the dove flew out when he stated the Mennonites could not condone speaking in tongues; Ward, *C. M. Ward Story* (Harrison, Arizona: New Leaf Press, 1976), 15–16; brought to my attention by Caleb Courtney, personal communication 14 June 2020, and the following reference on 6 July 2020.

81. Hawkes, "Pentecostal Assemblies," 11–12.

82. Burton, *Pentecost in Kitchener*, 15.

83. Earl R. Pannabecker, letter to the author from North Bay, 26 February 1986.

surrounded by people on the platform and front pews, unlikely as a place for confused birds to rest.

Ward Shantz quotes another version from C. N. Good, the Conference Secretary, who was present at the Conference as Chambers was (and who lived a long time in retirement worshipping at Bethany). Good also reported two pigeons flying in and alighting briefly on the *gallery* railing. "This was taken by the Conference as a sign that God was setting his seal of approval on the position taken in this matter."[84] After the birds flew out the same window Chambers added, ". . . Solomon Eby rose and said, 'Brethren, see these doves. Cannot we be at peace?'"[85]

Sam Goudie is not named in any of these versions. He would, however, have to be the "presiding elder" remembered by A. G. and Mary Ward announcing the decision of the Conference.

The majority of the Conference upheld the holiness interpretation of the *Discipline* articles as printed and the final resolutions of the Conference, which merely said, "Whereas, There is a difference of opinion in this Conference in the interpretation of article 5 page 15 and also article 12, page 18, therefore Resolved, That we recommend the General Conference [make] a more definite interpretation on said articles."[86]

As Chambers remembered it, eight other ministers (making nine) and two lady workers were nevertheless "given two alternatives: either to cease teaching, preaching and holding tarrying services in which people were encouraged to seek for the baptism of the Holy Ghost; and to move to another pastorate; or to be excommunicated from the fellowship of the Society."[87]

It was a tense Conference. At the end, Goudie wrote, "Conf. struggled on to a finish this eve about 7 p. m." After he reached home on September 29, he recorded for the next two days simply, "Spent the day at home."[88]

---

84. Shantz, *Bethany*, 25–26.
85. Chambers, quoted in Frodsham, *With Signs Following*, 55.
86. *Ontario Conference Journal 1908*, 28.
87. Chambers, *Fifty Years*, 14. Burton, *Pentecost in* Kitchener, 35, is the first Pentecostal author to get this right in one place, but misleads in another (p. 15). He was misled by his sources, Frodsham's version of 1928, 80, as quoted in Kulbeck, *Pentecostal Assemblies*, 116–17.
88. Sam Goudie, "Diary 1908," 28 September.

8

Who Left? Who Stayed?

CHAMBERS SAID "[T]WO BRETHREN compromised and recanted." I do not know who the two brethren were. It is sometimes claimed (for example, Chambers)[1] that Solomon Eby spoke in tongues at the New Year's meetings under Ward, but Eby himself did not claim that until 1912.[2] H. S. Hallman, treading a fine line between Pentecostal teaching and the holiness sanctification doctrine, may have been one of the "compromising" brethren. His wife was apparently attending Daniel and Lydia Hostetler's Pentecostal prayer meetings. The evidence is ambiguous, or Chambers did not remember well. Though called to account for refusing to stop printing articles for and against tongues, finally in mid-September Hallman agreed to submit until the October General Conference in Brown City, Michigan.[3] Hallman was not re-elected to the position of editor at the Brown City meeting, after twenty years at the post. He became the pastor of an independent, but C&MA-related church, the United Tabernacle in Columbus, Ohio, for a while, but somehow never lost the esteem of the Ontario Conference, nor of Goudie, continuing as a member of various boards and committees.[4]

1. Quoted in Frodsham, *Signs Following*, 55.
2. Huffman, *Mennonite Brethren in Christ*, 58 quotes a letter from Solomon Eby to J. A. Huffman stating clearly that he "was baptized in the Holy Ghost and fire on January 31 1912."
3. *Ontario Conference Journal 1908* 19.
4. Huffman, *Mennonite Brethren in Christ*, 240. The profile says he later became the "Superintendent of Publishing Business" for the C&MA in New York. He retired to

One other possible "recanter" was Elder Amos Eby. His wife, Esther (Moyer) Eby, was also remembered as attending the Hostetler meetings, but again, Amos himself did not identify with them publicly until about 1912.[5] Another possibility was David Fretz from Vineland whom Goudie visited in 1903 and other times, the missionary to Jews in Hamilton. Fretz had not resigned from the MBiC in September but did so before the end of the year. On his next visit to Vineland, Goudie again made a point of visiting Fretz.[6] David Brittain (1873–1935) is still another possible "recanter." Although assigned to Owen Sound, Squire and Dornoch in 1908, following A. G. Doner, and a conference evangelist later, he resigned in 1912 to serve the "Emmerson Avenue Church of the C&MA" (the sixth congregation organized fully subscribing to the C&MA constitution). He lasted one year there,[7] followed by Archibald Gormley Doner, one of those who did resign in 1908.

When those in favor of the initial evidence teaching saw that they were opposed by the majority, they prepared and submitted a resignation letter, printed without comment in the minutes of the ninth session. This letter has been much reprinted but the identities of those who signed it are not well understood, in particular, by Pentecostal writers, and were never commented on by MBiC/EMCC writers. I have studied the careers of the eight persons for over thirty years to get a better picture of what was going on, and I am still searching for more complete information. The spelling of the names go though curious variations in the reprinted versions.

As printed in the *Conference Journal*, the letter said,

> We, the undersigned do desire to herein express regret that owing to the attitude assumed by this Conference relative to the interpretation of the Church Discipline of article 5, page 15, also article 12 page 18, we desire to hereby submit our resignation, pending such

---

Kitchener, a member of Bethany, and died there in 1932.

5. Spaetzel, *Kitchener Gospel Temple*, 5. Amos Eby (1842–1923), in retirement, had serious disagreements with the leadership of the Ontario Conference from 1912 and was urged by a visiting committee to be reconciled. Both Eby cousins lived on Chapel Street, just down the street from Bethany. In the 1921 census, Amos Eby reported his religion as "Lutheran," not even Pentecostal.

6. Sam Goudie, "Diary 1908," October 19: "Bro [Christian] Raymer and I went calling . . . & had a talk with D. Fretz."

7. Reynolds, *Footprints*, 356–57. Brittain's wife was the former Johanna C. Krauth (1877–1963), a one time city mission preacher herself (1901–1903), almost certainly a sister of Charlie Krauth, as he had a sister "Hanah" two years younger in the 1891 Canada census.

time as the General Conference decision might effect the present interpretation of said Discipline. Yours in Christian love,

A. G. Doner, J. E. Ball, Geo. A. Chambers, C. R. Miller, E. M. Guy, M. M. Hisey, L. Homes, M. E. Ward.[8]

In the manuscript minutes, the names are given a little differently: "A. G. Doner, J. Ball, G. A. Chambers, C. R. Miller, Mrs. E. M. Guy, M. Hisey, L. Homes, Mrs. M. E. Ward."[9] I suppose that each in the group of eight signed the original hand-written resignation letter (now lost). In earlier times some spellings were never standardized as now, and children anglicized freely whereas now it costs immensely in time and money to alter identity documents. In addition, printers' devils delight in corrupting names in MBiC *Journals*, especially names with which the Secretary was unfamiliar. Poor Edgar Schlimm had numerous oddities in the printing of his surname in the few years it appeared in the proceedings, and city mission preacher Minerva Scheifele (Schiefly, Scheifly, Schufele, Schiefle). Schifele had to endure various mangling of her fine surname.

THE EIGHT WHO RESIGNED

Despite what Chambers said that eight male ministers and two women preachers were given an ultimatum, with two eventually "recanting," this list of eight actually includes the names of four men and four women, one of whom (Mary E. Ward, nee Markle) was not technically a member at the time, but she was an advisory member and the wife of an advisory member (A. G. Ward). The other women were members of the City Mission Workers Society and so could resign from that. The four men were all members of the Conference, and so could resign from that body. As Goudie noted in his diary, in practice, "4 preachers and 4 workers of the new school resigned."[10] No doubt there is a way to reconcile the two statements, if we knew more. It is possible Chambers' memory was hazy, fifty years later.

A. G. Doner

This man is Archibald Gormley Doner (1876–1951) (not "Donner" or "Donor" as in some works). As his name implies, he was from Gormley,

---

8. *Ontario Conference Journal 1908* 22.

9. *Minutes of the Proceedings of the Mennonite Brethren in Christ Ontario Conference 1898–1909*, 334, Box 4121, MCHT.

10. Sam Goudie, "Diary 1908," September 26.

Ontario, and grew up in the Gormley congregation of the Markham MBiC field. His parents were Josephus Doner and Mary (Steckley) Doner. He entered the ministry of the MBiC in 1900 and was ordained in 1904.[11] He had served at Hespeler (1901–1902) as a probationer, then was the pastor at The Twenty Mission (Vineland, Zion and Sherkston), assisted at first by Sylvester Fretz, and then for three years by Samuel A. Moyer (1845–1928). Both men from the Vineland area became elders in the MBiC. In 1906, he was transferred to Kilsyth/ Squire and Dornoch, from where he resigned in September 1908. Archibald Doner was remembered in later years as meeting with Pentecostal sympathizers in the countryside south of Owen Sound about 1909–1910, close to where he was formerly the MBiC pastor, and for a while he rented a hall in Owen Sound to preach the new teaching.[12] His reaction to the rejection of the Pentecostal baptism in the Spirit teaching by the MBiC may have been similar to George Chambers's: fight them! His desire may have been tempered with a feeling of obligation to continue to shepherd any who sympathized with the new teaching. From the MBiC side it would be a simple case of interfering in a circuit. There is no sign of the Doners in the 1911 Canada census; perhaps, as with George Chambers, they went to the US for a few years. He served Christian and Missionary Alliance churches at Toronto (1913–1914), Peterborough (Bethany Tabernacle, 1916–1923), London (a proto-Alliance fellowship that joined the C&MA in 1926), (1924–1926), Brantford (1926–?) and Windsor.[13] So despite the resignation over tongues, there is little indication he served Pentecostal churches as such, and Pentecostals do not know much about him. It is true that in the decade 1906 to about 1916, C&MA churches were in a theological flux, in which tongues-speaking was not officially forbidden, nor emphasized, which is the official policy today. He married his first wife,

---

11. "Obituary," *GB* (20 December 1951) 15, says that A. G. Doner was educated in Kansas City, Missouri, and was ordained in the Baptist Church there, which does not fit easily with the MBiC *Conference Journal* records. While the obituary writer shows signs of personal acquaintance with Rev. Doner in his later years, the person seems not to know that the churches Doner served in Hespeler and Vineland were in fact MBiC. The obituary also states that in retirement Doner was active in "the local Mennonite Church" in Markham which is ambiguous, but possibly means Gormley MBiC.

12. *Anniversary Week April 5 to April 12 1964, Pentecostal Tabernacle, Owen Sound*, 1. In PAOC Archives, Mississauga, Ontario. Rudd, *Early Years*, 270.

13. See Reynolds, *Footprints*, Toronto: 466, Peterborough: 465. London and Brantford: see Reynolds, *Rebirth*, 159–60. The Peterborough and Brantford churches maintained strong independence stances even though officially C&MA branches; Reynolds, *Footprints*, 295.

Melissa Moyer (b. 1880), on July 6, 1899, and many years later, after her death, her sister, Phoebe Ann (Moyer) Raymer, in November 1950. A niece remembered him as one the relatives joked about because they thought his stories were exaggerations,[14] but he had traveled "extensively in Canada and the United States." An obituary writer found Doner to be "a great student of the Bible and of all good reading." He was also "a keen observer, he could converse on any given subject which made it a pleasure to visit him." Doner retired to Gormley and is buried at Heise Hill Cemetery. He left three sons and two daughters.[15]

J. E. Ball

This is John T. Ball (1875–1955), who joined the MBiC ministry in 1898, and was ordained an elder in 1903. The middle initial stood for "Thomas." I don't know where the "C" in Kulbeck's book comes from, or the "E" in the *Conference Journal*, though handwritten names were frequently misinterpreted in the compositing room. He was born of Irish Methodist parents (William and Sarah) who came to Canada before their first child was born, settling as farmers in Bentinck Township in Grey County. Many Germans settled in that area. He was married to Margaret "Maggie" Robinson on August 7, 1901. They had two children, Reva and Harold.[16]

His probationer years were spent at the Shrigley field under Sam's brother Henry Goudie (1898–1899) and then John A. Sider (1899–1902). From 1902 to 1904 he served the Sunnidale Township. circuit (Ebenezer, 9th Line, Glencairn) just to the east of Stayner in Simcoe County. In 1903–1904, he had T. W. Brook as a helper.[17] Moved to the Stayner Mission next door in 1904, Ball served the charge with local help until 1907,[18] when

---

14. Doris Hoover, interview by the author, 18 January 1986. "Obituary," *GB* (20 December 1951) 15.

15. "Obituary," *GB* (20 December 1951) 15.

16. Information from Canada census of 1881, 1891, 1911 and 1921. The two children are named in an obituary clipping from Oshawa in 1956, John Thomas Ball Personal Papers, PAOC Archives, Mississauga, Ontario.

17. A certain T. W. Brook was recorded as a member of the Ontario Conference of the Pentecostal Holiness Church, who died in Toronto in 1956, Pentecostal Holiness Church, *Forty-First Session*, 4. It is an unusual name; this probably is the MBiC T. W. Brook. I have not been able to identify him in Canada census records.

18. In Stayner he suffered from a complication of a typhoid infection that gradually reduced his hearing. George A. Chambers, "Canadian Workers You Should Know," *Pentecostal Testimony* (June 1938) 5. Reva J. (Ball) Irvine, Transcript of Oral Interview with

he was transferred to the large Markham field, which included Mt. Joy, Dickson Hill, Bethesda, 3rd Line (that is, Gormley) and Vaughan (that is, Edgeley Meeting House [Schmitt's], Vaughan Township.), with many local helpers, such as the widow preacher Euphemia (Pool) Guy, Daniel Barkey, and retired men John H. Steckley and Moses Weber. As we have noted, those who were appointed to large fields such as Markham were considered by the Stationing Committee as capable people.

I have already described the circumstances in which John Ball became a Pentecostal in outlook in 1908. When he resigned from the MBiC, the Markham members who favored the tongues experience called on him to continue with them. In October 1908 items in the local newspapers announced the start of a new congregation in Markham village, about 1 km south of Mt. Joy, which he led until about 1916 or 1917.[19] This congregation continued as a Pentecostal Holiness congregation, as mentioned earlier, that survived until 1937 at least, perhaps into the 1950s.[20] The split, as could be expected, caused hard feelings in some families whose members continued in the two congregations. Missionary Church member Doris Hoover said the division was never talked about in any gathering of her relatives. She sensed from her family that they considered the action of those who joined the Pentecostals as "near betrayal and disloyalty."[21] No PAOC congregation in Markham village in 2024 is a direct outgrowth of the PHC congregation, so far as I have been able to tell, though doubtless some families did go into the PAOC later.

Jim Craig, 6–7, John Thomas Ball Personal Papers, PAOC Archives, Mississauga, Ontario.

19. *Markham Economist,* (15 October and 29 October 1908), *Markham Sun* (29 October 1908). R. E. McAlister, "Obituary," *Pentecostal Testimony* (February 1956) 9, G. A. Chambers, "A Tribute to John T. Ball," *Pentecostal Testimony* (May 1956) 26.

20. A notice in the *Markham Economist and Sun* in 1937 names "Geo. Hall" as pastor of the Pentecostal Holiness Church on Church Street. George Hall (d. 1970) was a highly honored minister of the Ontario Conference of the Pentecostal Holiness Church in Ontario, ordained in 1929, secretary and treasurer of that Conference for twenty-eight years, Pentecostal Holiness Church, *Forty-First Session,* 3–4. Kulbeck does not mention the PHC connection. Rudd, *Early Years,* 275–76, retells John Ball's story in Markham, but does not connect it to any current PAOC work in Markham. Flora (Elmore) Barkey remembered names of people who attended the Markham PHC: Boyd, Timbers, and Clodd families, Thomas Hastings (a nephew of the Pool sisters), Wilmot Raymer and some Moyers; Flora Barkey, telephone conversation with the author, 17 January 1987. The building was used as a Brethren assembly's building in more recent years; James McDowell, who grew up in Markham, conversation with the author, in Kitchener, ON.

21. Doris Hoover, interview by the author, 18 January 1986.

From Markham, Ball went briefly to lead a church in Toronto (Zion Pentecostal Mission), which after many changes became Danforth Gospel Temple.[22] While still a pastor in Toronto, he held meetings in Mount Forest, which the Pentecostal Assembly (PAOC) in Mount Forest in 2012 noted.[23] He moved to Owen Sound in 1917, invited by a Mount Forest man, perhaps to follow up small Pentecostal beginnings coming out of the Owen Sound MBiC Mission and others.[24] The Owen Sound PAOC church became quite large and sent out a good number of Christian workers. Later he established thriving churches in Pembroke (1923–1924 and 1925–1932, but spending one year back in Owen Sound, 1924–1925), and Oshawa (1932–1941).

In response to John Ball's stance in Markham, the Stationing Committee (Goudie and C. N. Good both being members) sent C. N. Good to the field. Finding the Mt. Joy group especially depleted, Good set about holding evangelistic meetings and so built up the membership that the numerical losses to the new assembly were replaced by the time he moved on and Ephraim Sievenpiper came in 1910.[25]

The PAOC praise John Ball as a vigorous church planter, and he was, but his repute in the MBiC became different, certainly with Sam Goudie, who looked on him as an opportunist and rival as far as the MBiC was concerned. While in Markham, Ball helped organize Pentecostal camp-meetings in the very woodlot that the MBiC had been using for some years—on the Moyer farm right across the road from the Dickson Hill church building.[26] The MBiC in later years used that same lot again. Hoover felt that her mother's generation of MBiC members were adversely affected by the split. Perhaps here is a sample which helps to answer Eileen Lageer's question. Hoover's mother believed the reluctance of the Dickson Hill members to speak up in testimony meetings was a sign of their unease: they were

---

22. Bundock, "Danforth Gospel Temple," 1. Zion may have been the remnants of the Hebden Mission. A Raymer family were part of Danforth Gospel Temple.

23. Not noted in Brown, *Fifty Years*, 96–97. In Ball, "Early Days," John Ball indicates he was in Mount Forest for brief special meetings and from there was urged by a man in Mount Forest to go to Owen Sound, which he did right away. A 100th anniversary book produced by the Mount Forest Pentecostal Church dates the first meetings of a Pentecostal nature to 1912 and names several people who led them or were involved. Ball was included, "Mt. Forest," PAOC Archives, Mississauga, Ontario.

24. Brown, *Fifty Years*, 108–09; see also Fuller, "Holiness People," 24, and Storms, "Calvary Church."

25. McDowell and others, *Markham*, 29.

26. Called "Meyer's" in Kulbeck, *Pentecostal Assemblies*, 109.

fearful of self-expression and a reaction to their own earlier and Pentecostal "manifestations."[27] Perhaps a set of expressive people left, leaving the less demonstrative. On the other hand, her friend and relative Mrs. Flora (Elmore) Barkey (b. 1906) did not remember bad relations between the MBiC and the Pentecostals. She liked an occasional "Amen!" or "Hallelujah," but not too often! She did remember, as unusual, old Christina ("Teeny") (Sherk) Weber, Moses Weber's second wife, whom she called a "shouting Mennonite."[28] Mrs. Weber did not join the Pentecostals, however. Sarah Pool, her sister Euphemia, and Mrs. Ben Reesor were also remembered as demonstrating their "happiness." And they did join the Pentecostals.[29]

In Owen Sound, Ball's efforts gathered the family of Herbert H. Barber, later of Winnipeg, who were converted through the MBiC Mission.[30][31] Reuben Eby Sternall, whose father Conrad Steuernagel had been an Evangelical Association ordained preacher (1865–1880),[32] was converted at the Chippawa Hill school house site of the Port Elgin field in 1901 or 1902,[33]

---

27. Doris Hoover, interview by the author, 18 January 1986. A daughter of C. N. Good, Mrs. Clayton W. (Grace Good) Cressman, also thought "possibly there was some restraint on emotional expression" as a reaction to the "excessive emotionalism of the Pentecostal element," Ward M. Shantz, letter to the author from Kitchener, ON, 28 January 1986.

28. Flora (Elmore) Barkey, telephone conversation with the author, 17 January 1987. The same memory of Mrs. "Teeny" Weber appears in Mrs. Albert Hawkins' memoir quoted in McDowell and others, *Markham*, 35.

29. McDowell and others, *Markham*, 35. Mrs. Reesor "ran around the aisles"; Sarah Pool "danced quietly up and down."

30. Ball wrote, "The message we preached had been a neglected one by the neighbouring Churches and stirred the whole city." He said all denominations had their people in his meetings: "Mennonites [that is, MBiC certainly], and Salvation Army and Anglicans, Methodists, Presbyterians, Catholics." Ball, "Early Days." Ellis A. Lageer said he was a friend of H. H. Barber at Owen Sound in the Young People's Society of the MBiC. In those days, Barber was embarrassed by antics of preachers in the pulpit. The Owen Sound church in the 1930s had much better relations with the Alliance Church in town than with the Pentecostals, even though there was a "second wave of Pentecostal interest and experiences" then; Ellis Lageer, former member from Owen Sound MBiC Church, and Emmanuel Bible College president, letter to the author, 6 May 1986.

31. Storms, "Calvary Church." A relative, Mrs. William Barber, had even donated the chairs for the Owen Sound mission hall in 1903.

32. Stapleton, *Evangelical United Church*, 349, 426. Last mentioned in 1880 as "locating," that is, resigning from itinerant ministry to settle somewhere.

33. P., R. E., "Pentecostal Pioneer: Rev R. E. Sternall," *Pentecostal Testimony* (November 1973) 6. Conrad and Magdalena Sternall, both (approximately) 69, and "Mennonite" were living in Owen Sound in 1921. The Canada census records them in 1901 with the spelling Steurnagel in Saugeen Township. Sam Goudie was their pastor in 1893.

and attended the Owen Sound MBiC church, briefly serving the MBiC under the Upper Canada Tract Society in the summer of 1907. He was out of Canada at the C&MA school at Nyack when the Pentecostal crisis arose in the MBiC, and along with many at that school, accepted the Pentecostal tongues-message at meetings in Rochester, New York. Back in Canada, he was an early pastor of the Berlin Pentecostal Assembly (now Kitchener Gospel Temple), and married Daniel and Lydia Hostetler's youngest daughter, Ella Mae, in December 1911.[34]

While John Ball was at Owen Sound, Alvin (or Alphin) Sternall, a brother of Reuben Sternall, invited Ball to come to Southampton, the town near his farm, to open meetings. This was close to Port Elgin, and at times the location of an MBiC City Mission. This he did in 1919.[35] While visiting Stayner about February of 1919, Sam Goudie heard rumors of Ball thinking to go to Stayner "to open fire." Goudie considered any such action by Ball as intentional aggression in a location Ball once served as an MBiC pastor. In a letter to C. N. Good, Goudie advised Good to warn the pastor at Port Elgin and Chippawa Hill to be on his guard: "I hope Schlimm and his wife [Clara (Eby) Schlimm] keep their balance & don't flop over to the Rollers . . . I wish you may find Schlimm's in a better state than one might look for; if you see Ball you tell him his place. I would if I met him."[36] (Goudie's emphasis)

John Ball spent about eight years total in Owen Sound and left an assembly in good condition while he went to Pembroke for nine years, and then to Oshawa for new church starts before continuing with evangelism in Ontario.[37]

G. A. Chambers

George Augustus Chambers left a number of short historical memoirs, mostly in the *Pentecostal Testimony*, but also in his book, *Fifty Years in the*

"Sternall" is an anglicized version of the family name.

34. Storms, "Calvary Church," lists Sternall as one of their members who were preachers "sent out" from the church. This suggests by then a level of respect had been achieved between the MBiC and Sternall. Sternall's call to Berlin: Burton, *Pentecost in Kitchener*, 21.

35. Brown, *Fifty Years*, 125. Ball in Toronto and Mount Forest: Miller, *Canadian Pentecostals*, 50.

36. Letter of S. Goudie to C. N. Good, from Stouffville, ON, 14 March 1919 (Everek Storms Collection, Missionary Church Archives, Mishawaka, Indiana).

37. John Ball, "Early Days" in John T. Ball Papers, PAOC Archives, Mississauga, ON, 2, 10–11.

Service of the King 1907–1957, published in Toronto in 1960.[38] We have been quoting him already. Sam Goudie had Chambers preach at the West End Mission in June 1903, and that day "received him into church fellowship," that is, membership. His wife Ida followed in August (She had been ill).[39] From MBiC records, he was licensed as an applicant to the Ontario Conference in 1904, and was assigned to the Guelph Mission, which was not that year a City Mission, staffed by women, but a Conference Mission field, staffed by men. Since Chambers says he was converted about 1898–1899 under the ministry of Charles Tobias Homuth,[40] it could have been Homuth who recommended Chambers apply to the MBiC, as he himself did. From 1905 to 1908, Chambers served the East End Mission of the MBiC on Parliament St., Toronto. The first year he was supervised by Sam Goudie's brother, Henry, who was at the West End Mission.[41] Chambers was never ordained an Elder in the MBiC. He was working his way through the Probationers Reading Course and passed all his first-year exams (squeaking by in Church History, but fine in the others), but he did somewhat poorly in the second year, failing in the exams on Richard Baxter's *Reformed Pastor*, the second part of Church History, and Sell's *Bible Study*, though doing well in Bible and an apologetics text.

After his suspension, Chambers continued to attend the East End Mission, but when he resigned, he and Ida prayed about what to do and his response was to fight the MBiC by opening up a Pentecostal mission just a few blocks north along Parliament Street. (He was at #375, the MBiC was at #266/268.) Many from the MBiC went with him, as frequently happens in splits, and the MBiC East End Mission was seriously destabilized, so that Sam Goudie and the others on the Stationing Committee considered turning the mission into a rescue mission only. A rescue mission was eventually opened elsewhere, but the East End Mission limped along for a few years and then was shifted to a site on Jones Avenue and the mission left the past more or less behind. Chambers left Toronto after a couple of years for a church in Elkland, Pennsylvania, leaving his mission in the hands of a Mrs. Grant, a mission which eventually disappeared.

---

38. Interestingly, the Holiness Movement Church also had a "(Rev.) Geo. Chambers" at this very time, whose testimony appears in Christie, *Out of Bondage*, 187–89.

39. Sam Goudie, "Diary 1903," 26 June and 7 August.

40. Chambers has "Hometh."

41 In 1906 he was assisted by Beniah Bowman, and in 1907–1908, by T. W. Brook. Sarah Pool was the slum worker who worked in the area.

Chambers' wife was Ida Williamson (1882–1970). They had at least four children by the 1911 census, including a son born in the US in 1910, the year they returned to Canada. Ida's daughter Viola married Roy C. Spaetzel, author of the Kitchener Gospel Temple history of 1974. The Chambers are buried at Memory Gardens, on Highway 7 between Breslau and Guelph, Ontario.

C. R. Miller

Christian "Chris" Roth Miller was born in 1867 or 1868 in Baden, Wilmot Township, Waterloo, the youngest of a family of eight. He married Elmina Shantz of Bridgeport, then a village on the east side Berlin on the Grand River, on March 5, 1895. Her father, Isaac Shantz, was the owner of a foundry in Berlin and for a time, a town councillor. Her father died 11 January 1908, at the start of the controversial Bethany New Year's meetings. Miller's middle name reflects that his family was part of the original Amish community in Wilmot Township.[42]

Miller entered the MBiC ministry in 1895 on the Bethel (New Dundee) field as a helper to Solomon Eby. There were six appointments in four townships that year on the circuit: Bright, (Blenheim, now in Blandford-Blenheim) Mannheim (Wilmot), Union (west of Roseville in North Dumfries), New Hamburg and New Dundee (Wilmot) and Poole (in Mornington, now part of Perth East). In 1896 until 1898, the year he was ordained, he was given charge of the newly re-organized Bright Mission, consisting of Bright and Burford (Brant County, west of Brantford, a short-lived appointment). In the second year he shared care for "Hamburg" (New Hamburg) with Solomon Eby. From this place he was switched to Sherkston, as we saw, for two years (1898–1900), Manitoulin Island for two years (1900–1902), then to Kilsyth Mission for three years (Kilsyth and Dornoch 1902–1903, Kilsyth and Benallen 1903–1904, Kilsyth and Vandusen School House 1904–1905). In 1905–1906, he was appointed a Tabernacle worker and evangelist for the Conference. He served on the Elmwood circuit which included Hanover and Allen Park for one year, 1906–1907. In the long Conference year of 1907 to 1908, he was a Conference evangelist again.

I do not know why Miller was moved after two years several times, and once after just one year. Perhaps the Stationing Committee saw him as more effective as an evangelist. Miller and his wife were involved in the

---

42. www.generations.regionofwaterloo.com.

Berlin Orphanage around 1907. A photograph of him on the front steps has a caption saying he worked tirelessly for the Children's Aid Society to be established in Waterloo County.[43] In the 1911 Canada census, he was recorded as a Pentecostal, and an inspector for the CAS. He traveled far and wide on behalf of the Society for several years, going for example to Winnipeg and Sault Ste. Marie in 1909, and Elmira in 1912. In 1912, he was paid a small amount for services as a "Constable" of the County, clearly an occasional duty for him. In the 1911 census, he and Elmina were recorded having one daughter, born in 1906.

The histories of Kitchener Gospel Temple suggest Chris Miller was a non-ordained lay-preacher.[44] Maybe he seemed that way to the Berlin Pentecostal Assembly, but in fact he was an experienced MBiC preacher from 1895 to 1908, ordained in 1898 and no wonder he was selected as one of their early "elders."[45] He was without support from a church in the years after 1908, so maybe that was how he was remembered. As the Agent for Waterloo County of the CAS from 1908, he was referred to as Rev C. R. Miller. He retired from the CAS in 1917 due to ill health,[46] and fades from the history of KGT, so he is not as well remembered in their community as others. The Canada census of 1921 locates Christian and Elmina Miller in Parkdale, Toronto, with their daughter Ruth. He is listed as a "Gentleman" which typically meant he was retired, though only fifty-three years

---

43. Printed in Walker, *Waterloo County Album*, 71, and also in Hoffman and Taylor, *Much to Be Done*, 128; original in the National Archives of Canada. In recent times the Family and Children's Services in Waterloo thought they started in 1908 with Miller, but later thought it began in 1896 (celebrating a centennial in 1996) probably with the start of the Berlin Orphanage, and still more recently discovering a document showing something like Children's Aid activity in the mid 1880s! Proof that historical records, or lack of them, can "change" history. Information from newspaper clippings which are on file in the Grace Schmidt Room at the Kitchener Public Library. The township societies were coordinated in 1908 to have better service for the CAS in Waterloo County.

44. Spaetzel, *Kitchener Gospel Temple*, 5.

45. The other early leaders were the deacon Daniel Hostetler (1848–1924); Nathaniel Eby (1890–1961), nineteen in 1908, from a Mennonite (non-MBiC) background; and Aaron S. Shoemaker (1871–1928), who had a probationer's license from the MBiC in 1906. Nathaniel Eby had a career of ministry, as a pastor of a Pentecostal church in Picton, ON, and then in New York City. He is buried at the cemetery of First Mennonite Church in Kitchener.

46. *K-W Record*, (22 March 1950), n. p. Clipping in "Children's Aid" file, Grace Schmidt Local History Room, Kitchener Public Library, and Elmina Miller's obituary presumably from the *Kitchener Daily Record* of 1945, clipping in Catherine (Baer) Bowman "Scrapbook," 156, Box 6500, MCHT.

old. They had lodgers. Two of them, young adults, were Pentecostal. But the interesting fact is the Millers' religion: it is given as "Christian Miss. All.": that is, Christian and Missionary Alliance.

An obituary for Elmina Miller, who died 29 July 1945, stated the couple left Toronto for Florida in 1925, establishing a "resort" for seafarers at St. Petersburg called The Seamen's Haven. C. R. Miller died on Monday, November 16, 1953.[47]

M. E. Guy

Euphemia M. (Pool) Guy (1858–1941), was a widow at the time of the 1908 Conference. Her husband Jesse Samuel Guy (b. 1862) died in his thirty-fifth year in 1897 of TB while the couple were serving the Nottawasaga field based at Stayner. She was from a large Presbyterian family, mostly daughters, who grew up on a farm just south of Markham village. She met Jesse when he was stationed as a probationer on the Markham field in 1887. He was ordained in 1890 and served with Daniel Barkey and Christian Raymer under Peter Cober. Euphemia married Jesse on June 4, 1888. How a Scottish Presbyterian girl met a Mennonite holiness preacher (though in his case of English ancestry) is one of life's mysteries that nevertheless happens all the time.

Euphemia herself became a probationer in the MBiC in 1888. This happened in the earliest days of the MBiC's acceptance of women evangelist-preachers and the gradual transition of them from church-planting evangelists to preaching-evangelist pastors, though they were not directly called pastors. She was fully a partner with Jesse in evangelizing, judging by the number of reports they each sent to the *Gospel Banner*. She served with him at Dornoch and Kilsyth for four years (1888–1892), assisted by Ebenezer Anthony the first year and John N. Kitching in the fourth. From 1892 to 1895, they were at The Twenty, and from there they went to Nottawasaga mission, renamed Stayner field in 1896, with Charlie Krauth as helper the first year.[48] At her husband's death, Guy settled back in Markham as a

---

47. "Obituary: Mrs C. R. Miller," [*Kitchener Daily Record*,] (1945). In Florida, they were members of a Glad Tidings Assemblies of God Church, as recorded Chris Miller's obituary in *The Tampa Bay Times* (Nov 17, 1953). I thank Caleb Courtney for forwarding the text of this document, May 14, 2022.

48. Records for the stationing of Canada Conference personnel 1889 and 1890 are not available at this time, but that Jesse and Euphemia continued at Kilsyth and Dornoch is fairly clear.

local preacher or as a Conference evangelist some years. When the City Mission system of the Canada Conference was organized in 1898 and the Society in 1902, she was often an examiner for the women's reading course, almost the same as for the men, which led to a status created in 1905 of "Approved Ministering Sister," which she herself had. That stage was set off by a "dedication" ceremony that paralleled ordination. She was an exuberant worshipper, and who gave a "positive confession," as some call it now, several times to the *Gospel Banner* in the year after Jesse's death. The only evidence I have of her career after 1908 is that she spoke at the Markham MBiC sixtieth anniversary in 1937.[49]

M. M. Hisey

M. Martha Hisey also had a surname with multiple spellings possible (Haisi, Haisey, Heisey), but this form is correct. She came from the Brethren in Christ Nottawa District, from Creemore, Ontario. In the 1901 Canada census, she is listed among her five brothers and sisters along with her parents John and Frances Hisey and her father's mother, another Martha Hisey. Her birth date was given as May 9, 1883. All the family were recorded in the census as Dunkard (should be Tunker) except, intriguingly, the two Marthas, who were recorded as "Mennonite," almost certainly meaning Mennonite Brethren in Christ. The older Martha seems to have had an independent character—and wrote to the *Gospel Banner* from Nottawasaga, Ontario, on March 24, 1900 with a testimony.[50]

The younger Martha Hisey entered the City Mission Workers Society in 1906, appearing first in the *Conference Journal* in 1907. She was sent as a team leader to Winnipeg, with Maude McClelland as helper. To be sent that far away and immediately made a leader suggests she had more experience than Ontario Conference records show.

After resigning from the MBiC, Hisey immediately appeared as a candidate for missionary work to go to Liberia with the (now former) American Methodist Episcopal missionaries, John M. L. Harrow, John M. Perkins of Owen Sound and his German-Canadian wife Miriam (from Keppel Township, near Owen Sound) and four others. They participated in a convention in a Christian Workers Church which is assumed by Pentecostal writers at this point to be a Pentecostal assembly. This was on Concord Ave., Toronto,

---

49. McDowell and others, *Markham*, 36.
50. Family details: Canada Census 1901; Martha Hisey, "Letter," *GB* (30 April 1900) 15.

and was being led by a Mr. and Mrs. George Murray, remembered as "returned missionaries from India," though under what agency is not recorded by William Miller.[51] It was from this mission that "Sister Edmund [variant spelling, see below] (Hisey)" left for Liberia late in 1908 in later memory. Among her supporters was a Mr. Troupe, "a prosperous fruit farmer" from Vineland and occasionally a congregational delegate at MBiC Annual Conferences, who also gave for Ruby Reeve, an MBiC City Mission preacher who went to India in 1908.[52] The Berlin Pentecostal Assembly also sent Hisey funds in 1910.[53] I was happy to discover in the Missionary Church Inc. Archives in Mishawaka, Indiana, a friendly letter to Hisey from Emma Hostetler, Hisey's former co-worker in Winnipeg. At the time, Hostetler was in Nigeria with the MBiC mission, and Hisey was in Liberia, just up the coast, with the Pentecostals.[54] Yet they apparently kept peace between themselves, otherwise o than some of the men. I am also happy to note that Sam Goudie with C. N. Good paid a visit to the Daniel Hostetlers after the death of their daughter Emma in Nigeria from smallpox in 1912. Sam had known the deacon Daniel and Lydia since 1893 at least. The visit could have been a formality, but some relationships do not end even when good people disagree. Daniel Hostetler was given an obituary in the *Gospel Banner*, 16 years after leaving for the Pentecostal Assembly, which suggests the continuing high esteem by some in Kitchener for their former deacon.[55]

51. Lindsay, *Footprints*, 257, reports Rev. George A. and Mrs. Murray were advertised for a C&MA convention in June 1906 as being from Hebron, Palestine. Miller, *Canadian Pentecostals*, 42–43, claims there were "at least six Latter Rain/ Pentecostal congregations in Toronto" within a short period of time. George Fisher (b. 1853) was one of the ex-Salvation Army officers leading a Christian Workers Church and probably did cooperate with the movement from the Hebden Mission, but he cooperated with the C&MA, too, and other evangelical holiness efforts, such as the MBiC. Designation that a certain assembly was a "Latter-Rain" congregation could be over-precise.

52. Manuscript notes by Chambers, George A., PAOC Archives, Series 2, Writings/ Key Persons, 8. "Troupe" was probably James Troup; Moyer, *Vineland*.

53. Burton, *Pentecost in Kitchener*, 17. Martha Hisey also visited the new Vineland Pentecostal Assembly on an early furlough.

54. Contrary to Miller, *Canadian Pentecostals*, 71. Emma Hostetler never joined the Pentecostals, in fact in a letter to the Conference in *Ontario Conference Journal 1908*, 33, she specifically said she praised God "for my home church, for its teachings. I am still in line with it all . . . ." This was a natural disclaimer, given that her parents and younger sister had joined the Pentecostal Assembly in Berlin, in fact were hosting them. Emma's other sister, Rebecca Hostetler (1881–1944), was an MBiC city mission worker, and remained so for the rest of her life.

55. Sam Goudie, "Diary 1912," 22 April., "Obituary," *GB* (20 March 1924) 14.

In Liberia, the party was kindly received by the American Methodist Episcopal missionaries, and they were assisted to choose their own sphere for mission work.[56] Despite deaths and illness forcing some staff to return to North America, Hisey and another were able to survive on their own station, and see a move to God in 1913, just before her furlough. She returned to Liberia in 1915 with two more Canadian women for another term. In 1924 Martha Hisey married a Franklin Edmand, a widower insurance agent from Cashtown, Simcoe County. Both bride and groom stated their religious affiliation as "Christian Workers Pentecostal."[57]

L. Homes

This person has been the most shadowy of all. Since "L. Holmes" appeared in the *Conference Journal* among the city mission women, I assume these are one and the same. Even this does not take us far, since L. Holmes entered the City Mission ranks in 1907 as a helper to Sarah McQuarrie at the Ingersoll mission and resigned in 1908. She wrote some subjects of the first year of the reading course as reported in 1908. Who was she? What happened to her after 1908? Some *Journal* statements mention an otherwise unknown Louise Holmes. Charles Gingerich found in the Minute book of the Miller Lake appointment of the MBiC Bruce Peninsula field that late in 1906, "Letitia Holmes" was recommended and accepted as a City Mission Society worker.[58] Goudie prayed for a Letitia Ann Holmes at Pine Tree in 1892, and there was even a "Holmes Settlement" around there, but she was a married woman (b. 1860).[59] Since the CMWS accepted only single women, widowed or never married, either this Letitia was recently widowed ("Letitia Holmes" was recorded in the 1901 Canada survey from Arran Township with a husband John and several children), or this is an otherwise unknown Letitia. In 1922 W. John Holmes started as a helper on the Bruce Peninsula under Nicholas H. Schwalm, and he continued as a helper even up to 1933 at least. There was W. John Holmes (b. 1890) in Bruce County—he could be the man, but that gets us no further. As we have seen, probationers usually started out on fields close to their home area. No Letitia or Louise Holmes of the right age appears in the 1911 Canada

56. Kulbeck, *Pentecostal Assemblies*, 231–32.

57. Marriage information from Ontario Registry forwarded to me by Caleb Courtney. They were married by A G Ward September 3, 1924.

58. Gingerich, *Peninsula Pilgrims*, 35.

59. Gingerich, *Peninsula Pilgrims*, 15.

Census, but a Letitia Holmes, widow, Mennonite, was living with her son in the Bruce North census area in 1921. She was listed as 70 years old, whereas the earlier Letitia mentioned would only be sixty. This could still be the "L. Homes," if census takers were shy about asking a woman her age and made a guess or made an error.

M. E. Ward

Mary Ellen (Markle) Ward was born in Walkerton, Ontario, in 1882. I have not been able to find her in Canada census returns until 1911. Then she was reported as having an Irish background. She applied to the City Mission Society in 1904, and went to Winnipeg with Emma Hostetler in 1905, as we saw. She took part in the holiness prayer meetings in the Alliance storefront mission with Ward, Andrew H. Argue, McAlister and others and at the home of some people called Lockhart and saw people speaking in tongues. She is said to have spoken in tongues at this time as well, while Argue was in Chicago seeking for the evidence of being baptized with the Spirit.[60] She and Alfred G. Ward were married in Elmwood, Ontario, on October 16, 1907,[61] and some of the events up to September we know. It would be no joy to have your husband at the center of a dispute. From September 1908 we can follow Mary's movements by where her husband went: for example, Vineland Pentecostal Assembly in the fall of 1908 until 1910; evangelist in Markham in June 1911. In the 1920s he was pastor of a church first led by George E. Fisher at 8 Robert St. in Toronto as a Christian Worker's Church, a mission which about 1930 joined the Pentecostal Holiness Church and became known after 1931 as the Toronto Gospel Tabernacle and (in the 1940s) as the Evangelistic Centre.[62] A. G. Ward led early camp-meetings at Moyer's Grove, Dickson Hill, Markham, and participated in early discussions to organize Pentecostal work in Canada.[63] At some point they were in the United States, but from 1932 to 1938, they were back in Canada. A. G. Ward served as the second Secretary-Treasurer and Missionary Secretary of the PAOC. Eventually the family ended up in the US, where Mary and

---

60. C. Morse Ward, "Yet Once More," *Pentecostal Testimony* (May 1956) 4–5, 13.

61. *Pentecostal Testimony* (October 1957).

62. Campbell B. Smith notes, written about 1945, PAOC Archives, Mississauga, Ontario. Many of the congregation's moves can also be followed through the annual *Might's Toronto Street Directories*.

63. Kulbeck, *Pentecostal Assemblies*, 131–32. G. A. Chambers led camps outside of Vineland. Organization: Miller, *Canadian Pentecostals*, 417.

A. G.'s son, C. Morse Ward, became famous in AoG circles for his radio broadcast, "Revivaltime."[64]

THE FASCINATION WITH TONGUES

Having surveyed the lives of the eight people who resigned from the MBiC Ontario Conference in September 1908, what can be said about the whole event? One question that comes to the twenty-first century mind is, was this Pentecostal movement in the MBiC partly a generational shift? And I wonder about that in two ways. First, was the older generation of sanctified members and leaders able to transmit their understanding of the sanctification experience to the next generation successfully, and if not, was the search for a new kind of baptism in the Spirit one result? I have already mentioned my suspicion that a second generation struggles to live up to or reproduce the *experience* of the pioneers in many movements.[65] It is not the fault of older or younger generations. The past is swiftly becoming a foreign country to the next generation, and many factors that encouraged one generation to move together are lost sight of even by the first generation themselves (if they were ever fully aware of the major factors) and unrecognized by the next generation. Perhaps there is another factor at work. Why can we not transmit the truth and our experience? Probably because you can transmit teaching, but not an experience for very long or accurately. I suspect that many younger members of the MBiC could not reproduce the experience testified to by their seniors, felt inferior, and therefore failures. They either tried to fake the experience (as Chambers reported he and a pastor confessed to each other when he was assigned to be an MBiC evangelist),[66] or gave up entirely, joining other church movements whose demands they could manage. A third path might be that the younger generation discovers some experience that is fresh to them, almost inevitably with its own theological curve, such as joining something more radical still, or shifting to a liturgical church. A drift can even occur in the religious society into formalism, deism or agnosticism, for example. It happens![67]

We can test this theory crudely by looking at the ages of those who chose the Pentecostal path from the MBiC credentialed ministry. Four

64. Ward, *A. G. Ward.*

65. Rawlyk, "Religious Awakenings," 37–60, has interesting comparative comments on the difficulty of passing on revival experiences in the Maritime provinces.

66. Chambers, *Fifty Years*, 10.

67. Explored in Cook, *Historical Drift.*

(Miller, Fretz, Guy, and Letitia Holmes—if indeed she is the lady for whom Goudie prayed for healing) were in their forties. Four (Chambers, Doner, Ball, and Shoemaker) were in their thirties, while six (Hisey, Dresch, Pike, Sherk, Alfred, and Mary Ward) were in their twenties. R. E. Sternall was in his twentie as well.[68] The Eby cousins who joined later were retired men (Solomon, 78 and Amos, 70 in 1912). This suggests but does not prove that a younger generation had a predilection to being attracted to the new experience. A majority were not attracted, but we are looking for pre-disposing factors. Against this is the tendency of younger people to be movable, as their choices in life are still somewhat unformed or unsolidified. But a generation shift is still possibly a factor. No one in the MBiC ministry who was in their fifties or sixties joined the Pentecostals, for example.

Another sociological question would ask about the insider/outsider status of those moved by the Pentecostal message: did these people feel outside the mainstream of their church? Chambers probably felt outside, coming out of Methodism, and not doing well in his reading course exams, despite training in a holiness school (God's Bible School, Cincinnati, Ohio). A. G. Ward had just recently joined. Some of the city mission workers were newcomers to the MBiC or at least from the smaller centers, recruited somehow by Henry S. Hallman or J. N. Kitching to the city mission work.[69] As women, they could also feel the subordination which the male ministers assumed was fitting (which even many of the women possibly assumed, but did not enjoy experiencing).[70] This could be true, despite the Wesleyan encouragement of women in public ministry, which the MBiC officially embraced and tried to put into practice. Mrs. Guy defended the "weakness" of women as used by God anyway in her 1896 sermon at Elmwood camp-meeting.

On the other hand, members at Bethany in Kitchener who spoke in tongues, could have felt themselves to be at the center of the Conference

---

68. T. W. Brook may be another who joined the Pentecostals later (PHC in his case), but I have no sure age or proof of his identity yet.

69. This is a puzzle awaiting original research. How did the MBiC Ontario Conference find these women, or if you wish, they find the MBiC? Hallman was the editor of the magazine, but I do not see "want ads." Perhaps the camp-meetings were a prime recruitment ground. Or probably word of mouth from other young women (suggestion from Jim McDowell).

70. The writer has heard EMCC women, one of whom was even a city mission worker, repeat the practical but non-biblical argument that if the men wouldn't do the work, God could raise up women to do it instead as a temporary expedient.

in a large church that was rapidly growing. They need not have feelings of alienation from the denomination. They might still have felt outside mainstream Canadian religious life, as members of a Wesleyan-holiness and Mennonite denomination, double minority believers.

Were they urban-oriented rather than rural? While nearly all the MBiC members were rural, it is noteworthy that most of those who turned to the Pentecostal movement did so in an urban environment (the old "church of the disenfranchised" thesis): Winnipeg and Toronto at first, followed by Berlin, and Toronto-related Mt. Joy. Owen Sound inhabitants behaved as townspeople, but Vineland and Kilsyth were not urban. Questions worth studying.

CHURCH GROWTH VIEWPOINT:
(1) CONGREGATIONAL MEMBERSHIPS DISTURBED

An analysis of the statistics of the five congregations chiefly noticed in the Pentecostal encounter and the overall growth of the Ontario Conference suggests that the shortterm effect on these congregations was negative. The three established churches (Berlin, Vineland, and Markham) experienced a rise and fall of membership peaking about 1908/1909. The Berlin church was seeing a steady growth throughout the decades 1890 to 1930: this could be part of the inflow of rural revived Mennonites into the large town. Daniel and Lydia Hostetler and the Eby cousins are part of this trend of retirement and switching to town life. The Pentecostal excitement and fallout were superimposed on this general pattern. After the start of the Great War and the policy of conscription seemed certain, most Mennonite Churches saw a rise in baptisms and memberships among young men, for carelessness on this point could cost them exemption from war duty, if their convictions were that way.[71] The Mennonite Brethren in Christ in areas where non-resistant convictions were strong probably saw growth for this reason. About the middle of the War, the Ontario Conference started to see steady modest annual increases in membership until by the end of the war (1918) it had reached 1,867 adult members. Before the War, however, after subtracting the membership moving to Alberta (143 at the time of the transfer to the new Conference), the Canada/ Ontario Conference was edging up to 1,600 in 1903–1905 to a peak of 1,690 to 1,680 in 1906–1908. Most of the following years Conference membership dipped to around 1,600, right

---

71. Steiner, *Promised Lands*, 202–3.

after the time of the Pentecostal challenge. For the two conference mission/city mission fields, the East End Mission and the Owen Sound mission with its nearby rural appointments, Kilsyth and Dornoch/Squire, the Pentecostal message knocked them from a peak membership of 61 and 48 in 1906 to 14 and 34 by 1912. In the case of Kilsyth, although sporting a healthy rural membership of 37 in 1905 and a history of several zealous preachers raised through its work since the ministry of Janet Douglas, migration of many members to Alberta and the attitude of Archie G. Doner, their pastor in 1907–1908, harmed the viability of the church community and by 1911, no pastor was even appointed. Owen Sound recovered, but the East End Mission had to relocate to survive after the war, basically a re-plant as we would call it today. We have noted the attempt to establish missions in Manitoba was completely halted, though no membership had yet been formed. The sum of losses in membership for the five centers due to withdrawal, expulsion or "dropped" in "normal" years were not great, for Markham and Vineland from 0 to 4 each, and 0 to 8 at Berlin except 1906 when 24 members were lost these ways. But in 1909, the year after the Pentecostal confrontation, 72 members withdrew or were dropped, 35 in Markham alone.[72]

CHURCH GROWTH VIEWPOINT: (2) CONGREGATIONS BEGUN

If we examine the results of the Pentecostal movement in the MBiC from a Pentecostal point of view, the results were promising. Four congregations started, although two ran into problems later. In Markham, a congregation with at least 24 adults started suddenly in October 1908, probably more, judging by the "35" dropped or withdrawn between 1908 and 1909. Chambers took the majority of the attenders from the East End Mission, over 30 at least. In Vineland, a small group started with about 20 adults, and in Berlin, about 20 as well, although Chambers said they were only a "baker's dozen" when he became their pastor in 1912. An unknown number of members left the Owen Sound area MBiC churches as Pentecostals, some of whom John Ball was able to gather up almost ten years later. In 1911, as the Canada census found, all across Canada, only 513 people identified themselves as "Pentecostal," but better days were definitely to come. By

---

72. All these statistics are derived from the *Conference Journals of the Canada/Ontario Conference* for 1905 to 1912. Unfortunately, in 1910, only a summary was published in copies I have seen.

the 1921 census, 7,003 were reported. As usual, this figure represents only those willing to use the "Pentecostal" label, whereas some of every group might prefer to assume "Christian" or "Gospel People" or something like that. "Apostolic Brethren" should probably also be a Pentecostal category, especially in western Canada in 1921 (848 counted).

CHURCH GROWTH VIEWPOINT: (3) THEOLOGICAL FACTORS

Some revival seasons produce no new theology and the groups involved continue on, enjoying the blessing of fresh vigor in witnessing or good works. In the case of Canadian Pentecostalism, those who joined the despised Pentecostals were convinced of the new truth of the evidence of the baptism with the Spirit as biblical. They had to, to face the opposition from their community, and continue. The rhetoric, as I call it, of the holiness movement and the Alliance Deeper-life talk was a short step away from the Pentecostal synthesis: healing and missions, the Lord's imminent return, tongues and prophecy were all in people's storehouses, waiting, so to speak, for a catalyzing doctrine and experience to arrange a new paradigm of Christian understanding and practice. Both Chambers and Ward attended the radically holiness God's Bible School in Cincinnati, Ohio (so did William Seymour of Azusa!)[73] before encountering the MBiC. Sternall attended the Toronto Bible Training School (later Toronto Bible College) 1906–1907,[74] and then the Alliance school in Nyack at the height of its openness to Pentecostal teaching. The Mennonite Brethren in Christ began as a revival of experience-oriented Christian piety and became saturated with the "Holy Ghost line," as Goudie called it from the beginning to the end of his life. Goudie's Conference has always been attracted to any lively message of the work of the Holy Spirit, and responded in prayerful evangelistic and missionary obedience. Creeds have not played a great role in governing church life, not even the articles of faith in the *Discipline* or

---

73. Pointed out to the author by Jim Craig, PAOC Archives, 2018. Alvin Traub, later a Presiding Elder in Alberta also attended God's Bible School, 1904–1907; Reimer, *Alvin Traub*, 11–12.

74. Along with a brother with the initial "I" probably Irvin or Ervin, *TBTS Recorder* (March 1907), or possibly an error for "Alvin." Goudie recorded a "bro. Irvine Stirnal" traveling with him to New Dundee and preaching January 1912, Sam Goudie, "Diary 1912," 23, 25 January. An "I. Sternall" was a member of the Gospel Herald Society in the Pennsylvania Conference around this time, W. G. Gehman, "PE Reports," *GB* (4 May 1911) 12.

Constitution.⁷⁵ Glenn Gibson noticed this as well: "I am convinced that we are more of a relational than a doctrinal denomination."⁷⁶ Goudie's own attempt to promote doctrine by a catechism did not attract much attention either. The Methodist organization was strong for the evangelistic purposes of the revived Mennonites that composed the MBiC, but vulnerable to change if other experiences became promoted.

OUTCOME OF THEIR LIVES: GOD RECEIVES GLORY

What can we say about the outcome of those who left the MBiC for the Pentecostal movement? Did they turn out well? Was God glorified in them? The answer is, mostly. Their communities, at least, honored the zeal and character of most of them.

One (G. A. Chambers) became a prominent leader in the Pentecostal movement in Canada, in the PAOC in particular. One became a prominent church planter in Ontario (John Ball) and later became associated with the PAOC; one a courageous Pentecostal missionary in Liberia (Martha Hisey), but her career there ended before the PAOC was formed in 1919, at least she is not listed as one of theirs. She and her husband continued in the PAOC as members. One man (Archibald G. Doner) moved to the C&MA rather than the Pentecostal movement as such. One became a competent elder in one Pentecostal assembly (Christian R. Miller), but perhaps left the Pentecostal movement in later years, only to return to a Pentecostal church in Florida. Amos Eby turned to the Lutherans, but his cousin Solomon was warmly remembered in the Berlin Pentecostal Assembly/KGT. Two women are scarcely heard from again (Euphemia Guy and Letitia Holmes). Mary Ellen Ward's contribution to the ministry in the Pentecostal movement in Canada and the PAOC is to be inferred by her husband's success. Unless they were missionaries, the MBiC women seemed swallowed up by their husbands' Pentecostal careers, but that is true of many MBiC women who supported their husbands' MBiC careers as well. On the whole, a moderately to fairly successful record of Christian ministry. The MBiC missed the services of these people.

---

75. The Pentecostal crisis of 1908 could be taken as demonstration that articles of faith did function to govern church life at least this once. Seen from the stand point of a few generations, however, rather large doctrinal changes have been accepted by the MBiC/ UMC/ MCoC/ EMCC.

76. Glenn Gibson, letter to the author, 28 November 1987.

Of those who were dismissed earlier, Mary Ann Dresch (b. 18 September 1884) became a missionary from about 1913, to Natal, South Africa. She served among the Zulu people with her husband, American Joseph K. Blakeney, under the Pentecostal Mission in South and Central Africa. They seem to have married about 1912.[77] Joseph traveled with an exploratory Pentecostal team to the southern Congo in 1915. After brief stints pastoring churches in Russell and Hamilton in Ontario, the couple transferred their efforts to southern Congo in 1921 under the Assemblies of God. From 1925, the family settled in Kitchener and attended the Kitchener Pentecostal Assembly (later called KGT), a member congregation of the PAOC from May 24, 1919.[78] Mary was the mother of seven children, one daughter at least being born in Natal in 1915.[79]

Of the young men, Jesse Ramer (Raymer) Sherk (1880–1953) and William Pike, there is also some news. Jesse, born in Nottawasaga Township, Simcoe County to a Mennonite family, married Emma L. Shelley in Toronto from Port Elgin and had six children, who were born in typical MBiC places such as Markham and Kitchener. In the 1921 census the family members were in Waterloo town, and listed as Pentecostals. He was buried in Kitchener's Woodland Cemetery. William Raymer Pike (1888–1954) taught school in Markham, as did his outstanding uncle, MBiC member and committee member for 50 plus years, Isaac Pike. William married Elsie Beall. He moved to Winnipeg, Manitoba, in 1909 and being ordained in a church there, taught and was principal in schools of the Home of the Friendless institution from 1911 to around 1928. For quite some time he was associated with the "Holiness Movement" (probably the Holiness Movement Church), and moved to British Columbia, where he served in the United Church of Canada. He died in Campbell River on Victoria

---

77. Snyder, *Schneider*, 328B, says Mary Ann Blakeney had seven children in all, although three had died by 1939. Mary A. Blakeney File, PAOC Archives, Mississauga, Ontario confirms this on her application for ministerial recognition when she was 48 (that is, about 1932).

78. *Canadian Pentecostal Testimony* (December 1920) [4]; Burton, *Pentecost in Kitchener*, 30.

79. Obituary of their daughter, Marjorie Priscilla (Blakeney) Hessenaur, who died in Oklahoma in 2011: www.waterloo.ogs.on.ca/mem_only/newspapers/Waterloo%20Region%20Record%20Newspaper%20Obituaries%202011-Sep.pdf. Joseph (1884–1961) and Mary Ann (d. 1952), Priscilla and a brother, Paul, are buried at Memory Gardens, near Breslau, Waterloo Region. Mary Ann's mother was Caroline Diefenbacher, whose father was German-born, and her father was Jacob Dresch, who had been born in Baden, Germany.

Island.[80] In other words, though he did not serve in a Pentecostal environment, he gave a lifetime of service to God and neighbor.

Another MBiC worker, Emma Good, dropped in 1908, is not identified with Pentecostalism. One time a member at Bethany, Kitchener, she was employed by the Home of the Friendless in Winnipeg before Pike was there. She managed to keep the lines of communication open with the Ontario Conference, though there was a glitch at the start. The President of the City Mission Workers, J. N. Kitching, made friendly reference to her: in his 1908 report he mentioned that "[s]ince Sister E. Good has gone to Winnipeg and has remained there without my consent, as President, I am therefore unable to use her in the work. I pray God bless her in her present work and calling."[81] In 1911, Kitching reported she had written a letter, and in 1921, Emma Good even addressed the Ontario Conference on her work.[82]

The missionary to Jews, David Fretz of Vineland, and others from nearby holiness churches in the Niagara peninsula visited the Hebdens's mission in Toronto in 1907–1908, and came back impressed by and convinced of the Pentecostal message. When the MBiC Ontario Conference rejected the tongues doctrine, the same response occurred in Vineland as in Berlin and Markham: prayer meetings and almost immediately, the formation of a Pentecostal fellowship. David Fretz owned an old schoolhouse on Victoria Avenue at Rittenhouse Road, Vineland, which was offered to the new group.[83] He is remembered as an important contributor to the Vineland Pentecostal Assembly locally. Fretz did not stay Pentecostal because by 1921, he and his second wife, Maggie, naming themselves "Pentecostal Saints" in 1911, were back to identifying as Mennonites in 1921, living in Toronto.

Here, too, there is an appearance of good. God knows the heart, of course. The MBiC had perceived themselves as God's radical obedient followers with a "full gospel of full salvation." There may have been some pride in that. Mennonites thought so at least—their usual charge against pietistic revival testimonies. Now in 1908, a new movement that saw itself as the real

---

80. www.mhs.mb.ca/docs/people/pike-wr.shtml.

81. *Ontario Conference Journal 1908*, 32.

82. *Ontario Conference Journal 1911*, 13; *Ontario Conference Journal 1921*, 29. Emma was a sister of Nancy Storms.

83. For location, see Gillham, *Vineland*, 11; for Fretz's ownership, see Miller, *Canadian Pentecostals*, 45.

radical "cutting edge" (our term) for God outflanked the holiness movement everywhere, MBiC included, and perhaps the MBiC could think of itself more soberly, as it ought to think. In Goudie's case perhaps for the first time a note of defensiveness creeps into his reports as we shall see.

Everek Storms said that in 1908 five ministers and about eighty MBiC members withdrew and joined the Pentecostal movement.[84] He was probably estimating from Conference records, or more specifically, losses of members in the three main churches affected which he gives as Markham, Vineland and Kitchener. He perhaps ignored therefore the East End Mission in Toronto, the weakened Owen Sound Mission and the Kilsyth field. I don't know which five ministers he counted; probably the four men who resigned and David Fretz. With the two Eby cousins leaving after 1912, Storms concluded seven ministers were lost to the Conference. As we have seen, if one counts ordained and licensed personnel, male and female, the number is higher, especially if we are willing, as Storms was, to go beyond the narrow September incident. In an earlier study of the crisis, I concluded that, in fact, eight male (now I would say eleven) and six female workers were lost, nearly a quarter of the licensed work force of the Conference, in addition to people like Reuben Sternall and T. W. Brook, who were deterred from continuing with the MBiC when the ruling was confirmed by the October MBiC GC.[85]

One final note. The 1908 dedication of the new Bethany building was commemorated by a special photograph—one of those immense panoramas that conferences like to take—"Hey, everybody, let's go outside for a photograph!" So they all stood outside on the Lancaster St. front and steps of Bethany's new building. It was one of the larger MBiC group photos. Usually Sam Goudie is present in such photographs, in the center as time went on, but in the early ones, he could be at the back or the side. I don't know what to make of it, but though I have searched this photograph carefully even in digital enlargements, I do not see Sam anywhere. It is speculation, but I wonder if the stress of the Conference issue was so great he just couldn't make it outside.[86]

84. Storms, *United Missionary Church*, 92.

85. Fuller, "Holiness People," 29.

86. The MCHT collection has several copies of this photograph; it would have been somewhat expensive. It is probable the photograph commemorated the Dedication of the Building on the Sunday previous to the Annual Conference, hence the large number of people, but Goudie was the featured preacher in the morning—he was there, but not in the photograph.

THE SEVENTH GENERAL CONFERENCE, BROWN CITY, MICHIGAN, OCTOBER 1908

Brown City was a small town with a population between six and seven hundred in the decade 1900–1910. It is mostly in Sanilac County at the base of the "thumb" of Michigan,[87] similar in size to Stouffville. It was fast becoming one hub of the MBiC in Michigan and hosted a camp-meeting for decades. As before, the quadrennial General Conference had delegates chosen at the various Annual Conferences of the MBiC. Ontario still had a large delegation of ministers and congregational people, eight in all. Of the ordained elders, there were John N. Kitching, Cyrus N. Good, and Peter Cober. Two "laymember" delegates were elected: Isaac Pike and Jacob B. Shantz. Alternates were Silas Cressman for the ministers and Ebenezer Dunnington for the laymembers. Sam Goudie and Ephraim Sievenpiper, the two Presiding Elders were *ex officio* members of the GC, as was the *Gospel Banner* editor, Henry S. Hallman.

Ebenezer Anthony, one of the Ontario-ordained Presiding Elders from the Michigan Conference, was elected the chair of this GC. All the Presiding Elders had the privilege of reporting briefly on their districts, and as in Annual Conferences in which resolutions from the Quarterly Conferences (the fields) were "entertained," so at General Conference, resolutions from the Annual Conferences were accepted for discussion. Goudie spoke for the Ontario Conference East District and reported no problems. The row at Bethany a month before? The eight resignations? No mention. They were not to be hidden though, and in 1912, Goudie referred to them, now a few years past.

Of interest to us are two requests from the Ontario Conference, the request for "more definite interpretation" of the two articles that touched on "Entire Sanctification," and the other was again "to consider the advisability of a Bishop."[88] Among resolutions from the other Conferences was an interesting one for us in the twenty-first century, from the Pacific Conference to revise the *Discipline* "so that recognition may be given our sister workers as members of Annual Conference,"[89] a question that sometimes came up in Ontario as well.

But first, the Reading Course. Pacific Conference wanted the whole course to be wrapped up in one year instead of three. (Not granted.)

---

87. Wikipedia, "Brown City, Michigan."
88. *Seventh General Conference 1908*, 10.
89. *Seventh General Conference 1908*, 10.

Michigan wanted a suitable theology book again, while this time the Indiana and Ohio Conference wanted to replace the *Lessons in Holiness* with a book on homiletics, and the general theology book (Henry T. Sell's *Bible Study by Books*) with a "good theology." (Implication: Sell's was not.) A "good theology" book was to elude the MBiC for a long time, in fact until today perhaps, certainly as long as the Reading Course continued. The MBiC/ UMC had to read books by Methodists, Nazarenes or Baptists, all of which were good, but had compatibility problems for some doctrines of the church. The obvious desirability of having one written by an MBiC member was never fulfilled, though J. A. Huffman finally published an extended "syllabus" of his theology classes, but not until 1959.[90] Goudie himself worked on a specialized sort of systematic theology project in the 1920s as we shall see.

Nebraska now wanted "Horch's" *Church History*.[91] Apparently Fisher's *Church History* had not been replaced in 1904 after all. The complaint about many text books was often that they were out of print, but theology was also behind the dislike of those recommended by some sections of the Church. Ontario did not have a textbook resolution for this GC. It had a real-world problem with another theology splitting the ranks.

Ontario's first resolution was dealt with carefully in a private session, and in a move similar to that at Berlin, "all ordained ministers and probationers members [GC's spelling] in charge of a work" were made advisory members, with the result that on the 31 October an uncommon recorded motion was passed that "the uniform interpretation be upheld since it has

---

90. Huffman, *Christian Doctrine*. The next one was perhaps Gerig, *Eden to Eternity*, also the result of collected theology lecture notes. Huffman also published a book on selected theological topics called *The Meaning of Things* in 1953. The Missionary Church issued a commendable study guide that included brief articles of systematic theology edited by Ralph Ringenberg, *Believers*. Pamphlets on certain issues were frequently reprinted in both the US and Canada, notably on *The Assurance of the Believer*, and *The Gifts of the Holy Spirit*. In Canada, apart from Goudie's catechism, the next work was in pamphlet form, Delsaut, *Christ at the Centre*, and the discipleship standard, "The Way of Jesus," developed in collaboration with national EMCC staff 2005–2018. This comment does not disparage theological contributions along the way by many wise pastor-theologians and Bible College teachers. A systematic theology for the denomination is something still needed.

91. It's not obvious what book Nebraska wanted. John Fletcher Hurst's one volume *A Brief History of the Church* of 1893 could possibly be meant, not his massive 2 volume book of 1900. He was a bishop of the Episcopal Methodist Church in the US. It is more probable the Nebraska request meant Mennonite John Horsch's 1903 *A Short History of Christianity*, which had just been published.

been uniform with a few exceptions." I guess you had to be there to know what the "uniform interpretation" was. It was of course, some form of the standard quasi-Wesleyan holiness view that the baptism with the Spirit was received by faith subsequent to justification and was the same as or a component of the experience of sanctification. The ambiguity of the expression probably held together the preferences of the "Keswick/ Christian and Missionary Alliance" Pennsylvania Conference and the more thoroughly theologically holiness Conferences. The thirty "yeahs" were all named and the one "nay" as well, though how that was known is a puzzle because the delegate was noted as being "absent"! He was Ebenezer Dunnington of Kilsyth, Sullivan Township, Grey County, Ontario, whose sister Mary Dunnington was a City Mission Worker from 1901 to 1917. And as usual Goudie had personal acquaintance with the Dunningtons: he had tea with Ebenezer's brother James Dunnington at Squire before Goudie moved on to see Ebenezer himself just a month before the GC on the Quarterly Conference tour.[92] I am also puzzled because it appears that all the Ontario delegates, alternate or otherwise were present and voted.

I would suppose that the recorded vote was to demonstrate to those back home that the decisions of Sam Goudie, the Reference Committee, and the Ontario Conference were not just the quirk of a stubborn few who wouldn't listen to the Holy Ghost, but the collective confession of the MBiC community who were also trying to discern the mind of the Spirit. Interestingly, Henry Schlichter Hallman, who lost his job as editor of the *Gospel Banner* at this GC, voted with the majority also. He had just been "passed" after examination, after his refusal in February, but submission in mid-September.[93] Charles Henry ("C. H.") Brunner (1864–1948) of the Pennsylvania Conference was elected *Banner* editor for the next GC term, starting 1 January 1909.

The Pacific Conference request was not accepted. Women workers were still not allowed to be members of Annual Conferences.[94] Elder S. Goudie was elected to the chair of the next GC, in 1912.

---

92. Sam Goudie, "Diary 1908," 17 September.

93. *Seventh General Conference 1908*, vote: 21, examination: 20. The denominational Executive Committee in a meeting 14 September in Berlin went on record that "we are grieved with our Editor for persisting in refusing to comply . . . by avoiding to publish such articles in the *Banner* as tend to controversies and misunderstandings more than for unity in the bonds of peace."

94. *Seventh General Conference 1908*, 23.

The General Conference decision may have settled the doctrinal direction of the MBiC for the present, but individual members voted with their feet, as we have seen. In the Eighth GC at Bethlehem, Pennsylvania, in October 1912, Goudie reported as Presiding Elder of the East District of the Ontario Conference,

> We have ten circuits and missions. During this term many were led away by the "Tongues Movement" together with four ordained ministers [Chambers was not ordained, but Fretz was] and some sister workers. Prospects are better now. The ministry is united and all in active work stand together. Our ministry is unconditional and mostly young.[95]

The fact that Goudie in 1912 could say most of his ministers were young suggests a generational shift was not sufficient as a factor in the attraction to the Pentecostal position. From my study, he was downplaying the losses, but as I have noted before, he is unusual among denominational officials in acknowledging problems publicly at all, as he had been in assessing the results of his fields' protracted meetings. It is not common or easy for organizations to report staff leaving because of differing views. In the church we have an additional awkward problem that in our disagreements, we often imply others are not listening to God. In the 1912 GC, at which Goudie was the chair, he also referred to "difference of conditions and circumstances existing with which they [that is, the presiding elders] must cope . . . and the Eastern Conferences subjected to keen competition in denominational and consequently doctrinal lines . . ."[96]

---

95. *Eighth General Conference 1912*, 13.

96. *Ninth General Conference 1916*, 20. The Executive Committee had had to meet in Cleveland, Ohio, on 14 November 1911 to discuss "concerning doctrine, failure of associate editors in their duties and apparent failure of the Executive Committee to come to the help of the publishers," (p. 23). Goudie was a member of that five-person Publishing Committee.

9

Meanwhile Back in Ontario

Picking Up the Pieces 1908–1912

WE HAVE TAKEN A long time to chronicle and interpret the 1908 crisis in the Mennonite Brethren in Christ Church in Ontario. The crisis had some further stages of note for Goudie. Soon after the General Conference in Brown City, Michigan, the very next Wednesday, in fact, the song leader at Mt. Joy, Dan W. Raymer, called on the telephone to alert Sam that there was "trouble at Mt. Joy over some people leaving the church." Goudie borrowed a horse and rig and with his daughter, drove down to Mt. Joy. They stopped in for tea at Moses Weber's. The next Sunday, Goudie preached at Mt. Joy in the morning, but allowed John Ball to preach his farewell sermon in the evening meeting, which Sam attended. The very next day, with C. N. Good and Livy on the way as soon as possible, Sam was looking around for a horse for his friend. On Tuesday, Sam attended a prayer meeting at Mt. Joy, and on Wednesday, he and Eliza again went the eleven kilometers to Mt. Joy with Dr. Storey's horse and rig to visit some more.[1]

In his Presiding Elder's Report on Quarterly Conference meetings at the end of 1908 at Scott, Stouffville and Markham, he reported about Markham in particular, sounding a little more confident the crisis was past.

---

1. Sam Goudie, "Diary 1908," 7, 11, 12, 13, 14 October.

This field has gained considerable notoriety in our conference during the past, especially since last New Year's time. Though we lost a few pilgrims here, yet the Lord is abundantly blessing the work and under the faithful and earnest labor of their new Pastor, C. N. Good, the work is going on. The financial reports were better than ever before. The Lord has given us a good deacon to fill the vacancy and under the special blessing of God, I fearlessly predict a revival all over the field. Sunday was a red-letter day. Glory!²

Goudie also reported cryptically that Vineland "in some respects I think is better . . . than for a long time."³ He is still clearly responding to the loss of David Fretz and other members. Of the East End Mission, Toronto, he wrote more extensively:

> The few pilgrims at this mission are standing by their pastor and the work nobly and we predict a bright future for them. The attendance at the Sunday services is increasing. The financial part of the mission has been left in bad shape and we shall have to come to the help of the pilgrims and help them over the present difficulty. Pastor Fidler is well received and is doing good work.⁴

Goudie had no disturbances to report at the other two sites in Toronto, at Bethel (West End) where Christian Raymer was stationed (he of the *Latter Rain and Fog*), and the Dundas St. Mission "where Sisters [Edith] Evans and McLelland [Maud McClelland] are doing good work. This was a real treat to us."⁵ McClelland had been in Winnipeg but showed no Pentecostal inclinations apparently. Edith Evans, from a Methodist congregation in Puslinch Township (Ellis Chapel), Wellington County (but converted in the Guelph MBiC mission), and the Hespeler MBiC, later went to Nigeria for a long missionary career there. In 1909, Sam had the pleasure of ordaining his older brother David Wanner Goudie as a deacon for the Bethel Mission (Toronto West).⁶

---

2. Sam Goudie, "PE's Report," *GB* (7 January 1909) 10.

3. Sam Goudie, "PE's Report," *GB* (7 January 1909) 10.

4. Sam Goudie, "PE's Report," *GB* (11 February 1909) 12.

5. Sam Goudie, "PE's Report," *GB* (11 February 1909) 12. In April, Goudie was still praying for restoration "to its former condition and may it, as in the past, be a soul-saving station," *GB* (29 April 1909) 11.

6. Harvey Fretz has uncovered Evans' family, church background and missionary career including her marriage in 1918 to Ira W. Sherk, and presented it in pubic lectures, so far unpublished. On D. W. Goudie's ordination as a deacon, see Sam Goudie, "Presiding Elder's Report," *GB* (20 May 1909) 14. I do not know the foundation of an assertion I

Goudie had become one of the four associate editors of the *Gospel Banner* along with Oliver B. Snyder (Michigan), Abraham B. Yoder (Indiana and Ohio) and Nicholas W. Rich (Nebraska), and as such, had the privilege and responsibility of contributing to the *Gospel Banner*. In February 1909, in a brief but scripture-filled article titled "Faithful," he quoted 5 texts, commented and then quoted five more, with particular reference to "faithful ministers." "Living for Christ" was another in March, a simple exhortation only three paragraphs long on Phil 1:21.[7] In April he contributed "We Would See Jesus," a non-controversial mediation which asked the question, "How do we see Jesus now?" and answered: (1) by the Word of God through the Holy Spirit; (2) through every Christian, every congregation; and (3) through every preacher. The same issue contained a report on the City Mission Workers Society convention at St. Catharines held that month at which he and "Bro. Raymer [Lewis P. Ramer] of Vineland" attended, that was tinged with echoes of the recent crisis, however: "Elder H. S. Hallman, ex-president [of the City Mission], gave us Bible readings each afternoon on the theme of Pentecost. Our hearts feasted on the good old doctrine of Holiness held up, and surely everyone who enjoyed the Baptism of the Holy Ghost felt the fire burning in their hearts."[8]

Once somebody starts referring almost nostalgically to something as "the good old doctrine" or "the old-fashioned" this or that, we know a decline or challenge has been perceived. In many early Pentecostal testimonies, as in many holiness ones, people could fall into the habit of describing events as "old-fashioned Methodism [or whatever]." The speaker is looking back, not forward, nor satisfied with the present. In Quarterly Reports in April, Goudie wrote of visiting Vineland and Sherkston, feeling a little sentimental perhaps at the decline of the Sherkston appointment from when he was still a bachelor there: "God bless dear old Sherkston." He referred to having fellowship with the River Brethren (Tunkers), visiting Titus Sherk and his wife, navigating the muddy roads, and feeling sad that though the attendance was holding "the numbers at best are few."[9] Of

---

have seen that D. W. was a deacon earlier. He had been a steward, a similar function some might confuse with a deacon in other traditions.

7. Sam Goudie, "Faithful," *GB* (25 February 1909) 4; *GB* (11 March 1909) 4. In the latter issue, Goudie also wrote (p. 12) that there were "efforts to stir up a feeling of dissatisfaction among the pilgrims."

8. Susie Bowman, "City Mission Report," *GB* (15 April 1909) 12.

9. Sam Goudie, "PE's Report," *GB* (29 April 1909) 11.

course Goudie was getting older, but not *that* old. In April 1909, he was only forty-two![10]

The Conference had decided to hold a camp-meeting in the Vineland area in 1909—only the second time they did in a century of camps. The selection was deliberate to counter the Pentecostal attraction and A. G. Ward who was pastor of the Pentecostal assembly in Vineland 1908–1910. Chambers was the next pastor. There was a Pentecostal camp-meeting at Vineland in 1911.[11] That also looks like a quite deliberately chosen counter action.

In announcing the Vineland camp for 2–9 June, Goudie wrote,

> Our coming together will not be to discuss theological questions upon which we may differ but our object and aim will be to lift up Jesus as a complete Saviour for a fallen race, and we expect souls to be saved, others reclaimed and sinners sanctified after a scriptural manner and baptized with the Holy Ghost . . . We predict victory for this camp in the name of the Lord.[12]

In a July issue, Goudie claimed his prophecy fulfilled: "The brethren and sisters in the ministry were united in their teaching. The trumpet had no uncertain sound . . . Oh, how different this is compared to what we have been forced to witness in the past when there was division in the camp."[13]

This is a significant admission. In August, Goudie was again reporting on the Quarterly Conferences at Vineland and the two sites in Toronto. His comments on the East End Mission contain a few curiosities.

> Though the numbers are not large at this mission, yet I believe there is a slight increase even in numbers. The Lord was manifestly with us. It makes me feel sad when I think of the very interesting mission we had here not many years ago, and to think that through the inconsistent and unwise methods of a few people the

---

10. Age does not seem to be all. Charles G. D. Roberts was only twenty-six when he lamented in a poem "Hands of chance and change have marred or moulded, or broken/ busy with spirit or flesh, all that I most have adored;" thoughts set in motion by changes he saw near the Tantramar Marshes, in New Brunswick. "The Tantramar Revisited," (first published 1886), Ross, *Poets*, 3–5.

11. Chambers' memories of his own lengths of stay in his early Pentecostal days are confusing, and he calls this the first Pentecostal camp-meeting (there had been two in Moyer's Grove 1909 and 1910), but he is correct on the year of this camp-meeting at Jordan Station, Chambers, *Fifty Years*, 19–20.

12. Sam Goudie, "[Announcement]," *GB* (20 May 1909) 14.

13. Sam Goudie, "Vineland Report," *GB* (1 July 1909) 13.

work has been so torn and blighted; but I am looking forward to brighter and better days. Bro. Thos. Kitching was elected delegate to Annual Conference, and Sister Grant was elected delegate to the Sunday School Convention.[14]

Only unwise "methods"? Goudie is rather mild to describe the doctrinal shift that way. Thomas Kitching could be a relative of the MBiC City Mission President (his father was a Thomas Kitching), and "Sister Grant" connects to the "Mrs. Grant" to whom Chambers said he handed his mission that he started in rivalry to the MBiC after October 1908. On Chambers's reckoning, he left Toronto after a little over eighteen months. It seems that this lady left the MBiC mission not long after Goudie's report.

Goudie's attention to the losses of the crisis showed in yet another report from Markham, where his friend C. N. Good was working hard:

> This field has gone through a strange experience during the past year but in spite of it all, the work has prospered more and better than almost anytime in the past . . . Fifty-four souls (adults) were received into church fellowship during the year [1909 conference reports were on hand for precise numbers!][15]

He did not say how many left, but about thirty-five did, as we saw.

PEARL ELIZABETH GOUDIE (1892–1910)

With a man like Sam Goudie, silences can mean much. He visited his district for their Quarterly Conferences, maybe sent a deputy sometimes, such as his Vice-Presiding Elder, Joshua Fidler, from the East End Mission. The reports kept coming. But the very day his report appeared on March 31 from a winter round of Quarterly Conferences, the *Gospel Banner* also printed a brief obituary for Eliza and Sam's daughter, Pearl, dead from spinal meningitis on her eighteenth birthday, March 20, 1910, which was also her parent's twenty-first wedding anniversary. She was well and in church one Sunday, and dead the next.[16]

> Sister Pearl E. Goudie died at her late residence, 33 Mill St., Stouffville, Ont., March 20, 1910 aged 18 years. Funeral from the residence, Tuesday, March 22, to Stouffville cemetery for

---

14. Sam Goudie, "PE's Report," *GB* (12 August 1909) 13.

15. Sam Goudie, "PE's Report," *GB* (30 September 1909) 11.

16. Eleanor (Goudie) Bunker, telephone interview by the author, 24 March 2011, from Minden Hills, ON.

internment. Memorial service to be held at Mennonite church Stouffville, Sunday Mar 27 at 2:30 pm. Funeral service was conducted by R. J. McLaren, assisted by Elder D. Brittain. She leaves a loving father and mother and two brothers to mourn her loss.[17]

Though this disease kills suddenly, we can imagine the efforts of the parents to help her get well. The Goudie's believed in "divine healing" and doubtless prayed for their daughter. They also believed in conventional medicine and used home remedies.[18]

Sam and Eliza were happy parents. In March 1902, on their wedding anniversary, Sam put in his diary, "I thank God for a good wife & a dear little girl 10 years old."[19] Pearl does not often appear in the diary, except when there were family picnics, or occasional school functions. Sometimes when she was older, he would mention going with her to the mission (in Toronto), or that she and Eliza were going shopping. In 1908, in Stouffville, he mentions the soon-to-be-sixteen Pearl going in the afternoon for what we might call a "sleepover" at her friend Louie Stouffer's on a day of "rain, rain, rain" as Goudie wrote. Spring cleaning had begun in the Goudie household that morning. Pearl had ironing to do when she returned and the cleaning continued.[20] Later that year, Pearl traveled with her father by boat to Hamilton, then to Beamsville by the Hamilton, Grimsby and Beamsville electric train, on a Quarterly Meeting tour to Vineland (and St. Catharines). They stayed with family friends and returned with a basket of cherries.[21] In September, Pearl went with her father to the 4th of Uxbridge meeting, and with Fletcher and her father to Bethesda. These reports of visits were not common, but casually mentioned as part of the family routine.[22]

One published article refers to Pearl's death from the Goudies in 1910. Sam and Eliza wrote thanking friends for their numerous cards and letters of condolence.[23] In June, Goudie sent to the church magazine the first part of a four-part meditation, "He is Able" on the subject of God's omnipotence. As Euphemia (Pool) Guy announced she had "the victory" soon after her

17. "GOUDIE. IN STOUFFVILLE, Ont.," *GB* (31 March 1910) 14.

18. Eleanor Bunker remembers they bought lemons and used the juice and baking soda to treat upset stomachs.

19. Sam Goudie, "Diary 1902," 20 March.

20. Sam Goudie, "Diary 1908," 7–10 March.

21. Sam Goudie, "Diary 1908," 3–6 July.

22. Sam Goudie, "Diary 1908," 3, 13 September.

23. Sam and Eliza Goudie, "Thanks," *GB* (28 April 1910) 12.

husband's death by TB in 1897, so I imagine this was Goudie's way of fighting back at the attacks of grief and discouragement.[24] In 1911, no special writings of Sam appear in the *Gospel Banner*, just "PE's Reports," except one late in the year.[25] In May 1912, however, Sam recorded that "This eve Allan & I wheeled up to the cemetery." No reason was given, but the Stouffville municipal graveyard was where Pearl was buried.[26]

Sam and Eliza's granddaughter Eleanor (Goudie) Bunker preserves Pearl's New Testament (from a Stouffville Sunday School teacher J[acob] Boadway), school notes, textbooks and her senior 4th (grade 8) report card from King Edward School, Toronto. The Bunker family also preserves an album of postcards from friends and relatives collected by Pearl, a common hobby at the time. It would seem that Eliza Goudie kept these tokens of her daughter's life. During her illness, no one was allowed in the house to visit Pearl except Jacob ("Jake") Reesor, a young man who had had hopes of marrying Pearl.[27]

Not much is recorded about Sam in 1911 other than routine Presiding Elder's reports in the *Gospel Banner*, recounting his Quarterly Meeting tours, or of those he sent to deputize for him. Perhaps he did not have energy for much else in the year following Pearl's death. He generally commented on the attendances he met on the field (sometimes affected by weather or sickness in the area), results of the annual Home Missionary meetings and offerings, and occasional special meetings on a field, for which he often assisted even for five or six days at a time. The Manitoulin Island appointments were cut off for a period each year when the ferries stopped running in the fall, so Goudie was able to visit about two times a year. He noted, joking, that he received such a welcome on the Island, that perhaps other fields would do the same if he stopped seeing them every three months![28] Goudie noted the summertime flight of Toronto's city dwellers was already well established, as people wanted to avoid the heat, dust and smells of the city for the countryside. In the trip between Toronto and Vineland he stopped in at

24. Sam Goudie, "God is Able," *GB* (2 June 1910) 4; *GB* (9 June 1910) 5; *GB* (16 June 1910) 4; *GB* (17 November 1910) 4.

25. Sam Goudie, "Getting Even—With What?" *GB* (21 December 1911) 2.

26. Sam Goudie, "Diary 1912," 15 May.

27. Eleanor (Goudie) Bunker, telephone interview, 24 February 2011. Pearl's books: Eleanor (Goudie) Bunker, notes for the author, March 2011, P. 3, from Minden Hills, ON. Memory of Jake Reesor: from his daughter, Mildred (Reesor, Thomson) James, telephone conversation with the author, January 2011, from Markham, ON.

28. Sam Goudie, "PE Report," *GB* (29 June 1911) 12.

the newest city mission in Hamilton, where Clara Brubacher and Melinda Devitt had been assigned a few months earlier. He was especially interested in seeing people whom he had known as members in Vineland twelve years before.[29] In several circuits, Goudie refers to discouraging circumstances and even opposition (Collingwood, Vineland, Bruce Peninsula) but commends the pastors for courage and pushing ahead anyway. What sort of opposition these congregations were experiencing, Sam did not say. He continued to comment where he thought revival was needed and where he thought the effect of special meetings showed by increased attendance and attention when he visited.

MORE PENTECOST TEACHING

In 1912, maybe as a result of the complaints of the Pennsylvania editor, C. H. Brunner, and some against him, four associate editors, all Presiding Elders, were appointed, Goudie being one of them again. In 1912 all of Goudie's ten articles started on the cover page. In February, Goudie started a major series[30] with what he acknowledged was a somewhat controversial subject (among holiness people), the spiritual state of the disciples before Pentecost. He said first that the disciples were evidently converted or regenerate before the day of Pentecost reported in Acts 20 and quoted several scriptures that demonstrated that to him. Then he moved to John 17 where Jesus prayed for the sanctification of his disciples. Goudie was able to quote many verses that identified some of the disciples' failures before Pentecost, and concluded the disciples were not yet sanctified. In the second part, he examined the effect on the disciples of the Pentecostal work of the Holy Spirit. The ten days' wait after the Ascension of Jesus was meant for them to get a proper attitude. He liked to hear of the rushing mighty wind,

> Would to God we had more sounds from heaven . . . Order is [good] but let us have the order of heaven, rather than the order of the cemetery . . . Pentecost meant more than a few manifestations and demonstrations of the Spirit, merely getting blessed, it meant cleansing, purifying their hearts. [quoting Acts 15:8–9] . . . It meant power for them, for Jesus said it would. (Acts 1:8) It meant blessing, too; they were all filled.[31]

---

29. Sam Goudie, "PE Report," *GB* (10 August 1911) 10–11.

30. The first two were Sam Goudie, "Before Pentecost," *GB* (15 February 1912) 1; "Pentecost," (7 March 1912) 1.

31. Sam Goudie, *GB* "Pentecost," (7 March 1912) 1.

In his third article, Goudie commented on why he wrote, using mostly quotes of Scripture (the plan of a "Bible reading-style sermon"). He noted another MBiC leader, W. S. Hottel, had submitted a similar essay, "The Spirit-filledness of Life," which though it used some different terms, was essentially the same. He went on to discover eleven points of similarity of his essay with Hottel's. Interestingly, an eradicationist view was not one of them (the view that in sanctification the person's built-in bent to sin was eradicated, so they could never sin again).

> [T]hough some may not define the work or experience of sanctification or baptism of the Holy Spirit just in the same terms . . . Some may be termed eradicationists, others suppressionists because of the different views maintained, yet they agree quite well as to the practical results of Pentecost . . . whatever differences they may hold regarding the crucifixion of the old-man or carnal mind, which has to do with the inner or heart condition of the believer after Pentecost . . . The sad intelligence reached my ears a few days ago of a preacher who said that it was a pity that the doctrine of sanctification had ever been taught in the MBC Church . . . thank God W. S. Hottel is not that preacher . . .[32]

Suppressionists could be represented by followers of Keswick theology, which was condemned in a *Gospel Banner* article about this time, but it is interesting that Goudie was flexible because he judged the outcome in behavior was in fact about the same as far as he saw.

Other topics Goudie wrote on were tithing, on which he testified that for twenty years his family had practised it and "the Lord has graciously and really kept His promise to us along this line" and on "Non-Conformity," that is, not conforming to the standards of the world turned away from God.[33] Though he admitted some have been extreme about non-conformity about dress (clothes), still it was an example of conformity he wanted to warn against.

GOUDIE AND THE *GOSPEL BANNER* INCIDENT, 1913

J. A. Huffman took over from Brunner as the editor of the *Gospel Banner* on January 1, 1913. A thirty-two-year-old studious pastor from the Indiana and Ohio Conference, he was the first member of the MBiC eldership

---

32. Sam Goudie, "Disciples of Jesus after Pentecost," *GB* (28 March 1912) 1.

33. Sam Goudie, "Tithing," *GB* (27 June 1912) 1; "Non-Conformity," *GB* (8 August 1912) 1.

to graduate with college degrees. His first was from Bonebrake Theological Seminary (a UBiC seminary in Dayton, Ohio) in 1909 with graduate studies at the University of Chicago (1915) and Bluffton College (1915) and others later on.[34] He quickly got himself in hot water with Goudie, though he explained himself and went on as editor for twelve years anyway. It seems in the May 1 issue, Huffman reprinted from some place (identified as "Selected"—maddening for those of us who want to know where things come from) a Question and Answer article that discussed the gifts of the Spirit, in which both responders—identified only by initials—implied that the gifts of the Spirit had ceased when the Bible was complete, technically called a "cessationist" viewpoint associated with Reformed believers or more particularly Christian Brethren dispensationalists, not an MBiC viewpoint.

Another issue in May also reprinted an article called "Why? Why?" which denied the immortality of the soul.[35] Goudie exploded with a most uncharacteristic "Public Notice" in the June 5, 1913 *Gospel Banner*, in which he as chair of the Ontario Conference rejected the teaching of both articles, the one as "nothing less than Higher Criticism," and the other as "rank Millennial Dawnism or No-hell-ism." Again, both responses are revealing. "Higher Criticism" in textbooks on the Bible is defined in a neutral fashion, and can refer simply to studies in the background, literary and historical, of any writing. We all do this consciously or unconsciously when we pick up a book or article to begin reading, to decide what to expect. It is defined in contrast to "Lower Criticism," studies in the text of documents, manuscript or print, to determine as closely as possible what an author originally wrote (if there has been copying of the text, especially if it is suspected that there were errors in the transmission of the text), and what the grammar and vocabulary mean. Obviously, Goudie objected to Higher Criticism when it was used, he believed, to undermine faith in the trustworthiness of Scripture or orthodox teaching. I have not seen evidence that the booklets called *The Fundamentals*, published beginning in 1910 to 1915 and distributed to hundreds of thousands of pastors, missionaries, YMCA leaders and other groups of Christian personnel, were in the hands of MBiC workers, but they probably were. Goudie's language here sounds similar to those opponents of modernism. Evangelical Christians had been

---

34. Huffman, *Mennonite Brethren in Christ*, 245. See his memoirs, Huffman, *Seventy Years*, 25–27, and the biography by his son Huffman, *Not of this World*, 84–89.

35. [Thoro Harris], "Why? Why?" *GB* (15 May 1913) 2–3.

complaining of the misuse of Higher Criticism for decades by this time, but normally the MBiC was definitely on the sidelines of the debate, isolated by language and limited educational attainments.[36]

In harsh words directed at the editor without naming him, Goudie said,

> Now we wish to say for our Conference that we are not Higher Critics nor do we accept much of what they teach, nor are we Russell-ites or Millennial Dawnists, and we positively will not stand for such teaching as appeared in the above mentioned articles but will denounce the same from our pulpits and with our testimony and pen.
>
> We have an abundance of such teaching in the form of tracts and papers and books in our fair land now without making use of our dear little church paper (the Gospel Banner) to scatter such misleading unscriptural and damnable heresy as No-Hellism ... If the Banner continues to bear such articles in the future, there will be no need of sending them to Ontario ... Your brother in defense of the Gospel Banner and Bible Truth.[37]

H. S. Hallman, the former editor, also wrote warning about the gifts article and its implied Higher Criticism in the same issue. Huffman replied by agreeing that the denials of "the immortality of the soul" were false teachings, and said denial implied annihilationism (for example, Adventism), future probation (such as Russellism) or no-resurrection (death ends all). I don't know Huffman's motives for including the articles. It is a custom of columnists and editors to use provocative language and to drop in counter articles to get responses, but perhaps that time, Huffman misjudged or forgot to frame the articles with cautions.[38] Goudie's angry response seems hasty and could have been moderated by first approaching the editor privately. However, I do not see any further repercussions in the pages of the *Gospel Banner*. When Goudie supplied a blurb about Huffman's newest book, *Upper Room Messages* in 1915, he said, "I have read your new book ... and can heartily recommend it to our people. It is (like all your

---

36. Each of the first four volumes of *The Fundamentals* contained a critique of the misuse of Higher Criticism, and Volume 7 of Millennial Dawnism (an early name for the teachings of Jehovah's Witnesses).

37. Sam Goudie, "Public Notice," *GB* (5 June 1913) 10.

38. H. S. Hallman, *GB* (5 June 1913) 3–4, J. A. Huffman, *GB* (5 June 1913) 2–3.

other books) very clear and sound in doctrine . . ."³⁹ Still later, Goudie and Huffman served together in the new inter-conference mission society, the United Missionary Society founded in 1921. Huffman was the first President and Goudie the first Vice-President.

BIBLE STUDY OUTLINES 1915-1919

While we are looking at the *Gospel Banner*, we note that beginning in 1915, Goudie started to contribute to a series organized by Huffman called "Department of Bible Study," outlines of sermons or Bible lessons evidently for use on Sundays. His topics included the following: salvation; abiding in Christ; advice to young converts; Abraham; friend of God; man's love to man; the believer's walk, and so on.⁴⁰ Other MBiC writers contributed and eventually the editor announced, "Because of the request which has come . . . we have decided to print [the Bible Study Outlines] in booklet form. Contributors for the last half of the year are as follows: S. Goudie, O. B. Snyder, Jacob Hygema, J[acob] N[elson] Pannabecker, L[ewis] J. Lehman, J. A. Huffman."⁴¹ When the third series was announced, Abraham Yoder was a writer but not Lehman this time.⁴² The series ended in 1919.

We have met Snyder and Yoder. O. B. Snyder attended high school in Ontario, and business colleges in Illinois and Indiana, before settling in pastorates in Ontario and Michigan.

A. B. Yoder (1867-1953) had a long and distinguished career mainly with the Indiana and Ohio Conference. He completed high school and was a teacher for sixteen years. He was a trustee of Bluffton College (a Mennonite college), an editor of the church magazine for nineteen years, a Presiding Elder for twenty-one years and engaged in many other energetic endeavours.⁴³

Jacob Hygema (1869-1951), born of Dutch background in Indiana, was an orphan early in life. He entered the ministry of the MBiC in the

39. Sam Goudie, "What Presiding Elder S. Goudie Says about *Upper Room Messages*," *GB* (25 November 1915) 8.

40. *GB* (3 June 1915) (for use on 4 July) 8, was the first one. An outline printed in 16 March 1916 is called "No. 16." Storms, *United Missionary Church*, 186, believed they were meant for young people's meetings.

41. J. A. Huffman, "Notice," *GB* (17 June 1915) 3. *Banner Bible Study Outlines* Series #2, (January-June 1916) survives in the David Sapelak Fonds, MAO, Waterloo.

42. J. A. Huffman, "Notice," *GB* (7 December 1916) 2.

43. Storms, *United Missionary Church*, 100-101, Huffman, *Mennonite Brethren in Christ*, 274-75.

Nebraska Conference in 1892 and was ordained in 1897. He had one term in a Free Will Baptist College, contributed to the *Gospel Banner* and often urged the MBiC to support opening a college or Bible institute. He taught in several short-term MBiC schools. A great reader, he donated many of his books to his son-in-law, Ray Pannabecker, the youngest son of the following man.[44]

Jacob Nelson Pannabecker (1866–1940), born in Wellington County, Ontario, moved to Michigan and was a pastor in the MBiC there. His father was Samuel Pannabecker, his mother Martha Cober. He had high school training in Owen Sound and was a trustee of Bluffton College. One of his sons, Ray, mentioned above, was a President of Bethel College, the United Missionary Church liberal arts college in Mishawaka, Indiana, and two sons (Lloyd and Floyd) were missionaries under the General Conference Mennonites, one a medical doctor.[45]

Lewis Lehman (1871–1950), born in Illinois, entered the ministry of the Mennonite Church in 1897, and his ordination was received by the MBiC in 1912. He, too, was a trustee of Bluffton College.[46]

Such were the writers and their educational attainments in 1915, slightly higher than many, but typical of MBiC ministers of the day, fitting into the general educational level of the churches. Goudie was there as well.

DEVELOPMENT OF THE ONTARIO CONFERENCE

During the Great War, Goudie and his co-Presiding Elders, Silas Cressman (1911–1917) and C. N. Good (1918–1919—Goudie was alone in 1917–1918), continued the administrating of a moderately growing Conference.

---

44. Huffman, *Mennonite Brethren in Christ*, 268. Also a profile by Ray Pannabecker, "Rev. Jacob Hygema," *GB* (30 August 1951) 3. Some of these books eventually reached the library of the UMCA Bible College in Tungan Magajiya, Niger State, Nigeria, by 2010. A biography of this man is needed.

45. Huffman, *Mennonite Brethren in Christ*, 259. Jacob was descended from the Tunker Pannabeckers of Puslinch Township, Wellington County, southwest of Guelph, Ontario. He was a close relative of the Pannabeckers who had the farm next to David Goudie, Sam's father. S. Floyd Pannabecker researched the origin of the MBiC in a thesis at Bluffton College which was incorporated in Huffman's 1920 *Mennonite Brethren in Christ*.

46. Huffman, *Mennonite Brethren in Christ*, 253. There was a serious attempt at that time to make Bluffton College the joint school of the General Conference Mennonites which started it, and the Mennonite Brethren in Christ and perhaps others. Huffman was part of that plan; Huffman, *Mennonite Brethren in Christ*, 219–20. See Storms, *United Missionary Church*, 198.

From 1914 to 1918, membership grew from 1,624 (1913) to 1,867 (1918), a 5-year growth rate of 12.8 percent. Specifically, the growth was a net increase of about 240 members in five years, about 48 members a year in a Conference of 26 circuits and city missions. Almost all the components of a typical denomination had been established, except a denominational mission Board, denominational colleges, women's and youth organizations. These would start to appear around the decade of the 1920s. The United Missionary Society was founded in 1921, and a Bible school was started in Edmonton in 1916 (closed in 1919 however), and another which lasted, in Didsbury in 1926. Ontario did not start a college until 1940, after Goudie's time as a Presiding Elder, though he was on the founding board. Although women in the congregations often worked together in projects such as for the Red Cross, organized Women's Missionary Societies began to appear only in the 1920s (again in Alberta, Conference-wide 1929, in Ontario not until 1939). Despite Goudie's doubts about a Young People's organization in the 1890s, one was initiated in Ontario in 1924 by Conference youth, a year after one was started in the Ohio district of the Indiana and Ohio Conference. Why Bible schools and women's organizations did not begin in Goudie's years as an influential presiding elder is not clear. He believed education for pastors was good.[47] He had various projects on the go as we will see. It is possible he was cautious or over-committed.

A large committee in the 1920 General Conference submitted a report that discouraged participation in theological or secular colleges, explicitly stating that all Christian colleges known to them were "honeycombed" with "apostasy, rationalism, materialism, higher criticism, and other anti-Christian tendencies," an obvious effect of the fundamentalist-modernist conflicts.[48] Goudie was not on that committee, but Good and Cressman were. It is perhaps significant that J. A. Huffman was also not on the committee, though he had the highest formal education in the denomination at the time. Huffman was a teacher at Bluffton College for eight years, when many hoped it could be an inter-Mennonite college. Huffman reacted to what he saw as growing liberalism in the new College and went to Marion College in 1922.[49] Huffman never gave up the hope of a Christian college

---

47. Sam Goudie, "Necessity of Ministerial Education," *GB* (28 October 1915) 11.

48. "Report on Education," *Tenth General Conference 1920*, 31.

49. Huffman, *Seventy Years*, 40–41. His son, Lambert is a bit more explicit in Huffman, *Not of this World*, 89. Marion College is now Indiana Wesleyan University.

for the MBiC, but his experience must have convinced many of the futility of the project, perhaps influencing Goudie or other leaders in Ontario.

ATTEMPTED RECONCILIATION: THE EBY COUSINS

In 1915, the simmering disagreement of the Conference with the two Eby cousins which we have mentioned began to reach a conclusion. Sam Goudie reported that there were, in particular, "difficulties between him and Elder A. Eby."[50] Goudie asked the Conference "Committee over the Presiding Elders," normally a routine committee with nothing to do, to investigate the complaint of Amos Eby. They listened to Amos Eby's side of the dispute, tried to persuade him he was in the wrong, but reported "they could do nothing with him." They appear to have taken Goudie's view of the dispute from the start, though what it was is not made clear by the published record. It may have had something to do with Amos' Pentecostal views, or it may not. The committee reported "he made very hard accusations against Bro. Goudie," and referred the case to the Conference.[51] Since Sam Goudie was involved in so many committees and boards, and so many leaders were his friends, it would have been very awkward for a conscientious leader to deal with. As chair of the Conference, Goudie normally appointed all the (temporary) Conference committees, while continuing ones were elected. The highest committee, which continued between Annual Conferences was the Reference Committee was composed of Sam Goudie (usually also the chair), John N. Kitching, Henry S. Hallman, Silas Cressman and Cyrus N. Good, all friends. These same five were also the Conference Foreign Mission Board for several years. The "Committee to Examine Ministers" was composed of Sam Goudie and Silas Cressman, the two Presiding Elders. The "Committee on Resolutions" which eventually summed up the Conference discussion, was made of Silas Cressman and C. N. Good. A new committee at this Conference, "appointed to make provision for our aged ministers [which would include the two retired Ebys] and minister's wives,"[52] were J. N. Kitching, Silas Cressman, Sam Goudie, Ephraim Sievenpiper and Simeon Schlichter Hallman (a representative of a congregation, at one time noted as being from Toronto West, brother of

---

50. *Ontario Conference Journal 1915*, 9–10.
51. *Ontario Conference Journal 1915*, 10.
52. *Ontario Conference Journal 1915*, 10.

H. S. Hallman). If someone were to complain that Goudie had a conflict of interest or something similar, one might be excused for thinking it.

The "Committee over the Presiding Elders" that year were three: John Bolwell (1852–1941), Milton Bricker and Charles Isaac Sinden (1875–1944). Bricker (1877–1967) was another good friend of Sam Goudie. Bolwell once had a difficulty with the Conference, but it was resolved by 1907 and he served many more years. Sinden was from South Norwich Township, Oxford County, and in 1915 was just finishing four years on the Bethel field (New Dundee).

The Resolutions Committee brought in two resolutions about the Ebys for the Conference to consider, one dealing with their doctrinal views, the other with Amos' relation to Sam Goudie and also C. N. Good, who was now involved. Both resolutions were accepted, but the one appointing a delegation for visiting Amos Eby, but which also threatened a suspension and church trial, was later reconsidered and a letter of notice of action was substituted.[53]

Solomon Eby was treated differently, and perhaps his relation to the Conference was more respectful, or the Conference found it perplexing to approach one of their founders with a complaint. Financial assistance to him as a retiree was continued by the Conference. In the resolution referring to "doctrinal views that are not in harmony with the teachings of the MBC Church," it said the "church has been lenient with them." "Resolved that we express our regret . . . and request these brethren to not make use of the said views in any way as to conflict with the MBC Church and, whereas they have arrived at a ripe old age, we unitedly pray the Lord bless and sustain them by grace Divine."[54]

Despite the efforts of the Annual Conference of 1915, both Eby men resigned from the MBiC before the 1916 General Conference.

THE MBIC MISSIONS IN WAR TIME

The Great War was starting to affect the Conference's missionary programs, as reported in the 1915 *Conference Journal*. The mission in Armenian Turkey (the UOMB) which had Canadian personnel was suddenly shut down by the Ottoman Empire entering the war in 1914 against the British Empire

---

53. *Ontario Conference Journal 1915*, 23.

54. *Ontario Conference Journal 1915*, 21, 10. The charge by Pentecostals that Solomon Eby was turned out by the church he founded is inaccurate and somewhat unfair, though understandable.

and its dominion Canada. The missionaries fled, a step ahead of Ottoman agents sent to detain them. Harold R. Pannabecker, a nephew of the missionary to Nigeria, Cornelia W. Pannabecker, was approved by the Ontario Conference to go to Nigeria in 1915, but it was 1917 before he got there. In the end he went, not under the MBiC Foreign Mission, but more of a private employee of A. W. Banfield for the Niger Press at Tsonga.[55] Ruby Reeve from Aylmer, they noted, had married during the past year, and was "out of active work" with the American Episcopal Methodist mission.[56] Her husband was a man from India, a Mr. Bose, and regrettably, notice of her ceases in MBiC publications, and practically anywhere else. Her mission supervisor wrote, "The work of the Hindustani Bible-women was carefully supervised by Miss Reeve. She was also a willing helper in our institution and our Conference has truly lost, through Miss Reeve's marriage, a most faithful and conscientious worker."[57] Any help in learning more of her life would be a great service.

With the Great War raging in Europe and elsewhere, the small MBiC missionary society largely based in Ontario—called, inaccurately, the African General Board—had at least two difficulties. One was trouble sending new recruits to Nigeria: no new appointees were sent from 1915 to late in 1918. In a "Special" report in the *Gospel Banner* in the summer of 1916, Goudie as secretary said they had accepted Elder Raymond G. Morgan (b. 1891) of the Michigan Conference as a missionary for Africa "if outfit is provided."[58] Miss Norah Shantz from Ontario was also accepted. Both Ira Sherk (from Michigan), the Nigeria field leader now that Alec Banfield was working for the British and Foreign Bible Society in West Africa, and Edith M. Evans (the former city mission worker from Puslinch/ Hespeler, Ontario), were in North America to report. The other difficulty of the MBiC General Foreign Mission Board was visible in this report, though disguised. A resolution noted the deep interest of the Indiana and Ohio Conference and the Michigan Conference in missions and asked them to each appoint representatives for the African Board. In other words, with the death of

---

55. Ira W. Sherk, letter to C. N. Good 6 August 1915, anticipating Harold Pannabecker's arrival, noted that Harold "will be separate tho [his spelling] we will think of him as one of us." in Missionary Church, Inc., Archives.

56. *Ontario Conference Journal 1915*, 13.

57. Mabel L. Eddy, "Evangelistic Work," *27th Bengal Women's Missionary Conference* (1915) 29, of the Women's Foreign Missionary Society of the Methodist Episcopal Church (USA).

58. Profile in Huffman, *Mennonite Brethren in Christ*, 257.

Ebenezer Anthony in 1914, and other circumstances, these two Conferences had neglected to continue to play a part in the fledgling mission.

Elder Morgan never made it to Nigeria, so perhaps the war, with its disruption of shipping prevented his travel, or perhaps the outfit was never provided. Norah Shantz did make it to Nigeria (in 1918) when an individual promised to support her. Even after her terms of service in Nigeria, she remained a supporter of missions for decades.[59] In the face of the regular request of the mission for men, it is regrettable Morgan did not go.

THE NINTH GENERAL CONFERENCE, NEW CARLISLE, OHIO, OCTOBER 1916

The 1916 General Conference was moved to Ohio for the sake of the American brethren, "[o]wing to conditions in Ontario on account of the war..."[60] Some American Mennonites found the Canadian border did not accept them.[61] Similarly, the Ontario Reference Committee decided "it did not seem advisable" to hold their 1916 camp-meeting at Berlin where anti-German sentiments were strong, but shifted it to more neutral Markham or Stouffville. Gormley, that is, Pike's Peak, on the farm of Isaac Pike, was chosen.

The Presiding Elder of the Nebraska Conference, Clifford I. Scott, was the chair of this GC. New Carlisle, Clark County, is in west central Ohio, then a rural town of just over 1,000. The Ontario delegation consisted of people from whom we have heard much: Sam Goudie and Silas Cressman as Presiding Elders, C. N. Good, Ephraim Sievenpiper and John N. Kitching as ordained elders, and Jacob B. Shantz, Isaac Pike and Abraham S. Stouffer[62] representing the fields.[63] Due to its small membership, the Canada Northwest Conference could only be represented by its Presiding Elder, Henry Goudie. Ontario brought only one request to the GC, a merely administrative one about the size of spaces on the denominational statistics form. Others wanted to discuss the *Discipline's* article about insurance (Michigan and "Alberta" that is, Canada Northwest), musical instruments

---

59. Goudie, Sam, "Special," *GB* (27 July 1916) 12.

60. "Report of the Executive Committee," *Ninth General Conference 1916*, 18.

61. Steiner, *Promised Lands*, 194.

62. A member of at least five generations of Stouffers was named "Abraham," with A. S. Stouffer III (a deacon at Stouffville MBiC from 1903) and his son "Abram" S. Stouffer IV (b. 1872) succeeding him at the father's death.

63. From Berlin, Markham, and Stouffville, respectively.

and choirs (Nebraska), the Reading Course (Nebraska), and the Indiana and Ohio Conference asked three issues to be discussed: the three-year limit on pastoral assignments (Michigan also asked about this), the eligibility of conditional workers being elected to various positions, and the Church's stand on militarism. Pennsylvania and Pacific Conferences had no requests at all.

When the Presiding Elders' reports were given, the GC secretary Abraham B. Yoder summarized everyone's oral reports. Sam Goudie, speaking of the East District of the Ontario Conference, referred obliquely to the effect of the war on his members, the only PE to do so. The US of course had not entered the war yet. "During the past two years the persecution has increased . . . We stand by the Mennonite doctrine."[64]

Although he was the chair of the Executive Committee, Goudie's part in that Committee's report is not clear. As chair, he would sign it, but in at least this case, all of the committee's members appended their name to the report. Who wrote the committee report? Goudie, or a secretary (none was recorded), or some other person or persons is disguised this way. This is entirely within the pattern of Goudie's leadership style. It is leadership by committee. It is very rare for his personal decisions to be isolated from the boards or committees he was part of. Correspondence might turn up with his views laid bare. Some of his committee style did get recorded in the minutes of the executive of the relief organization (the NRRO) of which he was a member from 1918, and it shows he regularly made motions or seconded them actively.

Perhaps there was another reason not to specify who phrased the report. The most contentious part of their report, which was as usual mostly about the *Gospel Banner*, dealt with the complaints at the start of Jasper A. Huffman's term, the 1913 fuss over the problematic articles. The report claims "The complaints made at the beginning of this GC term were adjusted by a special meeting . . ." Although the conference "reconsidered" the Executive Committee report, no resolution emerged from the private session. Later in the GC, resolutions in support of the editor, publisher and desire for the *Gospel Banner* to continue were all passed.[65] Huffman later said though, that secretly the Pennsylvania Conference was planning to make their own magazine, the *Eastern Gospel Banner*, which they did

---

64. *Ninth General Conference 1916*, 15.
65. *Ninth General Conference 1916*, 19.

publish for eight years before giving it up as a lost battle to gain readership.[66] In all this Goudie said nothing publicly. The "Alberta" and the Pennsylvania Conferences asked to be released from membership in the Executive Committee. Canada Northwest's request was almost certainly because of the cost of travel—in 1913–1916, the Executive held five meetings, all in Ohio. Pennsylvania Conference had no such excuse, but their action was probably related to its leaders' desire to chart a different course, and dislike of the *Gospel Banner* (at Pennsylvania's request, they were also released from responsibility from its debt, if it occurred).[67] Pennsylvania was fast becoming the largest and wealthiest conference of the MBiC: surpassing Ontario's membership of 1,783 in 1915 for the first time by 31 members at 1,814. Total offerings for all purposes in the years 1912 to 1915 in Pennsylvania were $288,173, compared to Ontario, the next largest, with $129,321. It was also the most urban conference.

Nebraska Conference's request about musical instruments and choirs reflected a gradual cultural shift, especially strong in the outlying conferences. Still contentious in the larger eastern conferences, the issue was too hot for general permission, so the GC gave each Conference authority to set the rules and that removed the GC from further discussion. On the request to add "an article defining our position on Militarism," the Conference also "Resolved, That this Conference deem it inadvisable to insert such a clause at this time."[68] No reason was given.

Goudie was the chair of the Annual Conferences in Ontario most of the years from 1905 to 1933, and he was normally the chair of the Reference Committee—that group which handled Conference business between Annual Conferences. The Reference Committee did not have the massive amount of business that later District Executive Boards had. Once under Goudie, they met once a year, but normally four to five times. In 1918, the question came to the Reference Committee whether organized City missions could send delegates to the Annual Conference since they were not exactly mentioned as such in the MBiC *Discipline*. The Reference Committee interpreted the church document to decide that an organized mission could send a delegate, since they too, were organized around a "class."[69]

---

66. Huffman, *Seventy Years*, 79.

67. C. H. Brunner referred to problems of MBiC unity in an editorial "A Bit of History," *GB* (17 October 1912) 6.

68. *Ninth General Conference 1916*, 23.

69. *Ontario Conference Journal 1918*, 9.

10

The Great War of 1914–1918

THE ONTARIO CONFERENCE, AFTER settling down from the challenge of the Pentecostal movement was again to be disturbed by world events, this time a war in Europe. The war divided Canada further along French-Canadian and Anglo-Canadian lines, it would kill almost 61,000 young Canadian men and some women and awaken some Mennonites to the need for Christian involvement in the world. Along with other Mennonites, the MBiC had to pay attention to the war. This chapter looks at some of their responses, and what Sam Goudie himself did.

Goudie and his Conference did not know—nobody publicly expected—that the European war would drag on and enmesh the whole country in a total war effort. Anabaptist groups in the US and Canada, except those more recently from Russia, had not needed to concern themselves with responding to war significantly since the American Civil War, which ended less than ten years before the formation of the Reforming Mennonites. The Evangelical Mennonites in Pennsylvania, a group with less than three hundred members then, and the New Mennonite Conference in Ontario of similar size, lived through the time of the American Civil War, but references to the war and any associated problems do not survive in their records. After the Civil War, Mennonites had been able to ignore conflicts involving their North American countries, such as the Fenian (Irish nationalist) raids on Canada from US soil (1866, 1870), many wars against

The Great War of 1914–1918

the indigenous peoples,[1] the Spanish-American War (1898), and the Boer War (1899–1902). Before the World War of 1914–1918, most Mennonites in Ontario had neglected preparing their congregations, especially their young men, for responding to militarism, as they sometimes called it. As a Mennonite body specializing in revivalist piety, holiness doctrine and pre-millennialism, the MBiC upheld the non-resistant teaching of her tradition, but it was not central, nor upheld by the holiness groups they thought of as their colleagues. Some pastors and members were convinced of the peace position, others were not active in explaining the church's doctrine. The Great War eventually involved massive mobilization in both countries and Mennonites started to worry about what to do if conscription came. Frank Epp for all of Canada and Samuel J. Steiner for Ontario have closely described the response of Mennonites, including the Ontario Conference of the MBiC.[2]

The Great War effected Goudie and the Ontario MBiC on several levels. Some of them are visible in relation to fashions of personal appearance, in rhetoric and more importantly in doctrinal change, inter-Mennonite cooperation and relief practices.

Steiner notes that whereas the Mennonite Conference of Ontario's experience in the war led to increasing stress on a few symbols of separation from the culture (clothing especially), the MBiC, on its journey to evangelical denomination building, continued to pick up features of the wider evangelical culture, sometimes in fundamentalist ways. Timothy Erdel affirms that while the MBiC "was never officially fundamentalist," at the same time it did adopt some fundamentalist attitudes.[3] The Ontario MBiC also gradually took on more Canadian culture in general. During the war, clean-shaven men's faces became more common and despite their claim to be non-conforming to the world, after the war numerous MBiC pastors drop any form of beard at all. Women's clothing styles were

---

1. Wars against indigenes: nearly twenty in the US, at least two against Metis and some Cree in Canada. Eaton and Boehner studied how the *Gospel Banner* used the rhetoric surrounding the Spanish-American War to approve of the opportunity for opening the Philippines to Protestant missions; Eaton and Boehner, "Missional Tensions," 217–36.

2. Steiner, *Promised Lands*, chapter 6 for World War 1, 189–230. For an example of US MBiC response to the draft, an odd mixture of patriotism and a non-resistant stance somehow opposed to the main Mennonite viewpoint, see the letters of Joseph Ummel to his Indiana MBiC family when he and his brothers were made to register in 1917; Overhulser, *Joseph Ummel*, 19–29. Denominational histories by the MBiC, UMC, Missionary Church and EMCC show very little interest in non-resistance.

3. Steiner, *Promised Lands*, 190–91. Erdel, "Evangelical Tradition," 81–82, 84.

modest, but I am certain any fashion historian could identify to the decade or half-decade when a photograph was taken, when involving young women of the church.

While reading through issues of the *Gospel Banner* published during the world war, I noticed that war-time rhetoric was gradually adopted by a wide variety of writers. It was topical and inevitable, and by no means confined to the *Gospel Banner*. Missions promoters in particular argued that if the world could expend billions on a destructive effort, why couldn't the churches rise up and put more into a thoroughly and eternally constructive struggle of world evangelization? Preachers and editorial writers urged all kinds of Christian efforts with conflict and military metaphors. A more casual and unconscious use of military language appeared. Goudie himself provided "Marching Orders," No. 21 in the Bible Study Outlines, in which the Christian life was compared to a soldier's career. There are "Rules and Regulations to be observed. Jesus Christ is the Captain of our salvation." His sub-points were labeled Halt, Attention, Quick March, and Forward.[4]

Nevertheless, at the start of the Great War, Quaker, Mennonite and Tunker churches hoped that the laws of Canada would still allow their members exemption from participating in combat, laws that built on British and Canadian legislation from 1793, 1808, 1849, 1868, 1878 and 1906.[5] The Government of Canada allowed itself unspecified conditions that they could impose even on exempted persons in war time, but the core was that Mennonites, Quakers and Tunkers need not bear arms.

We have seen that the MBiC had switched over to English for most purposes from 1890 to 1910, so on the surface they did not have to face anti-German *language* prejudice. The western US and Canadian Conferences feared that stereotypes about German Mennonites there were hampering their evangelism, but in Ontario, the church existed mostly in communities that knew them. The war was acknowledged in the September Annual Conferences in the final resolutions—in 1914 urging prayer for God to overrule and bring the carnage to an end, in 1915 prayer was urged "for the soldiers on the battlefield, the wounded and the homes that are sorrowing and destitute."[6] Relief work was encouraged and donations to the Red Cross suggested. Studies of the Ontario MBiC response suspect that as the war went on, and some young members joined the war effort,

---

4. Sam Goudie, "Marching Orders," *GB* (19 October 1916) 8.
5. Goudie and Good, *Non-Resistant Religious Societies*.
6. *Ontario Conference Journal 1915*, 24.

MBiC language about the war compromised to the point of praying for Allied victories.[7] On the whole though, the percentage of MBiC men who joined the armed forces was small.[8] According to the *Discipline*, no MBiC member was to participate in war, but that did not stop young men who were not yet members from signing up. John Kitching, during his pastorate of the Bethel Chapel in Toronto 1916-1918, allowed their young men in uniform to march into the services.[9] One licensed preacher, English-born probationer Thomas John Drinkall, did sign up in July 1916 and served in the Royal Army Medical Corps in France.[10] He was not openly disciplined, and after the war remained listed as "local help" in Stratford until 1921.

THE NON-RESISTANT RELIEF ORGANIZATION (NRRO)

In the summer of 1917, Ontario Mennonites saw that conscription in Canada was inevitable. They needed to confirm their historic position and clarify the procedures to follow to prevent their young men being harassed or arrested for failing to register or report for duty. This did start happening as early as November 10.[11] The Mennonite denominations used letters, ad hoc committees and one-time delegations to Ottawa to get answers to their questions. However, something more permanent did arise. An exploratory meeting was called for Tunkers and a few Mennonite groups by a Mennonite Conference of Ontario pastor, Lewis J. Burkholder, to meet at Wideman Mennonite Church in Markham Township. Sam Goudie, Ephraim Sievenpiper from Stouffville, and Milton Bricker from Markham joined seven others[12] to discuss forming a cooperative effort "for the purpose of considering ways and means by which the Non-resistant bodies ... might

---

7. *Ontario Conference Journal 1918*, 28–29.

8. Epp, *Separate People*, 365–89. Steiner thinks that in Ontario they were no more than a dozen men, *Promised Lands*, 195.

9. Epp, *Separate People*, 369, quotes Kitching confirming to a Toronto newspaper, *Toronto Daily Star* (25 November 1916) that the church still opposed war.

10. See Steiner, *Promised Lands*, 652, note 10, for references.

11. Conscientious objector status for individuals was not recognized in Canada in 1917 and objectors who were not members of the historic peace churches suffered abuse and even torture in Canadian barracks.

12. It is good to recognize these other men: Lewis J. Burkholder, Isaac Wambold (both Mennonite Conference of Ontario), Christian Gayman, Levi Grove, Thomas Reesor (all Old Order Mennonite), Fred Elliott and David W. Heise (both Tunker). All were living in Markham or Whitchurch Townships. These men and their denominations are all identified more fully in Steiner, *Promised Lands* in various places.

be able to express in some practical way to the Military representatives of Canada, their profound gratitude, and appreciation for the enjoyment of exemption privileges [that relieves] them from the performance of any class of military service."[13]

These men were sympathetic to a plan for an association of Mennonite Churches to offer gifts to the Government for war-related relief. Most of them were to become involved for many years.

In this meeting at Wideman Church, Sam Goudie was appointed to chair a committee to investigate for their denominations the state of the laws relating to non-resistant church members, to call a meeting to form a permanent group, and to select a name. The second exploratory meeting was held at Wideman on December 11 where the state of the laws was discussed. The official organizing meeting was held in Kitchener on 16 January 1918 at the home of C. N. Good, 26 Chapel Street, where they agreed to call themselves the Non-Resistant Relief Organization or NRRO. Sam Goudie may not have been at the founding meeting, however he was elected vice-chair of the NRRO anyway. Seventeen years later, Goudie and Good printed a collection of Canadian laws relating to the position of Quaker, Mennonite, and Tunker churches on participation in war, when the world situation made it seem necessary.[14]

THE 1920 NON-RESISTANCE PAMPHLET

Goudie was asked to prepare an essay for the Annual Ministerial Convention that preceded the Annual Conference in September 1920 on the topic of war and peace. He called it "A Scriptural Exegesis of the Doctrine of Non-Resistance." It is not clear who promoted the essay, but Goudie must have agreed strongly enough to go along with the Conference resolution that the essay be printed for distribution.[15] The Conference granted him

---

13. "Minutes of a Meeting," 17 November 1917; David L. Hunsberger Photographs collection, courtesy Samuel J. Steiner.

14. *Ontario Conference Journal 1934*, 34. Ontario Conference action made them a committee to publish, in 1934. No doubt the compilers used earlier collections of such laws. A similar pamphlet was compiled by Jesse B. Martin and Noah M. Bearinger (dated 26 May 1941) called *Laws Affecting Historic Peace Churches* for the Conference of Historic Peace Churches; in fact most of the wording is the same, just the most recent laws were added. Another telling of Goudie's involvement in the NRRO can be found at the YouTube video, Stouffer, Fuller and Fuller, "Sam Goudie and the NRRO."

15. The musician at Bethany that Goudie worked with, Peter Shupe, besides being the teacher in singing schools in the MBiC, also published a gospel song, arranged by H. D.

$35 from the Ministerial Convention treasury to print 1,000 copies of the essay in tract form. The essay is mostly a collection of scripture passages (readers who are used to "exegesis" meaning an author's critical comments and interpretation of Greek and Hebrew will be disappointed). It is an example of a Bible Reading type of sermon favored by some at the time. The Scriptures were assumed to be so plain, all one needed to do was collect and read verses on the particular topic. This is called pre-critical interpretation now and it is still widely practised. Students in Bible College and higher levels know it is a practice filled with problems, mainly because it assumes a particular tradition of interpretation ignorant of other traditions. But the past is a foreign country.

Many holiness groups were initially revolted by the war, and condemned participation in wars on moral or practical grounds.[16] The Mennonite Brethren in Christ could have been strengthened in their non-resistance theology by listening to their fellow Mennonites more, but that road was not maintained. A plain reading of the Sermon on the Mount has led more than one to condemn personal involvement, but it is hard to promote pacifism in a nation at war.[17] Few holiness groups achieved a thoroughly biblical foundation for non-resistance as the Mennonites did. Most holiness denominations modified their disapproval of militarism in the face of nationalist movements in war time and when they witnessed the monstrosity of aggressive enemies, through adoption of some form of just war theory.

Goudie began his pamphlet by saying, "Non-resistance is and has been one of the outstanding doctrines of the Mennonite Church . . . held in common by all branches . . . anyone who is not of the non-resistant faith or possessed of those principles is not a true Mennonite and is not worthy of the name." Goudie's first long quote, nearly a page of the eight-page

---

Huber, that deplored war, "Oh, Why Not Have Peace Instead of War? A Christmas Carol." The two men collaborated on at least two other songs, one written by "C M R," probably Cora Mae Rudy, copyrighted by H. S. Hallman in 1905. All in Box 7021, MCHT.

16. A good introduction to holiness and peace theologies is Hostetler, *Perfect Love and War*. Another example of how plain reading of the Sermon on the Mount can lead to pacifism is the newly converted John R. W. Stott. It caused a great strain on his relation to his father, an officer in the Royal Army Medical Corps in World War 2. Several years later Stott learned of just war theology and switched views; Dudley-Smith, *John Stott*, 110, 177–78.

17. Several Pentecostal churches in Canada and the US included pacifist statements in their organizational articles. Unfortunately, Canadian Pentecostals organized too late to benefit their members; Dempster, "Canadian Pentecostal Pacifism," 1–26.

tract, is from "that wonderful sermon recorded in Matthew 5th, 6th, and 7th, chapters" (followed by Matt 5:21–22a, 38–47; 6:12–14). This shows the Lord's instruction of the Sermon on the Mount was still definitive, as it was in early Anabaptism, at least for Goudie. The parallel passage Luke 6:27–37, 40, is quoted, then the pamphlet quotes from New Testament passages in Bible order:

> John 15:12, 18–20; 17:14; 18:36
>
> Rom 12:17–21; 13:9–10, 13–14; 1 Cor 13:4–8a; 2 Cor 10:3–4; Gal 5:19–20a, 22–26
>
> Eph 6:11–13; Phil 2:3–5; Col 3:12–15; 1 Thess 5:15; 1 Tim 2:1–3
>
> Jas 4:1–2; 1 Pet 2:13–23; 2 Pet 3:8–9, 13–14, 17; 4:12–15, 16–14, 19; 1 John 2:8–9; 3:14b–15

To Goudie, these scriptures are "the spirit of true Christianity, and is expected and looked for in the Christian by even worldly minded men, and justly so . . . This is none other than the spirit of Jesus and should be found in every one of his followers irrespective of name or creed . . ." Goudie was even bold enough to apply Paul's words in Rom 8:9 where it says, "Now if any man have not the spirit of Christ, he is none of his." After all the quotes, Goudie answers only one possible objection about non-resistance, as some might say that "does not the Old Testament teach war or resistance?" Again, he quotes Matt 5:38–39a, ending with Jesus' words: "resist not evil." No nuance here. Just plain Anabaptist plain interpretation. To Goudie, we are not living in the old dispensation, but in the new. That was all. "Any candid thinker will admit that the teachings of the New Testament [are] opposed to war or strife, either in the home, the church or state." One might wish Bible interpretation were so obvious to all.

Goudie was to be involved in the NRRO until 1944, as the vice-chair 1918–1923 and 1937–1941, and as the chairman 1923–1924 and 1941–1944. Until 1944, Goudie was always one of the three representatives to the NRRO from the MBiC. The others were his friends, men who saw things the same way he did, I suspect. When they (Silas Cressman in 1935, Ephraim Sievenpiper in 1943) passed from the scene, few were ready to continue their work, and those who did, such as J. Harold Sherk, must have felt rather alone. Rev. Percy G. Lehman, who replaced Sievenpiper in 1943, later a district superintendent of the United Missionary Church (the leadership title and church name changed in 1946 and 1947 respectively), was president of the NRRO 1951–1955. Their positions were annually ratified at the Annual Conference, even in peacetime, when the activities of the NRRO were greatly reduced, but Goudie was always a member 1918 to 1944. Unfortunately, whoever spoke to Conference (often Goudie) gave verbal reports that were unrecorded most of the time, so we don't know what was on their mind through those years. From the example of later years when not much was happening, the reports could simply have been "No actions to report this year."[18]

Before the NRRO's founding, Bishop Samuel F. Coffman, an American Mennonite living in Vineland, led many of the representations to the Canadian government in Ottawa over the generality and particulars of Ontario Mennonite relations to the war effort.[19] With the NRRO, the Ontario MBiC became organizationally connected for the first time to any outside body, so far as I can tell, except for the United Orphanage and Mission group, which was staffed, as mentioned, almost entirely by MBiC personnel from Canada and the US. For several years, H. S. Hallman was on the Board of the Africa Industrial Mission, but he did not represent the Ontario MBiC officially. Not even the temperance movement had received official participation at a Conference level. This NRRO co-operation is noteworthy in another way as many of the member bodies had divided from each other in earlier years: the New Mennonites, Reforming Mennonites and the Old Orders had all come out of the Mennonite Conference of Canada in the 1850s, the 1870s and the 1890s respectively. Later, the independent congregation Stirling Avenue Mennonite Church, which had broken away from First Mennonite (King St., Kitchener) in the 1920s, joined the NRRO. You can call it ecumenical behavior, as Steiner does in the recent *GAMEO* article about Sam Goudie,[20] or you can call it co-operation as the "ecumenically-shy" Missionary Church/ EMCC would tend to, it is still remarkable that *war* drove these sometimes rival Mennonite groups to do something together for *peace*, for the first time for some of them.

The major aim of the NRRO at first was to raise $100,000 from the 7,000 members of the seven or eight participating denominations for relief

---

18. See report of the Military Problems Committee, *Ontario Conference Journal 1947*, 38–39: "No particular problems . . ."

19. Samuel Frederick Coffman' s career parallel's Samuel Goudie's in several ways, such as the extent of their involvements in Conference, General Conference, and interMennonite relations. Coffman served 54 years, Goudie, 55. Coffman lived 1872–1954, Goudie 1866–1951. They both made visits to western Canada: Coffman in 1901, Goudie in 1905. They both liked Vineland, ON. See Koch, "Coffman."

20. Storms and Steiner, "Goudie, Samuel."

of people harmed by the war. The war ended before the collection was given, but soon after between $70,000 to $80,000 in donations were sent.[21] The resolution for the Memorial Fund, as the Ontario MBiC called it at the 1918 Annual Conference, was unanimously supported. Sam Goudie and Ephraim Sievenpiper were delegated to contact all the churches of Ontario's MBiC to solicit for the fund.[22] From September 1916 to September 1920, the Ontario Conference donated $4,474 to the Red Cross and the Memorial Fund. In the year of the Memorial Fund collection, $3,586 was donated, mostly for the Fund, far below the target of $10 per member.[23] After the war, but before the Second World War, fresh NRRO relief funds were sent for famines in China (1920) and Russia (1921), for Russian Mennonite immigrants to Canada (1923), sufferers in the Spanish civil war (1937), and drought in western Canada (1937–38).[24] Minutes of the NRRO are missing during David Heise's chairmanship (1924–1937) or non-existent, but little activity is visible from those years anyway. Nevertheless, the Ontario Conference elected their representatives annually as if needing to be ready. In 1934 Goudie wrote a fellow executive member, Thomas Reesor, asking for a list of all the monies collected and how much from each denomination and to which cause the funds were sent.[25] Recognizing that wars and rumors of wars were increasing, Goudie and C. N. Good contributed to the readiness of young non-resistant men in the 1930s by publishing the collection of Canadian laws concerning military service in 1934. The Spanish Civil War of 1937 gave an occasion for the NRRO to begin relief work again. The Ontario Conference Reference Committee began considering the situation 3 November 1937 at the request of Goudie, chair of the Committee and again on the executive of the NRRO. The Committee passed a resolution asking the NRRO to

---

21. Epp, *Separate People*, 377. Coffman, "Non-resistant Relief Organization," said "$70,000."

22. *Ontario Conference Journal 1918*, 11. Sievenpiper was sick in the intervening year, so Goudie did it alone during his rounds as Presiding Elder.

23. "Statistical Report," *Ontario Conference Journal 1920*.

24. Coffman, "Non-resistant Relief Organization."

25. Samuel Goudie to Thomas Reesor, 1934, Thomas Reesor fonds, Mennonite Archives of Ontario at Conrad Grebel University College. Reesor, a member of the Old Order Mennonites, is clearly the treasurer for the first year, signing the call for a Memorial Fund in 1918, though not recorded in the *GAMEO* article on the NRRO when accessed October 30 2018. The letter of 1918 is from the NRRO file in the Mennonite Archives of Ontario.

consider the war sufferers in the Spanish Civil War,[26] as American Mennonites were doing. Whether the Ontario Conference was first to urge the NRRO to act or not, it is remarkable that the MBiC in Ontario actually took this action, especially considering all the world conflicts they could have been addressing. I suspect that it was urged by the younger Elder, J. Harold Sherk, who as Conference secretary from the 1920s, was becoming influential in the Ontario Conference and had strong non-resistant convictions.[27] Sherk was not on the Reference Committee, however, so the action probably had Goudie's complete support.[28] The September 1938 Annual Conference accepted the NRRO's decision of January 7, 1938 to send relief to "war sufferers" and urged the Church to support war relief in Spain (and "clothing etc." to the drought-stricken Canadian North-West) by free-will offerings.[29]

The 1938 Ontario Annual Conference made other preparations for the probability of a new war. The Mennonite Church General Conference, meeting in Turner, Oregon, in 1937 had developed a long statement about "Peace, War, and Military Service." They invited other Mennonite groups to endorse the document, which became known as the Turner Statement. Samuel Goudie, J. Harold Sherk, and Milton Bricker were appointed by the Ontario Conference "to act in conjunction with representatives of other non-resistant Churches to present to the Prime Minister of the Dominion of Canada briefs stating our position as non-resistant Churches."[30] The new committee met and organized in Milton Bricker's home in Toronto on January 17, 1939 with Goudie appointed Chairman, and Sherk as the Secretary. The three went over the doctrine and history of the MBiC's relation to non-resistance and realized they could endorse most of the Turner Statement. Once the committee had agreed on a modified statement, they sent it to the Canada Northwest Conference and also decided to involve the Brethren in Christ in Ontario. Goudie, Sherk and Bricker held a number of meetings with the BiC bishop, Ernie J. Swalm, with S. F. Coffman present unofficially, and by August their statements were successfully conveyed to Prime Minister Mackenzie King. This was all done on behalf of the MBiC

26. *Ontario Conference Journal 1938*, 22.
27. Marr, "Sherk."
28. Members that year were Goudie, Bricker, C. N. Good, William B. Moyer and Sidney S. Shantz.
29. *Ontario Conference Journal 1938*, 24.
30. *Ontario Conference Journal 1938*, 37.

Ontario Conference which did not meet until ten days after Canada declared war on September 10, 1939. "The work of the Committee on the Memorial which was forwarded to the Prime Minister was endorsed by a unanimous vote of the Conference."[31] Frank Epp noted that the Turner paragraph the MBiC could not endorse for this war was the one rejecting humanitarian service under military control, such as Red Cross or YMCA work. The door was now open for MBiC young men to join the war effort as far as humanitarian service, even if under military direction.[32] Goudie, Bricker and Sherk did not give their reasons for accepting this change in policy, but they must have known what they were doing. Mennonite historians point to it as demonstrating the gradual assimilation of the MBiC to world culture which assumes countries must conduct wars to protect themselves and preserve freedom.[33] The Committee may have been bowing to the reality they knew in the MBiC by accepting the policy of western Canadian Mennonites.

THE CANADIAN MENNONITE BOARD OF COLONIZATION 1922–1925

The plight of Mennonites fleeing Lenin's "workers' paradise" in the early 1920s involved Sam Goudie in one more way. Steiner details the explorations Canadian Mennonites made to unify their approach to the Canadian government about a 1919 Canadian government ban on immigration of Mennonites and Hutterites, including those from the US. It was also becoming difficult for Mennonites and Hutterites to visit or study in Canada.[34] At the same time, some Mennonites in Manitoba were disturbed, as francophone Canadians had been, over the enforcement of English only as the language of education, contrary to the assurances they had been given on first migrating to Canada. The government pointed out the irony of some Mennonites wanting to come to Canada, and some wanting to leave.

---

31. *Ontario Conference Journal 1939*, 38–40. The Memorial stated that the MBiC was in continuity with the Dordrecht Confession of Faith with respect to doctrines of peace and non-resistance; Epp, *Struggle for Survival*, 567.

32. Epp, *Struggle for Survival*, 567–68. The writer's first pastor in the UMC, Earl Pannabecker, served as a stretcher bearer in the Red Cross in exactly this way in the Second World War. Several Mennonite groups in western Canada accepted a similar approach, mostly those from Russia, who had accepted medical work under the Tsars.

33. For example, Steiner, *Promised Lands*, 579.

34. Steiner, *Promised Lands*, 232–38.

As the noose tightened around Russian Mennonites, Canadian Mennonites petitioned the new government of Mackenzie King for the ban to be lifted. Goudie with Samuel Coffman was part of the delegation of western and eastern Canadian Mennonites, with Abram A. Friesen from Russia, who went to Ottawa on March 29, 1922 to see the minister of immigration and colonization, Charles Stewart, the minister of agriculture, William Motherwell, who was from Saskatchewan, and the Member of Parliament from North Waterloo, William D. Euler. The western delegate and the Russian Mennonite representative did most of the talking, according to Steiner, but on this occasion, Mennonite solidarity was achieved. The petition moved the government of Mackenzie King to lift the ban in June 1922.[35]

At the request of western Canadian Mennonites, Sam Goudie and Sam Coffman were appointed members from the MBiC and the Mennonite Conference of Ontario, respectively, on the Canadian Mennonite Board of Colonization, organized in May that year. The scheme did not have smooth sailing, logistically or financially. However, Russian (originally Dutch) Mennonites started coming in 1923, 3,000 of whom went to the west. In 1924, 5,000 more were able to enter Canada, 1,500 of whom were settled in Ontario. This situation, Steiner says, affected the Mennonite landscape in Ontario permanently, which had received mainly Swiss-South German Mennonites from Pennsylvania and Amish straight from Europe since the late 1700s.[36]

Kitchener's Bethany Church was the main MBiC congregation involved when on July 19, 1924, several hundred refugees (eight hundred fifty!) from the Ukrainian Mennonite colonies arrived by Canadian National Railways in Waterloo, co-ordinated by Erb Street Mennonite Church, Waterloo. Bethany was responsible for about one hundred refugees.[37] The move to Canada was disorienting to people torn from their comfortable settlements in Russia and taken into the rather different ways of far more rural Mennonites of Ontario.[38] Ministers Jacob P. Friesen and Jacob W. Re-

---

35. Steiner, *Promised Lands*, 236.

36. Steiner, *Promised Lands*, 236. More details are in Epp, *Struggle for Survival*, 157–77. An index reference to page 165 mistakenly attributes some opposition to the immigration to the MBiC. In fact it was the Mennonite Brethren, as the text shows.

37. Bethany's committee was helped (for German translation) by C. N. Good's wife, Livy (Hallman) Good, her daughter Grace (Good) Cressman (Clayton W. Cressman's wife), and Mrs. Joseph S. Shantz (probably Mary (Snyder) Shantz, Ward Shantz's mother). They spoke Pennsylvania "Dutch," not the same as the newcomer's High German, but it was better than nothing.

38. Shantz, *Bethany*, 45–46.

imer attended the 1924 Ontario Conference in September meeting in New Dundee. Reimer spoke of his community's experience of the past few years in a very moving way.[39] Rev. Peter Goertzen (Mennonite Brethren) gave a short address, interpreted by Silas Cressman, in the 1925 Annual Conference in Vineland.[40] This help continued until families were settled and the Mennonite Brethren congregations later meeting at, for example, Ottawa St., Kitchener, or Vineland in Niagara were established.

---

39. *Ontario Conference Journal 1924*, 10, 15, 31 and 34.

40. *Ontario Conference Journal 1925*, 25. I identify the three men from Steiner, *Promised Lands*, 256.

11

A History and a Mission

AFTER THE WORLD WAR, several matters engaged Goudie's attention. One of them, the Ministerial Conventions, were a continuation from the 1890s, but two were new. One was proposed by a colleague, and the other, the denominational mission, was a passion of Goudie's that needed the collaboration of many across the church to make happen.

BETHEL PUBLISHING AND HUFFMAN'S *HISTORY*

We have already mentioned several issues that were important in the 1920 General Conference in Kitchener, especially the establishment of a denominational mission, but there was more discussion on the reading course, something on the *Gospel Banner* and purchasing of Bethel Publishing.

J. A. Huffman founded many publishing efforts in his lifetime. Bethel Publishing Company was the first.[1] He used it to publish the *Gospel Banner* when he was elected editor in his second term beginning 1916. The MBiC leaders were persuaded by Bethel that the church could benefit by operating its own publishing company as most other denominations did, to offset *Gospel Banner* deficits. They set about purchasing Bethel in 1917 and for raising funds, the Executive Committee announced a "General Conference Forward Movement." To make Bethel profitable, Goudie urged the

---

1. Huffman, *Mennonite Brethren in Christ*, 174–75.

whole church to begin ordering all their church and Sunday School supplies from Bethel Publishing, beginning January 1918.[2]

One new long-lasting plan discussed in the Conference was a proposal to publish a denominational history. J. A. Huffman initiated this. The Executive Committee sometime in 1919 approved the history proposal and by 1920, Huffman reported that the work was at the galley proof stage, available for the conference delegates to inspect and approve.[3] The Ontario Conference in September 1919 in response to a communication from J. A. Huffman resolved to establish a committee "to prepare Biographical sketches for the Church History being compiled by the Bethel Publishing Co."[4] The two Presiding Elders, Goudie and Silas Cressman with Peter Cober were given this job. The format of the sketches in the history book strongly suggest a form was used, in fact in Eleanor Bunker's collection, a copy of such a form with entries in Sam Goudie's own handwriting still exists.[5] One might have thought H. S. Hallman, who preached in that General Conference, would have been an ideal member of the committee, having been closely connected with the denominational magazine for twenty intense years, despite his diversion into C&MA circles for a while, but perhaps he was not free to travel.

The Presiding Elders were in a good position to collect profiles, because in their quarterly meeting travels, they went over the whole Conference and could contact all the ministers selected for inclusion in the book. Peter Cober had a long acquaintance with the Conference, not least as a Presiding Elder from the earlier years. Ontario Conference, with its predecessor church (New Mennonite Church of Canada West and Ohio) had a longer history than most other districts of the denomination including Pennsylvania and supplied fifty of the one hundred twenty profiles. Nevertheless, they had to rely on memories for certain profiles, such as for Abraham (d. 1893) and Joseph Raymer (d. 1879). Some leaders such as Christian Troyer (d. 1883) and Samuel Schlichter (who died in 1873 before the forming of the Reforming Mennonite Society) are named in the book, but no profiles were provided.[6] There were some errors, which appear to be misread-

---

2. Sam Goudie, "Chairman Goudie's Announcement," *GB* (25 October 1917) 14.
3. *Tenth General Conference 1920*, 13.
4. *Ontario Conference Journal 1919*, 25.
5. Goudie's papers in the Eleanor Bunker Collection are planned to be kept at the Mennonite Archives of Ontario at Conrad Grebel University College.
6. Profiles for Troyer and Schlichter are now available in *GAMEO* articles.

ing of handwriting in the compositing room and have been noted in the present book. In other cases, the editing was faulty, for example, Amos and Solomon Eby, though in fact cousins a few times distant, are given the same parents. Both were out of the denomination at the time, and no one corrected the proofs for their sketches.

The exercise may have inspired Goudie for some historical reminiscence because when he visited New Dundee in 1921 to dedicate Bethel's new building, he typed out his address with brief memories from his own experience on the circuit.[7] If he wrote out similar historical addresses for other church dedications, they have not surfaced.[8]

MINISTERIAL CONVENTIONS

The "Minutes of the Ministerial Conventions of the MBC Church [Ontario Conference]" survives in the Missionary Church Historical Trust (MCHT) and has the tantalizing note by some secretary of the Ministerial Convention that it was "continued from previous book dated 1890–1916." Unfortunately, the fate of the earlier minutes book is unknown, though various components of those minutes are recoverable from agendas and notices in the *Gospel Banner* and occasional printed programs.[9] I have not seen any comment from any minister of the Ontario Conference, male or female, on the usefulness of the Ministerial Convention, but since it was an institution which lasted from 1890 to 1948, it must have been very helpful in the self-education and unity of the eldership and approved ministering sisterhood of the Conference. Amazingly, the Convention seems to have welcomed the contributions of the men and the women workers (not in proportion to their numbers however), both in the presentation of the essays[10] and significantly, the discussion after the essay was read. I assume many of the conventions of male-female relations from the period were observed, but the mere fact of the interaction of the genders in the forum is remarkable. Topics chosen were mainly practical ones for professional development, as

7. Goudie, "Bethel Circuit." Box 1015, MCHT.

8. C. N. Good provided some, for example, for meetings at St. Thomas and Listowel, because of his involvement with the City Missions which began those congregations, Box 6002, MCHT.

9. For example, a program of September 1900, preserved in a diary of Sam Goudie. The David Sapelak fonds of the Mennonite Archives of Ontario has the program for 1940, signed by Sam Goudie, who was on its planning committee.

10. For example, Maude Chatham presented on "Prayer: Its Varied Aspects and Modes" in 1900.

we would say, but some were straight theological subjects. I do not plan to analyze this whole document here—it is an opportunity for further study for someone some day. What I do wish to do is reflect on Sam Goudie's contributions at this period of his career, from Presiding Elder up to his return to the pastorate (1933) and eventual retirement from most of the work of an elder of the MBiC (1940).

Since the Ministerial Convention preceded the Annual Conference by one day, the dates were fixed in relation to the Conference, that is in this period, around late September of each year. There was an organizing committee, usually including a pastor or two from the area where the Conference was to be held. In 1918, for example, Goudie helped the pastors of Markham and Stouffville organize the convention and got into the minutes only when he spoke in the discussion after the seventh essay was read.

The first minute of this book is dated September 18, 1917. The convention was held at Kitchener (Bethany Church), with A. G. Warder as the secretary-treasurer. Sam Goudie contributed the second essay, titled "The Minister's Ability and Responsibility in and out of the Pulpit." Before his contribution, Martha Hood read her essay on the practice of the ministerial meeting itself,[11] the others were C. N. Good on camp-meetings, H. S. Hallman on retention of workers, M. Bricker on feet-washing, C. F. Krauth on country churches, and T. F. Barker on evangelistic and pastoral preaching: eight contributions, seven practical theology, and one probably theological (on feet-washing).

I am not sure how the topics were selected and assigned. Many conventions had a "Question Drawer" into which participants could literally put papers with questions they wanted answers to. Some were answered in the current convention, but some were probably turned into essay topics and, it appears, assigned by the organizing committee. In 1920, Sam Goudie and C. N. Good were the committee to answer questions.

In the 1917 convention, discussion was opened on Goudie's essay by Peter Cober, the secretary noted, adding unhelpfully that Cober was "followed by others." Who were they? What did they say? The final note was frequently, "The essay was accepted." Some essays, as we noted before, were selected by a committee for publication in the *Gospel Banner*, usually three to five a year. In 1920, Sam and Ephraim Sievenpiper were that committee.

---

11. Her remarks might have included evaluation of the usefulness of the Convention, but her essay has not survived.

Discussion time was normally about ten minutes each, but sometimes a topic struck a chord with the group and they voted to "extend the time."

The quality of the essays varied. As we have noted before, the average education of an Ontario MBiC pastor in the first generation was on par with the average education of Mennonites generally—grade 8. Gradually more attended high school, and in the 1920s a fair number of young probationers were going to Bible schools which were available for some further studies, still at a high school level. Pulpit preparation and the reading course, the *Gospel Banner* itself and other books and magazines gave other opportunities to improve. Many MBiC pastors and workers felt keenly their lack of further training, such as Isaac Brubacher.[12] In 1924 Ministerial Convention, Elder Harvey Frey mentioned one of the disadvantages of the MBiC was that they had no school. Elder Elmer Moyer in 1926 also said a Bible School should be included in the mission of the Ontario Conference. Sam Goudie himself wished he had had more schooling.[13]

While he was a Presiding Elder, Sam Goudie usually contributed essays—every other year—on pastoral theology. In 1920, however, we saw him write with feeling on the "Doctrine of Non-Resistance." Otherwise, he might give an impromptu talk as he did in place of Elder William Brown, who was sick, about the assigned topic, "The Divine Call to the Ministry and How to Distinguish between the call to the Home and Foreign Missionary Work," in 1921. This was the address in which, referring to his (Goudie's) own call to the ministry, the secretary recorded, "He briefly related his own experience."[14]

In 1922, Goudie was only recorded as praying at the end of the day, but in 1923 Sam read an essay titled "The Abilities and Qualifications that Constitute a Successful Ministry." In 1924, he did not have an essay, but opened the discussion of Peter Cober's called "Bible Landmarks that have identified the MBC Church in the Past and our Present Standing." This time the secretary provided longer notes on Cober's address and even notes on Goudie's response. Cober listed the MBiC's emphasis on "Fundamental doctrines—Repentance, regeneration, Entire Sanctification . . . Our integrity to these Fundamentals have kept us from being swallowed up in other

---

12. Lageer, *Merging Streams*, 146. Isaac Brubacher (1883–1950) entered ministry in 1908, ordained 1912; Huffman, *Mennonite Brethren in Christ*, 227. He is credited with making the first donation for Emmanuel Bible School.

13. Frey: "Ministerial Convention," 56–57; Moyer: p. 76. See reference mentioned before, "Necessity of Ministerial Education," *GB* (28 October 1915) 11.

14. "Ministerial Convention," 30.

organizations. The Spirit of devotion, as manifested in our camp-meetings, in prayer especially of many years ago has also been an outstanding feature." In response, Goudie "expressed regret that Bro. Cober had not had time to finish" (he had stopped suddenly when his allotted time expired, the secretary had noted). Goudie picked up other topics perhaps unrecorded by the secretary: "He [Goudie] specially emphasized the doctrine of separation, numerating and commenting on the doctrines of non-resistance, non-swearing of oaths, washing the saints feet, baptism by immersion." "A number of others took part. The essay and discussion were received. Two verses of the hymn "A Charge to Keep I Have" were sung."[15]

The use of the word "fundamentals" by Cober is probably influenced by the prominence of the word since the publication of the famous booklets (1910–1915) and subsequent movement, but it is remarkable that the five famous doctrines promoted by the movement, (inerrancy of Scripture, the Virgin Birth, substitutionary atonement, bodily resurrection, authenticity of miracles),[16] were not in Cober's or Goudie's minds. Those would be assumed by the MBiC and were not contested as they were in some larger denominations. The fundamentals for these leaders were "practised" in the daily church life: getting people to conviction of sin (leading to repentance), persuading people to seek the new birth (regeneration), and urging people to pursue holiness (sanctification). Goudie's list is heavily Anabaptist, except the baptism *by immersion* (most Mennonites practised effusion, that is, pouring). On an occasion such as this ministerial, Goudie was possibly emphasizing the doctrines he thought were in danger of being lost or reduced.

My experience with Christian students in Nigeria has blurred, for me, the distinction between doctrines and actions which the Missionary Church, and which many western church traditions make, as in "Articles of Faith *and Practice*." When we heard of a denomination restricting who may pass beyond an altar railing at the front of the church building to those who are wearing a suit and tie, my students would comment saying, "That is not our doctrine." And of course they are right—it is not our teaching. St. Paul said that we must only "do" what springs from "faith" (Roma 14:23). Any "practice" cannot merely be "things that we do" (customs) but represent real belief (teaching accepted, trust lived). The MBiC used somewhat

---

15. 1922: "Ministerial Convention," 1923, 1924: 52–53, Box 6001, MCHT.

16. Marsden, *Fundamentalism*, 117–23. The Presbyterian version. A later version replaced miracles with the premillennial return of Christ.

different language: the *Discipline* spoke of "Articles of Faith" and "General Rules for our Society." "Rules," like "duty," is a word twenty-first-century Christians in the west generally shy away from. Consider the topics of the "Rules" from a *Discipline* as late as 1951: General Services; Special or Revival Meetings; Prayer and Fellowship Meetings; Class Meetings; Duties of Members; Singing; Apparel; Intoxicating Liquors; Harmful Indulgences and Habits [mostly on tobacco]; Secret, Oath-Bound Societies; Conformity to the World; Divorce; and an article with a long title, on church discipline. Lots of room for legalism, but also an attempt to live holy lives, however limited. I don't know if all of the institutions, as I call them, such as class meetings, were still actually conducted in 1951, but the church considered that conduct did matter, in and out of the congregational setting. "These are the general rules of our society, all of which are in harmony with the spirit of the Word of God."[17]

Administrative "practice" (policies, procedures) are customs agreed upon for the time, yet even they must be derived somehow from beliefs about the way Jesus or the apostles did things or taught. To men like Cober and Goudie, believing and doing were practically one and the same.[18]

Later in the day, Sam's brother Henry, who had returned from Alberta about 1920, read his essay, "Plainness and Uniformity of Dress" in which "[t]he brother mentioned the unpopularity of the subject and told how the churches have drifted on this line. His time was extended and an interesting discussion followed."[19] Here is another case where belief turned into a practice. The MBiC knew the word "legalism" but they were less worried about it than instilling obedience, humility and contentment.

The 1925 Ministerial included as its fifth topic, Sam Goudie's essay, "The Why and How of the United Missionary Society." Goudie had been

17. *The Doctrines and the Discipline of the United Missionary Church 1951*, 37.

18. Interesting to compare this with Bill Hossler, US Missionary Church President writing in *Missionary Church Today* (Winter 2010) 3, "Rather than biblical distinctives being our primary denominational uniqueness, we coupled that with an insatiable passion to be missional in outreach. We have an unwavering desire to be biblical, but that desire raises the Great Commission into the cross hairs of what we do." (The image of "cross hairs" suggests a rather unfortunate allusion to gun sights to this reader.) Apparently some churches think they can declare their distinctiveness to be simply "biblical beliefs," without "biblical doing"? Hossler is correct in that in the Great Commission (Matthew 28:18–20), Jesus spoke of us making disciples by doing: going, baptizing and "teaching them to obey everything I have commanded you." The Great Commission inevitably leads directly to Holy Biblical Obedience.

19. "Ministerial Convention," 59.

President of the UMS for three years by that time and seemed to think that the ministerial members still needed him "to make clear what the society is and what it stands for and who the members and officers are." Goudie wanted people to know "the advantage thro' the Union of carrying on that which lone[-]handed none of our conferences would be able to do."[20] The UMS did not achieve a regular, effective way of publicity until the introduction of the *Missionary Banner* in 1938, but in any case missionary information, thinking and practice except some basics are not caught by most church members and even not all denominational leaders, immersed as they often are in their immediate church life, and their surrounding culture and events.[21] Hence repeated frequent statements and descriptions are appropriate to expose the why and the what of a mission society.

Goudie's next contribution was in 1927. This was a definitely a leader's talk: "The *Discipline*—Should it be Revised or Enforced," as someone who submitted to the church polity and who had to uphold it and did wholeheartedly. "The iscipline itself requires that its principles be strictly adhered to and carried out." Goudie said the *Discipline* needed to be more widely known. "The [d]iscipline is not perfect. It can be revised . . . ," but Goudie said the revision must be by the pattern laid down: recommendation from Annual Conferences and consideration by the General Conference.[22] Perhaps some members were asking questions or grumbling about the denomination but not understanding the way to go about constructive change. It is always discouraging in conferences to hear people ask about things that are already spelled out in documents that were distributed or revisit discussions that were already held, because they were not there or did not read the reports (Forgive me, I have done it myself). I do not know if Goudie was seeing those situations, but it sounds as if he were.

In 1930, Goudie led a round table discussion on the need for a "Minister's Superannuation Fund" and in 1931, the administrative question of "Proper Representation in the Conference Bar."[23] In 1934, Goudie, back in place as a pastor in Toronto, read "The Apostle Paul, An example for the Present Day Minister, Experimentally, Doctrinally and Practically." In

---

20. "Ministerial Convention," 66.

21. I accept Ralph Winter's view, at least as an observation, that people who make a second commitment to missions after their conversion are often needed for missions to flourish; in Winter, "Two Structures," B-47. See also Fuller, *Missions*, 127.

22. "Ministerial Convention," 81–82.

23. 1930: "Ministerial Convention," 108, 1931: p. 114.

1937, Goudie again led a round table talk on "Why Preach Holiness." This was his last substantial contribution, according to the minutes, though he read scripture and made remarks in 1941.[24] By this time the ministerial convention had fewer topics treated (down to only two in 1944), and thereafter was basically a special sermon by outside speakers. There is no record of Goudie participating past 1946 in his eightieth year, when he prayed. The institution practically ended after 1948 when other activities replaced it, as far as I can see.

Thus, in the thirty-two years covered by this minute book, Sam Goudie contributed ten times, but after 1934, he contributed only once. During the years he was a Presiding Elder, he contributed about once every two years. Two of these ten were Round Table moderations (one pastoral theology, one doctrinal); of the rest, seven were mainly pastoral issues, and only one (non-resistance) was more doctrinal. His last contribution (why holiness) could have been doctrinal, but by the title could be simply pragmatic: why is it useful.

GOUDIE FAMILY EVENTS, 1918–1929

Goudie family events in 1918, in the midst of the organizing of the NRRO and before the end of the war, included the weddings of Sam and Eliza's two sons within a month of each other. Fletcher Smith Goudie married Ina Dorcas Mertens, daughter of a pioneering family whose farm was on the immediate southwest edge of Stouffville, a Christian Church family, on March 27, 1918. Howard Allen Goudie married Edith Jackson (b. 1890 in Toronto) on April 24, 1918.[25] Before these happened, Sam's brother, David W. Goudie the deacon, died on February 5, 1918, at his wife's place in Markham.

A few years later, the wife of Sam's brother Henry, Sarah (Wildfong) Goudie, died on September 26, 1921, while Henry was serving as the pastor for the Aylmer field. She was buried with other Goudies[26] in Wanner Men-

---

24. 1934: "Ministerial Convention," 134, 1937: p. 154, 1941: p. 175.

25. Fletcher (d. 1983) and Ina had four children. After Ina's death, he married Rita (Paisley) Barnes in 1966. Allen (d. 1982) and Edith (1890–1978) had no children. Some of his career, Allen worked on Great Lakes ships; Allen P. Stouffer, comments on a draft, 14 January 2019. Genealogical information from Eleanor (Goudie) Bunker and Bunker, *Hugh Goudie Family*, 122–29; Reta Barnes: Eleanor Bunker, typescript notes for the author, March 2011, [4].

26. By 1921, others buried at Wanner were at least Benjamin (in 1846) not quite 2 years old; Tobias (d. 1858), who had lived not even a month; David Senior and Nancy

nonite Cemetery, across the road from the Wanner Church, just north of Hespeler. Henry continued as the pastor at Aylmer, until he was transferred to Hespeler in 1923. About that time he married Mrs. Susannah (Doner) Lageer (b. May 4, 1864) on October 16, 1923.[27] She was the mother of several Lageers in MBiC history: Edith Myrtle (Lageer) Good, a City Mission Worker who served 1918–1930; Russell G. Lageer, a probationer briefly around 1920; and Wilmot E. Lageer who was a pastor (1914–1918) and a missionary in Nigeria (1918–1921). Sadly, Susannah died in 1925. Henry retired from active ministry in 1926 except for a half-year at Gormley (March to September 1929). For a while he lived with his daughter Annie (Mrs. Arthur Clendenen) at Box Grove, three km southeast of Markham village. Still quite healthy at eighty-seven, he was living with another daughter in Kitchener in 1938 when the *Kitchener Daily Record* interviewed him.[28]

Meanwhile, Goudie's long-term desire to see a denominational missionary society finally took shape 1918–1921.

AN ALMOST DENOMINATIONAL MISSION BOARD, 1921

The 1916 MBiC General Conference had said nothing about missions except a parting resolution calling on the MBiC to pray for foreign missionaries. With the war, and the difficulty of sending new personnel, perhaps the time was not ripe to plan new structures. The *Gospel Banner* editor, J. A. Huffman, wrote an open letter in early 1918 calling for readers to send in comments about a denominational mission society. His call was immediately answered by the Nebraska Conference Presiding Elder, Clifford Scott, who advocated such a mission. Other readers wrote in support, mainly serving or former missionaries, and leaders of the smaller conferences. Sam Goudie also wrote in support.[29] The response in the magazine was unanimously in favor, appearing from March 1918 to September 1920, and Huffman added favorable comment to several of them.[30] The 1920 GC finally authorized forming a missionary society to which the various conferences

---

(1896 and 1906 respectively); Helena Caroline (Snyder), James' wife who died in 1909. Later James was buried in Wanner's (1931) and finally Henry in 1942.

27. The widow of a member of the Brethren in Christ, Peter John Lageer of Stayner.

28. "'Let Your Beards Grow' Church Head's Advice," *Kitchener Daily Record* (22 March 1938) page not available.

29. Scott, "Letter," *GB* (21 March 1918) 4; Goudie, "General Conference Foreign Mission Board," *GB* (29 August 1918) 3.

30. Fuller, "Nigeria," 87n101.

could belong through representatives elected by them. As mentioned, there was resistance in some parts of the church, especially the Pennsylvania Conference, to mandate a society which could recruit, raise money, set plans and policy outside the control of the individual Conferences. In fact, there were heated words about Pennsylvania Conference and an attempt to bring a charge of failing the denomination by a member of the General Conference. In the last sessions, the Resolution Committee introduced an apology aimed at Pennsylvania Conference, and a prohibition of any other attempt by any but a whole Annual Conference or the Executive Committee to bring a charge or accusation against another Conference. Pennsylvania asked to be excused from representation on the Executive Committee and was granted that privilege as well as the option to not be involved in the UMS.[31] Goudie could not have been unaware of the serious damage to the unity of the MBiC Church these actions by Conferences and individuals were producing both ways.

The proposal was to form a mission governed by a Board structure, that is, directed by a group who did not have to be accountable to another denominational level, though they might communicate information, and would represent the desires of the Conferences which elected the members. Sam Goudie was appointed to arrange for the organizing meeting. Goudie was Chairman of the MBiC Foreign Missionary Society (General Board) at the time and seemed to have experience in managing a mission organization for the MBiC. Abraham B. Yoder, the long-time secretary-treasurer of the UOMB, probably had equivalent experience. The authorizing resolution directed that each Foreign Mission committee of each Conference should appoint a member to meet in Elkhart, Indiana, "at a time appointed by the chairman [of the MBiC Executive Committee]."[32]

The representatives met in January 1921 as planned and developed a constitution for comment and ratification by the Conferences. Five of the seven MBiC Conferences accomplished this in time for an inaugural meeting at Goshen, Indiana, on October 5, 1921. A sixth Conference joined later.[33]

The organizing conference elected officers, with J. A. Huffman (then teaching right there at Goshen College and Seminary) as President, Sam Goudie as Vice-President, Clifford Scott as recording secretary, Abraham B. Yoder (a Presiding Elder of Indiana and Ohio) as the corresponding

31. *Tenth General Conference 1920*, 36–38.
32. *Tenth General Conference 1920*, 27.
33. Goudie, "United Missionary Society," 7.

secretary, and Ontario's Cyrus N. Good as treasurer. The new United Missionary Society inherited the work of the MBiC Foreign Missionary Society (General Board) in Nigeria, with fifteen missionaries directly under it. The UMS initially did not inherit the work of the largely MBiC-staffed United Orphanage and Mission Board, (six missionaries in 1921) on which several UMS board members were simultaneously serving. The UMS published letters from the UOMB missionaries in its two yearbooks of 1928 and 1930, however the UOMB did not merge with the UMS until 1932.[34]

With the organizing of the UMS, some MBiC members who were serving in India under other missions desired to be affiliated with it. Frances Matheson was the first to be so appointed in 1921. In 1924, under Goudie's presidency, the UMS board instructed former Hephzibah Faith Missionary Association missionaries from the MBiC Nebraska Conference, Rev. Walter E. Wood and his wife Mary (Dayhoff) Wood, who had gone to India in 1916, to acquire a comity territory in India.[35] Eventually, a 1,500 square mile zone (about 3,900 square kilometers) west of Kolkata (Calcutta) in West Bengal was designated for them among Bengali-speaking Hindus and the Santal (Santhal) people around the city of Purulia. The territory assigned, at one time in Bihar, is now part of the westernmost part of West Bengal and was formerly allotted to a German Lutheran mission, but removed from them after the first World War. Frances Matheson stated that at her station near Balarampur, the people were mainly Santals, "Bhumys and Mahatahs" [terms not used now] before Hindus and some Mohammedans migrated there for business purposes.[36] Goudie could report in 1924 that the UMS had opened its second field.

The 1930 *UMS Yearbook* also carried a report of the African Evangelistic Mission, a "full Gospel Holiness mission" which was led by Isaac O. and Annie Alice (Heise) Lehman. These MBiC members from Nebraska, formerly missionaries of the Brethren in Christ in Matopo, Rhodesia,

---

34. Storms, *What God Hath Wrought*, 93. Several publications state the UOMB ceased when the Ottomans closed the mission in 1914 in Turkey but this is not true.

35. "Comity" was the term for sharing responsibility for introducing missions into separate areas with no churches to prevent overlap and competition. This policy made great sense for efficiency in pioneering new areas. It cannot be used in places and times where members of various denominations have migrated and mingled on their own.

36. The territory was nearly doubled in 1948, when the HFMA wound down their mission in India and merged their territory with that of the UMS which was adjacent to them; Storms, *United Missionary Church*, 247. At the time, there were approximately 400,000 people in the district, 30% being animist Santals. Matheson, "My Word," 96.

started what became a family-run mission based in Johannesburg, South Africa, in 1901. By 1930 the AEM had twenty "mission rooms" around Johannesburg and over twenty in Eastern Transvaal, Portuguese East Africa (now Mozambique) and Rhodesia (now Zimbabwe). They were acting organizationally on their own, though reporting their 218 members with another 210 probationer class members as "MBC."[37] When the Nebraska Conference applied for the AEM to be recognized as part of the MBiC in 1936, the General Conference suggested instead that Nebraska could take them on as a Conference-supported mission conference.[38] This did not happen. The family still reported cheerfully from time to time to the *Gospel Banner* (eleven times 1927 to 1960). Eventually their mission was merged with that of the Church of the Nazarene in southern Africa.[39]

UMS PUBLICITY EFFORTS

The MBiC Foreign Mission Board (1905–1921) used the pages of the *Gospel Banner* to publish letters from missionaries and occasional articles. Missionaries also reported to the Conference of which they were members in annual reports often published in their Conference's journals. This added to the practice of reprinting missionary news and teaching from other magazines since the founding of the *Gospel Banner* in 1878.[40] As time went on the letters in the *Ontario Conference Journals* were abbreviated and eventually omitted. The UOMB had effective writers in some of the staff (especially Rose [Lambert] Musselman, Katie [Bredemus] Weaver, Blanche [Remington] Eby and Dorinda Bowman) and a regular newsletter, *Our Bi-Monthly Letter* (1915–1938) was sent to supporters, but neither

---

37. Lehman and Lehman, "African Evangelistic Mission," 89–94.

38. *Thirteenth General Conference 1936*, 24, 28.

39. Here is still another story waiting for research. Why the UMS declined to get involved in a field that was practically given to them is not clear. I suspect there are still people in the US Missionary Church who know. Perhaps the UMS did not feel right in accepting the work of missionaries who did not submit to the BiC mission? The Lehmans' daughters Faith, married to Thomas Sorenson, and Eunice Francis, married to Abraham E. Zook, continued the mission leadership. In 1949, Isaac Lehman, retired to Pennsylvania the year before, petitioned the UMS to help the AEM with some missionaries, but the UMS declined "because of present commitments," *Journal of the Proceedings of the United Missionary Society 1949*, 22. See also Engle, Climenhaga and Buckwalter, *Africa and India*, 362–63.

40. The missions content of the *Gospel Banner* waxed and waned as different editors saw fit. Some statistics on frequency are in Fuller, "Nigeria," 21, 23, 39 n. 75, but some variation may merely reflect the incompleteness of the index database.

the MBiC FMB nor the UMS managed anything regular for a long time. After the Armenian mission merged with the UMS, a 16-page booklet, *To Bind Up the Broken-Hearted* was prepared with illustrations and a map and published in 1936 summarizing the nearly forty-year effort.[41] For Nigeria, a pamphlet similar in style to an early SIM annual report was issued for the MBiC FMB by H. S. Hallman in 1908. The UMS Board authorized a quarterly newsletter, "The United Missionary Call" in May 1924 to be edited by Goudie, and the UMS published *Yearbooks* in 1928 and 1930, edited by Yoder.[42] The Depression discouraged continuing publications of that size. In 1930 the Nigerian field began producing their own "Nigeria Tidings," normally published in the pages of the *Gospel Banner*.[43]

It was only in Goudie's last year as President of the UMS (1938), that a 20-page trial magazine called *Missionary News*, exclusively for missionary reports and editorials, principally of the UMS, edited by Russell P. Ditmer of Ohio, was issued. It received such strong support that the monthly *Missionary Banner*, parallel to the *Gospel Banner*, was launched later that year. It may be wondered why the UMS did not produce a magazine as so many mission societies automatically did, and why Goudie, as president, did not promote such a magazine earlier. In his president's letter "To the Whole Constituency of the United Missionary Society," on the cover, Goudie's theme was "continued help in the future," openly meaning, keep supplying finances among other helps, please! The magazine also printed his article on prayer called "How to Get Things from God," which concluded with the need to pray for missions.[44] I speculate that since Goudie as chair of the denominational Executive Committee was frequently involved in handling the chronic deficits of the *Gospel Banner*, I imagine Goudie was reluctant to plunge the MBiC into further financial embarrassment. The UMS operated without debts. As it turned out, there was no debt from the publication of

---

41. Copy is in the David Sapelak fonds at the Mennonite Archives of Ontario at Conrad Grebel University College, Waterloo, ON. The United Orphanage and Mission Board awaits a full history. Another challenge for a book, project or thesis!

42. "Minutes of the UMS 1924," [in the Everek Storms Collection at Bowen Library, MCI Archives, Mishawaka, IN: "Resolved that we have an annual report and that A. B. Yoder [corresponding secretary] edit the same." and "Resolved that we publish an eight page Quarterly Bulletin and that S. Goudie edit the same."

43. Fuller, "Nigeria," 88 n. 115, 116, 117. Ditmer, "Banner Beginnings," 2. Storms, *What God Hath Wrought*, 158, lists a publication called *The Missionary* (1909–) from Berlin, ON, in his bibliography which did not continue either.

44. Sam Goudie, "How to Get Things from God," *MB* (September 1938) 4.

the *Missionary Banner*. The period immediately before the Second World War and during the war saw an increase in income for many in North America. There was money available after the war, too, enough to fund the sudden increase in young people applying for missionary service and founding many new societies. Actually, mission finances had been increasing for numerous mission societies during the war, but they had restricted opportunity to use the money, obviously.[45]

---

45. Pierard, "Evangelical Missionary Advance," 163.

12

Friendly Visitors, Mennonite Unions, Holiness Affairs

DURING SAM GOUDIE'S YEARS as a leader in the Ontario Conference and the MBiC denomination, a number of relations with other ecclesiastical bodies arose. Some were merely friendly relations, some were explorations looking for cooperation in a project, some were more ambitious. This chapter follows several activities relating to these affairs from 1910 to Goudie's retirement from the Presiding Elder's chair.

As early as 1910, the *Conference Journal* of Ontario reported Free Methodist Rev. Albert Sims presenting his Conference's resolution urging promoting holiness and unity between the two Conferences.[1] The resolution was welcomed and a fraternal delegate to the Free Methodists, Sam Goudie, was appointed.[2] In 1911, Sam reported that he did not go as planned and explained why to the satisfaction of the Conference, recorded only as "for lawful reasons."[3]

---

1. In 1895, Albert Sims was Kingston District Elder of the Eastern Ontario Conference of the Free Methodist Church. He operated a printing establishment in Toronto around 1900, and continued associated with the Eastern Ontario Conference, as the East/ West conference boundary was just west of Toronto; Sigsworth, *Free Methodist Church*, 105, 181–82.

2. *Ontario Conference Journal 1910*, 22–23, 29.

3. *Ontario Conference Journal 1911*, 15. The Goudies' daughter had died in 1910, and perhaps lingering grief prevented further travels.

In the middle of the first World War, in 1916, the second "All-Mennonite Convention" was held in Carlock, Illinois, with five delegates from the MBiC including J. A. Huffman and Sam Goudie.[4] To those who initiated the Conventions in 1913, the aim was "discussing common problems in the hope that such discussions would bring about greater unity among the various groups." Although not directly fulfilling the hope of unity, one result was that J. A. Huffman of Bluffton and Jacob Snyder of Pennsylvania went to Washington, DC, to present resolutions to US President Wilson urging legislation to accommodate young men of non-resistant churches if conscription should be implemented.[5]

A MODEST MENNONITE MERGER PROPOSAL

An interesting exploration of Mennonite union occurred after the First World War, and one may wonder if the experience of cooperation in relief services as well as other inter-Mennonite cooperative efforts in the US encouraged its promoters in 1920. Daniel Brenneman, who had facilitated several of the early mergers for the MBiC, had died in 1919. At the 1920 General Conference, two representatives from the Defenseless Mennonite Church, Joseph K. Gerig and Emanuel Slagle, addressed the Conference and included suggestions for a "union."[6] They apparently hinted that other Mennonite groups were interested in discussing union, too. The Conference was intrigued and set up a small committee to suggest a way forward. The chair of the Conference, A. B. Yoder, called on Sam Goudie, and C. I. Scott, who had spoken in favor of a union, to help. At the next session, the two reported:

> We recommend that this Conference appoint a Committee of five from the several Conferences more centrally located, and this Committee be authorized to meet a Committee from each of those churches that have expressed a desire to form a union, that the Committee be empowered to take such steps; and if necessary

4. The others were Sidney Lambert, A. B. Yoder, and Norah Lambert.

5. *GB* (3 August 1916) 2. Huffman's role in 1916 and reported in 1919 in Noah E. Byers, "All-Mennonite Convention," *Mennonite Life* (July 1948) 7–8, 10, at https://ml.bethelks.edu/store/ml/files/1948jul.pdf.

6. The Defenseless Mennonite Church ("Egli Amish") was the "parent" denomination of the Missionary Church Association, and continues to this day (2024) as the Fellowship of Evangelical Churches. For the MBiC, it would be a delicate discussion, since as we saw, they also discussed cooperation with the MCA, with which the MBiC, by then known as the United Missionary Church, eventually did merge, although only in 1969.

shall instruct the chairman of the Executive Board [that would be Sam Goudie!] to call a conference of delegates chosen by the above mentioned churches, to adjust differences and perfect an organization . . .[7]

This report was accepted.

The suggested conference was held at Elkhart, Indiana, and representatives of four bodies did meet on January 6, 1921. The groups were: the Defenseless Mennonites, again represented by Gerig and Slagle; the Missionary Church Association, represented by David Roth (another delegate was "called away owing to an accident at home"); and E. R. Augsburger from the Central Conference of Mennonites, a group of about twelve Amish-descended churches informally known as the "Stuckey Mennonites" which was centered in Illinois.[8] Two other Central Conference delegates were "deprived of being present on account of duties at home." There were five from the MBiC however: J. A. Huffman, A. B. Yoder, Nicholas W. Rich, Benjamin A. Sherk, and Sam Goudie.[9] Considering the number of Mennonite Conferences and denominations at the time, four are not very many, but their affinities are interesting. At least three of these small bodies were heavily influenced by evangelical revivalism (all but the Central Conference Mennonites—at least the *GAMEO* article does not reveal any particular affiliations apart from missions and institution-building after 1908),[10] three were descended from Amish (all but the MBiC), and two were additionally influenced by Wesleyan holiness (the MBiC) and the Christian and Missionary Alliance (the MCA) movements.

This group actually managed to draft a constitution and by-laws for united efforts in foreign mission work, a logical extension in some ways of the arguments Goudie had made for the formation of an MBiC General Mission in October 1920. The group urged the four churches to send five delegates each to a further conference in Goshen, Indiana, on October 5, 1921 for follow up discussions. Sam Goudie was among the delegates chosen to represent the MBiC. He seems to have timed the organizing meeting

7. *Tenth General Conference 1920*, 27.

8. A good history of the Defenseless/ Evangelical Mennonite Church is Nussbaum, *Born Again,* and see comments, including on the Missionary Church Association split of 1896, by Erdel, "Better Right Than Mennonite," 467–87.

9. "Minutes of a Meeting to Consider the Matter of Union, January 6, 1921," on MBiC Missionary Society General Board letterhead, dated February 1921. This document was brought to my attention by Timothy Erdel in 2002.

10. Weaver, "Central Conference," *GAMEO.*

of the UMS to close to the union consultation-no doubt to save money on the fares to the US! In fact, the committee of five reported in the 1924 General Conference that no delegates from any of the other three churches appeared. So those discussions died. No explanation was recorded.[11]

HOLINESS MERGER EXPLORATIONS

The committee continued to explore talks with still other churches, including the Pilgrim Holiness Church in June 1923, and the Wesleyan Methodist Connection of America. The Defenseless Mennonites again sent Joseph Gerig and Emanuel Slagle to address the MBiC in the 1924 General Conference. The Wesleyan Methodist Connection sent a fraternal delegate, Rev T. P. Baker.[12]

MBiC Union enthusiasm had considerably cooled by 1928. In Canada, "Church Union" talks between the Congregational Union of Canada, the Presbyterian Church of Canada and the Methodist Church of Canada, off and on for a generation, did finally culminate in the June 1925 union of the three denominations to great enthusiasm. Yet not all was well, as a sizable portion (about 40 percent) of the Canadian Presbyterians, especially in Ontario, declined to enter the United Church of Canada. Some of those who rejected the union spoke of it as illegal, or a betrayal of Presbyterian standards and tradition (there were various reasons for opposition). It is speculation, as I have not seen any direct comment good or bad from Goudie or the MBiC about the United Church union, but the noise about the union could not have left the MBiC Ontario Conference unmoved. There were congregations of the merging denominations near every MBiC field. The major Protestant bodies in Canada had long been accused of compromise over scriptural authority and worldly behavior by groups like the MBiC. In these very years, the Canadian Baptist conventions had also witnessed bitter words over liberal theology[13] especially coming from Thomas Todhunter Shields of Toronto's Jarvis Street Baptist Church. Any acrimony in church affairs would leave members of the Mennonite Brethren in Christ Church unwilling to get involved in similar conflicts. What dangers for the MBiC could lurk in mergers with allied denominations is not obvious.

11. *Eleventh General Conference 1924*, 13.
12. *Eleventh General Conference 1924*, 13–14.
13. Using a definition provided by Olsen, *Mosaic*, 62, "maximal acknowledgement of the claims of modernity," in which "modern reason and investigation—including science, philosophy and sociology—play determinative roles . . . they are regulative."

Some compromises in polity and favorite emphases, even points of doctrine, typically occur for unions to work. Liberalism would not likely be an issue. There were probably MBiC members who sympathized with liberal theology, but they were so few they have left scarcely a sign of their presence.[14] Evangelicals have plenty of other issues to disagree over.

In another generation, United Church liberal theology was reported with dismay if not alarm in the *Gospel Banner* at how far the UCC had departed from evangelical Christianity.[15] Without participating in any fundamentalist organizations officially, the MBiC would normally side with fundamentalist evaluation of liberal theology. Wesleyan holiness churches' priorities and theology did not regularly mesh with the Baptist-Presbyterian-Christian Brethren core of fundamentalism, either.[16] I do not know how events were felt in the MBiC Conferences in the US over various schemes of union and Federal Council of Churches activity in the 1920s and 30s. The MBiC did not join the Federal Council but did become a member of the (American) National Association of Evangelicals when it started in the 1940s, supplying some key staff members at times.[17]

In the 1928 MBiC General Conference, fraternal delegates to the Wesleyan Methodist Connection and the Defenseless Mennonites (A. B. Yoder and Clifford Scott, respectively), reported vaguely why they did not go to those churches' conferences as planned in 1924, and the Union Committee reported no actions.

The Missionary Church Association (ex-Defenseless Mennonites) and the MBiC had informally discussed merging since the 1898 formation of the MCA,[18] and other Mennonite groups perhaps met future partners

---

14. This could be a topic of study by a future historian. The EMCC of the early twenty-first century, having more experience with cultural assimilation, exhibits more signs of modern theological movements than the MBiC in the early twentieth.

15. The schizophrenia in the United Church of Canada over evangelical piety versus modernist theology is well studied by Redeemer College professor Kevin N. Flatt, *United Church*.

16. See for example, Bassett, "Fundamentalist Leavening," 65–91; Ingersol, "Strange Bedfellows," 123–41. See also Marsden, *Fundamentalism*, 73–74, 93–96. Jasper Abraham Huffman firmly rejected the Scofield Bible's dispensational schema as "erroneous," Jasper A. Huffman, "Editorial," *GB* (13 January 1913) 1, and Huffman, *Christian Doctrine*, 192.

17. Erdel, "Better Right than Mennonite," 83.

18. In the 1943 General Conference, after Goudie's last year as chair of the Executive Committee of the MBiC, there was another attempt to begin union talks through the Indiana and Ohio Conference. Still another attempt got as far as voting in each denomination in the 1950s, which lost by a few percentage points.

in these sessions, but the Mennonite habit of division continued. A different trend occurred among holiness groups in Canada, as many from the small Georgian Bay area Gospel Workers Church (founded around 1900) joined the Nazarenes in 1955,[19] and the declining remnants of the Holiness Movement Church joined the Free Methodists in Canada (1958). The Pilgrim Holiness Church, which had a few congregations in Ontario, and the Wesleyan Methodist Connection which also had a few, eventually merged in the US in 1968, becoming the Wesleyan Church, and their constituents in Canada similarly merged. Most recently, the Standard Church of America also joined the Wesleyan Church in 2006. Often, each merger left remnants unwilling to join, which turned independent or disappeared.

Oddly, the Canada Conference of the Evangelical Association (all in Ontario), which became Evangelical United Brethren, also merged in 1968, but with the liberal UCC. A number of EUB members and congregations, not liking merger with the UCC, chose to join the Ontario District of the United Missionary Church about that time.[20]

Thus, Sam Goudie did not see any mergers of the MBiC in his time of ministry, though he helped explore them. Cooperation continued, and over the years, the Ontario Conference camp-meetings made use of evangelists from kindred groups, mostly holiness groups and the Christian and Missionary Alliance. They were invited by the Reference Committee, of which, as we saw, Goudie was normally the chair.

---

19. Ably described in Hobbs, "Gospel Workers Church," 201–18. The merger with the Church of the Nazarene is described in Parker, *Nazarene*, 70–71.

20. One congregation, in Arnprior, joined the Wesleyan Church. Of the rest, 1) the majority of the Wilmot Centre church in Waterloo County, 2) many members of the Pembroke EUB, 3) Rye/ South River EUB, although the switch for some families happened some years later, 4) around 5 families of Floradale EUB, and 5) some members from Calvary EUB, Kitchener, became the nucleus of Missionary Churches in Wilmot Centre, Pembroke (First Missionary), Sundridge (Almaguin), Elmira (Emmanuel), and Waterloo (Lincoln Heights), respectively about 1968–69. Augsburg and Killaloe in the Ottawa Valley joined later, straight from the Evangelical Church based in western Canada in 1993. Several Ontario EUB pastors also joined the UMC in the 1960s; [Storms, Everek R], "Former EUB Congregation Joins the Missionary Church," *GB* (9 January 1969) 5. In the US, there were a few additions such as in Michigan (photo caption, *GB* (3 October 1968) 15; *Emphasis* (15 July 1969) 18, and later at Cloverdale, Kentucky, *Emphasis* (15 April 1975) 14.

ANNUAL CONFERENCE VISITORS

The Annual Conference continued to recognize visits from clergy of neighboring congregations, and sometimes officials from sympathetic denominations. Visitors from the MBiC Conferences, led by Michigan Conference (29 appearances), followed by those from Canada Northwest (10) were most numerous in the twenty-eight years of 1906 to 1933. All the rest combined were no more than 11 from three other Conferences. These visitors were nearly always received as advisory members of the Canada/Ontario Conference. Albert Sims and evangelist Levi Ecker of the Canadian Free Methodists (all FM visits numbered 24)[21] were almost regulars to the Ontario Annual Conferences for a time.[22] H. S. Hallman regularly sold Sim's books through the pages of the *Gospel Banner* up until 1908. The United Brethren in Christ "Radical" branch recorded a total of 9 visits over all years in the same period.[23] This custom of fraternal delegates became rarer.[24] Visitors continued, especially as staff of various organizations which had displays close to the conference hall.

21. By a "visit," I count every individual who attended in any year, and count them again in any other year they attended.

22. It might be significant that the Canadian Free Methodists made a move in 1920 to distinguish Canadian FM conferences from their much more numerous American co-members, but efforts stayed small until 1974. Was a possible merger one of their motives? See Kleinsteuber, *Renewal of Methodism*, 100–12. See also Sigsworth, *Free Methodist Church*, 216–23. Many Canadian components of binational churches, including the Missionary Church, were thinking of setting up national denominational structures in the 1970s. For the Missionary Church in Canada, the first steps came in 1975, with incorporation in 1979 and a national church in 1985.

23. Statistics: All denominations with visitors during Goudie's years: 17, four of which were represented by one visitor each. Some of these were individuals interested in joining the MBiC. The rest were: Mennonites (including one visit from a Stirling Ave. leader, and two Mennonite Brethren) (8), Baptists (5), Brethren in Christ (4), Evangelical Association/ Church (4), Christian and Missionary Alliance (4). Many recorded 3 "person-visits" or less: Christian Church (3), Church of the Nazarene (C. W. Ruth 2 times), Congregationalist (S. Sanderson 2 times), Salvation Army ("Sister Thompson"), Presbyterian Church of Canada, Pilgrim Holiness Church, the mission SIM (R. V. Bingham once) and the Canadian Bible Society.

24. From 1965, the Ontario District of the United Missionary Church gave serious effort to merging with the eastern Canadian section of the Christian and Missionary Alliance, but the talks collapsed when they realized that C&MA districts had no power to merge independently of their binational denomination. *Ontario Conference Journal 1965*, 40, 43. In the twenty-first century, Canadian C&MA and the EMCC are nudging closer again, sharing credentialing and educational institutions.

Before Sam Goudie's time as Presiding Elder, all visitors to the Canada/ Ontario Conference were voted advisory member status. During his years, the Conference added a category of "introduced" visitors, which did not give permission for them to speak in the conference. In the last nine years of Goudie's term, 32 of 35 non-MBiC guests were "introduced" instead of voted advisory membership in the Conference, compared to 25 out of 26 for MBiC members from other Conferences who were voted to be advisers. The First World War severely reduced the number of visitors, no doubt due to travel-related rationing. As visits resumed in the 1920s, attention from the Evangelicals and the United Brethren fell away.[25]

In the 1930s, the Free Methodists in Ontario were hoping the MBiC would join them in building up their college (founded in 1926) in Lorne Park, near Port Credit, now in southwest Mississauga, Ontario. Many FM pastors and school officials visited the Ontario Conference. Some MBiC members went to the school to study, and the Free Methodists were hopeful, inviting the Ontario Conference to visit and evaluate, which they did, while Goudie was chair of the Conference. The Brethren in Christ also started a school in Gormley in 1932, the Salvation Army had its Davisville Training School (Toronto)[26] and several MBiC young people attended Toronto Bible College (started 1894) and other schools in the US. The Depression affected the FM, BiC and Salvation Army schools adversely. MBiC students attended all these schools at one point or other.

In the end however, the Conference decided in 1938 to establish its own Bible school, to begin in 1940, which became Emmanuel Bible College.[27] Free Methodist visits dried up in the years after Goudie retired from being Presiding Elder (1933). By 1940, Sam Goudie was reducing his participation in many Ontario Conference affairs. He continued as chair of the Reference Committee until 1941. When an EBS Board photograph was taken, he was not present.[28]

---

25. All statistics derived from *Canada/ Ontario Conference Journals* 1898–1941.

26. Founded in 1915, Moyles, *Blood and Fire*, 285, the Davisville School was not the first Canadian Salvation Army training institution. Some were closed during the depression; Davisville for two years.

27. Fuller, "Emmanuel Bible College," unpublished paper requested by EBC for its 50th anniversary in 1990, in Box 4202, MCHT.

28. *The Pilot*, 10.

13

Conference Matters 1924–1933

SAMUEL GOUDIE WAS TO see further Conference structures established in his last ten years as Presiding Elder. This chapter looks at three of them: Campgrounds, the Young People's Society and the provision of a Catechism. A fourth institution, the Ontario Conference Women's Missionary Society, although established outside this time period in 1939, is examined to see what part, if any, Goudie as a missions leader had in founding the WMS.

CAMPGROUNDS

A felt need of the Ontario Conference was to have permanent camp-meeting land. Other denominations had them, and as early as 1883, according to Lloyd Brubacher and others, the idea of buying Moses Burkholder's land at Breslau was talked about and even a committee formed to see about it, but nothing developed.[1] While the Conference owned no land for a camp-meeting, they made use of that freedom to move around the province. Fields could make requests through their Quarterly Conferences to host a camp-meeting. The tabernacle (tent) meetings were used more for direct evangelism, but in a way, they were like mobile camp-meetings as well, so acquiring permanent campgrounds was not urgent. Several privately owned camp grounds were favored for periods, such as the Schneider's woods along Mill St., Kitchener, a site now partly represented by a

---

1. Brubacher and others, *Camp Meetings*, 7.

small park and lawn bowling court.[2] Pike's Peak on the Isaac Pike farm near Gormley, Moyer's bush on the Moyer farm at Dickson Hill and the Maple Valley site in Dufferin County have also been mentioned. Not all the sites they used are known today. The place along the Nith River near New Dundee where Sam Goudie preached his first sermon and was baptized is not known, for example, unless local memory still has it. A photograph in the MCHT is labeled "Hespeler Camp," which is an unknown site, though named twice in the camp-ground booklet in 1914 and 1920. The Reference Committee also had the option of choosing available sites across the Conference to expose the church and teachings of holiness to new areas.[3] I don't see Goudie often taking a visible lead in the strategy of East District camp-meeting locations. Local committees made preparations, but the Presiding Elders were definitely involved in camp leadership and continued to report on them in the *Gospel Banner*.

The Canada East camp-meeting Centennial booklet refers to attempts to buy land in 1909, 1914, 1916 and 1921. Sam Goudie was on the committee in 1914 "to search for a property to buy." They reported on a possible property at Bridgeport, Waterloo County, in 1915, but no more mention was made of it.[4] As a Conference leader, Sam Goudie was often involved through the Reference Committee, or received reports from committees investigating properties that they had heard about or that people offered to sell to them. For some years they negotiated with a Mr. Moss in Kitchener.[5] Then J. Hubert Sherk offered to sell a field on his Centreville farm where Fairview Rd. and King St. intersect now in Kitchener. The search took a lot of turns and delays, and from this distance in time it does not seem obvious what was the cause of the delay and hesitation. Certainly, cost was one of the factors. The tabernacle tents were a continual care, keeping them in repair, storing them, and buying new ones, but a permanent campground would also need maintenance and the members knew that.

Finally, land was bought (1925) at Stayner and shortly afterward from John Moss on Weber St. at what was then still called Centreville,

---

2. The photograph of a camp-meeting scene in Huffman, *Mennonite Brethren in Christ*, 148, is at the Schneider's maple woods site by the railway crossing on Mill St., Kitchener.

3. See the list in Brubacher and others, *Camp Meetings*, [12–13]. This list is nearly complete, and deserves study to discern the overall plan of the camp locations.

4. *Ontario Conference Journal 1915*, 8.

5. For example, *Ontario Conference Journal 1922*, 11–13, *Ontario Conference Journal 1925*, 13. Some of Moss family were members of Bethany.

Waterloo Township, outside Kitchener at the time. The site was named "Beulah Grove" in 1929, though the name fell out of use.[6] A campground was nearly purchased in the Markham area about the same year.[7] At both places camp-meeting committees, and later, Camp Boards watched over them. Sam Goudie was not normally involved in the committees. He and the Reference Committee spent much time arranging for camp evangelists, however.

YOUNG PEOPLE'S SOCIETY

We saw that Sam Goudie early on (1893) was opposed to forming young people's societies of the kind that were then becoming popular among the Methodists and others in the 1880s.[8] Many in the denomination at the time agreed with him, for no mention of distinct youth activities appears in the *Gospel Banner* or the *Journals* of the Conferences except to discourage them.[9] Huffman's 1920 *History of the MBiC Church* likewise does not refer to youth organizations as institutions of the denomination. This does not mean that youth were ignored because from the start, the MBiC had enthusiastically promoted Sunday School classes for all, and many youth classes (split along gender lines) banded together with their teachers in closer attachments than usual today. Some groups gave themselves names and continued as age-mate groups for a generation or more. Eliza Goudie taught such a woman's class at Stouffville for a number of years.[10]

J. A. Huffman's Bible Study series printed in the *Gospel Banner* 1915–1919 were apparently meant for youth meetings, among other uses.[11]

---

6. Recognized by David Doherty, 16 January 2020, in "History: Revival on the Emmanuel Grounds," <emmanuelbiblecollege.ca/history_revival_on_the_emmanuel_grounds>

7. Brubacher and others, *Camp Meetings*, [7].

8. Canadian Methodists started their Epworth League (1889) in direct response to the growing popularity of the inter-denominational Christian Endeavour group (started 1880–1881 in the US). The MBiC did not welcome Boy Scouts either (founded in Canada 1914), nor Boy's Brigade (founded in 1889 in Canada), because of their quasi-military programs.

9. The Indiana and Ohio Conference, as quoted in Storms, *United Missionary Church*, 185, resolved, "[W]e as a conference do not recognize or encourage young people's meetings such as Christian Endeavour, Epworth League, etc."

10. The number of Sunday school class studio photographs surviving from around 1900 in the MCHT suggests the level of identification class members had with each other, at the bigger churches such as Bethany, Markham and Stouffville.

11. See Huffman, *Mennonite Brethren in Christ*, 158–59, for J. A. Huffman's own comments, followed by Storms in his book.

Huffman, born in 1880 and teaching in colleges and seminaries from 1914, was already seeking solutions to the Christian education of youth in the denomination that the church was reluctant to attempt. Storms thought there was "little demand" for Bible Studies (by youth?) and that is why the series was discontinued. Goudie contributed to the series, however, so he would have known that he was supporting youth Bible study classes at least.

After the First World War a new generation of youth were entering the church, and they saw things differently. Everek Storms, who grew up in a large and vigorous youth fellowship in the Owen Sound MBiC in the 1930s, looked back on the "foreign country" of just a few years previous in his 1958 history of the UMC/ MBiC: "The same denomination that left the (Old) Mennonite Church because it would not adopt such progressive means as Sunday schools, prayer meetings, and revival services, was itself quite hesitant about introducing young people's societies."[12]

While some MBiC members probably framed their decision to leave the Mennonite Conference in terms of methods ("means"), as we have seen, the change is better interpreted as a change of "pieties" as Steiner says, involving both theology and practice. There was a change of basic theological priorities involved, with the means to an end, which was increasing numbers of conversions, held as more important than conformity to (or submission to, depending on how you saw it) a community's consensus, for example.

Storms assumes that Goudie, who in 1893 said he would have to change his mind greatly to agree to youth meetings, did change his mind by 1924 when Ontario, following the lead of the Indiana and Ohio Conference in 1923, organized a Conference youth society. In Ontario the impetus came from the already organized local youth groups with a request to the 1923 Ontario Annual Conference. Bethany Church in Kitchener had a young people's group started sometime in the first world war, followed by New Dundee (1921)[13] and Stouffville (before 1923), so, under local control, youth groups did get underway.[14] The 1923 Annual Conference asked the youth to clarify their verbal request and draw up an organizational proposal, which the Bethany, Bethel and Stouffville youth groups supplied in

---

12. Storms, *United Missionary Church*, 185.

13. Hoover, *Bethel*, 27.

14. Shantz, *Bethany*, 53. These nevertheless seem to be exceptions, as a quick survey of centennial local church histories suggest. Many refer to youth groups starting only after the Conference authorized them to.

1924, signed by Gordon H. Good and Dora Thede of Bethany. A conference committee was set the task of recommending some response to the youth resolution. (Goudie was not one of them). The committee was favorable to the youth, and the conference acted rather decisively, immediately electing a superintendent of the youth with power to settle on a constitution with them. Since Goudie's friend Silas Cressman was elected by the Conference to superintend the societies, the Conference was acting cautiously.[15] That year, both Cressman and Goudie turned fifty-eight years old. Cressman had just completed the standard five years as a Presiding Elder.

WOMEN'S MISSIONARY SOCIETY

Although a field (Quarterly Conference level) could encourage or permit any activity such as women getting together for any godly purpose, any organization at an MBiC Annual Conference level needed sanction from the Annual Conference. Again, this seems baffling, by the twenty-first-century assumption of EMCC congregationalism and our cultural exaltation of innovation. Huffman's history of 1920 does not mention the existence of women's groups in the MBiC, but my experience and reading suggest that formally or informally, women will work together in church-related activities anyway. Community quilting bees could quickly be adapted for congregational or field-related needs and were in the MBiC. Whenever a project like a camp-meeting was hosted on a field, you can be sure the men would count on the women to cook together for guests who did not have family present, as they were used to doing for funerals. Fannie Raymer mentioned she and daughters in Sunnidale Township, Ontario, quilting with their minister's wife when the lady, Mrs. [Rachel] Clark, came for the day.[16] The caption to a photo of seven women standing on steps outside the Vineland MBiC in 1922, with the four in front wearing aprons assumes they had been cooking together.[17]

In Ontario generally, "Ladies Aid" or "Auxiliary" societies in the major denominations to support the local congregation's physical plant arose

---

15. *Ontario Conference Journal 1923*, 17–18, 25, 28–29.

16. Fannie Raymer "Diary 1906," 22 March. The women finished the baby quilt for Mrs. Clark that very day. Photocopy in Box 6050, MCHT.

17. Including Ida (Troxell) Brown, wife of the pastor 1920–1924, Elder William B. Brown. The caption misidentifies her as Mrs. W. C. Brown, who came with her husband, Wm. B. Brown's son, Pastor William C. Brown, only in 1957–1961.

early.[18] Women's societies in support of *missions* emerged in Protestant denominations later, in the second part of the nineteenth century. Shortly before, interdenominational groups such as the Young Woman's Christian Association (1870), and the Young Women's Christian Temperance Union (1874) had come to Ontario from England and the US.[19] The women's missionary movement was different from, but parallel to, the impulse that saw women preaching which resulted in the deaconess societies and city missions. The Methodist Episcopal Church of Canada had founded their women's missionary societies in 1876,[20] and the main Canadian Methodist Church established their Woman's (not "Women's") Missionary Society in 1881. Evangelical Association women in the cities in the US organized their first EvA local societies in 1878 as a movement among young women to support their denomination's new mission to Japan in 1875. After 1884, when a denominational Women's Missionary Society was authorized, women's societies spread throughout the EvA, including Canada.[21]

These societies had missions as their focus from the start, some as fund raisers for a denominational agency, some as missionary sending agencies on their own. All became involved in educational efforts.[22] Generally, women's societies were successful in raising funds. The Canadian Presbyterians watched as their WMS eventually accounted for two-thirds of their general mission budget, and consequently the Presbyterian WMS was able to influence and choose what activities to support with their money. I have heard men joke that the women's money all came from one pocket (theirs) but historically that is not true. Mission Boards have worried that women's offerings would simply dig into the total donations. But this also has not proven to be the case.[23] Women have often found alternative sources of income from their husbands, even if family income was mainly from a "head of the house."

---

18. Grant, *Profusion of Spires*, 57.

19. Steiner, *Promised Lands*, 176–78. See Cook, "Temperance Union," and Pederson, "True Christian Women."

20. Semple, *Canadian Methodism*, 279–80. Canadian Presbyterian women were organized by their churches also in 1876, Gregg, *Presbyterian* Church, 240.

21. Albright, *Evangelical* Church, 321–22.

22. For example, Albright, *Evangelical Church*, 333; Semple, *Canadian Methodism*, 280. The MBiC WMS immediately initiated annual missions study programs.

23. Board-level opposition to the founding of the Evangelical Association's WMS was exactly along this line. Eller, *Evangelical Missions*, 37–38. The fears were groundless. Canadian Methodist experience was the same: Semple, *Canadian Methodism*, 280.

Among Mennonites generally, women's organizations emerged only after 1908 in response to the Mennonite city mission in Toronto, when a staff member returned to her Waterloo congregation and continued advocating to support its needs.[24] A similar story can be traced in the MBiC. As soon as the Waterloo Orphanage was announced in 1895, Markham women organized a "Sister's Union" to support it.[25] The MBiC women who worked with orphans in Turkish Armenia (1898–1914) were helped by women in the Canadian fields who collected children's clothing for them. Yet strangely, although missionary activity was established in the MBiC in 1905, both foreign and domestic, women's groups in support of missions did not form until years later.[26] During the First World War, sewing circles in the churches for the Red Cross were common, including the MBiC.[27] Steiner found evidence of women's groups in Ontario MBiC in the 1910s. For example, in 1916 the Markham church "Women's Auxiliary" formed and began producing quilts and clothing for "an Edmonton organization" (said to be Hope Mission).[28] Gormley women also organized the "Willing Workers' Sewing Circle" which converted into a WMS branch.[29] Fannie Raymer opened her home for the founding of a women's "Missions Circle" on the Sunnidale circuit in 1924.[30] Only in 1931, when the Canada Northwest Conference organized a Conference-wide WMS,[31] or the Ontario Conference in 1939, did the pattern of a general Women's Missionary Society take hold. By then, the society plan could have been well understood through examples from neighboring congregations of other denominations.

24. Erb St. Mennonite; Steiner, *Promised Lands*, 176.

25. "Sisters' Union," *GB* (10 December 1895) 8.

26. Storms, *United Missionary Church*, 189 n33. Steiner, *Promised Lands*, 178, collects several early MBiC references from 1910 onward.

27. Some women of the earliest Pentecostal assemblies likewise worked together sewing for the Red Cross, as in Winnipeg in 1915; Kulbeck, *Pentecostal Assemblies*, 39.

28. McDowell and others, *Markham*, 18. The Hope Mission traces its work to that of the Rev. Harold Edwardson, originally an MBiC licensee, and to 1929, so this memory is unclear evidence of a women's society before the organizing of women's groups in Canada Northwest; www.hopemission.com. I suspect there is an error here, and Beulah Home or its affiliates started by Maude Chatham is meant, but support continued in later years by adding or switching to Hope Mission.

29. Yake, "Women of Gormley," 1, Box 3052, MCHT.

30. Chester, *Stayner*, 11.

31. Maconochie, *Missionary Women*, [4], affirms there were Sewing Circles in nearly all of the Canada Northwest Conference circuits by 1921 which prepared materials for the Red Cross, missionaries and both Beulah Home and Hope Mission in Edmonton.

The leaders of the Ontario WMS included former missionaries and leading pastors' wives: Director Mrs. Allan Hoover (Bertha Fidler), had served under the UOMB in Syria five years (1925–1930), Norah (Shantz) Shuert, had been in Nigeria two terms (1918–1925), and Margaret (Kercher) Purdy, with her husband was beginning four years as a missionary to Chippewas on the Kettle and Stoney Point Reserves in Ontario.[32] Steiner speculates that a distinct Conference-sponsored women's organization was fairly late in being organized in MBiC Conferences because women had relatively more opportunities to serve in the holiness MBiC, where evangelizing women worked alongside (though not quite equally with) the men.[33] According to the *Ontario Conference Journal* of 1939, only Sam Goudie, as secretary of the Conference Foreign Mission Board, noted the formation of the Ontario Conference MBiC WMS: "Just recently a Women's Missionary Society was organized, and no doubt after this society begins to function properly there will be a marked increase in interest and giving."[34]

Why did he say that? He was right, the Ontario WMS took off in the war years quite quickly and they did become strong missions supporters. However, Goudie had been a mission executive for thirty-five years by 1939, eighteen as president of the UMS. That year he retired from the position, though not yet from membership on his Conference's Foreign Mission Board. He could have seen the benefits of WMS groups for other missions, even if only through extracts printed in the *Gospel Banner*. It is puzzling that only in 1937 did the UMS General Board recommend the organizing of Conference WMS organizations at the request of the women with the possibility of a "marked increase in interest and giving."[35] I don't think it was ignorance, there may have been another policy Goudie believed was better up to that point. At one time Mennonites were reluctant to divide their community by age and gender organizations. Perhaps Goudie had that same thought. I have not seen published "missions theory" writings from Goudie. He managed, he implemented. He did not try to innovate.

32. "Minutes of the Ontario WMS 1939–1958." Box 3051, MCHT.
33. Steiner, *Promised Lands*, 647 n. 48.
34. *Ontario Conference Journal 1939*, 66.
35. Storms, *United Missionary Church*, 190. The women's initiative is mentioned in the "WMS History" leaflet (1985), through a request from MBiC women of several Conferences to the UMS Board in June 1937. In Ontario, this was followed up by a request to the Ontario Foreign Missionary Board. C. N. Good, chair of the Ontario Board, encouraged their petition.

Although old and retired from practically everything by 1944 (he was Vice-President of the UMS until 1945), Goudie does not seem to have been invited to speak at Ontario WMS activities. His death in 1951 passed without notice in WMS executive minutes.

BOOK OF RELIGIOUS INSTRUCTION

A project that involved Sam Goudie for nearly ten years as a Presiding Elder does not even seem to be originally his plan. In the 1924 Ontario Annual Conference, a request came from the Canada Northwest Conference, that the two Conferences each petition the General Conference in the following month to prepare a catechism.[36] This was accepted, with the slight difference that the Canada Northwest Conference petition indicated they thought it would especially benefit younger children or youth. The GC of 1924 meeting at Brown City, Michigan, accepted the plan in principle, but gave the task of preparing a catechism back to representatives of the two Conferences, who were to report to the Executive Committee, which was given authority to act. The Canadians Sam Goudie, Silas Cressman and Alvin Traub (Alberta) were appointed.[37] Curiously, I have seen one letter to the editor in the *Gospel Banner*, in which M. A. Zyner of Center Valley, PA, urged the value of a catechism with a suggested outline almost exactly as Goudie's booklet eventually followed.[38] Perhaps the suggestion stuck in Goudie's mind, or an exemplar catechism was the first he saw in the early days of his ministry, and its plan commended itself to him and others in the church.

In the following General Conference (1928), Alvin Traub[39] and Sam Goudie reported that they had found a book of instruction and added a few paragraphs but had failed to follow the resolution instructions to submit it to the Executive Committee for action. Silas Cressman's role is not mentioned. Since Goudie was the chair of the Executive Committee, he could only confess it was by oversight, not with any reluctance that they failed to

---

36. *Ontario Conference Journal 1924*, 32.

37. *Eleventh General Conference 1924*, 43–44.

38. M. A. Zyner, "Letter," *GB* (1 April 1892) 4–5. Zyner, an Elder of the Pennsylvania Conference, read an essay on "The Use of the Reading Course," in his Conference's Ministerial Convention on the value of knowing doctrine, with the Holy Spirit, *GB* (7 March 1893) 9.

39. On the life of this western Canadian MBiC leader, born and raised in Elmwood, Ontario, see Reimer, *Alvin Traub*.

do so.⁴⁰ Goudie, although chair of the top Executive Committee, submitted to the rules. This reference to "finding a book" says that Traub and Goudie followed the honorable practice of many catechism writers of revising a useful catechism for the needs of the new times and the new group.⁴¹ I wish we knew now what work they used, especially if they selected from a Mennonite, Evangelical/United Brethren, Methodist, Free Methodist or other source. That could be an interesting search for someone in the future.⁴²

The book that was eventually published in 1933 contains two further notes on the history of the text.⁴³ In 1930, Alvin Traub wrote an introduction that acknowledged that Sam Goudie did most of the editing of the catechism. He made it plain by his language that he hoped that the catechism would at least "counteract the many false teachings which are so prevalent." Traub, the Alberta Presiding Elder and by then a main instructor at his Conference's Mountain View Bible School in Didsbury, Alberta, expected the book by positive teaching of the "fundamental doctrines," would fortify MBiC members "against the awful ravages of destructive criticism and other false doctrines." In fact, Goudie, in his report to the 1928 General Conference as Presiding Elder for four years of the West District of the Ontario Conference (his only years not the PE of the East District), said, "Our laity and ministry stand together unitedly in doctrine, I know of no modernism or modernistic teaching among our people. We stand for the fundamental teachings of the Word of God."⁴⁴ The raging fundamentalist-

---

40. *Twelfth General Conference 1928*, 44.

41. The Evangelical Association issued at least five catechisms between 1809 and 1905, Albright, *Evangelical Church*, 215–17. The new constitution United Brethren had Charles Warren Brewbaker, *Christian Growth and Conduct: A Book of Religious Instruction for Our Youth* (Dayton, OH: Otterbein Press, 1922) and a catechism from 1897.

42. It does not follow standard Mennonite catechisms such as the three reprinted in Wenger, *Doctrines*, named Roosen's, the Waldeck, and the Shorter ("Brief Instruction for Youth from the Scriptures") Catechisms. The Free Methodists published their first catechism in 1890, Marston, *Free Methodism's First Century*, 499, 502. Baptists, though respected, (and there were German Baptists in Waterloo County) were not at that time a strong influence on the MBiC, except for the Arminian Free-will Baptists in Michigan in the matter of female preachers. See Gingerich,"Experiment in Denominationalism," 47.

43. The Ontario Reference Committee, October 26 1932, authorized publishing, and paying the total cost of printing 2,000 copies. Neither Michigan nor the Canada Northwest Conference were mentioned. *Ontario Conference Journal 1933*, 13. The Reference Committee members that year were S. Goudie (chairman), Secretary-Treasurer William H. Yates, Silas Cressman, C. N. Good and Milton Bricker. It was to be sold for 25 cents.

44. *Twelfth General Conference 1928*, 30.

modernist controversies of the day are clearly reflected in such language by Goudie and Traub.

There follows a further note that the MBiC Executive Committee permitted the publication of the work, but this is dated September 28, 1932. Finally in 1933 Goudie issued the pocket-sized 110-page *Book of Religious Instruction*. Oddly, Goudie is described on the title page as the Publisher and Editor of the book, where one might expect a statement of the denomination's authorization (however, on the cover it says, "Published by the Authority of the Executive Committee"). There is no place of publication or printer. I infer that there were elements in the church that could not endorse the theology (or custom) of the book wholeheartedly and so allowed the two Conferences to go ahead, but they did not want to openly reject the project, either. I guess that since their chairman Sam Goudie was the top promoter of the book, no one wanted to oppose it directly. The Executive Committee did not provide any funding for the project, but said it was up to the two Conferences to pay for and accept all "other obligations." In the end, Ontario paid for it all. Storms reports that 2,000 copies were printed, but "for various reasons" which he does not state, which perhaps he guessed but could not prove, it "was never widely used."[45] Prejudice against the practices of more liturgical churches, and prejudice against doctrinal study probably reduced the acceptance of the project, even though Goudie supplied only scripture references throughout to support the answers given in the book.

The catechism was read and understood in a few places at least. I have a copy owned at one time by an Ontario pastor's wife, which was altered in the 1950s when the UMC changed the status of the "sacrament" of washing the saints' feet to a practice, or perhaps in 1962 when all mention of the ordinance was dropped from the UMC Articles of Faith and Rules for the Society. The owner scratched out in blue ball-point ink the heading, "The washing of the Saints feet." Another user was a member of the MBiC in Toronto, Robert Grove, who says he treasured the book as a young believer at the Jones Avenue church of the MBiC, where Goudie was pastor in 1933–1936.[46] Some pastor was promoting the book at least. The MCHT has other copies originally owned in Stratford and two in Breslau, one of which has a few study notes in the margin.

---

45. Storms, *United Missionary Church*, 216–17.
46. Grove, *A Dedicated Life*, 3, Box 6042, MCHT. Goudie probably was that pastor!

Goudie's catechism includes many typical features. Traub wrote that "no pretence has been made at originality, except in a few doctrinal points." As in most catechisms since the Reformation, it begins with a statement of authority: the Word of God, before exploring the Bible's teaching under nine headings: God and His Attributes, Creation, Man's Fall and Sinful State, Our Redemption Through Christ, The Holy Spirit, Salvation and Its Conditions, The Church and the Means of Grace, The Christian's Duties Toward God and Man and finally, The Last Things. Before the statements on the Word of God, however, are printed The Lord's Prayer, The Apostles' Creed and the Ten Commandments. The Lord's Prayer will show up under the "Means of Grace" as a model of prayer. The Ten Commandments will also show up again, in catechism fashion, in the section on the Christian's duties. For ages, Christians included duties as a normal part of Christian discipleship. Luther's catechisms included questions on the Ten Commandments. We are in a foreign country from that perspective, disparaging "duty" in our fear of legalism and emphasis on love and relationships above rules. Karl Barth in the twentieth century was thought to be doing something new when he integrated ethics into his *Church Dogmatics*, but Methodist systematic theologies normally did this, not just holiness ones.

I would like to emphasize the implications of printing the Apostles' Creed. The Creed grew to its present form over a few centuries in the early Church, but the Creed is not a Bible passage. Everywhere else Goudie relies on Bible verses to support the answers to the catechism questions. He does not, as many catechism writers do, provide any questions on the Creed. Nevertheless, by including it, Goudie declares that the MBiC is orthodox or part of the Christian Church's "Great Tradition," a phrase from Roger Olsen.[47] Though sociologists once dismissed the smaller churches as "sects," Goudie did not claim that only the MBiC was the True Church. Even the cooperation with revival-minded Mennonites or holiness denominations was not the limit of his circle of "true Christians." As early as 1895, in a Ministerial Convention essay on who are true Christians, Goudie had dismissed as errors that (1) we can't know; or (2) my denomination's members are Christians and others are not. He believed the distinction could nevertheless be seen in seven ways: (1) a righteous life; (2) love; (3) humility; (4) plainness; (5) unselfishness; (6) forbearance; and (7) forgiveness.[48]

---

47. And earlier; Olsen, *Mosaic*, especially 32-39.

48. Sam Goudie, "Marks of Distinction Between the Children of God and of the World," *GB* (18 May 1895) 3-4.

These are behavioural, not doctrinal tests! The MBiC had their quarrels with other churches and movements but did not by that write them off as all non-Christian, all non-believers. Other MBiC leaders obviously thought the same, from Daniel Brenneman referring to the "dear Mennonite brethren,"[49] or the constant reprint of useful articles in the *Gospel Banner* from various church magazines by successive editors, to the textbooks required for probationers to pass exams on. In 1905, Sam Goudie attended a Christian Alliance Convention in Toronto and described one meeting as "very good," and the next day A. B. Simpson and Dr. Henry Wilson's[50] messages on Divine Healing as "grand." Goudie even went to talk to Dr. Wilson about Lydia, his sister-in-law, Abram's wife. Next month he was at Cooke's Presbyterian Church to hear Mr. William R. Newell, and "it was very good."[51] In 1907 he attended a Society of Friends (Quakers) meeting in Newmarket on a Sunday.[52]

The *Book of Religious Instruction* is divided into thirty-seven lessons and begins with the question made famous by the Shorter Westminster Catechism (1643–1648), "What is the chief end of man?" which nearly every branch of Protestantism in English has found commendable, not just the Reformed. After each question and brief answer, Goudie collects and prints out up to six verses or passages of scripture (usually KJV but occasionally the Revised Version of 1885) without comment, assumed to be sufficient proof of the answer. "Proof texting" is normally rejected in today's Bible study environment, but to those who believed the Bible was sufficiently clear for faith and practice, perfectly acceptable. By printing the scripture, its authority is visibly (and conveniently) demonstrated. Goudie's texts are different from the Westminster Catechism[53] and quickly the questions go to different topics, with occasional returns to the Reformed standard or more than likely, some alternative. As expected in a work first intended for children, the language is simple. The thirty-seven lessons contain three hundred seven questions, an average of just over eight per lesson, which

---

49. Brenneman, "Letter," 50.

50. Rev. Henry Wilson DD, Canadian Anglican (1841–1908), was healed of chronic illnesses in a Simpson meeting in NY in 1884. While remaining an Anglican, he served in numerous C&MA organizational roles; Reynolds, *Footprints*, 116, 211, 247, 256–59.

51. Sam Goudie, "Diary 1905," 9–10, 14 February and 2 March.

52. Sam Goudie, "Diary 1907," 24 November.

53. However, one supporting scripture is common, that is, 1 Corinthians 10:31.

seems like a heavy investment in memorization for youth, but perhaps we are the strange generation that can't believe we can do it.

Goudie's questions assume an evangelical Mennonite Wesleyan-Arminian framework with an MBiC twist: baptism is by immersion,[54] for believers, washing of the Saints' feet is taught, the atonement is for everyone, the order of salvation is Arminian (conviction, repentance and faith leading to justification, regeneration, sanctification),[55] sanctification is explained in detail, as a full cleansing (the only scripture printed in capital letters! from 1 John 1:7, 9), subsequent to regeneration, possible in this life, yet leaving the believer open to temptation and lapsing (that is, this is not sinless perfection), apostasy is possible and divine decrees for salvation or eternal condemnation are not mentioned.[56]

The explanation of the Ten Commandments and the Lord's Prayer, typical of many catechisms, and the attention given to Christian life throughout, fits the discipleship assumptions of Anabaptists. From the third commandment, the swearing of oaths is forbidden, supported by Sermon on the Mount and Jas 5 in the standard Anabaptist understanding. At the sixth commandment (do not kill), one question supports non-resistance.[57] There is no reference to the ban, which Huffman noted in 1920 was not continued by the MBiC anyway.[58] In a concluding lesson on the commandments, one question asks about our duties toward magistrates and

---

54. Immersion beliefs came very early into the MBiC, even as early as 1875. Menno Bowman and his wife had chosen to be baptized by immersion in the Grand River as early as 1863, so there were those who had preference for that mode. Bowman was an influential leader in Ontario. Storms tells of the question being left open in the union of Reforming and New Mennonites. John McNally, former New Mennonite leader, baptized people by immersion through the ice in Schneider Creek, Berlin, in the middle of February in 1878 according to a celebrated account, Shantz, *Bethany*, 10, also in Storms, *United Missionary Church*, 227. This cannot be the influence of Simpson, who was still a Presbyterian minister at the time. Perhaps the influence of Tunkers in Niagara and Waterloo and York Counties? In the union of 1883, the persuasion of the Swankite Brethren in Christ, a Tunker group, definitely turned the MBiC to immersion as the preferred mode, which became fixed in the *Discipline* by 1896, Huffman, *Mennonite Brethren in Christ*, 156–58. "Trine immersion baptism"—going under the water three times—was not adopted, however.

55. Believers: *Religious Instruction*, 73–74; feet-washing: 74; universal atonement: 51, 57; order of salvation: 58–62.

56. Sanctification: *Religious Instruction*, 64–67; subsequent: 65; apostasy: 67–68.

57. Oaths: *Religious Instruction*, 93; non-resistance: 98.

58. Huffman, *Mennonite Brethren in Christ*, 148.

rulers. We should obey the government under which we live is the reply, with Romans 13:1–3 quoted in support.[59]

Surprisingly for a leader in a church excited by premillennialism, very little is said about the last things. Only four questions touch simply on Jesus' return, the resurrections, the judgment and nothing much about heaven or hell ("He descended into hell" does not even appear in the Apostles' Creed as printed), as in the Dordrecht Confession of 1632. A millennium is described in the very last question, which is not normally part of Mennonite eschatology. It is not in the Dordrecht Confession. The answer allows two possibilities of who will accompany Jesus—the church or ten-thousand saints: an option showing Goudie (or his church?) was not decided on this question of end-time staging. Earlier, the answer to a question about "Thy kingdom come," in the lesson on the Lord's Prayer, also introduced a "future literal kingdom on earth," as additional to the older understanding of a kingdom of grace prevailing in us and everywhere now.[60]

Prayer for the sick has been a standard of all branches of Christianity from the time of the New Testament. Of nineteenth-century issues and innovations in theology, the question "is there healing in the atonement?" introduced by Charles Cullis, Alexander Dowie, but especially A. B. Simpson and others is answered positively,[61] with the option of calling on elders to use oil, prayer and laying on of hands as in James 5. One other question to which Goudie answered simply and strongly "no," is whether "there is any evidence in the Scriptures that the extraordinary power over unclean spirits and the healing of diseases was transferred by the Apostles to their successors in the Christian ministry?" The catechism says that there is no evidence for it.[62] The question suggests that members of the MBiC were confronted by people claiming exorcism or healing powers due to office

---

59. Duties to government: *Religious Instruction*, 106.

60. End times: *Religious Instruction*, 110; earthly kingdom: 81.

61. Healing in the atonement: *Religious* Instruction, 51. This doctrine was introduced officially to the MBiC *Discipline* in 1888 and continued to 1969 at least; Storms, *United Missionary Church*, 226. "Healing in the atonement" language came in a little later, probably in response to A. B. Simpson's writings; Blowers, "Practice of Healing," 7–20. R. V. Bingham accepted this doctrine in the early part of his career, but his experience with malaria turned him to re-examine it and reject it; Bingham, *Bible and Body*. In the Missionary Church era, *Manual and Constitution*, 7, stated that "[i]n the redemptive work of Christ" [not "in the atonement"] "provision has been made for man's physical healing." A similar statement, "Provision is made in the redemptive work of the Lord Jesus Christ for the healing of the mortal body," occurs in the C&MA brochure "Statement of Faith."

62. Apostolic healing: *Religious Instruction*, 71.

in the church, probably Pentecostals. It is not a classic catechism concern that I am aware of. The charismatic movement of the late twentieth century has convinced many evangelical people, including many in the EMCC, that in fact the answer should be that any prepared Christian (since we are all ministers) may cast out spirits. An interesting shift.

While the catechism was waiting for the go ahead to be published, Goudie was writing one of his few purely doctrinal essays for the *Gospel Banner*. It could be that preparing the catechism suggested the topic or the need for it, because it defends "The Divinity of Christ" in a fundamentalist manner. Goudie provides a medley of scriptures, a Bible Reading, in response to some unnamed author who claimed that the divinity did not matter "neither d[id] the location of Jesus' resurrected body matter." Goudie answers via the testimony of seven witnesses (God, the angels and so on) by quoting scriptures and Bible references for readers to look up. The method works for those who assume the trustworthiness and clarity of Scripture, that is, the vast majority of *Gospel Banner* readers. "[T]his has been a source of pleasure and spiritual benefit to myself and I believe will be so to all others . . . ."[63] This is a true testimony to the effect of good theology on the hungry seeker.

SUMMARIZING TWENTY-EIGHT YEARS

According to reports in the *Conference Journal*, during the twenty-eight years of his Presiding Eldership, Sam Goudie preached 3,519 sermons. No doubt some of them were repeats. From a minimum of 84 (1930) to a maximum of 243 (1908–eighteen months), he was a speaker. Although the Conference ruled that Presiding Elders were exempt from regular visiting, I see no let up by Sam. He continued to report hundreds of visits on the various fields, from a low of 166 in 1923 (records must have been lost in 1920, because the column is blank), to 744 in the early year of 1906–1907. Normally he averaged 300 to 400, with a median of 335 visits per year. His annual salary varied, dependent on Conference offerings—usually shared equally with his co-Presiding Elder—from a low of $259 in 1907 to a maximum of $1,179 in 1929. After 1929, the depression hit and the salary sagged, and reached a low of $860 in 1933, his last year. The first World War showed a rapid rise, reflecting the growing farm prices (and inflation) of the war-time economy.

---

63. Sam Goudie, "The Divinity of Christ," *GB* (11 September 1930) 3–6.

RESUME HERE There will be more analysis of the progress or lack of it during Goudie's years as the chief Presiding Elder in a later chapter. For the moment here are the fields and personnel in 1933. In terms of responsibilities in the Conference, C. N. Good had the heavier load:

Circuits	Number of Appointments	Appointments	Members 1933	Pastors (1932–1933)	Helpers (1932–1933)
Stouffville	2	Stouffville, Altona	188	Silas Cressman	Lloyd Hoover
Markham	4	Mt. Joy, Dickson Hill, Gormley, Bethesda	250	Alonzo T. Gooding	Local help
Vineland	1		151	Lewis R. Pipher	
Owen Sound	1		70	Sidney S. Shantz	
Aylmer	1		55	Harvey R. Frey	
Elmwood	2	Elmwood, Hanover	66	Ephraim Sievenpiper	
Port Elgin	2	Port Elgin, Chippawa Hill	24	Herbert Shantz	
Maryboro	2	Maryboro, Wallace	31	Harold R. Brown	Harvey S. Hallman
8	15		835	8	2

Table 1. West District (Served by Samuel Goudie 1932–1933)

Circuits	Number of Appointments	Appointments	Members 1933	Pastors (1932–1933)	Helpers (1932–1933)
Kitchener	1		361	William H. Yates	
Bethel	2	Bethel, Bright	183	William Brown	
Toronto West	1		95	Elmer B. Moyer	
Toronto East	1		59	Charles T. Homuth	
Stayner	2	Stayner, 2nd Line	85	Nicholas H. Schwalm	
Breslau	1		54	Milton Bricker	
Hespeler	1		58	Russell J. Pike	
Manitoulin	3	Long Bay, Salem, Monument Church	30	Percy G. Lehman	
Sunnidale	4	Ebenezer, 9th Line, Glencairn, (4th site not named)	72	J. Harold Sherk	Charles Milsted
Scott	2	Scott, E. Gwillimbury	56	Isaac Brubacher	
Collingwood	2	Collingwood, Clarksburg	39	J. Henry Good	
Bruce Peninsula	4	Ferndale, Stokes Bay, Miller Lake, Hay's Sch. H.	48	Ernest Lucas	John Holmes
Shrigley	2	Shrigley, Mt. Pleasant	36	Arthur D. Lehman	? not named
13	26		1176	13	3

Table 2: East District (Served by C. N. Good)

Mission	Members 1933	Leader 1, 1932–1933	Leader 2, 1932–1933
Stratford	49	Annie Yeo	Hazel Scouler
Petrolia	21	Mildred Spies	Ethel Snider
Listowel	34	Annie Shrigley	Muriel Alexander
St. Catharines	20	Edith Raymer	Vera Schwass
St. Thomas	23	Hazel Rogers	Rosaline Sargeant
Wingham (new)	—	Jessie E. Peard	Rebecca Hostetler
6	147		Total 12
27 fields in 47 appointments	2158 total members		

Table 3: City Missions

As in 1905, there were workers, some of them declaring themselves unconditional, that the Conference was not able to use, listed under the heading "To Labour as the Lord Directs": Henry Goudie, Flavius J. Lehman, Lloyd Cressman, Peter Cober, Ernest Harvey, Leslie Grove, and V. Clarence Shantz. There were also the "local preachers": John Bolwell, Jacob B. Detwiler, Robert Eltherington, Sylvester Fretz, T. Ford Barker, Joshua E. Fidler, Dr. Isaac H. Erb, and Charles I. Sinden.

Foreign missionaries were remembered as well: William and Mary Shantz (C&MA, China), Martha Hood (UMS, Nigeria), Frances Matheson (UMS, India), Bertha Fidler (UMS, Nigeria), and G. Max Powers (UMS, just returned from Nigeria).

Among the women workers, Annie Alexander had stated herself as unconditional, but she was not placed. Eight women stated they were conditional (some were retired, others not well): Annie Bowman, Jennie Little, Martha Doner, Ethel Eastman, Bessie Plant, Maggie Neill, Winnie Barfoot, and F. Willison, who was new and never mentioned again.[64]

Thus, there were 21 active itinerants, 4 probationers serving as helpers, 7 unconditional men not placed 8 retired preachers, and two presiding elders (42 in all). Of the women, there were now 12 placed in city missions, 8 with conditions, and one able to work but not paired in a mission with another, 21 in all, half the number of the men. There were 21 fields with 41

---

64. Flossie Willison from Aylmer, mentioned as sixteen years old in the 1921 census, whose Scotch father is listed as "Mininight" (Mennonite), the French-origin mother and the rest of the family as "Mission" adherents, almost certainly the MBiC city mission (see Jean, ed., *History*).

appointments in 1933, plus six city missions, making 47 appointments in total. There were now 2,158 members.

14

Return to the Pastorate 1933–1940

CONSISTENT WITH HIS CONVICTIONS, Sam Goudie remained submissive to the will of the Annual Conference when the Conference did not elect him to be a Presiding Elder in 1933. All indications are, as this chapter records, that he entered into his return to the pastorate with energy.

In the 1931 annual elections for the two Presiding Elders, eight candidates (a typical number) were informally nominated for two PE positions, and C. N. Good was elected right away. However, Sam Goudie and Milton Bricker were each supported well, but neither name could achieve a two-thirds majority to be declared elected according to the *Discipline*. After seven ballots, five of which gave Goudie more than Bricker, the conference decided to award the Presiding Eldership to Sam Goudie. He was immediately re-elected as Conference chair as well.[1]

For twenty-six years, Sam Goudie had been re-elected as one of the two Presiding Elders in the Ontario Conference almost automatically, except for two years when he had been alone in that position. He was sixty-five in 1931 and maybe there was a feeling in some that it was time to give him a rest. Goudie remained "unconditional" and there is no murmur or hint from Goudie that he thought he was being disregarded for all his labor. In 1932, seven candidates were nominated for election. C. N. Good and Sam Goudie were elected immediately, and again Goudie was immediately elected chair of the Conference. Nevertheless, a change was about to come.

---

1. Ontario *Conference Journal 1931*, 31–32.

Perhaps Sam Goudie had hinted that he was ready to let others do the work, though he remained "unconditional" as always.

The 1933 Ontario Conference was held in Gormley. The chair (Goudie, of course) opened the assembly with a reading from 1 Pet 5 and emphasized v. 2, the instruction to elders to "feed the flock of God in your care" and noted the verse about obeying one's elders and everyone being "clothed with humility" (v. 5). Conference secretaries (Russell J. Pike was secretary in this Conference) often recorded the scriptures the chair read, but typically merely reported that he said, "appropriate remarks." I wonder if the comments were noted because everyone knew this might be Goudie's last year as chair of the conference. The Scripture seems especially significant for an elder thinking about handing over to others, about his own role and position in the conference structure after so many years. Some people in Goudie's position, thinking hierarchically, cannot "go down" to a mere pastorate, and return to submitting to people who were his juniors. In some cultures, this would be very difficult for the juniors as well as the seniors. Some organizations solve the problem by making their top leaders ordained or emeritus for life—they never back down the ladder. But Mennonites, and Goudie was one, see humility as a pattern Jesus himself displayed. Jesus' action was awkward for his disciples' culture when he washed their feet, a slave's job no one chose normally.

In 1933, the Conference minutes did not record candidates nominated for Presiding Elders, which is unusual. It all looks somewhat orchestrated. Instead, it has first that C. N. Good was elected and then the Conference business was suspended so they could conduct a memorial service for the late Rev. Robert Eltherington, led by Sam Goudie and C. N. Good. This unusual suspension allowed Sam to conduct one last memorial service as a Presiding Elder. When Conference business resumed, Milton Bricker was elected the second Presiding Elder.

> If this story of Sam Goudie were a fictional drama, we could write this as a palace coup in slow motion. The longest serving Presiding Elder in the history of the Ontario Conference of the MBiC was unseated at sixty-seven by perhaps a younger set of pastors and delegates who thought it was a "time for a change," a useful but content-less political slogan. But I don't see the drama playing out that way. The *Conference Journal* is maddening in its laconic record. After the vote: "S. Goudie, retiring Chairman, addressed the Conference; C. N. Good took the chair and addressed the

Conference; M. Bricker, newly elected Presiding Elder, addressed the Conference."[2]

What did everyone say? It clearly was an emotional moment for many in the assembly. Sam Goudie did not go away. He was appointed the pastor of the Jones Avenue MBiC in Toronto, the continuation of the MBiC East End Mission. It was not a big congregation and involved no great amount of travel to serve. Goudie remained a member of the Reference Committee, member of the Conference Foreign Mission Board, and continued on so many things. He was still busy as President of the UMS in the depth of the Depression and Chair of the denominational Executive Committee. Although the NRRO was more or less dormant until 1937, as we saw, in that very year, 1933, Goudie finally got the catechism published, and the next year, he and C. N. Good got the leaflet on Canadian laws that affected Non-Resistant Religious bodies printed and distributed.[3] When the NRRO was re-organized in 1937, he was active in it, even as Chair from 1941–1944.

562 JONES AVENUE/GRACE CHAPEL 1933–1936

Sam and Eliza served the Jones Avenue congregation for the standard three years. The last time we noted the East End Mission, it had lost a majority of its members to George Chambers's rival mission further up Parliament St., and the Reference Committee considering closing the mission or switching it to a rescue mission for orphans at least. A rescue mission was in fact started a few blocks away from Danforth Avenue (Berechah Home),[4] but the Parliament St. mission was continued after all, run by the City Mission Workers after 1911. J. N. Kitching gave a report on the Sunday School run there in the spring of 1911. The women rounded up children from the neighborhood, "white, some black and some not quite white," many needing clothes and shoes. Maggie Neill and Olive Baalim were present from the CMWS, but also Ethel Foote, a young Anglican dressmaker who briefly wore the uniform, at least for a CMWS group photograph about that year. The mission continued at 266 Parliament St. before disappearing from there in the Toronto Street Directories.[5]

2. *Ontario Conference Journal 1933*, 24.

3. *Ontario Conference Journal 1934*, 29.

4. *GB* (15 August 1912) 11. Annie Bowman and Edna V. Jacobson served that year at 297 Withrow Avenue. The C&MA had a famous city mission in New York also called Berechah Home.

5. John N. Kitching, "Ontario City Mission President's Report," *GB* (27 April 1911) 13.

Return to the Pastorate 1933–1940

At some point, the Conference disposed of the Parliament St. property and bought a tiny lot at 562 Jones Avenue just south of Danforth Avenue in East York which had a small hall already built on it. This was only a few blocks away from the rescue mission. The women lived in a small apartment above the hall. Though not far geographically from Parliament St. between Dundas and Shuter St., likely few old attenders migrated with the congregation.[6] However, membership gradually grew under the city mission workers to about 40 with an average Sunday School attendance of around 60. In 1925, the Conference decided to send Silas Cressman's eldest son Lloyd Silas Cressman to lead the congregation, who had just graduated from the Chicago Evangelistic Institute, a holiness Bible school. He married Bertha Lamb on June 2, 1926. Lloyd Cressman left for further studies to the US again, never to return to Canada (a loss, since there was no place for people with degrees in the Ontario MBiC). For some reason it was left under the administration of the City Mission Workers Society until the end of his three years, when it was returned to the status of a Conference Mission.

The church had no pastoral care for some of 1927–1928 until Max Powers, a probationer, was appointed briefly before he left for missionary work in Nigeria under the UMS. Charlie Homuth, back from some years in the Canada Northwest Conference, a former missionary to Nigeria and one-time Christian Workers Church pastor, was appointed for 1928 and he stayed an unusually long term of five years, as allowed by the *Discipline* if the Conference so chose. Under him the membership grew to 59, though the Sunday school dropped to the 40s and rose back to 60 again. This was the congregation Sam and Eliza met in the fall of 1933.

Sam Goudie's sons were married and living in Stouffville. Eliza and Sam left Stouffville for the first time in twenty-six years and had to adjust to being a congregational pastoral couple again. He had thought about that: "I sometimes wondered if I could fit in again as a pastor, but I am trying my best and the Lord is helping."[7] He rejoiced in a church anniversary for the East End Mission with C. N. Good on November 12, and concluded his report with an optimistic prayer request, "[H]elp us to stand together as one man and push the battle to the gates."[8]

---

6. "Grace MBiC/ United Missionary Church Membership Record," 4, notes Thomas Kitching still there in the 1920s. Box 1022, MCHT.

7. Sam Goudie, "Toronto East," *GB* (30 November 1933) 14.

8. Sam Goudie, "Toronto East," *GB* (30 November 1933) 14.

Sam's tours to the quarterly conferences ceased, and with it his numerous reports in the *Gospel Banner* (22 in 1932!). He made only 9 reports on his church over the three years in Toronto. Goudie continued to be a member of the Reference Committee which sometimes came to their Toronto building for meetings. In 1934, he reported they had one other ordained elder, one approved ministering sister and one probationer, recommended by the congregation, probably Frank Huson. He had baptized 4 believers in the year, and received 8 new members, while 2 transferred elsewhere, leaving a net gain of 6 to reach 65 members. He had preached 88 times and made 253 pastoral visits, down from his Presiding Elder's pace (427 in 1932–33). Two of the people converted during his years at Jones Avenue, were Alex and Agnes Brown. Alex trusted in Jesus in a home prayer meeting.[9]

In 1934, Goudie wrote an obituary for one of his colleagues in the United Missionary Society, their recording secretary from 1921 to 1933, Clifford Isaiah Scott (1871–1933), a one-time Presiding Elder of the Indiana and Ohio Conference (1906–1908) and later of the Nebraska Conference (1915–1933).[10]

He also contributed roughly an article a year to the *Gospel Banner*. His first had begun as a Ministerial Convention essay on St. Paul as an example for pastors.[11] In it, Goudie identified the ministry as a trust. "Christ has made Repositories of men. I recall hearing Dr. G. D. Watson say one time, "That God had made Paul a banker, He committed to him a Great Trust [emphasis Goudie's]." Goudie wanted ministers "to recognize that the church itself . . . is the primary and paramount object of our care and prayer." He insisted the pastor's ministry is not to nations, civilization, nor institutions, but rather to the Body of Christ. He could not encourage a Christian minister to assume responsibility to society or the state rather than care for the church, nor "educational over evangelistic, material over the spiritual, forms and institutions" over the church's "power and sanctification." That would be to Goudie an abnormal ministry. I agree with Goudie on the central importance of the church for God as well as for the Christian public ministry. Many downplay the role of the church or broaden it to include all kinds of human endeavours. The church is the bride of Christ

---

9. Isabel (Brown) Morby, conversation with the author, 21 April 2016 at Faith Missionary Church, Kitchener, ON.

10. Sam Goudie, "A Great Man has Fallen," *GB* (5 April 1934) 3.

11. Published in two parts, Sam Goudie, "The Apostle Paul an Example for the Present Day Minister, Experimentally, Doctrinally and Practically," *GB* (3 January 1935) 3–4 and *GB* (10 January 1935) 2. The paragraph's references are to these two articles.

that will not disappear after the marriage supper of the Lamb, and it will continue to show the wisdom of God for all ages. It is not temporary nor an interim solution to Jewish rejection of Jesus on Palm Sunday. The church continues the people of God, started in Eden. The church does have a large responsibility for those who are not followers, of course. Probably Goudie made a distinction between the *pastor's* ministry to the congregation and the *Church's* mission to the world.

Evangelicals have been convinced, most of them anyway, that an "every member ministry" is the intention of Eph 4:11-16, Goudie's main text in this article. Goudie followed the KJV punctuation, as nearly everyone did, and made a distinction between the ministry of the ministers and the work of the congregation's other members, "the laity."

Goudie's second article was a re-working of his 1920 pamphlet on Non-Resistance.[12] His third was an article on gratitude. Interestingly, he noted that the aboriginal peoples of Canada, the Huron and Iroquois nations, practised thanksgiving seasons.[13] The United Missionary Society was not forgotten. Each year he wrote once about the UMS General Council, once about mission finances, and then news of UMS appointments.[14]

During the years at Jones Avenue, Goudie's great friend and fellow in so many Ontario affairs from the Reference Committee to the NRRO, Silas Cressman, grew sick and died in pastoral work in Stouffville (1935). Goudie did not miss the chance to speak about his friend at the memorial service. One achievement of Silas and Sarah that he especially praised, was that all of Silas' children followed him in Christian faith.[15]

While at Jones Avenue, Goudie led the congregation in 1935 to take a name change. Instead of East End Mission, they chose "Grace Chapel." I suppose they decided to forget about the past and rely on God's grace to go ahead. In 1936, a milestone in Goudie's own life was recognized by the members and adherents of Grace Chapel. On March 22 after a Sunday service in which his brother Henry, now well over eighty, preached, there was a special celebration. Sam Goudie had reached fifty years in the service of the

---

12. Sam Goudie, "What the Scriptures Teach on Non-Resistance," *GB* (14 November 1935) 2, perhaps issued to correspond with Armistice Day (Remembrance Day) on 11 November.

13. Sam Goudie, "Thanksgiving Day," *GB* (28 November 1935) 2-3, timed to match American Thanksgiving.

14. Sam Goudie, "General Council," *GB* (15 November 1934) 13, *GB* "Lest We Forget," (7 March 1935) 15; "Missionary News," (6 February 1936) 13.

15. [D. V. Nolan], "Beloved Pastor . . . ," *Stouffville Tribune* (12 September 1935) 1.

gospel through the Mennonite Brethren in Christ. The congregation read out an appreciation to their "Dear Reverend Sister and Brother in Christ," including Eliza Goudie in their congratulations, remembering in particular the many years during which she had remained at home in Stouffville, "long and loving vigils of solitude awaiting your return," as the letter colorfully, but accurately noted.[16] The Ontario Conference also noted Goudie's perseverance, by including in the Annual Conference and in the *Conference Journal* of 1936 a photo and summary of his career along with three others: his brother Henry, Jacob "J. B." Detwiler and Peter Cober.[17]

On leaving Grace Chapel in the fall of 1936 when the Conference moved them again, Goudie wrote he had a "note of praise." "Through this time we learned to know and love our people, not only the church members but attendants as well, and entertained a good hope that we might stay a year or two longer." The farewell service was good, he said, and a love offering for them was large.[18]

VINELAND YEARS AGAIN 1936–1940

At seventy, Goudie remained unconditional to the ministry of the Ontario Conference. I cannot prove it, but I suspect that the stationing committee may have asked him where he wanted to go next. Vineland seems to have held his affection somehow. He had an early association with the Niagara peninsula church. He spent three years at Sherkston as a probationer (1888–1891), and then three years more as pastor with Eliza (1897–1900). Vineland was usually included in the East District, so for many of his twenty-eight years as a Presiding Elder, he would visit Vineland four times a year, as he would the others, of course. Now he finished his active ministry with four years at Vineland. A few people still remember him from those days, nearly eighty years later. One who was a young boy then did not perceive him as a dynamic or emotionally warm man, but rather dour, if that is the right word.[19]

---

16. B., W. C. [W. Cecil Brown?], "Congratulations, Felicitations, etc.," *GB* (7 May 1936) 2.

17. Ontario *Conference Journal 1936*, 35, 43. Goudie had the opportunity to give the address of appreciation for Peter Cober in the Ontario Conference, *Ontario Conference Journal 1941*, 47. Cober had died March 23 that year.

18. Sam Goudie, "Vineland," *GB* (26 November 1936) 13. "Love offering," is evangelical jargon for a free-will offering, not budgeted.

19. Harvey T. Fretz, conversation with the author, 2015, Kitchener, ON.

Goudie was not the only pastor to finish at Vineland. Before him had been Alonzo T. Gooding, who concluded his twenty-eight years as an MBiC elder at Vineland, 1934–1936, but at the relatively young age of fifty-two. He left the Vineland Church in good shape with 152 members and an average of 116 attendance in the Sunday school and stayed in the community for two more years not in good health.

Sam wrote ten more reports about his congregation from those four years. He contributed only one more ministry article,[20] and another one for another missionary board member and friend, A. B. (Abraham Bixler) Yoder and his wife Mary (Myers) on their golden wedding anniversary.

From the start, Goudie kept up the pastoral pattern by engaging the Rev. William H. Yates as an evangelist. "Will you join us in prayer for a revival, we need it."[21] Just over a year later he was reporting about another three weeks of special evangelistic meetings (no longer called protracted meetings, note), with the Rev. James Smith Wood from Michigan. He was Ontario-born (b. 1883), who preached "good doctrine in a good spirit and it made a good impression."[22] He happily reported 25 people responded to appeals for salvation, though he realistically noted most were converted before. One young man on the last night "prayed through to victory." Standard holiness language.[23]

To Goudie's satisfaction, he was able to report at the end of the summer:

> Most of the young people who were saved last winter in the special meetings are continuing to take their place and are doing fairly well. Ten of them were baptized, also four young converts from the St. Catharines Mission were baptized at the same time and place. While I do not teach baptismal regeneration nor do I believe that doctrine, yet I do believe and teach that every true convert should follow his Lord and Master in water baptism. A number joined in church membership with more to follow.[24]

Goudie was not willing to let up: "We are planning evangelistic meetings . . . [with] C. W. Ruth . . . September 25 . . . Pray . . . resulting in the

---

20. Sam Goudie, "Gospel Field," *GB* (25 February 1937) 11, a Bible study on evangelistic work.

21. Sam Goudie, "Vineland," *GB* (26 November 1936) 13.

22. And married to the former CMW Clara Brubacher; Huffman, *Mennonite Brethren in Christ*, 273.

23. Sam Goudie, "Vineland, Ontario," *GB* (17 March 1938) 13.

24. Sam Goudie, "Vineland, Ontario," *GB* (1 September 1938) 14.

conversion of many."²⁵ He noted competition from the fruit harvest kept some people away.

The Vineland church witnessed more evangelistic meetings while Goudie was pastor: a Mr. Roy Pitts of Hamilton, preached from February 15 to 27. As ever, Goudie did not refrain from evaluating the response: "good messages... sorry there was not more visible results." Some meetings were well attended in some stormy weather, but some were not. "We are not discouraged but are hoping to see a real awakening take place in the future."²⁶ In a fall series of meetings with Irish evangelists Mr. and Mrs. T. H. Ritchie, again "visible results not what we longed for, yet we are glad to report a man and his wife, also a boy were reclaimed, and two young married women were saved."²⁷

Sam and Eliza reached another family milestone while at the Vineland church: they celebrated their 50th wedding anniversary. A front page notice of the *Gospel Banner* mentioned that Rev. William J. "Hiltz" [Hilts], who was Eliza Jane Smith's pastor on the Greenwood, Brown City and Lamotte field in the Michigan Conference, had conducted the joining in St. Clair County.²⁸

Despite the steady revival activity, the Vineland church, which had a membership of 152 in 1936 (up from 82 in 1905), the congregation saw three yearly modest increases and one large drop during Goudie's term as pastor. The year 1940 ended with a membership of 147 when he handed over to the next appointee, a much younger man, Harvey S. Hallman (b. 1907). In 1937, Goudie baptized four, fourteen in 1938, four in 1939, and nine in 1940.²⁹

---

25. Sam Goudie, "Vineland, Ontario," *GB* (1 September 1938) 14.

26. Sam Goudie, "Vineland, Ontario," *GB* (16 March 1939) 13.

27. Sam Goudie, "Vineland," *GB* (30 November 1939) 13. How far I am from Goudie's frame of mind, when I judge even two converts in special meetings as remarkable. He seems to be in a foreign land to me.

28. Abraham B. Yoder, "50th Wedding Anniversary," *GB* (16 March 1939) 1. A contemporary newspaper clipping used in Gillham, *Vineland*, 56, misspelled Hilts' name, and got the wrong wedding date, which of course was 20 March 1889.

29. David B. Marshall reflects on the declining influence of revivalism in the twentieth century in urban Canada in his 1992 book, *Secularizing the Faith,* especially chapter 8: "Why No Revival?" "Indeed, revivalism had failed as a method to reach the new and ever-expanding urban population and to halt secularization." Secularization theory has been challenged globally, but Canadian evangelicals perceive that the Christian faith continues to be marginalized in Canada.

In conformity to the recommendation of the UMS made in 1937, a Women's Missionary Society formed in Ontario in 1939, and subsequently in Goudie's last year as a pastor, a local society formed in Vineland 18 January 1940 with Mrs. Ernie D. Shuert (former Norah Shantz) as president. She was to become the Conference WMS President as well.[30]

By September 1940, Goudie had turned seventy-four. Countries were at war, the NRRO was in high gear packing up relief materials to send across the ocean, and the Peace Problems Committee of the Ontario Conference was advising young men how to respond to a new Canadian government demand for recruits. He finally turned his face to retirement from pastoral assignments, and returned to the house on Mill St., Stouffville. Yet even now he became, as mentioned, chair of the NRRO from 1941 to 1944.

A BIBLE SCHOOL AT LAST

We have partially traced some of the movements toward biblical/theological education while Goudie was the chair of the Canada/Ontario Conference, but a school was not started until January 1940. Again, why the glacial approach is surprising. Huffman wrote in his chapter on Education: "No church can hope to maintain itself aggressively which does not provide for the training of its leaders," a proposition which I fully endorse.[31] The Canada Conference in 1882 was the first to suggest establishment of a reading course, which the General Conference of the Evangelical United Mennonites initiated later that year.[32] The Indiana and Ohio Conference vigorously discussed the school question in the 1890s, with many writers to the *Gospel Banner* in proportion 1 for to 3 against a college. The Canada Northwest Conference had experimented with a Bible Institute at Edmonton, (Maude Chatham's school 1915–1919), and then Alvin Traub's Mountain View Bible College from 1926. Perhaps the founding of Mountain View Bible School spurred probationer J. Harold Sherk's round table talk in the 1927 Ministerial Convention, "Advantages and Adv[isability] of a Bible School for the Young People of the Ontario Conference." That same day, Lloyd Silas Cressman read his essay, "The Advisable Preparations

---

30. Gillham, *Vineland*, 21.

31. Huffman, *Mennonite Brethren in Christ*, 221.

32. Huffman, *Mennonite Brethren in Christ*, 214–15. Huffman's evaluation of the program ("more valuable has the course become . . . that probationers have been obliged to pass examinations on the books prescribed . . .") suggests the "But . . ." with which he continues, people felt the need for something better still, that is, colleges.

for the Gospel Ministry," which recommended Bible School studies. Lloyd Cressman was a probationer at the time (entered 1925), and was attending the Chicago Evangelistic Institute, the same school Sherk had graduated from in 1924.[33] Yet nothing was done.

Goudie was a young pastor during the period when suspicion of formal schooling in the MBiC was strong enough to discourage those who hoped to see it, such as Daniel Brenneman, J. A. Huffman, Jacob Hygema, and others.[34] The discouragements expressed toward the Bible Training School at Elkhart, Indiana (1900–1904)[35] may have convinced him the time or need wasn't right. Yet some of his fellow pastors in Ontario expressed a wish that they had had more training (e.g., Isaac Brubacher).[36]

Goudie apparently did not commit himself to working toward establishing a school for pastoral leadership or biblical studies. He himself had grade 8 education and went through the Probationer's Reading Course. Perhaps he thought that was sufficient. As the chair of the denominational Executive Committee, he saw how the texts of the Probationers Reading Course were a source of contention among the Conferences, with books falling out of print or out of date, some wanting Keswick/Christian and Missionary Alliance or even more Calvinistic texts, others objecting to more theology, and of course the fundamentalist controversy and battles for control of seminaries between liberals and evangelicals were heating up from 1910 onward.[37] The majority of the rural Ontario MBiC membership were also completing grade 8 and no further, so in most of his pastoral

---

33. Cressman later earned a doctorate and became President of the Friends University, Witchita, Kansas. See also Marr, "Sherk." In 1925, four students from the Chicago Evangelistic Institute were applicants in the Ontario Conference: Lloyd Cressman, Percy G. Lehman, Harold Brown and Henry Good, *Ontario Conference Journal 1925*, 14.

34. Storms, *United Missionary Church*, 194. A brief history of early schools is in Erdel, "Insisting Upon Higher Education," 153–56.

35. Huffman, *Mennonite Brethren in Christ*, 216–17. Huffman catalogs the efforts of western US Conferences to meet their leadership needs by a succession of short-lived Bible Schools in Washington, Idaho, and Nebraska, 217–18. See Storms, *United Missionary Church*, 195.

36. Lageer, *Merging Streams*, 146.

37. In 1936, Pennsylvania Conference wanted to use Evan Hopkins' 1884 book, *The Law of Liberty in the Spiritual Life*, a Keswick classic. Hopkins was an eyewitness-participant of the Welsh Revival of 1904–1905 and among those who wrote about it. By 1949, the Pennsylvania Conference preferred to read William Evans' *The Great Doctrines of the Bible*, first edition 1912, a dispensationalist classic which came out while he was teacher of English Bible at Moody Bible Institute. A revised edition was issued in 1949, a year before Evans' death.

experience, higher education might have seemed unnecessary or too distancing (and expensive) to be useful for the church he knew. Nevertheless, Goudie saw an increasing number of young men were going to some sort of Bible school before applying to be workers in the Conference. He was at times either the examiner on the *Discipline* of the MBiC many years (until 1938), or on the committee that gave credits to applicants coming with formal education to be exempt from studying various reading course books.

So, in 1936, in response to a recommendation that came out of the 1936 Ministerial Convention, the Ontario Conference finally set up a committee to study the need for a Bible School. The members were C. N. Good, J. Harold Sherk, Sam Goudie, P. G. Lehman, W. H. Yates, M. Dedels, and M. Alexander (the latter two being City Mission Workers). Apart from recommending some short Bible study classes with Dr. Peter Wiseman, a Holiness Movement Bible School principal from Brockville/Ottawa, to be held in Stouffville and Kitchener, the committee promised to study the matter. Eileen Lageer says they did not meet until the following year, and all they did was report that people who attended said Wiseman's classes were great blessings, and asked that their committee be made a standing committee. They were, with C. N. Good dropping out and William B. Moyer being added.[38]

Reflect a moment on the ages of these Conference committee members: Sherk (34), Moyer (45), Goudie (71), Percy G. Lehman (35), William H. Yates (51), Marjorie Dedels (possibly 31), and Muriel Alexander (34). Goudie stands out as the elder on this committee. His presence on the committee reflects his standing in the Conference, but as what? Wise counsellor? Voice of caution? As usual, Goudie the committee member did not leave a "memo trail." He stood by the decision of the committee.

The same committee finally recommended in 1938 that a Bible school board be appointed and given power to launch the school. The *Journal* simply says, "The report was adopted." J. Harold Sherk was the Conference secretary at the time. He could have recorded "after much discussion . . ." or something, but not so. The first Board of ten was appointed by the Conference.[39] Somebody must have noticed the need for people of "practical affairs" (meaning: businessmen) because in 1939, prominent MBiC

---

38. *Ontario Conference Journal 1937*, 30.

39. Members were Milton Bricker, Sidney S. Shantz, Ward M. Shantz, Sam Goudie, C. N. Good, J. Harold Sherk, P. G. Lehman, William H. Yates, Dr. Isaac H. Erb, William B. Moyer. *Ontario Conference Journal 1938*, 44.

members were added who were not ordained,[40] and the members were put into staggered terms. Sam Goudie's term was to end in 1941. He did not continue, because as far as I know, his work with the NRRO and the Peace Problems Committee were taking his attention. Thus, the Ontario Conference Emmanuel Bible School finally started in January 1940 in Stouffville where Ward Shantz was the pastor and school principal.

---

40. *Ontario Conference Journal 1939*, 45. J. Henry Good, William H. Yates, Samuel Norman Doner from Gormley (1886–1976) (ending 1940), Sam Goudie, Paul Boadway from Stouffville (1898–1962), Emerson Krupp Bock from New Dundee (1878–1951) (ending 1941), Lewis Raymer Pipher, Dr. Isaac H. Erb a pathologist from Toronto, Herbert Detwiler Huber in manufacturing from Kitchener (b. 1880) (ending 1942), with Ward M. Shantz, principal and J. Harold Sherk, faculty, as advisory members.

15

Family and Last Things 1940–1951, 1957

REACHING THE AGE OF seventy-four in 1940, Sam Goudie was to be active in a number of ministries for a five more years, but not as a pastor. He would shed some other roles especially after a broken hip in the first part of 1944. However, a granddaughter's account shows he and Eliza were engaged as ever in being grandparents.

HOME LIFE, GRANDCHILDREN

Sam and Eliza were becoming grandparents in the twenties and thirties. Fletcher's wife Ina gave birth to Ivan Goudie in 1919, Eleanor in 1927, Helen in 1931, and Donald (nicknamed "Sam") in 1935. While Sam was posted to Jones Avenue and then Vineland, Fletcher's family lived in the Mill St. house in Stouffville. Eleanor remembers it then and from later visits to her grandparents. She gives a completely different kind of memory of the senior Goudies, which is a good correction to the more formal official documentation with which we mostly have to work. Eleanor Goudie, who married Mervyn Bunker and lived for many years around Altona, just southeast of Stouffville about three to four kilometers, did not recall as much about her Goudie grandparents as her Mertens grandparents who farmed near Stouffville. She later learned the reason:

> I don't remember too much about Grandma and Grandpa Goudie before Donnie was born. But since reading grandpa's diaries, I realized that he was away a lot—preaching—not only at his own

church but travelling to other churches as "Presiding Elder" of the Mennonite Brethren in Christ Church—a position he held for 2[8] years. They had lived on Mill St. Since 190[7]—moving there from Toronto—Dad [that is, Fletcher], Uncle Allen and Pearl their daughter who we never knew. She died of spinal meningitis on her 18th birthday, Mar. 20, 1910. Pearl was a special friend of Louie (Stouffer) Forsyth and Jake Reesor. Dad (Fletcher) and uncle Allen chummed with the Reesor kids—Jake and Adah (Mrs Stanley Lewis) and their siblings, Charlie Barkey, the Stouffers and all the families that we grew up with. Grandpa was well-known and respected. A tribute to him when he died—all the Ontario Mennonite [MBiC] ministers except three lined the walkway from the church to the hearse in his honor. From grandpa's diaries I realized grandma stayed at home while he travelled and had many boarders. Grandpa had a huge (perfect) garden—no weeds. Their big brick house and lot surrounded by cedar hedges—all neatly trimmed. A beautiful yellow rose bush (very prickly) grew out by the grey painted 2 holed shanty. A sidewalk led from the house to a two storey barn. Grandpa kept chickens and at one time raised mink.[1] We had a great spot in the hedge to climb or play house and a big lawn to play ball or croquet. When we stayed overnight with grandma and grandpa, after breakfast, it was time for grandpa to read the Bible then each one got down on their knees at their chair while grandpa prayed. Both our sets of grandparents were very religious people. I never heard a cross word from any of them. Grace was always said at the table too.

Grandpa was preaching in Vineland (the second time) when Donnie was about 2 years old. We visited there often—a big field of grapes grew just next door and even some in his garden. The Culp and High families were friends too that we visited at Jordan Station close by. It was wonderful to be able to eat your fill of peaches—just fallen from the tree—so ripe and juicy. Mom used to drive to Vineland in later years and bring a car full of peaches back to Altona for all of us and some neighbors to preserve.[2]

Eleanor had happy memories of a tourist camp her parents—really, her mother—ran on a western arm of Lake Nipissing in northern Ontario during the Depression. The war ended the running of the camp. Things were not easy for them; the girls only had one outfit each, made by their mother or an aunt. Their home economy was constrained, but she remembered

1. After retirement; Bunker, notes for the author, March 2011, "P. 5."
2. Bunker, *Memories*, 13–14.

striped flannel nighties and grey fleece-lined petticoats edged in a red blanket stitch that her Grandma Goudie made for each of the two sisters.³

Eleanor also got to visit her grandparents in Toronto, that is, 1933 to 1936, when Eleanor was six to nine years old.

> Grandpa Goudie was still preaching. Vineland and Jones Avenue in Toronto are the places I remember best. Helen and I stayed for holidays in Toronto—I never really liked being away from home. The best part was being able to go into the church and play the piano (or pretend). They had such beautiful music in that church. Percy Lehman led and Violet Lehman played the piano—very lively—especially for Mennonites. That's where I first remember Rev. and Mrs. Huson—they were Salvation Army people at that time.⁴ Grandma kept a parrot for a lady for a while—that bird could sing "Jesus Loves Me"—great fun! Grandma's treat was a chocolate roll cake with marshmallow filling—I'd love one now—so good! Helen and I could get 2 ice cream cones for 5 cents at the next-door grocery—those double cones with a scoop on each side. I wonder if the church is still there.⁵

Time does funny things. The building is there and still (as of 2024) used for Christian things: Holy Trinity Christian Ministries, which is connected to an Estonian Evangelical Covenant Church. Grace Chapel, however, migrated to O'Connor Hills in Don Mills in 1961, becoming O'Connor Hills United Missionary Church, then Grace Memorial Missionary Church and sadly closed (about in 2006), after many wonderful years of ministry to its neighborhoods.

Eleanor also remembered her grandmother in other ways:

> Grandma was a tiny lady—by the time my children were about 10 years old, they were as tall as grandma. She was a pernickety housekeeper. It seems she must have had boarders as over the years I heard and read in the diaries of different people staying there. Evelyn (Gooding) Milstead [Milsted]—sister of Dorine Doner was always there it seemed. Another sister Dorothy Winger was my good friend and neighbour at Minden and said she lived at grandma's while she went to Teachers College. Their dad was Rev. A. T. Gooding—a Mennonite minister [MBiC] at Gormley.

---

3. Bunker, *Memories*, 17.
4. Frank (1905–1979) and Catherine Huson.
5. Bunker, *Memories*, 17.

> I remember Grandma making soap—she washed my long hair with it—smelled good. I think she put sassafras in it.
>
> Grandma dressed very plainly ["being a Mennonite but didn't wear Mennonite style dresses"]—no wedding ring. I had 2 of her pearl brooches—gave one to our daughter. She had an atomizer on her dresser with Old English Lavender in & when we were good she'd give us a spritz on our Sunday School hankie—where we tied pennies in the corner. On Sunday if we sat in church with her, she'd give me a whole clove to suck on—no gum or candy to chew. Grandma and Grandpa were in Toronto and Vineland preaching, our family lived in their home on Mill St . . . I had to wash dishes at an early age because I could reach grandma's sink—low for her. I wished she had been taller.[6]

Mrs. Bunker inherited a number of the grandparents' household items, dishes and so on, including an organ stool and a "wooden pedestal bowl and matching candle-sticks—always sat on organ with waxed fruit."[7] This is interesting, too, because while the Mennonite Brethren in Christ banned musical instruments from their worship services for a long time, pianos and organs were known in their homes. The 1916 General Conference turned over authority to allow instruments to the Annual Conferences, and the Annual Conferences in turn allowed the Quarterly Conferences to handle this sticky question by votes for which large percentages were needed. Seven of the Goudies' hymnbooks have also survived, two of Sam's and two of Eliza's, plus one from a congregation.

Eleanor Bunker had still other memories:

> At Grandma G's house, we could have coffee for breakfast. She perked it and the milk was added to the coffee pot . . . I wonder if it was because she was from the U.S.A. that we had coffee so much. She would make chocolate pudding—from scratch— like everyone did. She served it in pretty flow-blue bowls—I wish I had them now—I have no idea where they went. At their house on Sundays or holidays, meals were served in the dining room. Plates were heated at the oven door and grandpa served all the first course and grandma the desert. Always on a white tablecloth on the table and at each end white embroidered cloths—in case of a spill. No jumping up and down at the table—good manners were expected. Kids were to be seen and not heard.

---

6. Bunker, letter to the author, March 2011, from Minden Hills, ON.
7. Bunker, letter to the author, March 2011, from Minden Hills, ON.

> It was fun when we lived in grandma's house and no one was around. We got to slide down the stairs on our bum or ride the banister—a good way to keep them dusted. Otherwise I had to use a goose wing to do it. Later on it was my job to clean the French door windows into the parlor . . .
>
> Grandma wore a "switch" on her hair so she had enough hair to wear it in a knob at the back of her head. She would twist strands of her hair at the front, back and forth over hair pins—the tortoise shell kind, when she went to bed—then she had a few wavy pieces to comb into the front.[8]

Eleanor's experienced her "Grandpa Sam," or "Grandpa Goudie" (to distinguish him from other grandfathers), as a "quiet kind of man—I never heard him say a cross word." He used to "rock me on his knee and play 'See-Saw—Dickity-Daw,'" and he did the same with her own older children twenty years later. "Another game was 'Conny over the Stones,' the road got better so he'd bounce me faster." She recalled, "Grandpa was never one to preach to us—you should do this or that."[9]

Sam Goudie was away from Stouffville a lot. Eleanor saw however that "[h]e always helped ma-ma when he was home." In fact the diaries show him doing just that whenever he was in Stouffville.

As for Sam and Eliza's grandchildren, in the 1940s, one grandchild attended United Church programs in Stouffville, though later that family did go to the Christian Church-United Missionary Church at Altona. Fletcher's oldest son Ivan went to the Conscientious Objectors' camp in northern Ontario because of the grandfather's influence. As with some other MBiC youth,[10] when the term of service was lengthened unexpectedly by the government, the prospect of an indefinite term of service in the bush was too much. Ivan quit the Montreal River Camp and joined the Royal Canadian Air Force after all. Probably the Canadian government hoped for such a reaction, but most objectors held to their convictions. Grandpa Goudie may have been disappointed, but he continued to love his grandchildren. He conducted Ivan's wedding in 1943.[11] A photo of Ivan in uniform with his grandparents still exists in the family.[12]

---

8. Bunker, *Memories*, 19–20.
9. Bunker, notes for the author, March 2011, P. 5, from Minden Hills, ON.
10. Steiner, *Promised Lands*, 269 n. 53.
11. Bunker, letter to the author, March 2011, from Minden Hills, ON.
12. Bunker, *Memories*, 22–23. Photo in the Eleanor Bunker Collection.

The Smith and Goudie relations were not forgotten in the Stouffville household. Eleanor recalled her (great) Aunt Clara, from a few visits the Reichards made from Michigan, and a few visits Eleanor and her sister Helen made to Port Huron to see their cousins Velma and Margaret. "Grandma was so much like her sister—Aunt Clara—but she thought Aunt Clara wore too fussy clothes and hats."[13]

Eleanor was also aware that her Grandfather Goudie had a lot of brothers, but she only met a few of those relatives:

> Ethel was the cousin we knew best—uncle Jim's [James Goudie's] daughter. She worked and lived in Stouffville for years[14] and was always with our family at Christmas etc.... Uncle Abe [Abraham Goudie], grandpa's brother, and Aunt Frances lived in Toronto and our family visited them quite frequently. Wilfred[15] was their son—his wife Mary... Their kids were Charles, Evelyn, Elsie and George—the same age group as our family. George rode his bike from Toronto to our house in Stouffville when we were teens... Uncle Henry Goudie, a minister, was another of grandpa's brothers. I remember him when he preached at Mount Joy (Markham). His daughter Annie married Art Clendenen and lived at Cedar Grove by the lane to "Cedarena" where we had skating parties. In later years I learned he had married Audrey Lageer's grandma—their second marriages.[16]

Mrs. Bunker did not meet the other uncles because John lived in Michigan, dying in 1936 in Caro, Tuscola County, Michigan and buried at Brown City. His wife Margaret (Cober) died in Brown City in 1924. David W. died in 1918, retired from retail sales at the Toronto market and living with Martha in Markham on land she inherited, and he was buried in Kitchener.[17] Again, I do not know where his second wife Martha died in 1928, but probably in Markham. Isaac died in 1941 in Kitchener, having been busy with the department store associated with his name and that of his son Arthur R. Goudie. His wife Susannah (Witmer) died in 1930 in Kitchener. After her death, he married Olive N. Knowles. Jacob died in the Kitchener area in 1937 after his wife Rebecca (Hembling),

---

13. Bunker, *Memories*, 20.

14. She was a registered nurse; Bunker, *Hugh Goudie Family*, 110. She never married.

15. Wilford, married Mary Oldford in Toronto in 1914; Bunker, *Hugh Goudie Family*, 106.

16. Bunker, *Memories*, 21.

17. Bunker, *Hugh Goudie Family*, 68.

who died in 1934 in Waterloo County, buried at Breslau's Cressman Mennonite Cemetery. Uncle Jim (James) died in 1931 at his son Elton's[18] in Tuckersmith Township (now part of Municipality of Huron East), Huron County, near Seaforth, so Mrs. Bunker knew only the daughter Ethel. His wife Carrie (Snyder) died as early as 1909, buried in the hilltop cemetery in Blair (Old Blair Memorial Cemetery). Waterloo Generations erroneously places Abraham's death occurring at Verona Mills, Michigan, where he farmed for some years, and does not know of his second marriage to Frances (Geddes) Benson and life in Toronto later. He died in 1938, and Frances in 1948, both dying in Toronto.[19]

SOME EVALUATION. SAM GOUDIE THE MAN, THE MINISTER, THE LEADER AND HIS CHURCH

Membership

When Sam Goudie was elected one of two Presiding Elders in 1905, we found the membership of the Canada/ Ontario Conference of the MBiC was 1,730. The next year 143 were released from the Conference as the nucleus membership of the Canada Northwest Conference centered on Didsbury, where his brother Henry had gone to give leadership. This left about 1,587 members in Ontario. In the table below we can compare the changes over 28 years:

---

18. Bunker, *Hugh Goudie Family*, 110.

19. Most of these family events are from Bunker, *Hugh Goudie Family*, 99–101, with some help from www.generations.regionofwaterloo.com.

	1905	1933	Comments
City Missions	9	6	
Membership	89	147	
Sunday school av. att.	139	321	
Workers	22	21	12 in missions, nine resting (1933)
East and West Districts	22 in 52 locations	21 in 47 locations	(fields, appointments)
Districts Membership	1498	2011	
Sunday school av. att.	1206	2011	
Workers-ordained	27	34	
Probationers in field	10	5	
TOTAL membership	1587	2158	Difference: 571 (about 20.4 members per year)
TOTAL Sunday school	1345	2342	Difference: 997 (about 35.6 members per year)
TOTAL workers available	59	60	

Table 1. Membership

Church growth evaluation

As Glenn Gibson noted, this record of church growth is not explosive.[20] At 1.28 percent per year, it is not even in keeping with the growth rate of Canada, which from 1901 to 1931 was 2.9 percent, 2.0 percent, and 1.7 percent in each of the three decades. The decade 1931 to 1941 was a dismal one for Canada's population growth at 1.2 percent per year, and for the MBiC which grew by only 0.75 percent.[21] Ontario's statistics suggest what was going on. Urban population numbers in Ontario surpassed the rural population at the 1911 Canada census and made only modest increases and even one ten-year decrease (1941 to 1951). The places where Ontario's MBiC churches served were continually losing population to the urban centers, but the MBiC did not follow them to the cities much. Only three completely new congregations were started in these years, if you count Stratford (1906), Petrolia (1920), and Listowel (1926), all started by the City Mission Workers Society. The City Missions tried hard at other places (Toronto-Dundas, Wiarton, Wingham, probably Guelph should be here, although that was sometimes a Conference mission.) Many did not succeed. None

20. Gibson, "Church Planting," [6–7].
21. Canadian statistics from www12.statcan.gc.ca/census-rencensement/2001/as-sa/.

of the Conference Missions (by men) attempted in the years 1905 to 1933 survived. The average members per appointment increased, as the rural members gradually drifted to fewer locations, and they did retain some of the younger generation or attract new members. Some of this consolidation is due to the spread of motor vehicles replacing horse-powered transport. Over Goudie's twenty-eight years, the number of new churches coming into the Conference simply replaced those appointments that closed.

The number of ordained Elders and Approved Ministering Sisters stayed about the same. Everek Storms commented on this static pattern and assigned the problem to (1) rural focus, (2) neglect of the Sunday School, (3) the 1908 Pentecostal schism, and (4) isolation of many congregations on the edges of the core membership areas of Waterloo, Lincoln and York Counties. I would agree with (1), (3), and (4) as factors but not (2). Sunday School growth was the driving force in the 1950s when Storms was writing, but it neglects the power of the birth rate in those decades, which included a long period in which it was the lowest in all of Canada's history. I would add the following factors: (5) the caution of Sam Goudie and his colleagues; (6) the inherent flaws in the policies toward women preachers and church planters who were the most able in starting new churches for the Conference in Gibson's second period;[22] and (7) competition from the Pentecostal and other evangelistic churches.

Sam Goudie did not address the issue of supporting women's pastoral calling in his ministry that I can see. He must have seen the declining number of young women entering the ministry in Ontario, and their aging CMWS membership. We have seen that he enthusiastically encouraged the "mission girls" as he sometimes called them and visited and preached in the missions on his Presiding Elder rounds, even though they were, strictly, supervised by a President. I have never seen any hint that the CMWS Presidents, who were his friends, thought he was straying into their "territory," on the contrary, probably they were happy he lent his support to the missions and workers. However, better theological underpinning for the position of women workers does not seem to have concerned him. This is an argument from silence, so it is not strong. He supported the *Discipline*, which had a path for women to become ministering sisters. I would be happy to see this question researched more.

22. Gibson, "Church Planting."

Mission Administrator

Goudie was also on the Board of a multi-Conference mission society (MBiC FMB) for sixteen years and then president of the denominational mission, the UMS, for all but one year from 1921 to 1939. After 1939, he continued as the chair of the Home Council, a kind of executive committee to care for business between Annual General Meetings of the UMS Board, until his fall in early 1944, when he sent Reginald Beech as his proxy to a Council meeting.[23] In Nigeria, the results after thirty-five years were not immediately impressive. Statistics comparable to the Ontario Conference's fields, membership, attendances and Sunday schools are hard to come by from the mission, in fact they seem to be an afterthought when they are given. As early as 1916, field treasurer Cornelia Pannabecker was apologetic about including statistics of their activities: "I have not given these figures to make a show, but thought it might be of interest and hope you will be as agreeably surprised as I was . . . I notice other societies do it and if we can boost our work in this way it will be worthwhile . . . ."[24]

I find it astonishing that the mission board did not require the missionaries to report useful statistics, and that neither Alexander W. Banfield nor Ira Sherk collected them normally. Ebenezer Anthony was the chair of the MBiC FMB from 1905 to about 1913; policies could have been in place. By 1938, near the end of Goudie's service as UMS President, the UMS reported 7 mission stations, 16 "outstations" (missionary jargon for places where no missionary resided, but some people met every Sunday to listen to somebody preach, foreign or local agents)—with no assurance that any of the hearers were counted as believers, much less members. In 1935, Goudie reported that the Nigerian mission was busy: they had held 2,247 "services," counted 77,412 people attending in those 2,247, recorded 20,657 in Sunday Schools, administered over 25,000 medical treatments and "taught in day school, 35,428."[25] These massive numbers are uninformative on their own.

---

23. *UMS Journal 1944*, 1.

24. Letter of Cornelia W. Pannabecker to C. N. Good from Nigeria, 3 August 1916. In Everek R. Storms Collection, MCI Archives, Mishawaka, Indiana. She was still remarking about keeping statistics in a letter of January 1917: "I think it would be a good thing if the Board would ask it of the missionaries." Letter of 4 January 1917 to C. N. Good, from Shonga, Nigeria. Hint! Hint! Nobody took the hint, it seems.

25. *Ontario Conference Journal 1935*, 60. Donald McGavran described the "fog of busy-ness" that could distract a mission from asking themselves what was going on in their mission and why and where they were or were not seeing a harvest; McGavran, *Understanding Church Growth*, 67–82.

Much more useful would have been, how many worshipping groups met every Sunday, how many did they baptize in the year? The Syrian field reported 106 baptisms, why not something similar from Nigeria? What tribal groups were responding and where? Goudie implied the Nigerian field reported the number of converts, why did he not quote it? The attendees and services suggest that the Nigerian mission had an average of 34.5 people attending their meetings, but it does not say whether these were mainly one-time preaching tours in marketplaces, or regular discipling/ training activities or a mix of events like those. One place, Jebba, more or less the mission headquarters, had an average attendance of 400 in 1935. Assuming they lumped the various language services at Jebba as one service a Sunday, that removes 20,800 attendees from the 77,400, and the average attendance of all the rest reduces to 25.6 per location per meeting. Jebba was a bright spot (there were children boarding for a school there), but with even one or two other large meetings (for example by 1944 Igbeti had an average of 500 per Sunday), the number per service drops even further. In 1933, Joseph Ummel reported an average of 10.5 people per meeting in the Salka area, little more than a compound (family group) of people per meeting.[26] The statistic demonstrates activity by the mission but not effectiveness. Goudie did not mention that in the Zuru area, young men were just starting to accept the gospel in 1933 after seven years of the young staff learning the language and teaching as best they could. In 1938 someone reported "100 Christians at Zuru," which should be interpreted as a surprising work of God. I never understood the attitude of some commentators on missions in Nigeria who belittled missions like the UMS for making no converts in the first seven years, though there were 100 by the thirteenth year, converts from people who knew absolutely nothing about the gospel in 1925. Few congregations in Ontario could match that kind of result, who work with people who had no language barriers and few cultural ones. The mission perhaps hesitated to affirm the conversion of Nigerians because they did not see the same spiritual journeys with which they were familiar in North America. Eventually they did affirm conversions.[27]

26. Overhulser, *Joseph Ummel*, 397.

27. See Storms, *What God Hath Wrought*, 69, which gives just a hint of the awakening in Zuru. Overhulser, *Joseph Ummel*, 397–98, 404, 410, notices some of the steps through the letters the Ummel brothers and their wives wrote to their families in the US. See also Lageer, *Ask of Me*, "Zuru" (unpaginated); and (in Hausa), Rikoto, "Ekklesiyar Kasar Zuru," 2–3; in Box 7211, MCHT. Sakaba Rikoto and his twin brother Zomi were among the first three to "repent" and preach the gospel to their own people, credited by the

India was opened as a field in 1924 but did not see equal numbers of missionaries sent there. It was farther away and more expensive to get to, but I do not know other reasons for the different treatment. A proper history of the UMS in India has never been written—a shining omission in MBiC history writing, despite introductory chapters in Storms' and Lageer's books, and the booklet by Pronoy Sarkar which focus, understandably, on the field activities and personnel, rather than context, the society's administration, strategy, growth, and indigenous leaders.[28] Membership statistics are equally hard to come by as from Nigeria.

All this simply shows that Sam Goudie was a competent administrator (for example, the UMS operated with no debts—and salaries were cut by a third in the Depression to keep going and avoiding dismissing any staff member), financial reports were reliably prepared and reasonable adjustments made when transfers were lost, or unusual circumstances forced new plans. Missionaries were loved and prayed for, mourned when they died or resigned in ill health.[29] Reports were required from the mission's agents regularly. Appeals for new missionaries were sent out frequently. There were persistent efforts to get out missionary news and requests.

I don't think Goudie was a harsh leader by any standard. Staff were sent whenever money was available, which was never fast enough for the fields' opportunities. The MBiC had a tiny membership base to operate a foreign mission. Goudie was a spiritual leader who regularly thanked God for missionary health and safety, called for days of prayer and judged as best as he and his board could about the abilities of those they interviewed to send to the fields of India, Syria or Nigeria. Few missionaries had to be recalled for incompetence or immoral behavior. However, Goudie could not really interpret what the mission fields were achieving. Reading his report to the Tenth Annual Session of the General Board of the United Missionary Society, I believe it is plain Goudie could not give much strategic direction to the Board or the Mission.[30] Here is where educational limitations of

---

Ummels with stirring the awakening in Zuru.

28. Storms, *What God Hath Wrought*, 95–112; Lageer, *Merging Streams*, 210–21. Lageer, *Common Bonds*, 135–41; Sarkar and Lageer, *Missionary Church in India*, is a booklet of 12 pages. Weyburn C. Johnson's 2013 memoir *This is my Story*, goes a long way to fill in some of the gap.

29. While he was alive, Ebenezer Anthony, Goudie's chair in the MBiC FMB, even traveled with new missionaries as far as the port of Boston to see them off; Cornelia Pannabecker, "Diary 1906," 24 July. Goudie does not seem to have traveled in this way.

30. Sam Goudie, "Report of the President of the United Missionary Society," *GB* (11

the leadership as well as the missionaries, which they all shared, may have reduced the progress of the UMS. Some will immediately reject this suggestion and remind me that the leadership of the Holy Spirit is paramount in the Church, not education, and that the missionaries were fully consecrated (most of them clearly were), but wisdom is assisted by knowledge as well. The field leaders probably had a good idea what was working and what was not if they were asked and had a shrewd idea why, but for the sake of reporting the good story to the church back home, which paid the bills, they might not say everything on their mind. Goudie was probably following the pattern of evangelical missions that he read about in their literature. On the other hand, a loose administration from the homeland can be useful to allow field administrators to handle the field situation without interference from the board which did not know the field firsthand, the China Inland Mission pattern. Goudie never traveled to see Nigeria or India or Syria, the way some mission leaders did, who were much more directive in style, or whose missions were personality-driven. Travel was expensive.[31]

Goudie's home Conference was heavily invested in the UMS, judging by the donations reported. The wealthier Pennsylvania Conference reported its finances of missions separately. In 1924, for example, the Ontario Conference alone supplied over half of the whole UMS budget ($8,380 to total income of $15,431, Indiana and Ohio gave $3,955).[32] Even in 1936 in the Depression, Ontario continued to lead the offerings for the UMS, while the next largest donor Conference, the Indiana and Ohio, was closing the gap. (Ontario: $8,411 to Indiana and Ohio's $7,524 out of a total income of $23,495. Indiana and Ohio now had five missionaries in Nigeria, up from three in 1924, their whole missionary force. Pennsylvania Conference added $700 that year). This suggests Goudie was a motivator for giving to missions, or if he was not the chief one in Ontario, his presidency did no harm. In 1924, three UMS personnel in Nigeria plus one in India were Ontario people. Two others who had married men from other Conferences were supported from their husband's place. Two couples (William and

---

June 1930), 13–14.

31. Such as The People's Church's Oswald J. Smith, Methodist Episcopal William Taylor, Nazarene leader Hiram F. Reynolds, The Evangelical Alliance Mission's founder Fredrik Franson, or Hudson Taylor, China Inland Mission. Even A. B. Simpson of the C&MA took one journey in 1910 to mission fields in Latin America.

32. "Minutes of the General Board of the UMS," 1924. Everek Storms collection, MCI Archives, Mishawaka, Indiana. I do not know how they adjusted for the ever-changing difference between the American and Canadian dollars.

Mary (Davidson) Shantz of the C&MA, and Alex and Ella Banfield with the British and Foreign Bible Society), were supported from the Ontario Conference, but not through the UMS. Ontario congregations were well motivated to support their people. In 1936, five missionaries were supported from Ontario: two were in Nigeria, two in Syria, and one in India.[33]

Another telling statistic is that even in 1951, the year of Goudie's death and six years after his last membership on the UMS board, his home congregation, Stouffville, was the single largest donor to the UMS in Ontario, even leading the much larger Bethany congregation in Kitchener.[34]

The Character of an Unconditional Elder

Remembering that in all but two of his twenty-eight years as a Presiding Elder, Sam Goudie was one of two district overseers, still, since he had an increasingly senior role in the Conference leadership, we have to suspect that what happened in the Ontario MBiC was flavoured with Goudie's ways. Remember, too, that he had to be elected *annually* to this position. When I realized this only a few years ago, I marvelled at the "stick-to-itiveness" that Peter Cober recognized when he visited him in 1896 at the Maryboro field. Why did the Conference keep on re-electing him? The Conference was not being coerced by him or his relatives. True, for a brief period his older brother Henry was in the leadership and during it Sam Goudie was elected a Presiding Elder, but Henry soon left for Alberta. In another MBiC Conference, Pennsylvania, the leadership was dominated by a web of family connections for eighty years or more.[35] This did not happen in Ontario. True again that Goudie served with a circle of competent pastors who were also his age-mates, friends that included people we have met repeatedly in this story, especially Silas Cressman, C. N. Good, Ephraim Sievenpiper and Milton Bricker. It is possible that our post-modernist suspicion of every authority structure as inherently coercive would lead us to believe that Goudie was a supreme manipulator to ensure his re-election year by year. I think it is simply that Sam Goudie received the confidence of the Conference. He was steady, he was trustworthy. And he liked committee work! He did not complain of the constant travel involved in the PE's work.

---

33. Pipher, L. R., "Report of the United Missionary Society Treasurer," Ontario *Conference Journal 1936*, 71.

34. Storms, *Yearbook 1952*, 24.

35. Storms, *United Missionary Church*, 70–71.

Add to this record, that he was elected chair of the denominational Executive Committee for an even longer period (1912 to 1943), seven times. These elections were only at the General Conferences, every four years, (longer during the Depression), plenty of time for new leaders and agendas to come to the top and relieve the incumbent.

Goudie was not a charismatic leader who spoke in grand visionary terms, though he was hopeful for the future. He was modest about his own abilities. On his thirty-seventh birthday after eighteen years of public ministry, he wrote in his diary, "[W]ould to God that I might be able to please Him. Hitherto my life appears to be a blank. I pray that it may be made fruitful . . ." These might be conventional meditations, but he had what he thought was evidence: "Who ever would have expected to hear that I was called upon to help in evangelistic meetings?" he wrote in 1922:

> But the unexpected does happen sometimes. I was actually invited to assist the Workers at St. Catharines, Ontario, in a special effort . . . a few were saved, some reclaimed and several very definitely sanctified, if no one else got any good of the meetings, I can truthfully say that it was a grand treat for me. I enjoyed bringing the word of God to the people . . .[36]

Someone must have recommended him despite his misgivings because at least once more he was called to be an evangelist for special meetings: Edith Raymer and Mrs. W. H. French wrote in 1924: "The Lord willing we begin special meetings here from February 20th to March 9th with Rev. S. Goudie as Bible teacher and evangelist. Then our [City Mission] President C. N. Good will continue from March 13 to 23rd. Will [you] continue to pray for Owen Sound?"[37] Edith Raymer was an evangelist in her own right and C. N. Good was the Ontario Conference evangelist many years, so he was moving with the "upper leagues" here. Goudie tried it again in 1928 to assist Max Powers, a probationer fresh at the East End Mission on Jones Avenue.

---

36. Sam Goudie, "Presiding Elder's Report," *GB* (1 March 1922) 13. On a Quarterly Conference tour in 1916 he returned to Stouffville to find "Pastor Sievenpiper engaged in special meetings at the Altona appointment, and we endeavoured to assist him as best we could, and though we were never possessed of any great evangelistic talent yet we always enjoy getting into a revival meeting." Sam Goudie, "Presiding Elder's Report," *GB* (6 June 1916) 10. The first quote in the text is from Sam Goudie, "Diary 1903," 13 August.

37. Edith Raymer, and Mrs. H. W. French, "[Notice]," *GB* (14 February 1924) 13. I have not been able to identify Mrs. French further. She served just the one year.

Here I spent two weeks, one before and one after the quarterly meeting, holding evangelistic meetings every night (except Saturday night.) The attendance was small except on Sundays we had a very nice turn out, a few of the Bethel Chapel people gave us good service several nights. The visible results of the meetings were not what we hoped for, only four professed conversion, a few of the pilgrims were helped in their Christian life; and I enjoyed laboring with our young pastor, G. M. Powers. Here, too, is a good Sunday School.[38]

Assessment for the Church of the Twenty-first Century

Sam Goudie knew he was part of a "small society" of Christians, not a mighty triumphal army such as the Canadian Methodists saw themselves to be at the end of the nineteenth century, nor was he a blaze of prairie fire, which some church leaders seem to need to be.[39] The rise of Pentecostals out of their church in 1906–1912, and leaving it, chastened the MBiC to think more soberly of themselves, at least in Ontario. Goudie did not exaggerate the results of the present. We have noted his realism in assessing congregational situations, while remaining hopeful of better things. We have seen him confront sinful behaviors in the eldership and maintain the procedures of the MBiC *Discipline*, which he submitted to, even when not convenient. He showed patience concerning his projects, such as organizing a General Mission, or the printing of the catechism. Probably due to his moderation as chair of the Executive Committee, some of the tensions between the Pennsylvania Conference and the rest of the Conferences were reduced and ways to co-operate were found. Some initiatives he promoted did not get denominational support, such as producing new editions of a denominational hymnbook, or upholding non-resistance as important as holiness, or adopting catechetical practices, but he did not resign and start up a ministry of his own. He was not an entrepreneurial leader. He worked by consensus in committees and co-operation in the Conferences.

---

38. Sam Goudie, "Presiding Elders' Report," *GB* (2 February 1928) 13.

39. See for example Horner, *Ralph C. Horner Evangelist*, 74–112 especially, where he repeatedly describes the results of his evangelistic preaching as accompanied by "cyclones of converting power" and dozens of people prostrate under the power of the Holy Spirit wherever he went. That book is now admirably superseded by Laurence Croswell and Mark Croswell, *Lift Up a Standard: The Life and Legacy of Ralph C. Horner* ([Belleville, ON: Wesleyan], 2012).

He exhibited the characteristic seen in the title of Eugene Peterson's book on Pss 120–134, *A Long Obedience in One Direction*.[40]

This book demonstrates Sam Goudie was as Mennonite as anybody in the Mennonite Churches. He was as "holiness" and as Arminian as the Wesleyans. He upheld plainness, non-conformity to the world, non-resistance, washing of the Saint's feet, and he was humble without worrying about it. I have related controversies Elder Goudie was involved in, but I have uncovered no scandal due to impropriety or schemes for personal gain. He seems to have been a genuinely converted man, saved by grace, even if others now despise his morality. He was zealous in the work of God as he understood it, even if unspectacular in his way of fulfilling his calling as a servant of God.

It is time to assess the witness of the Mennonite Brethren in Christ Church in the time of Samuel Goudie. We have to remember that Sam Goudie's Mennonite Brethren in Christ Church is a foreign country. Their context is not our context. There is no need to idealize the "founders" of the MBiC, the MCA or the Evangelical Association or to try to reproduce their church life. It is worth asking what we can retrieve from the five (or six) traditions we now have, consciously, not flopping over to every wave of fashion or culture.[41]

Eleanor Bunker remembered her grandmother Goudie admitting that the MBiC as a church was "too hard" in some ways. Rules that potentially crowd out grace are a common failing of holiness churches according to the critics.[42] I have already given a review of Wesleyan holiness theology (chapter 4), revealing my own bias: the Methodist optimism that the will of God can be fulfilled in us while recognizing that we are still unprofitable servants.

---

40. Peterson, *A Long Obedience*.

41. I did not take on a consciously Anabaptist or a Wesleyan identity through the preaching or church life I grew up with. Possibly singing from the 1963 UMC *Hymns for Worship* was as powerful as my pastors' preaching. For some of the rest of the story, see Fuller, "Waking Up," 135–38.

42. The writer remembers an almost casual remark of Dr. Ian Rennie, Dean of Ontario Theological Seminary, Willowdale, Ontario, a kindly Presbyterian church historian, in the Canadian Church history class. He said in effect that all holiness churches lean to legalism and that the period between the world wars was the era of strongest legalistic practice. Since I agree that legalism contradicts God's mercy in salvation, the judgment made me unhappy and made me wish to disprove or diminish it. On the question of legalism, see also Blowers, "Practice of Healing," 18.

Structures for Unity

Mennonite writers note that the MBiC was highly organized in comparison with their Mennonite forebears, with institutions, as we have seen, stemming from the Evangelical Association model and others from the holiness movement. They had a lot of committees.[43] Annual Conference oversight of the movement of ministers, camp-meetings, quarterly visits by the Presiding Elders, and especially the *Gospel Banner*, all these institutions contributed to a feeling of moving together. In the beginning the majority of members were Swiss-South German-origin Mennonites who already had a sense of community. Now they had similar experiences of emotional release, sense of sins forgiven, assurance of salvation sought and found, and joy in subsequent sanctification, feelings of assurance in the protracted meetings and the testimony prayer meetings. Frequent member check ups in the class meetings gathered people to experiences which were similar enough to encourage unity in the denomination. In the first years of the MBiC there were many marriages between members of the movement, as the profiles often show.

If denominations of like-minded and like-experienced people are valuable groupings of Christians, then the MBiC were building a strong and helpful Christian community for the spiritual formation (discipling) and mission of its members. If a denomination is also effective in penetrating the world around it, locally and globally, then change will be inevitable, as new experiences and cultural assumptions will be introduced through the converts and their host communities. That may work against close community feelings, but it may be simply the price of success. There may be other unintended side effects toward cultural and theological assimilation, some of which may be helpful, but possibly also harmful.

This can be seen in the name change debate.

The Church Name Change, 1947

The movement to change the church name rose up rather suddenly in the Ontario Conference. After "special prayer," somebody presented an essay in the 1944 Ministerial Convention on the topic "Name of our Church-An Asset or Liability?" Sam Goudie moved that the convention extend the time for discussion, because the paper seemed favorable to changing the name. Goudie's motion suggests he thought the paper should not pass without

---

43. Noted with some amusement in Epp, *Struggle for Survival*, 506.

comment and perhaps opposed dropping the word "Mennonite." No one objected to "Brethren in Christ." It was the word "Mennonite" that was thought to be the problem. The secretary, Reginald A. Beech, did not record who composed the paper, or what Goudie contributed.[44]

The ending of World War Two relieved the pressure to keep the Mennonite name as evidence of being a "peace church." To many young church members, that war seemed to fit just war theology. The percentages of those enlisting in both Canada and the US were higher than in World War One. About 90% of American MBiC young men enlisted rather than sign up for non-military Civilian Public Service. In Canadian MBiC Conferences, 50% registered as Conscientious Objectors[45] Leaders teaching non-resistance such as Silas Cressman and Sam Goudie were dead or in retirement. Some of the western conferences, the Canada Northwest, for example, supported a change. In fact, even in 1922 there were letters to the *Gospel Banner* urging that "Mennonite" be dropped, some suggesting "Missionary Brethren in Christ." Ontario Elder Harvey R. Frey, however, considered their name an advantage when he read an essay to the Ministerial Convention of 1924.[46] In Alberta, Alvin Traub had complained the "Mennonite" label was a detriment to their evangelism and reputation as early as the 1928 General Conference.[47]

The Ontario Conference was under no particular pressure to change the denominational name. In a 1945 poll of Ontario Conference members, 55% even said "Mennonite" was an asset, but had no strong attachment to the MBiC name either—66% said if the General Conference chose another name, they would accept it. They were persuadable, in other words. Steiner believes that for Ontario, the Mennonite name could have lasted another decade or two.[48] The mission society had so fulfilled the image of the church that a name derived from the society was eventually chosen. I don't know if this has ever happened elsewhere in denominational name changes, that a group actually chose a name based on their mission society. For Goudie, being Mennonite was no problem, as his commitments in writings on non-resistance and non-conformity show. Goudie was no longer

---

44. "Ministerial Convention Minutes," 187–188.

45. Kevin Blowers, e-mail to the author, 6 July 2017. See also Steiner, *Promised Lands*, 195, 323.

46. "Ministerial Convention Minutes," 56–7.

47. Lageer, "Name Change," 3.

48. Steiner, *Promised Lands*, 341–45, 473, 579.

expressing the teaching of a Conference united on Mennonite distinctives, and only three years later, with Goudie also no longer chair of the General Conference Executive Committee, change came. According to the work of Kevin Lageer, the name change made very little difference in the growth of the districts.[49] If growth continued to be slow, it might be that people switched to other objections to the Church's gospel message. "Mennonite" was not really the problem.

For some reason I do not understand, the Pennsylvania Conference opposed the name change and again, negotiated permission to retain the name from 1947 to 1952. Some say it was because they wanted to remain Mennonite, but subsequent events do not support this. In 1952 they finalized their decision not to participate in the United Missionary Church any more and that was accepted by the rest of the Church. The Pennsylvania churches dropped the MBiC name themselves in 1959, to become the Bible Fellowship Church, which they are still called in the twenty-first century.[50]

The Assimilation Theme

A major theme of Samuel J. Steiner's book *In Search of Promised Lands* is assimilation of the Mennonite communities of Ontario to the dominant cultures (religious or otherwise). In his typology, the Old Orders (whether on Mennonite, Brethren in Christ, Amish, or Hutterite foundations) stand at one end of a spectrum, and churches such as the MBiC-UMC-EMCC close to the other. One strength of this analysis is that a Mennonite writer recognizes that *all* Mennonite groups have been assimilating to some extent, not just the MBiC.[51] I suppose Mennonites who leave the Christian faith entirely would be one outer extreme. In his study, some version of

---

49. Graphs in Lageer, "Name Change," [14].

50. For some of the story, see Storms, *United Missionary Church*, 70–75, and Gerber, "Pennsylvania Conference," 32–37, and the bibliography noted there. The BFC, once a fast-growing Conference of the MBiC, remained static in membership (around 4,600 in 44 congregations) for the generation after the separation; Wagner, "Evangelism," 271; but since the 1970s has returned to church planting growth with 65 congregations, 7,700 members and over 10,000 worshippers per Sunday; www.mybfc.org. Though Reformed in doctrine now, they continue to baptize believers only. God bless them. They have an active Historical Society.

51. Two student essays followed this path in describing the MBiC *from* Mennonite *to* something else, negatively described as "non-Mennonite"; Knowles, "Mennonite," in Epp, *Struggle for Survival*, 505, 534 n. 20, copy in David Sapelak Fonds, MAO; and Lageer, "Name Change." The Old Order groups need not be interpreted as representing the "core" of Mennonitism, if there ever was only one core, as in Harold Bender's "Anabaptist Vision."

Mennonitism would be the core, more or less, from which assimilation moves.[52] There are of course, other continua that churches and individuals are constantly moving along. Practically all Anabaptists were European Roman Catholics at one time, for example.[53] And Mennonites may be moving closer to or farther away from evangelicalism or orthodoxy. Sam Goudie's family were assimilated from Presbyterianism to the Mennonites in the life of the Scot David Goudie. And the MBiC was assimilating to a Wesleyan holiness evangelicalism.

If a culture which values differences and diversity, individualism and congregational autonomy in Church life replaces that earlier Mennonite and Wesleyan connectional consensus, then a rather different church life would result. The new worldview will enforce and defend itself and see more faults and weakness in the earlier pattern than the current pattern. And vice versa.

Evangelism and blessings

Church growth is a complex business and every time and situation is a mix of shifting factors.[54] For Sam Goudie's Conference, it would take more study than we can give it here. We have noted the tendency of the MBiC to shift from evangelistic organizational structures to favor the needs of established congregations. The Ontario MBiC's periods of growth, according to Gibson, corresponded to times when several factors, some of them outside the Church's control, provided occasions for growth that the Church was able to make use of, such as available "manpower" and culturally suited methods. They grew at first by providing a home for revivalistic Mennonites, until the Mennonite Church in Ontario itself adopted in the 1890s many of the means the evangelical Mennonites desired in the 1850s and

---

52. Which "Mennonitism" is itself a question. As long ago as 1990, James Reimer discerned at least 14 different kinds of Mennonite theology and four "stances" with respect to theology, Reimer, "Mennonite community," 13. Steiner's typology of Mennonites in Ontario, *Promised Lands*, 589–93, grouped the thirty Ontario Anabaptist denominations in four types: Assimilated Mennonites, Separatist Conservatives, Evangelical Conservatives, and Old Order. He did not include the EMCC in the four types.

53. In the intellectual sphere, Friesen, *Erasmus*, demonstrated that many Anabaptists were extending Erasmus of Rotterdam's version of Catholicism, rather than mainly Lutheran or Reformed theology. Outwardly, of course, Anabaptists themselves conformed to some variety of the culture of the countries in which they arose (cooking, clothing, occupations, buildings, customs, thought patterns and so on).

54. McGavran, *Understanding Church Growth*, 30.

1870s. During the city mission era, the MBiC turned its attention to the small towns and had some modest success, although Gibson saw a weakness in that the rural MBiC could not consistently adapt to small town or city ways and did not support the women they depended on sufficiently.[55]

At a congregational level, Goudie himself pushed evangelistic events. In Vineland when he was pastor in 1936–1940, the revivals the church arranged did not produce sustained growth in the congregation's community. Fourteen converts did not translate, as one would have hoped, into fourteen new members. The link between conversion to Jesus and identifying with Jesus' Church was somehow weak. In an era when we are urged that the Church's task is not seek members but to bless in the effort to lead others to faith, the link might be weaker still. The words of Marshall McLuhan, the Canadian philosopher and media theorist, often seem so right, "The medium is the message." What delivers the message is often taken as part of the message, mostly unintentionally and inescapably so. If the congregation's church life is uninvolved in the conversion of people and incorporation into the faith, then the converts attachment to the church will be that much weaker. Christian literature is full of suggestions on how to fix the weaknesses of the church. We have been bombarded (for a couple of generations) with tiring (and often contradictory) messages that whatever we have been doing has been wrong and everything has to change. Some movements still stumble across growth and think they know what made it happen. Some may actually be right.[56]

It is still God's intention that Jesus build the Church (Matthew 16:18) through us, and the gospel bear fruit and grow in the whole world (Colossians 1:6).

Final Years

Sam's brother Henry died in Markham in the winter of 1942, on 19 January, three days after his ninety-first birthday.[57] He and Sarah, his first wife, had raised two sons and five daughters. The two sons were in Alberta (Edmonton and Didsbury) at the time of his death, four of the daughters were scattered

---

55. Gibson, "Church planting," [6–7].

56. Dr. Rennie, who had made renewal a special area of study, in Canadian Church History class at Ontario Theological Seminary said that in a period of decline, the Church needs to work, be faithful, and pray.

57. Abraham B. Yoder, "In Memoriam: Elder Henry Goudie (1851–1942)," *GB* (30 April 1942) 1–2.

from Markham, to Kitchener, to British Columbia. It is remarkable how many young preachers we have noted were supervised in their probationary year or years by Henry Goudie. This says something good about him as a "father" or "shepherd" in the church, and suggests that churches need people gifted to encourage young preachers.[58] Henry is mentioned in this connection more often than his brother Sam. Funeral services for Henry were held in MBiC Markham (Mt. Joy), and in Wanner Mennonite Church, Hespeler. Presiding Elder Milton Bricker led both services, with Percy G. Lehman preaching at Markham and C. N. Good at Wanner. You can find Henry's gravestone in the Wanner Cemetery where his parents, two baby brothers, his brother James and James' wife Helena Caroline and his own wife Sarah (Wildfong) Goudie are also buried. Many tributes of love were given for this servant of God. At Henry's death, the obituary mentioned Sam Goudie as the only member of the family of eleven children surviving.

Goudie continued to preach on invitation. In 1943 he reported preaching forty-five times, but only six in 1944. Allen Stouffer as a boy noted that the old white-haired minister with round spectacles, who always wore his clerical collar and black coat to church, was often away and supposed that Goudie missed church at times because he was still off on church business, which was somewhat true.[59] That boy from the Stouffville MBiC remembers Goudie only vaguely, though he lived on the farm at the end of the Goudies' street.[60] Sam did not impress, but Eliza was somewhat of a "character" to him as she lived longer. He does not remember talking to the old preacher, or remember any sermon. Allen Stouffer describes Sam Goudie as a "retiring" man, not outgoing like Milton Bricker or some other Conference leaders.[61]

Sam stopped writing for the *Gospel Banner* after 1940 except for one testimony of healing in answer to prayer in 1949. In that letter he acknowledged cards and gifts Sam and Eliza received for their sixtieth wedding anniversary which they had observed that March. The testimony is the only place I have seen in which he refers to and dates his sanctification experience. The occasion for the letter was recovering from "a severe illness

58. More biblical terms than the Greek legend-based "mentor" or sports-related "coach."

59. Dr. Allen P. Stouffer, who grew up in the Stouffville MBiC church in the 1930s and 1940s, conversation with the author, 1 April 2017, in Kitchener, ON.

60. The farm lane did not come out on Mill St., but on Ninth Line. Allen Stouffer, comments on a draft, to the author, 14 January 2019.

61. Stouffer, conversation with the author, 1 April 2017 in Kitchener, ON. He remembers anecdotes told about Eliza Goudie in the community.

that came upon me August 12th, last, and almost cost my life, but through the mercy of God in answering the prayers of God's children I have been spared." He wanted to testify that God had converted him, 15 June 1884, sanctified him in May 1885, that God was willing to forgive and regenerate, cleanse and baptize with the Holy Ghost, "and down through the years I have experienced His power to heal the body, and thank God He is just the same today."[62] By the time of writing he was walking with a cane, but he says while for three months he had been unable to read anything, he was again reading. He was still not able to get to church, which he missed, and missed as well the fellowship of brethren he had worked with so closely in the Conference Executive and the Foreign Mission Boards.

As to the anniversary, "We had a wonderful day."

> The weather was nice and everything passed off fine. We did not put on the celebration. It was done by our children [granddaughter Eleanor Bunker remembers cutting a huge number of sandwiches[63]] and friends. About 130 signed the guest register. We were greatly encouraged by receiving so many cards and letters from people as far south as Florida and as far north and west as British Columbia, Washington and Alberta. We received about 250 cards, some letters, two telegrams from Ontario and a cablegram from Africa.[64]

And there were a lot of flowers.

Honoured

When Sam died in the summer of 1951, as Eleanor Bunker said, practically the whole eldership of the United Missionary Church in Ontario turned out to honor him. Nobody specified if any of the former city mission workers were present, but I suspect many were. The *Missionary Banner* editor wrote a eulogy-like front page recognition of Sam Goudie.[65] I was disappointed that there were no stories about Goudie as a Mission leader, but what we have is also valuable, a character study: intensely interested in missions, zealous and pleased with any news of advancement, a friend of missionaries. At first I guessed that the editor actually did not know Goudie at all, for there was no

---

62. Sam Goudie, "Testimonies," *GB* (14 April 1949) 6.

63. Bunker, Eleanor, telephone conversation with the author from Minden Hills, ON, 28 June 2018.

64. Sam Goudie, "Testimonies," *GB* (14 April 1949) 6.

65. Ditmer, Russell P., "A Great Friend of Missions," *Missionary Banner* (August 1951) 2.

analysis of his achievements. But Russell P. Ditmer, a superintendent from Ohio, did know the UMS, as editor of the *Missionary Banner* from its start in 1938 and as the UMS Foreign Secretary for 1943–1952. Sam Goudie was the Vice-President of the UMS 1939 until the middle of 1945, though he stopped attending meetings after he fell and broke his hip in early 1944.

The *Gospel Banner* editor also supplied an obituary for Sam Goudie. Ray Pannabecker could actually claim he was Goudie's relative, through his Uncle David Pannabecker's marriage to a Wanner, a sister of Sam Goudie's mother, but instead he announced on the cover page:

> A mighty warrior in Israel has fallen in the passing of Rev. Samuel Goudie. Of the older ministers of the United Missionary Church few have given more generous and faithful leadership to the Church. He was president of the United Missionary Society for seventeen years, Chairman of the General Executive Board for thirty-one years and a member of eight General Conferences, the Chairman of one, in 1912.[66]

In the actual obituary, giving Goudie's age in the old customary way, Pannabecker wrote,

> Death came on Monday, July 2, 1951, at the age of eighty-four years, ten months and twenty-one days. He leaves to mourn their loss his widow and two sons, Fletcher and Allan.
>
> Funeral Services were conducted in the Stouffville Church on July 5 with Rev. H[arvey] S. Hallman in charge. Rev. P. G. Lehman, Conference Chairman, delivered the sermon; Rev. C. N. Good read the Scripture and Rev. M. Bricker offered the closing prayer. Almost the entire ministerial membership of the Conference were present.[67]

Eliza continued living in Stouffville and died on 5 November 1957 following an illness of about six weeks. Her pastor, Frank C. Huson, the one who had pleased the Goudies' granddaughter at Jones Avenue in the Depression with his singing, conducted the funeral at the Stouffville United Missionary Church. Somebody wrote, "Mrs. Goudie found the Lord young in years and kept faithful to Him unto the end." She was buried by her husband and her daughter, Pearl, in the municipal cemetery in Stouffville near the eastern entrance.[68]

66. Ray P. Pannabecker, "Samuel Goudie 1866–1951," *GB* (19 July 1951) 1.
67. Ray P. Pannabecker, "Obituary," *GB* (19 July 1951) 15.
68. "Deaths," *GB* (5 December 1957) 14–15.

Appendix A

GLOBAL REACH OF MISSIONARY CHURCHES

THE LARGEST MEMBER OF World Partners International, started by the binational mission, the Nigerian United Missionary Church of Africa, has about 1,000 congregations and preaching points and a constituency of at least 200,000. Next would be the American Missionary Church, Inc., which in 2010 reported 423 congregations and 63,775 adherents (from Association of Religion Data Archives). One website claims the "Missionary Church" is now present in 100 countries, has 20,000 congregations and has 2,000,000 adherents, but does not reveal the basis of those estimates (see mcusa.org).

Canadian Pentecostalism, with a broader initial source from Canadian Methodism and several holiness churches, encouraged large Pentecostal communities around the world which include tens of millions of believers alongside the other Pentecostal communities conducting missions. All told there are hundreds of millions of Pentecostal believers, when independent Pentecostal churches are included. One Pentecostal denomination (the Pentecostal Assemblies of Canada—PAOC) is the leading evangelical church in Canada, reporting 235,000 attendees in over 1100 congregations (see paoc.org). The Pentecostal Assemblies of Kenya had about 5,000 congregations and a constituency of about 500,000, following the missionary efforts of the PAOC since 1910.

Self-declared Pentecostals of all kinds in the last Canadian census which asked "What is your religion?" numbered 478,185 (2011 Canada census). The EMCC, even with a church merging the Evangelical Church of Canada and the Missionary Church of Canada only received 7,820 acknowledgements in the 2011 census, far below the attendances reported. From denominational data for 2015, I estimate average weekly attendance to be around 24,000 per "Primary Worship Service;" (116 congregations reported 21,507, out of about 150 congregations in the denomination). Community size would therefore be an unknown amount higher than this, since not all of the community attend every Sunday.

Non-Pentecostal evangelicals, though divided into many denominations and present in most of the mainline denominations, maintain their numbers. Three of the top groups are the Salvation Army, the Fellowship of Evangelical Baptists and the Christian and Missionary Alliance Canada. The Salvation Army has over 300 churches (corps) in Canada and was named by 70,955 people as their religion. The Fellowship Baptists do not have statistics from StatsCanada, however, they report "over 500" congregations and "over 80,000" attendees per Sunday (see fellowship.ca). The Christian and Missionary Alliance reports about 440 congregations. The 2011 census reported 50,725 naming the C&MA as their church (see cmacan.org).

Appendix B

TIMELINE OF IMPORTANT EVENTS OF SAMUEL GOUDIE'S LIFE

1810	Wanner family migrated to Waterloo from Pennsylvania
1816	David Goudie Senior born in Scotland
1822	Sarah Fathers born in Canada West
1825	Nancy Wanner born in Waterloo Township, Waterloo County
1828	Hugh and Jane Goudie migrated to Wellington County, Canada West
1832	Orrin Smith born in South Norwich, Oxford County
1841	David Goudie married Sarah Fathers
1842	Emily Goudie born in May; Sarah died in August
1843	David married Nancy Wanner, eventually bore ten sons
1848	David W. Goudie born
1851	Henry Goudie born
1852	New Mennonite Church began to ordain and organize in Canada West
1855	Jane (Aird) Goudie died
1859/1860	Orrin Smith married Margaret Weaver in Ontario

Appendix B

1866	Samuel Goudie born (August 15), in Waterloo Township, Waterloo County
1867	Smith family moved to St. Clair County, Michigan
1868	Eliza Jane Smith born
1870	Henry Goudie converted in Wismer prayer meetings
1872	Henry married Sarah Wildfong
1874	Reforming Mennonite Society (Reformed Mennonite Church) formed, May, in Eby's Meeting House, Berlin, Waterloo County
1875	Reforming Mennonites merged with New Mennonite Church at Bloomingdale, Waterloo County to form United Mennonite Church. Margaret (Weaver) Smith died
1879	United Mennonites merged with Evangelical Mennonite Church of Pennsylvania, forming the Evangelical United Mennonite Church. Orrin Smith married Elizabeth Pritchett
1883	Evangelical United Mennonites merged with Swankite Brethren in Christ (Ohio) to form Mennonite Brethren in Christ Church (MBiC)
1884	Samuel Goudie converted (June 15) in Galt, Waterloo County, through the Salvation Army
1885	Sam Goudie baptized (May 10), joined MBiC (May 24), sanctified June, called to preach
1886	Sam accepted as a probationer (April), sent to Nottawasaga, Simcoe County, Ontario
1887	Sam sent to St Clair County, Michigan, Greenwood area
1888	Sam sent to Sherkston field, Welland County, Ontario
1889	Sam married Eliza Jane Smith at Greenwood, Michigan (March 20)
1891	Sam ordained an elder in the MBiC, sent to Port Elgin mission, Bruce County
1892	Pearl Elizabeth Goudie born (March 20)
1894	Sam sent to Maryboro mission, Wellington and Peel Counties

Appendix B

1895	Fletcher Smith Goudie born (July 24)
1896	David Goudie Senior died (Dec 25)
1897	Sam sent to The Twenty mission (Vineland), Lincoln County
1898	Howard Allan born (June 23)
1900	Sam sent to Berlin station (Bethany), Waterloo County; Henry elected a Presiding Elder
1903	Sam sent to Spadina (West Toronto) mission
1905	Sam Goudie elected Presiding Elder; MBiC Foreign Mission, General Board formed, northern Nigeria field opened
1906	Nancy (Wanner) Goudie died; Sam elected chair of Ontario Conference; Henry appointed Presiding Elder, Canada Northwest Conference.
1907	Goudies moved to Stouffville, Whitchurch Township, York County; *MBC Hymnal* published with Oliver B. Snyder, Ebenezer Anthony, and Peter Cober
1908	Pentecostal crisis divided the Ontario Conference
1910	Daughter Pearl died of meningitis (March 20)
1912	Sam elected chair of MBiC Executive Committee (continued until 1943)
1917	Sam helped found the Non-Resistant Relief Organization (member until 1944)
1920	Non-Resistance tract published
1921	United Missionary Society formed (Sam was Vice-President or President until 1945)
1923	Sarah (Wildfong) Goudie died
1924	UMS opened India field, West Bengal
1932	United Orphanage and Mission Board Syrian (Armenian) field assumed by UMS
1933	"Laws Affecting Non-Resistant Religious Societies" booklet published (with C. N. Good); Sam ended position as Presiding Elder, sent to Jones Avenue mission, Toronto
1934	*Book of Religious Instruction* published (with Alvin Traub)

Appendix B

1936	Sam sent to Vineland field
1939	Sam resigned from UMS presidency, became a Vice President and chair of the management committee
1940	Sam retired from itinerant ministry, returned to Stouffville
1944	Sam broke a hip, resigned from NRRO
1945	Sam resigned from UMS
1947	MBiC changed name to United Missionary Church; Pennsylvania kept the MBiC name
1951	Samuel Goudie died on July 2 in Stouffville
1952	Pennsylvania Conference formally left the MBiC
1957	Eliza (Smith) Goudie died on November 5 in Stouffville

Appendix C

SELECT LIST OF GOUDIE'S WRITINGS

1886–1894	"Pastor's Diary"—Eleanor Bunker Family Collection
1887	"From [Greenwood,] Michigan," *GB* (June 1) 10.
1887	"Repentance," *GB* (September 1) 8. MCE.
1888	"Question of Holiness," *GB* (May 15) 10.
1889	"Non-Conformity to the World," *GB* (July 1) 14.
1891	"Bohlender," *GB* (June 1) 16 (obituary).
1891	"Obituary. Bro. Amos Bowman," *GB* (December 1) 16.
1892	"The Influence of the Sabbath School," *GB* (March 15) 4.
1893	"Christian Endeavour, Epworth League and Young People's Societies," *GB* (April 25) 2. MCE.
1893	"Testimony," *GB* (November 14) 14.
1895	"Marks of Distinction Between the Children of God and of the World," *GB* (May 21) 3.
1896	"Elmwood Camp-Meeting," *GB* (September 29) 8.
1896	"Elmwood Camp-Meeting," *GB* (October 6) 8.
1899	"Testimony," *GB* (January 17) 15.
1899	"Model Presiding Elder," *GB* (December 12) 3. MCE.
1901	"Our Individuality," *GB* (November 2) 3.
1902	"Compromising to Gain Influence," *GB* (January 4) 8–9.

Appendix C

1903	"Whoso Offereth Praise, Glorifieth Me," *GB* (March 14) 13.
1907	*Hymnal for MBC* (co-edited).
1909	"Faithful," *GB* (February 25) 4.
1909	"Living for Christ," *GB* (March 11) 4.
1909	"We Would See Jesus," *GB* (April 15) 4.
1909	"Sympathy," *GB* (August 12) 2.
1910	"God is Able," *GB* (June 2) 4.
1910	"God is Able," *GB* (June 9) 5.
1910	"God is Able," *GB* (June 16) 4.
1910	"God is Able," *GB* (November 17) 4.
1911	"Getting Even—With What?" *GB* (December 21) 2.
1912	"Our Sufficiency is of God," *GB* (February 1) 1.
1912	"Disciples of Jesus before Pentecost," *GB* (February 15) 1.
1912	"Pentecost," *GB* (March 7) 1.
1912	"Disciples of Jesus After Pentecost," *GB* (March 28) 1.
1912	"Zeal," *GB* (May 9) 1.
1912	"Lord's Festivals," *GB* (May 30) 1.
1912	"Testimonies on Tithing," *GB* (June 27) 1.
1912	"Non-Conformity," *GB* (August 8) 1.
1912	"Have Ye Understood?" *GB* (September 5) 1.
1912	"Unconditional Ministry and Laity," *GB* (October 12) 1.
1913	"Public Notice," *GB* (June 5) 10.
1914	"Holiness—Its Godly Walk," *GB* (November 26) 10.
1915	"Salvation," *GB* (June 3) 8.
1915	"Abiding in Christ," *GB* (June 10) 8.
1915	"Advice to Young Converts," *GB* (June 17) 8.
1915	"Abraham: Friend of God," *GB* (June 24) 8.
1915	"Necessity of Ministerial Education," *GB* (October 28) 11.

Appendix C

1915	"What Presiding Elder Goudie says about *Upper Room Messages*," *GB* (November 25) 8.
1915	"Man's Love to Man," *GB* (December 30) 8.
1915	"Believer's Walk," *GB* (December 30) 8.
1916	"Life Separated unto God," *GB* (January 20) 8.
1916	"Evil Speaking," *GB* (March 16) 8.
1916	"I Wills . . ." *GB* (September 14) 8.
1916	"Marching Orders," *GB* (October 19) 8.
1916	"Swarms of Honey B's without Stings," *GB* (November 8) 8.
1917	"Six 'One Things' of the Bible," *GB* (February 22) 4.
1917	"Believer's Walk," *GB* (March 22) 4.
1917	"Privileges of Partakers," *GB* (May 4) 4.
1917	"Answers to Prayer," *GB* (June 21) 4.
1917	"Consecration," *GB* (August 9) 4.
1917	"Bible 'All's,'" *GB* (September 27) 4.
1917	"Chairman Goudie's Announcement," *GB* (October 25) 14.
1917	"Minister's Ability and Responsibility in and out of the Pulpit," *GB* (November 1) 2. MCE.
1917	"Minister's Ability and Responsibility in and out of the Pulpit," *GB* (November 8) 3. MCE.
1917	"Daniel," *GB* (November 15) 4.
1918	"Saving the Children," *GB* (May 9) 4.
1918	"Some Things Worth Knowing," *GB* (June 6) 8.
1918	"Purity," *GB* (July 18) 8.
1918	"Answers to Prayer," *GB* (September 26) 8.
1918	"Closet Prayer," *GB* (October 31) 8.
1918	"Consecration," *GB* (November 14) 8.
1919	"Prayer Meeting and its Benefits," *GB* (January 2) 8.
1919	"Christian's Conversation," *GB* (February 13) 4.
1919	"A Word of Encouragement and Advice," *GB* (February 20) 13.

1919	"Conditions of Prayer," *GB* (March 20) 4.
1919	"Sabbath in the Home," *GB* (May 8) 5.
1919	"Faith," *GB* (May 15) 4.
1920	"Parental Compensation," *GB* (May 6) 6.
1920	*A Scriptural Exegesis of the Doctrine of Non-Resistance* (Stouffville, ON)
1921	"Place of the Young in the Church," *GB* (May 5) 9.
1921	"History of the Bethel Circuit" (compiled and read on Nov 6, 1921, at the Dedication of the New Church [Mennonite Archives of Ontario]).
1921	"Church Dedication," *GB* (November 24) 14.
1923	"Call to Prayer," *GB* (April 12) 11.
1924	"[Criticism]," *GB* (April 17) 2.
1924	"Cliques," *GB* (May 29) 2.
1925	"New Year Greetings," *GB* (January 8) 1.
1925	"Apology," *GB* (December 17) 2.
1927	"Thanksgiving," *GB* (November 24) 2.
1927	"Consecration," *GB* (December 22) 11.
1928	"Origin of the UMS" (in *Yearbook of the UMS 1928*).
1930	"Divinity of Christ," *GB* (September 11) 3.
1930	"Outline of a Sermon on Acts 1:8," *Ontario Conference Journal 1930*, 42.
1931	"Church Dedication, Gormley, Ont.," *GB* (December 17) 1.
1933	*Book of Religious Instruction* (edited with Alvin Traub).
1934	"Great Man is Fallen," *GB* (April 5) 3.
1934	*Laws Affecting Non-Resistant Religious Societies* (edited with C. N. Good).
1935	"The Apostle Paul an Example for the Present Day Minister, Experimentally, Doctrinally and Practically," *GB* (January 3) 3–4.

1935	"The Apostle Paul an Example for the Present Day Minister, Experimentally, Doctrinally and Practically," *GB* (January 10) 2.
1935	"Lest We Forget," *GB* (March 7) 8.
1935	"What the Scriptures Teach on Non-Resistance," *GB* (November 14) 2.
1935	"Thanksgiving Day," *GB* (November 28) 2.
1937	"Gospel Field," *GB* (February 25) 11.
1937	"How to Get Things from God," *MB* (September) 4.
1939	"Golden Wedding Anniversary," *GB* (August 24) 1.
1942	"Sermon Notes on Thot," *GB* (April 2) 7.
1942	"Special Attention," *GB* (September 24) 14.
1949	"Testimonies," *GB* (April 6) 6.

Bibliography

Airhart, Phyllis D. "The Eclipse of Revivalist Spirituality: The Transformation of Canadian Methodist Piety 1884–1925." PhD diss., University of Toronto, 1985.
Aitken, Kate. *Never a Day So Bright*. Toronto: Longmans, 1956.
Akenson, Donald Harman. *The Irish in Ontario: A Study in Rural History*. 2nd ed. Kingston: McGill-Queen's University Press, 1999.
Albright, Raymond W. *A History of the Evangelical Church*. Harrisburg, PA: Evangelical, 1942.
Allen, Richard. *The Social Passion: Religion and Social Reform in Canada 1914–1928*. Toronto: University of Toronto Press, 1973.
Ambrose, Rosemary Willard. *Waterloo County Churches: A Research Guide to Churches Established Before 1900*. Kitchener, ON: Waterloo-Wellington Branch Ontario Genealogical Society, 1993.
Anthes, Jacob. "Anthes Family Letters." Online: http://www.uwaterloo.ca/library/special-collections-archives/collections/digital-collections/waterloo-county-anthes-family-letters.
Anthony, Ebenezer. "Cass River Camp-meeting." *GB*, October 3, 1893.
———. "Letter." *GB*, May 1, 1892.
Atkinson, John. *The Class Leader: His Work, and How to Do It; with Illustrations of Principles, Deeds, Methods, and Results*. Toronto: Samuel Rose, 1875.
Ball, John Thomas. *Early Days of Pentecost*. Personal Papers: John T. Ball, n.d.
Barkey, Jean, ed. *Stouffville 1877–1977: A Pictorial History of a Prosperous Ontario Community*. Stouffville, ON: Stouffville Historical Committee, 1977.
Bassett, Paul M. "The Fundamentalist Leavening of the Holiness Movement." *Wesleyan Theological Journal* 13 (1978) 65–91.
Bassler, Gerhard P. "German Canadians." *The Canadian Encyclopedia*. Online: http://www.thecanadianencyclopedia.ca/en/article/german-canadians.
Bender, Harold S. "Evangelism." In *The Mennonite Encyclopedia*, edited by Cornellus Krahn, 2:269–73. Scottdale, PA: Mennonite, 1972.
Bennett, Daniel, Thomas Fuller, and Clare Fuller. "Ontario Church Stories Episode 3: Three Generations of Hostetlers." *YouTube*. http://www.youtube.com/channel/UCxBx4rLwIpnyXxrlsrmhj6g.
Benson, Joseph. *The Life of the Rev. John W. De La Flechere: Compiled from the Narrative of the Rev. J. Wesley, A. M*. London: Wesleyan-Methodist, 1860.

BIBLIOGRAPHY

Beverley, James, and Barry Moody, eds. *The Journal of Henry Alline*. Wolfville, NS: Lancelot, 1982.

Bingham, Rowland V. *The Bible and the Body: Healing in the Scriptures*. 3rd ed. London: Marshall, Morgan and Scott, 1939.

Black, Marieda. "The History." In *Mount Pleasant Missionary Church: A Church for All People, 100 Years 1889-1989*, edited by Ilah Weller, 11–18. Ravenshoe, ON: Mount Pleasant Missionary Church, 1989.

Bloomfield, Elizabeth. *Waterloo Township through Two Centuries*. Kitchener, ON: Waterloo Historical Society, 1995.

Bloomfield, Elizabeth, and Linda Foster. *Families and Communities of Waterloo Township in 1861*. Guelph, ON: Caribou Imprints, 1995.

———. *Waterloo Township Schools 1842-1972*. Guelph, ON: Caribou, 1995.

Blowers, Kevin. "Jesus Christ, the Same Yesterday, and Today, and Forever: A Brief Look at How the Practice of Healing Has Changed over Time in the Missionary Church." *Reflections* 18–19 (2016–2017) 7–20.

Bowman, Hezekiah J. *Voices on Holiness from the Evangelical Association*. Cleveland, OH: Evangelical, 1882.

Bowman, Menno. "Presiding Elder's Report." *GB*, May 8, 1894.

Brenneman, Daniel. "Letter from Daniel Brenneman to C. Henry Smith." *Reflections* 6 (2002) 41–50.

Bricker, Irvin Charles. "History of the Gowdy-Goldie-Goudie Family." *Waterloo Historical Society Journal* (1938) 20–37.

———. "The History of Waterloo Township up to 1825." *Waterloo Historical Society Journal* (1934) 84–122.

Brown, Elaine S., Kimberly Brander, and Anne Kuykendall. "Connecting through History: A Visual Timeline from Common Bonds." In *Common Bonds: The Story Of The Evangelical Missionary Church Of Canada*, edited by Eileen Lageer. Calgary, AB: Evangelical Church Of Canada, 2004.

Brown, Victor G., ed. *Fifty Years of Pentecostal History 1933-1983*. Burlington, ON: Pentecostal Assemblies of Canada, 1983.

Brubacher, Lloyd. *100 Years of Camp Meetings 1881-1981*. Kitchener, ON: Centennial Committee of the Canada East District, Missionary Church, 1981.

Brunner, Charles Henry. "Oliver B. Snyder P. E. of Michigan." *GB*, 1909, 10.

———. "[Samuel Goudie]." *GB*, December 23, 1909.

Bumsted, John Michael. *The Peoples of Canada: A Post-Confederation History*. 2nd ed. Don Mills, ON: Oxford University Press, 2004.

Bunker, Eleanor. *Memories*. Minden Hills, ON: For the Author, 2010.

Bunker, Tom. *The Hugh Goudie (Gouldie) Family of Wellington and Waterloo Counties*. Bracebridge, ON: For the Author, 2017.

Burkholder, Lewis J. *A Brief History of the Mennonites in Ontario*. Markham, ON: Mennonite Conference of Ontario, 1935.

Burton, Richard. *The Lord Has Helped Us: 100 Years of Pentecost in Kitchener 1909- 2009*. Kitchener, ON: For the Author, 2008.

Burwash, Nathaniel, ed. *Wesley's Doctrinal Standards Part I: The Sermons, with Introductions, Analysis and Notes*. Toronto: William Briggs, 1881.

Byer, Lillian. "Canada Conference Proceedings." *GB*. April 15, 1891.

Chambers, George Augustus. *Fifty Years in the Service of the King 1907–1957*. Toronto: Testimony, 1960.

BIBLIOGRAPHY

Champion, Isabel, ed. *Markham 1793–1900*. 2nd ed. Markham, ON: Markham Historical Society, 1989.
Chester, Edward N., ed. *Great Is Thy Faithfulness: Centennial Celebration Stayner Missionary Church 1890–1990*. Stayner, ON: Stayner Missionary Church, 1990.
Chester, Leonard J. "A History of the Puslinch Community Brethren in Christ Church Formerly Known as the Puslinch Union Church." n.d.
Christie, George A., ed. *Out of Bondage into Liberty*. Ottawa, ON: Holiness Movement Church, 1912.
Church, Gormley Missionary. *The Word for 100 Years: 1873–1973*. Gormley, ON: Gormley Missionary Church, 1973.
Clark, Samuel D. *Church and Sect in Canada*. Toronto: University of Toronto Press, 1948.
Coffman, Barbara F. "Samuel Fry the Weaver and Mennonites of the Twenty." *Canadian-German Folklore* 8 (1982) 169–209.
Coffman, Samuel F. "Nonresistant Relief Organization (NRRO)." *Global Anabaptist Mennonite Encyclopedia Online*. Online: https://gameo.org/index.php?title=Nonresistant_Relief_Organization_(NRRO)&oldid=135601.
Cook, Arnold L. *Historical Drift: Must my Church Die?* Camp Hill, PA: Christian, 2000.
Cook, Sharon Ann. "The Ontario Young Woman's Christian Temperance Union: A Study in Female Evangelicalism, 1874–1930." In *Changing Roles of Women within the Christian Church in Canada*, edited by Elizabeth Gillian Muir and Marilyn Fardig Wheatley, 299–320. Toronto: University of Toronto Press, 1995.
Creighton, Luella. *High Bright Buggy Wheels*. Reprint. Don Mills, ON: Oxford University Press, 1951.
Cressman, John Gordon. "Developing Confidence and Competencies of Church Board Chairs: Designing, Facilitating and Evaluating a Training Course to Develop Church Board Chairs for Effective Leadership in Their Local Churches." DMin diss., Tyndale Seminary, 2016.
Croswell, Laurence, and Mark Croswell. *Lift Up a Standard: The Life and Legacy of Ralph C. Horner*. Brockville, ON: Wesleyan, 2012.
Dayton, Donald W. *Theological Roots of Pentecostalism*. Peabody, MA: Hendrickson, 1987.
Delsaut, Phillippe Gerard. "Christ at the Centre." Calgary, AB: Evangelical Missionary Church of Canada, 2000.
Dempster, Murray W. "The Canada-Britain-USA Triad: Canadian Pentecostal Pacifism in WWI and WWII." *Canadian Journal of Pentecostal-Charismatic Christianity* 4 (2013) 1–26.
Dillistone, F.W. "Max Warren—1904–1977." In *Missionary Legacies: Biographical Studies of the Leaders of the Modern Missionary Movement*, edited by Gerald H. Anderson, 616–23. Maryknoll, NY: Orbis, 1994.
Ditmer, Russell P. "Banner Beginnings." *Missionary Banner*, September 1968, 2.
Doctrines and Discipline of the Evangelical Church 1939. Harrisonburg, PA: Evangelical, 1939.
Doherty, David A. "The Emergence of the United Mennonites in Ontario." *McMaster Journal of Theology and Ministry* 20 (2018) 45–80.
Dow, Thomas Edward. *When Storms Come: Another Look at Job*. 2nd ed. McMaster Ministry Studies Series 1. Eugene, OR: Pickwick, 2010.
Dudley-Smith, Timothy. *John Stott, the Making of a Leader: A Biography, the Early Years*. Downers Grove, IL: InterVarsity, 1999.

Bibliography

Dunae, Patrick A., and George Woodcock. "English Canadians." *The Canadian Encyclopedia.* Online: https://www.thecanadianencyclopedia.ca/en/article/english.

Dunning, H.Ray. *Reflecting the Divine Image: Christian Ethics in Wesleyan Perspective.* Downers Grove, IL: InterVarsity, 1998.

Dyck, Cornelius J., ed. *An Introduction to Mennonite History: A Popular History of the Anabaptists and the Mennonites.* 3rd ed. Scottdale, PA: Herald, 1993.

Eaton, Matthew, and Joel Boehner. "Practising Peace, Embracing Evangelism: Missional Tensions in the Mennonite Brethren in Christ." In *The Activist Impulse: Essays on the Intersection of Evangelicalism and Anabaptism,* edited by Jared S. Burkholder and David C. Cramer, 217–36. Eugene, OR: Pickwick, 2012.

Eby, Solomon. "[Notice]." *GB,* June 6, 1893.

———. "Port Elgin Camp-Meeting." *GB,* July 4, 1893.

———. "Presiding Elder's Report." *GB,* May 15, 1891.

Eby, Ezra E., Eldon D. Weber, and Joseph Buchanan Snyder. *A Biographical History of Early Settlers and Their Descendants in Waterloo Township.* Kitchener, ON: Eldon D. Weber, 1971.

Eleanor Bunker Family Collection. Minden Hills: ON, n.d.

Eller, Paul Himmel. *History of Evangelical Church Missions.* Harrisburg, PA: Evangelical, 1942.

"EMCC Restructuring Proposal." *Canada East District Conference Journal,* 2004.

Engle, Anna R., John A. Climenhaga, and Leoda A. Buckwalter. *There Is No Difference: God Works in Africa and India.* Nappanee, IN: Evangelical Visitor, 1950.

Epp, Frank H. *Mennonites in Canada, 1786-1920: The History of a Separate People.* Toronto: Macmillan, 1974.

———. *Mennonites in Canada, 1920-1940: A People's Struggle for Survival.* Toronto: Macmillan, 1982.

Epp, Marlene. "Port Elgin Mennonite Church (Port Elgin, Ontario, Canada)." *Global Anabaptist Mennonite Encyclopedia Online.* Online: https://gameo.org/index.php?title=Port_Elgin_Mennonite_Church_(Port_Elgin,_Ontario,_Canada)&oldid=114490.

———. "Wallace Mennonite Brethren in Christ Church (Palmerston, Ontario, Canada)." *Global Anabaptist Mennonite Encyclopedia Online.* Online: https://gameo.org/index.php?title=Wallace_Mennonite_Brethren_in_Christ_Church_(Palmerston,_Ontario,_Canada)&oldid=78565.

Erdel, Timothy Paul. "'Better Right Than Mennonite': From 'Egli Amish' to the Defenseless Mennonite Church, to the Evangelical Mennonite Church to the Fellowship of Evangelical Churches." *Mennonite Quarterly Review* 89 (2015) 467–87.

———. "The Evangelical Tradition in the Missionary Church: Enduring Debts and Unresolved Dilemmas." *Reflections* 13 (2011) 74–109.

———. "Holiness among the Mennonites." *Reflections* 10 (2008) 5–42.

———. "I Wish I'd Been There." *Mennonite Historical Bulletin* 62 (2001) 8–9.

———. "Insisting Upon Higher Education." *Reflections* 7 (2003) 153–56.

———. "Pedagogy, Propaganda, Prophetic Protest, and Projection: Dangers and Dilemmas in Writing an Authorized Denominational History." In *Conference on Faith and History.* Huntington, IN: Huntington College Press, 2002.

Failing, George E. "Developments in Holiness Theology After Wesley." In *Insights into Holiness: Discussions of Holiness by Fifteen Leading Scholars of the Wesleyan Persuasion,* edited by Kenneth Geiger. Kansas City, MO: Beacon Hill, 1962.

BIBLIOGRAPHY

Fairbairn, Charles V. *I Call to Remembrance*. Winona Lake, IN: Light and Life, 1960.

Faupel, D.William. "Glossolalia as Foreign Language: An Investigation of the Early Twentieth-Century Pentecostal Claim." *Wesleyan Theological Journal* 31 (1996) 95–109.

Flanagan, Thomas. "Aboriginal Title." In *An Introduction to Canadian History*, edited by Arthur I. Silver, 454–79. Toronto: Canadian Scholars, 1991.

Flatt, Kevin N. *Beyond Evangelicalism: The Sixties and the United Church of Canada*. Montreal and Kingston: McGill-Queen's University Press, 2013.

Flood, Cynthia. "Introduction to the Wynford Edition." In *High Bright Buggy Wheelsh*, edited by Luella Creighton. Don Mills, ON: Oxford University Press, 2013.

Fretz, Joseph C., and Marlene Epp. "Sherkston Mennonite Church (Sherkston, Ontario, Canada)." *Global Anabaptist Mennonite Encyclopedia Online*. Online: https://gameo.org/index.php?title=Sherkston_Mennonite_Church_(Sherkston,_Ontario,_Canada)&oldid=114491.

———. "Wallace Mennonite Church (Palmerston, Ontario, Canada)." *Global Anabaptist Mennonite Encyclopedia Online*. Online: https://gameo.org/index.php?title=Wallace_Mennonite_Church_(Palmerston,_Ontario,_Canada)&oldid=114484.

Friesen, Abraham. *Erasmus, The Anabaptists and the Great Commission*. Grand Rapids: Eerdmans, 1998.

Frodsham, Stanley Howard. *With Signs Following: The Story of the Pentecostal Revival in the Twentieth Century*. 3rd ed. Springfield, MO: Gospel, 1941.

"From Our Fields of Labor." *GB*, July 15, 1884.

Fuller, James Clare. "Banfield, Alexander Woods (1878–1949)." *Global Anabaptist Mennonite Encyclopedia Online*. Online: https://gameo.org/index.php?title=Banfield,_Alexander_Woods_(1878–1949)&oldid=132566.

———. *Banfield, Nupe and the UMCA*. Ilorin, Nigeria: World Partners, 2001.

———. "Barker, Ada Moyer (1875–1982)." *Global Anabaptist Mennonite Encyclopedia Online*. Online: https://gameo.org/index.php?title=Barker,_Ada_Moyer_(1875–1982)&oldid=135915.

———. "Chatham, Maude Elizabeth (1870–1951)." *Global Anabaptist Mennonite Encyclopedia Online*. Online: https://gameo.org/index.php?title=Chatham,_Maude_Elizabeth_(1870–1951)&oldid=132853.

———. "Cressman, Silas Shantz (1866–1935)." *Global Anabaptist Mennonite Encyclopedia Online*. Online: https://gameo.org/index.php?title=Cressman,_Silas_Shantz_(1866–1935)&oldid=132546.

———. "Detweiler, Noah (1839–1914)." *Global Anabaptist Mennonite Encyclopedia Online*. Online: https://gameo.org/index.php?title=Detweiler,_Noah_(1839–1914)&oldid=135607.

———. "Emmanuel Bible College," n.d.

———. "Go and Proclaim: Ministering Sisters in the Missionary Church 1885–1987." Missionary Church, Canada East District, n.d.

———. "Holiness People in Early Canadian Pentecostalism 1906–1919," n.d.

———. "Pool, Sarah Ann (1862–1913)." *Global Anabaptist Mennonite Encyclopedia Online*. Online: https://gameo.org/index.php?title=Pool,_Sarah_Ann_(1862–1913)&oldid=133259.

———. "Schlichter, Samuel (1821–1873)." *Global Anabaptist Mennonite Encyclopedia Online*. Online: https://gameo.org/index.php?title=Schlichter,_Samuel_(1821–1873)&oldid=135612.

———. "Shantz, Ward Montford (1910–2009)." *Global Anabaptist Mennonite Encyclopedia Online*. Online: https://gameo.org/index.php?title=Shantz,_Ward_Montford_(1910-2009)&oldid=132007.

———. "Shantz, William Albert (1866–1936)." *Global Anabaptist Mennonite Encyclopedia Online*. Online: https://gameo.org/index.php?title=Shantz,_William_Albert_(1866-1936)&oldid=134703.

———. "Waking Up in the Missionary Church." *Reflections* 13–14 (2012) 135–38.

———. "We Trust God Will Own His Word: A Holiness-Mennonite Mission in Nigeria 1905–1978." MTS thesis, McMaster Divinity College, 2004.

Fuller, Lois K. *A Biblical Theology of Missions: God's Great Project for the Blessing of All Nations*. Bukuru, Nigeria: African Christian Textbooks, 2005.

Gauvreau, Michael. *The Evangelical Century: College and Creed in English Canada from the Great Revival to the Great Depression*. Montreal and Kingston: McGill-Queen's University Press, 1991.

Geissinger, Andrew F. "The Hymnody of the Evangelical Mennonites of Pennsylvania and the Mennonite Brethren in Christ, Pennsylvania Conference 1858–1917." PhD diss., University of Southern California, 2008.

Gerber, Wayne. "Whatever Happened to the Pennsylvania Conference?" *Reflections* 3 (1995).

Gerig, Jared F. *The Conflict from Eden to Eternity*. Elkhart, IN: Bethel, 1990.

Gibson, Glenn Alexander. "Methods, Momentum, and Manpower: A Study of the Church Planting History of the Missionary Church, Canada East 1875 to 1980." Toronto: Ontario Theological Seminary, 1986.

———. "Urbanization in a Rural Denomination: A Study of Pastoral and Congregational Values in the Missionary Church—Canada East District." Ontario Theological Seminary, 1992.

Gillham, Skip, ed. *The Church on the Hill: Vineland Missionary Church 1881–1891*. Vineland, ON: Vineland Missionary Church, 1978.

Gingerich, Charles S. "An Experiment in Denominationalism: A History of the Missionary Church of Canada, Ontario Conference, 1849–1918." MA thesis, Wheaton College, 1994.

———. *The Peninsula Pilgrims: A History of Bethel Church*. Lion's Head, ON: RDP Graphics, 2007.

———. "Pietistic and Wesleyan Influences in the Mennonite Brethren in Christ." *Reflections* 4 (1996) 18–23.

Gingerich, Melvin, Timothy Burkholder, Paul Voegtlin, and Samuel J. Steiner. "Northwest Mennonite Conference." *Global Anabaptist Mennonite Encyclopedia Online*. Online: https://gameo.org/index.php?title.

Gingerich, Orland. *The Amish of Canada*. Kitchener, ON: Herald, 1972.

Good, E. Reginald. *Frontier Community to Urban Congregation: First Mennonite Church, Kitchener, 1813–1988*. Kitchener, ON: The Church, 1988.

———. "Joseph Witmer." *Ontario History* 71 (1979) 191–204.

Goudie, Henry. "Detwiler." *GB*, November 28, 1893.

Goudie, Sam. "Christian Endeavour, Epworth League and Young People's Societies." *GB*, April 25, 1893.

———. "From Michigan." *GB*, June 1, 1887.

———. "From Port Elgin, Ont." *GB*, March 1, 1892.

———. "From Port Elgin." *GB*, March 7, 1893.

———. "Holiness." *GB*, January 31, 1893.
———. "The Influence of the Sabbath School." *GB*, March 15, 1892.
———. "Non-Conformity to the World." *GB*, July 1, 1889.
———. "Over Two Years Ago." *GB*, November 19, 1895.
———. "Pastor's Report, Port Elgin." *GB*, March 6, 1894.
———. "Testimonies." *GB*, April 14, 1949.
———. "Testimony." *GB*, November 14, 1893.
———. "A Trip Northward." *GB*, November 1, 1892.
———. "Unconditional." *GB*, September 12, 1912.
———. "Visit to the Pennsylvania Conference." *GB*, November 4, 1909.
Grant, John Webster. *The Church in the Canadian Era*. Rev. Burlington, ON: Welch, 1988.
———. *A Profusion of Spires: Religion in Nineteenth-Century Ontario*. Toronto: University of Toronto Press, 1988.
Gregg, William. *Short History of the Presbyterian Church in the Dominion of Canada from the Earliest to the Present Time*. Toronto: For the Author, 1892.
Groh, Ivan. "Uncle Hannes and Levi." *Canadian German Folklore* 3 (1970) 11–62.
Grove, Robert. *A Directed Life*. Brampton, ON: For the Author, 2008.
Hallman, Henry Schlichter. *Annual Report of the Mennonite Brethren in Christ Missionary Society*. Berlin, ON: Mennonite Brethren in Christ Missionary Society, 1908.
———. "Editorial." *GB*, June 15, 1892.
———. "Editorial." *GB*, June 20, 1893.
———. "Editorial." *GB*, September 12, 1893.
Handy, Robert T. *A History of the Churches in the United States and Canada*. Oxford: Oxford University Press, 1976.
Harper, Nancy. "A Very 'Good' Tradition Indeed." 2014.
Hawkes, Paul. "Pentecostalism in Canada: A History with Implications for the Future." DMin thesis, San Francisco Theological Seminary, 1982.
———. "The Pentecost Assemblies of Canada Organization and Growth." 1965.
Hayes, Geoffrey. *Waterloo County: An Illustrated History*. Kitchener, ON: Waterloo Historical Society, 1997.
Henry, George W. *Demonstrations of the Spirit: Originally Called Shouting, Genuine and Spurious, Rechristened and Re-Printed by W. G. Burns*. Ottawa, ON: Holiness Movement, 1859.
Hiemstra, Rick. "Evangelicals and the Canadian Census." *Church and Faith Trends*. Online: https://www.evangelicalfellowship.ca/getattachment/About-us/About-Evangelicalism/About-Evangelicals/Evangelicals_Canadian_Census.pdf.aspx?lang=en-US.
Hill, Valerie. "Goudie's Descendants Meet for the First Time Thanks to Old Photo." *Waterloo Region Record*, October 24, 2016.
Hilts, Joseph H. *Experiences of a Backwoods Preacher: Or, Facts and Incidents Culled from Thirty Years of Ministerial Life*. 2nd ed. Toronto: Methodist Mission Rooms, 1892.
History of Benton Street Baptist Church Kitchener, Ontario and Program of the Seventy-Fifth Anniversary of the Founding of the Church, September 26th, 27th and 28th. Kitchener, ON: Benton Street Baptist Church, 1926.
Hobbs, Helen G. "'What She Could': Women in the Gospel Workers Church 1902–1955." In *Changing Roles of Women within the Christian Church in Canada*, edited by Elizabeth Gillan Muir and Marilyn Fardig Whiteley, 201–18. Toronto: University of Toronto Press, 1995.

Hobbs, R. Gerald, and Helen Hobbs. "Holiness Churches." In *Canadian Encyclopedia*, 1091–92. Toronto: McClelland and Stewart, 1999.

Hoffman, Frances, and Ryan Taylor. *Much To Be Done: Private Life in Ontario from Victorian Diaries*. Toronto: Natural Heritage/ Natural History, 1996.

Holmes, Letitia Ann. "Letter from Pine Tree, Ont., of June 4th." *GB*, July 1, 1892.

Hoover, Muriel I. *A History of Bethel Missionary Church*. New Dundee, ON: Centennial Committee of Bethel Missionary Church, 1978.

Horner, Ralph C. *Horner Evangelist: Reminiscences from his Own Pen Also Reports of Five Typical Sermons*. Brockville, ON: Mrs. A. E. Horner, n.d.

Horst, Isaac R. *Close Ups of the Great Awakening*. Mount Forest, ON: For the Author, 1985.

———. "Mennonite Settlement in Port Elgin." *Ontario Mennonite History* (1997) 25–27.

———. *Up the Conestogo*. Mount Forest, ON: For the Author, 1979.

Hossler, Bill. "Go In Strength; Am I Not Sending You?" *Missionary Church Today* 42 (2010) 3.

Hostetler, Paul E., ed. *Perfect Love and War: A Dialogue on Christian Holiness and the Issues of War and Peace*. Nappanee, IL: Evangel, 1974.

Huffman, Jasper Abraham. *A Comprehensive System of Christian Doctrine: A Syllabus*. Winona Lake, IN: Wesley, 1958.

———, ed. *History of the Mennonite Brethren in Christ Church*. New Carlisle, OH: Bethel, 1920.

———. *Profile of a Modern Pentecostal Movement*. Elkhart, IN: Bethel, 1968.

———. *Seventy Years with Pen, Pointer and Pulpit: Memoirs of Jasper Abraham Huffman*. Elkhart, IN: Bethel, 1968.

———. *Speaking in Tongues*. Dayton, OH: Bethel, 1910.

Hunking, Leaman. *Home Spun Flashbacks of Shrigley and Community 1893–1995*. Mount Forest, ON: For the Author, 1995.

Ingersol, Stan. "Strange Bedfellows: Nazarenes and Fundamentalism." *Wesleyan Theological Journal* 40 (2005) 123–41.

Jesske, Theodore E. *Pioneers of Faith: A History of the Evangelical Church in Canada*. Medicine Hat, AB: Evangelical Church of Canada, 1985.

Job, John B. *What Warmed John Wesley's Heart?* Ibadan, Nigeria: Daystar, 1971.

Johnson, Weyburn C. *This Is My Story: The Road I Traveled*. n.d.

Jones, Charles Edwin. *The Wesleyan Holiness Movement: A Comprehensive Guide*. 2 vols. Lanham, MD: Scarecrow, 2005.

Katz, Michael. "The People of a Canadian City, 1851–2." In *An Introduction to Canadian History*, edited by Arthur I. Silver, 300–322. Toronto: Canadian Scholar's, 1991.

Kaufman, Edmund George. *The Development of the Missionary and Philanthropic Interest among the Mennonites of North America*. Berne, IN: Mennonite Book Concern, 1931.

Kleinsteuber, R.Wayne. *More Than a Memory: The Renewal of Methodism in Canada*. Minneapolis: Light and Life, 1984.

Koch, Roy S. "Coffman, Samuel Frederick (1872–1954)." *Global Anabaptist Mennonite Encyclopedia Online*. Online: https://gameo.org/index.php?title=Coffman,_Samuel_Frederick_(1872–1954)&oldid=112892.

Kulbeck, Gloria Grace. *What God Hath Wrought: A History of the Pentecostal Assemblies of Canada*. Toronto: Pentecostal Assemblies of Canada, 1958.

Lageer, Edith Eileen, ed. *Ask of Me the Heathen for Thine Inheritance*. Elkhart, IN: United Missionary Society, 1959.

BIBLIOGRAPHY

———. *Common Bonds: The Story of the Evangelical Missionary Church of Canada.* Calgary, AB: Evangelical Missionary Church of Canada, 2004.

———. *Merging Streams: Story of the Missionary Church.* Elkhart, IN: Bethel, 1979.

Lageer, Kevin. "The Pragmatics and Excuses for a Name Change: Mennonite Brethren in Christ to Missionary Church." Research paper. University of Waterloo, 1982.

Lambert, David U. "[Report]." *GB*, October 15, 1881.

Lehman, Isaac O., and Alice Lehman. "African Evangelistic Mission." In *United Missionary Society Yearbook 1930*, edited by Abraham B. Yoder, 89–94. Elkhart, IN: United Missionary Society Board, 1930.

Losch, Ted. *Breslau Missionary Church 1882–1982: 100th Anniversary.* Breslau, ON: Breslau Missionary Church, 1982.

Lugibihl, Walter H., and Jared F. Gerig. *The Missionary Church Association: Historical Account of its Origin and Development.* Berne, IN: Economy, 1950.

Macdonald, Norman. *Canada Immigration and Colonization: 1841–1903.* Toronto: Macmillan, 1966.

Mackey, Lloyd. *These Evangelical Churches of Ours.* Winfield, BC: Wood Lake, 1995.

Maconochie, Jean, ed. *Missionary Women of Canada: Canada West District 1931–1991.* Missionary Women of Canada, Canada West District, 1991.

Mandryk, Jason, ed. *Operation World.* 7th ed. Colorado Springs, CO: Biblica, 2010.

Mann, William E. *Sect, Cult and Church in Alberta.* Toronto: University of Toronto Press, 1950.

Manual and Constitution of the Missionary Church of the United States and Canada. Fort Wayne, IN: The Missionary Church, 1977.

Marks, Lynne Sorrel. *Revivals and Roller Rinks: Religion, Leisure, and Identity in Late-Nineteenth-Century Small-Town Ontario.* Toronto: University of Toronto Press, 1996.

Marr, Lucille. "Sherk, J. Harold (1903–1974)." *Global Anabaptist Mennonite Encyclopedia Online.* Online: https://gameo.org/index.php?title=Sherk,_J._Harold_(1903-1974)&oldid=117484.

Marsden, George M. *Fundamentalism and American Culture: The Shaping of Twentieth-Century Evangelicalism: 1870–1925.* New York: Oxford University Press, 1980.

Martin, Jesse B., and Noah M. Bearinger, eds. *Laws Affecting Historic Peace Churches.* ON: Conference of Historic Peace Churches, 1941.

Matheson, Frances. "My Word Shall Not Return unto Me Void." In *United Missionary Society Yearbook 1928*, edited by Abraham B. Yoder, 96–97. Elkhart, IN: United Missionary Society Board, 1928.

McDowell, Clarence. *Built in This Place, Centennial 1877–1977: Markham Missionary Church.* Markham, ON: Centennial Historical Research Committee, 1977.

McGavran, Donald. *Understanding Church Growth.* Grand Rapids: Eerdmans, 1970.

Miller, Thomas William. *Canadian Pentecostals: A History of the Pentecostal Assemblies of Canada.* Mississauga, ON: Full Gospel, 1994.

———. "The Canadian Azusa: The Hebden Mission in Toronto." *Pneuma* (1986) 5–26.

"Ministerial Conference Minutes 1917–1948." Mennonite Brethren in Christ, Ontario Conference. Box 2500, n.d.

"Minutes of the Ministerial Conventions of the MBC Church, 1917–1948." Mennonite Brethren in Christ, Ontario Conference. n.d.

Montgomery, Margaret H., and Winnie Srigley. *Celebrating Our Heritage: Palmerston Evangelical Missionary Church 1874–1999, 125 Years Under God's Leadership.* Palmerston, ON: Palmerston Evangelical Missionary Church, 1999.

Bibliography

Motz, Arnell, ed. *Reclaiming a Nation*. Richmond, BC: Church Leadership Library, 1990.
Moyer, Don. "Abraham's Children," 1994.
Moyer, H. Kenneth. *60 Years of Pentecost in Vineland 1908–1968*. For the Author, 1968.
Moyles, Russell Gordon. *The Blood and Fire in Canada: A History of the Salvation Army in the Dominion 1882–1976*. Toronto: Peter Martin Associates, 1977.
Murphy, Terrence, and Roberto Perin, eds. *A Concise History of Christianity in Canada*. Toronto: Oxford University Press, 1996.
Musselman, W.B. "A Trip to Canada." *GB*, July 11, 1893.
Neill, Stephen, and Owen Chadwick. *A History of Christian Missions*. 2nd ed. London: Penguin, 1986.
Newcombe, Hiram K. "Among the Farmers: History of Breslau and Sketches of Its Nearby Farmers—Our German and Swiss Ancestors." In *The 1890 Waterloo Farmers Directory*. Berlin, ON: Union, 1890.
Nienkirchen, Charles W. *Simpson and the Pentecostal Movement: A Study in Continuity, Crisis, and Change*. Peabody, MA: Hendrickson, 1992.
Nigh, Harold. "The Lost Tribes of the Niagara Plain Folk." *Mennogespräch*, September 1986.
Noll, Mark. *A History of Christianity in the United States and Canada*. Grand Rapids: Eerdmans, 1992.
Nussbaum, Stan. *You Must Be Born Again: A History of the Evangelical Mennonite Church*. Fort Wayne, IN: Evangelical Mennonite Church, 1980.
Oke, Edward. "A Theological History of the Evangelical Missionary Church of Canada." In *Common Bonds: The History of the Evangelical Missionary Church of Canada*, edited by Edith Eileen Lageer, 362–73. Calgary, AB: Evangelical Missionary Church of Canada, 2004.
Olsen, Roger E. *The Mosaic of Christian Belief: Twenty Centuries of Unity and Diversity*. Downers Grove, IL: InterVarsity, 2002.
100th Anniversary 1838–1938 Zion Evangelical Church, Kitchener, Ontario. Kitchener, ON: 1939.
"Ontario Church Stories Episode 4: Sam Goudie and the NRRO, 2017." *YouTube*. https://www.youtube.com/channel/UCxBx4rLwIpnyXxrlsrmhj6g.
"Ontario Heritage Trust." *Heritage Trust*. Online: https://www.heritagetrust.on.ca/en/oha/details/file?id=1432.
Overhulser, Josephine Marie. *They Called Him Mallam: The Biography of Joseph Ummel, A Pioneer Missionary to Northern Nigeria, West Africa*. Carmel, IN: Cork Hill, 2005.
Packer, James Innell. *Keep in Step with the Spirit: Finding Fullness in Our Walk*. 2nd ed. Grand Rapids: Baker, 2005.
Panabaker, Cornelius Arthur. *The Barefoot Farm Boy: Boyhood Reminiscences*. Kitchener, ON: Waterloo Historical Society, n.d.
Pannabecker, Cornelia. "Diaries." Chester-Hunking Family Collection, n.d.
Parker, J. Fred. *From East to Western Sea: A Brief History of the Church of the Nazarene in Canada*. Kansas City, MO: Nazarene, 1971.
Pearce, Jean, ed. *History of the Aylmer Missionary Church 1900–1990: 90 Years*. Aylmer. ON: Aylmer Missionary Church, 1990
Pedersen, Diana. "'The Power of True Christian Women': The YWCA and Evangelical Womanhood in the Late Nineteenth Century." In *Changing Roles of Women within the Christian Church in Canada*, edited by Elizabeth Gillan Muir and Marilyn Fardig Whiteley, 321–37. Toronto: University of Toronto Press, 1995.

Bibliography

Peters, John Leland. *Christian Perfection and American Methodism*. Grand Rapids: Zondervan, 1956.

Peterson, Eugene. *A Long Obedience in the Same Direction: Discipleship in an Instant Society*. 2nd ed. Downers Grove, IL: InterVarsity, 2000.

Pierard, Richard V. "Pax Americana and the Evangelical Missionary Advance." In *Earthen Vessels: American Evangelicals and Foreign Missions, 1880–1980*, edited by Joel A. Carpenter and Wilbert R. Shenk, 155–79. Grand Rapids: Eerdmans, 1990.

Porter, David K. "Shaping the Missionary Identity of the Pentecostal Assemblies of Canada: Spirit Baptism and Eschatology in the Writings of George A. Chambers and Robert E. McAlister." ThM thesis, Wycliffe College, University of Toronto, 1997.

Powers, George Maxwell. "Greetings." In *United Missionary Society Yearbook 1930*, edited by Abraham B. Yoder, 66–69. Elkhart, IN: United Missionary Society Board, 1930.

Poythress, Vern S. "Nature of Corinthian Glossolalia: Possible Options." *Westminster Theological Journal* 40 (1977) 130–35.

Quantz, William A. "Diaries 1872–1945." Online: https://www.quanz.net.

Ramseyer, Macy Garth, and Joseph E. Ramseyer. *Yet Speaking*. Fort Wayne, IN: Fort Wayne Bible Institute, 1945.

Ratcliff, Carolyn, ed. *One Hundred Years of Faithful Ministry: Stouffville Missionary Church*. Stouffville, ON: Stouffville Missionary Church, 2003.

Rawlyk, George A. "New Lights, Baptists and Religious Awakenings in Nova Scotia 1776–1843: A Preliminary Probe." In *Prophets, Priests, and Prodigals: Readings in Canadian Religious History, 1608 to Present*, edited by Mark G. McGowan and David B. Marshall, 35–60. Toronto: McGraw-Hill Ryerson, 1992.

Rawlyk, George A., ed. *The Canadian Protestant Experience 1760–1990*. Burlington, ON: Welch, 1990.

Raymer, Christian. *Latter Rain and Fog*. Berlin, ON: For the Author, 1908.

Raymer, Fannie. "Diaries." Raymer Family Collection, n.d.

Reamon, G. Elmore. *A History of Vaughan Township: Two Centuries of Life in the Township*. Vaughan Township, ON: Vaughan Township Historical Society, 1971.

———. *The Trail of the Black Walnut*. Toronto: McClelland and Stewart, 1957.

Redinger, Lauren K. *A Tree Well Planted: The Official History of the Christian Workers' Churches of Canada and the Associated Gospel Churches of Canada 1892–1993*. Burlington, ON: Associated Gospel Churches, 1995.

Reid, W. Stanford, ed. *The Scottish Tradition in Canada*. Toronto: McClelland and Stewart, 1976.

Reimer, Earl. *Alvin Traub: Iron Will and Iron Hammer*. Elkhart, IN: Bethel, 1962.

Reimer, James. "Thoughts on Current Theology in the Mennonite Community." *Christian Week*, August 28, 1990.

Reynolds, Lindsay. *Footprints: The Beginnings of the Christian and Missionary Alliance in Canada*. Toronto: The Christian and Missionary Alliance in Canada, 1981.

———. *Rebirth: The Redevelopment of the Christian and Missionary Alliance in Canada*. Willowdale, ON: The Christian and Missionary Alliance in Canada, 1992.

Ringenberg, Ralph E., ed. *Believers in the Missionary Church*. Elkhart, IN: Bethel, 1976.

Robertson, Heather. *The History of Port Elgin*. Port Elgin, ON: For the Author, 1975.

Rosen, Anne Faris. "A Brief History of Religion and the U.S. Census." *Pew Forum*. Online: https://www.pewforum.org/2010/01/26/q-brief-history-of-religion-and-the-u-s-census.

Ross, Malcolm, ed. *Poets of the Confederation*. Toronto: McClelland and Stewart, 1960.

Bibliography

Rudd, Douglas. *When the Spirit Came upon Them: Highlights from the Early Years of the Pentecostal Movement in Canada*. Burlington, ON: Antioch, 2002.

Sangster, William E. *The Path to Perfection: An Examination and Restatement of John Wesley's Doctrine of Christian Perfection*. London: Hodder and Stoughton, 1943.

Sarkar, Pronoy, and Eileen Lageer. *Missionary Church in India*. Fort Wayne, IN: World Partners, 1993.

Sauder, Dorothy. *Trail's End: The Oxbow*. Bloomingdale, ON: Bloomingdale Mennonite Church, 1972.

Sawatsky, Rodney James. *History and Identity: American Mennonite Identity Definition through History*. Kitchener, ON: Pandora, 2005.

Sawin, John. "The Fourfold Gospel." In *The Birth of a Vision*, edited by David F. Hartzfeld and Charles Nienkirchen, 1–28. Regina, SK: Canadian Bible College and Canadian Theological Seminary, 1986.

Schaller, Lyle E. *The Middle Sized Church: Problems and Perspectives*. Nashville: Abingdon, 1985.

Semple, Neil. *The Lord's Dominion: A History of Canadian Methodism*. Montreal and Kingston: McGill-Queen's University Press, 1996.

Shantz, Ward Montford. *A History of Bethany Missionary Church*. Kitchener, ON: Bethany Missionary Church, 1977.

Sherk, F. Arthur. *Keeping Faith: A Centennial History of Banfield Memorial Church*. Willowdale, ON: Banfield Memorial Church, 1997.

Shupe, Peter. *Oh, Why Not Have Peace Instead of War?* 2nd ed. Berlin, ON: H. S. Hallman, n.d.

Sider, E. Morris. *Be In Christ: A Canadian Church Engages Heritage and Change*. Oakville, ON: Be In Christ Church of Canada, 2019.

Sider, E. Morris. "Zook, John Roel (1857–1919)." *Global Anabaptist Mennonite Encyclopedia Online*. Online: https://gameo.org/index.php?title=Zook,_John_Roel_(1857-1919)&oldid=122611.(1989).

Sigsworth, John Wilkins. *The Battle Was the Lord's: A History of the Free Methodist Church in Canada*. Oshawa, ON: Sage, 1960.

"Smith-Freeman-Burnham-Hoffman-Hartleb-Family Lines." *Free Ancestry Family Tree Software*. Online: http://www.mfhn.com/Hoffman_Smith/fren12.asp.

Snyder, Miriam Helen, ed. *Johannes Schneider and His Wife Catharine Haus Schneider: Their Descendants and Times 1534–1939*. Kitchener, ON: For the Author, 1939.

Spaetzel, Roy C. *History of Kitchener Gospel Temple 1909–1974*. Kitchener, ON: Kitchener Gospel Temple, 1974.

Stackhouse, John G., Jr. *Canadian Evangelicalism in the Twentieth Century: An Introduction to Its Character*. Toronto: University of Toronto Press, 1993.

Stapleton, Ammon. *Annals of the Evangelical Association of North America and History of the United Evangelical Church*. Harrisburg, PA: Evangelical United Church, 1900.

Steckley, John H. "Letter." *GB*, July 11, 1893.

Steinacher, C. Mark. "The Homogenization of Methodism: An Examination of the Convergence of Aspects of Polity and Revivalist Practice in Upper Canadian Methodism 1824–1884." ThM thesis, Emmanuel College, University of Toronto, 1992.

Steiner, Cyrus Nathaniel "C. N. Samuel J. Good." *Global Anabaptist Mennonite Encyclopedia Online*. Online: https://gameo.org/index.php?title=Good,_Cyrus_Nathaniel_N.%22C._N.%22_(1869-1967)&oldid=165088.

BIBLIOGRAPHY

Steiner, Samuel J. "Effects of the 1870s New Mennonite Division on Bloomingdale Mennonite Church." *Ontario Mennonite History* 15 (1997) 28–31.

———. "Hall, Janet Douglas (1863–1946)." *Global Anabaptist Mennonite Encyclopedia Online*. Online: https://gameo.org/index.php?title=Hall,_Janet_Douglas_(1863-1946)&oldid=165056.

———. "Hoch, Daniel (1805–1878)." *Global Anabaptist Mennonite Encyclopedia*. Online: https://gameo.org/index.php?title=Hoch,_Daniel_(1805-1878)&oldid=165022.

———. *In Search of Promised Lands: A Religious History of Mennonites in Ontario*. Kitchener, ON: Herald, 2015.

———. "Review." Online: https://www.goodreads.com/book/show/17616894-high-bright-buggy-wheels.

———. *Vicarious Pioneer: The Life of Jacob Y*. Winnipeg, MB: Shantz, n.d.

Stephenson, John W. "Choosing the Right Metaphor: Did a Bomb Go Off or a Light Turn On? Mennonites and Pentecostals in Southern Ontario." ThM thesis, Wycliffe College, University of Toronto, 1993.

Storms, Everek R. "Cober, Peter (1853–1941)." In *Global Anabaptist Mennonite Encyclopedia Online*. Online: https://gameo.org/index.php?title=Cober,_Peter_(1853-1941)&oldid=113762.

———. *History of Calvary Church*. Owen Sound, ON: Calvary Church Board, 1942.

———. *History of the United Missionary Church*. Elkhart, IN: Bethel, 1958.

———. *What God Hath Wrought: The Story of the Foreign Missionary Efforts of the United Missionary Church*. Springfield, OH: United Missionary Society, 1948.

———. *Yearbook [of the Mennonite Brethren in Christ] 1952*. Kitchener, ON: Trinity, 1951.

Storms, Everek R., and Samuel J. Steiner. "Goudie, Henry (1851–1942)." *Global Anabaptist Mennonite Encyclopedia Online*. Online: https://gameo.org/index.php?title=Goudie,_Henry_(1851-1942)&oldid=165658.

———. "Goudie, Samuel (1866–1951)." *Global Anabaptist Mennonite Encyclopedia Online*. Online: https://gameo.org/index.php?title=Goudie,_Samuel_(1866-1951)&oldid=165702.

Storms, Everek R., and Richard D. Thiessen. "Eby, Solomon (1834–1931)." *Global Anabaptist Mennonite Encyclopedia Online*. Online: https://gameo.org/index.php?title=Eby,_Solomon_(1834-1931)&oldid=102370.

Stott, John R.W. *The Baptism and Fullness of the Holy Spirit*. London: Inter-Varsity, 1964.

Swalm, Ernie J. *A History of the Brethren in Christ Nottawa District 1878–1978*. For the Author, 1978.

Swalm, Noah, and Pearl Swalm. *History of the United Missionary Church Canada Northwest District 1894–1962*. Calgary, AB: Canada Northwest District, 1963.

Swartz, David R. "Woman, Thou Art Almost Loosed! The Rise of Women Ministers in the Nineteenth-Century Mennonite Brethren in Christ Church." *Reflections* 9 (2007) 19–40.

Synan, Vinson. *The Holiness-Pentecostal Movement*. Grand Rapids: Eerdmans, 1971.

The Pilot 1944. Kitchener, ON: The Student Body of Emmanuel Bible School, 1944.

Tiessen, Hildi Froese. "A Mennonite Novelist's Journey (from) Home: Ephraim Weber's Encounters with S. F. Coffman and Lucy Maud Montgomery." *Conrad Grebel Review* 24 (2006) 84–108.

Tracy, Frank Basil. *The Tercentenary History of Canada from Champlain to Laurier 1608–1908*. New York: P. F. Collier and Son, 1908.

Wagner, C. Peter. "Why Body Evangelism Really Works." *Global Church Growth* 20 (1983) 271–72.

Walker, Stephanie Kirkwood. *Waterloo County Album*. Toronto: Dundurn, 2008.

Walsh, Henry Horace. *The Christian Church in Canada*. Toronto: Ryerson, 1956.

Ward, C. Morse, and Doug Wead. *A. G. Ward: Intimate Glimpses of My Father's Life*. Springfield, MO: Assemblies of God, 1955.

———. *The C. M. Ward Story*. Harrison, AZ: New Leaf, 1976.

Watson, David Lowes. "Methodist Spirituality." In *Protestant Spiritual Traditions*, edited by Frank C. Senn, 217–73. Mahwah, NJ: Paulist, 1986.

Watson, George Duncan. *Love Abounding: And Other Expositions on the Spiritual Life*. Boston: McDonald, Gill, 1891.

Weaver, William B. "Central Conference Mennonite Church." *Global Anabaptist Mennonite Encyclopedia Online*. Online: https://gameo.org/index.php?title=Central_Conference_Mennonite_Church&oldid=115173.

Weeks, Ken. "The Legacy of Fetter's Grove." *Reflections* 4 (1996) 4–10.

Wenger, John Christian. "Documents on the Daniel Brenneman Division." *Mennonite Quarterly Review* 34 (1960) 48–56.

———. *The Doctrines of the Mennonites*. Scottdale, PA: Mennonite, 1950.

———. *Introduction to Theology: A Brief Introduction to the Doctrinal Content of Scripture from the Anabaptist-Mennonite Tradition*. 2nd ed. Scottdale, PA: Herald, 1975.

Wesley, John. *A Plain Account of Christian Perfection*. Kansas City, MO: Beacon Hill, 1966.

Westfall, William. *Two Worlds: The Protestant Culture of Nineteenth-Century Ontario*. Montreal and Kingston: McGill-Queens University Press, 1990.

White, Charles Edward. *The Beauty of Holiness: Phoebe Palmer as Theologian, Revivalist, and Humanitarian*. Grand Rapids: Frances Asbury, 1986.

Wilkens, Robert. *A Historical Sketch of New Dundee Baptist Church*. For the Author, 1977.

Winter, Ralph D. "The Two Structures of God's Redemptive Mission." In *Perspectives on the World Christian Movement*, edited by Ralph Winter and Steven C. Hawthorne, 45–57. Pasadena, CA: William Carey Library, 1992.

Yake, Reta, ed. *A History of the Missionary Work Done by the Women of Gormley Missionary Church*. Gormley, ON: Gormley Women's Fellowship, 1989.

Names Index

Airhart, Phyllis D., 33, 83
Aitken, Kate, 158
Alexander, Annie, 282
Alexander, Muriel, 282, 295
Alline, Henry, 72, 73
Ambrose, Rosemary W., 33
Anthes, Jacob, 61
Anthony, Ebenezer, 66, 90, 118, 131, 132, 156, 173, 190, 204, 225, 306, 308
Argue, Andrew H., 194
Atkinson, Dick, 150
Atter, Gordon, 175

Baalim, Olive J., 286
Backus, W., 113
Baker, August, 52
Baker, Lavina, 64
Baker, T. P., 259
Ball, John T., 139, 150, 167, 171, 172, 180, 182–86, 196, 198, 200, 208
Ball, Margaret R., 167, 182
Banfield, Alexander W., 4, 118, 141, 224, 306, 310
Banfield, Althea, 140, 141, 174, 310
Barber, Herbert H., 185
Barber, William, 185
Barker, Ada (Moyer), 118, 174
Barker, T. Ford, 118, 128, 244, 282
Barkey, Charlie, 298
Barkey, Daniel, 60, 183, 190
Barkey, Flora (Elmore), 183, 185
Barkey, G. Wilmot, 139
Barley, Robert, 166
Barnes, Rita (Paisley), 249

Barth, Karl, 275
Bartleman, Frank, 164
Bates, Hattie, 42
Baxter, Richard, 103, 187
Beall, Elsie, 201
Bear, John, 27, 29
Beasley, Richard, 18
Bedingfield, xi, 79, 80, 82
Beech, Reginald, 155, 306, 315
Beese, William E., and Barbara M., 145, 146
Beeshy, Jared, 52
Bell, Alexander, 79, 80, 81, 108
Bender, Harold, 121, 316
Benner, Lorne, 138
Benson, Frances (Geddes), 21, 303
Bergey, David, 25
Biehn, Barbara, xii
Bingham, Rowland V., 112, 118, 126, 127, 262, 278
Blake, Carol (Sherk), 43
Blakeney, Mary Ann (Dresch), and Joseph K., 201
Block, Emma, 120, 127, 140
Bloomfield, Elizabeth, 12, 22, 36
Blowers, Kevin, 98, 315
Bloye, Robert, 139
Boadway, Jacob, 214
Boadway, Paul, 296
Bock, Emerson Krupp, 156, 296
Bock, Moses, 135, 156
Bolender, Conrad, 42
Bolender, Mark, viii
Bolwell, John, 121, 223, 282

Names Index

Booth, Katherine, 42
Booth, William, 161
Bose, Ruby (Reeve), 140, 192, 224
Bowman, Amos, 62
Bowman, Anna, 174
Bowman, Annie, 104, 282, 286
Bowman, Beniah, 2, 187
Bowman, Benjamin, 92, 10
Bowman, Catherine (Baer), 189
Bowman, Dorinda, 253
Bowman, Hezekiah, 103
Bowman, Menno, 20, 26, 27, 36, 39, 40, 44, 53, 54, 58–60, 63–66, 70, 71, 73, 75, 80, 90, 92, 95–98, 101, 107, 111, 113, 120, 137, 139
Bowman, Samuel, 2
Bowman, Susannah, 27, 277
Bowman, Susie, 97, 104, 120, 135, 140, 162
Bowman, Thomas, 65
Bredemus, Katie, 253
Brengel, Samuel Logan, 85
Brenneman, Daniel, 29, 31, 32, 71, 92, 94, 102, 110, 113, 257, 276, 294
Brenneman, Phoebe, 90, 132
Breyfogel, Silvanus C., 128
Bricker, Irvin Charles, 16
Bricker, Milton, 98, 114, 120, 138, 155, 223, 231, 237, 238, 244, 273, 281, 284–286, 295, 310, 319, 321
Bricker, Samuel, 2
Brittain, David, 139, 179, 213
Brook, Thomas W., 140, 172, 182, 187, 196, 203
Brown, Alex and Agnes, 288
Brown, Harold, 280, 294
Brown, Ida (Troxell), 268
Brown, W. Cecil, 268, 290
Brown, William B., 40, 139, 245, 268, 281
Brubacher, Clara Rudy, 215, 291
Brubacher, Isaac, 245, 281
Brubacher, Lloyd, 83
Brubacher, Nancy, xii
Brunner, Charles Henry, 91, 206, 215, 216, 227
Brunner, William M., 67

Bumsted, John Michael, 2
Bunker, Eleanor (Goudie), 11, 12, 16–18, 35, 157, 212–14, 300, 302, 303, 313, 320
Bunker, Mervyn, 297
Bunker, Tom, 11, 56
Bunyan, John, 73
Burkholder, Daniel, 62
Burkholder, Lewis J., 4, 28, 79, 231
Burkholder, Moses, 40, 41, 264
Burley, S. D., 113
Burton, Richard, 176, 177
Burwash, Nathanael, 85
Bushart, Tillie and sister, Maggie, 144

Calvin, John, 48
Carey, William, 48
Carlton, Fred, 128, 129
Carlton, Robert and Elizabeth, 129
Carmichael, Mahlon J., 147
Chambers, George, 187
Chambers, George A., 127, 128, 139, 161, 164–66, 171, 172, 174–78, 180, 181, 186–88, 194–96, 198–200, 207, 211, 212, 286
Chambers, Ida (Williamson), 165, 187, 188
Chatham, Ed, 101
Chatham, Maude E., 77, 79, 81, 96, 124, 139, 140, 147, 243, 270, 293
Cherry, Sarah, 76
Clark, Joseph, 139
Clark, Rachel, 268
Clark, Samuel D., 113
Clendenen, Annie (Goudie), 250, 302
Clendenen, Arthur, 302
Cober, Margaret, 20, 302
Cober, Martha, 220
Cober, Peter, 54, 66, 69, 76, 77, 79, 82, 90, 91, 98, 124–27, 132, 135, 137–39, 142, 144, 146, 149, 156, 170, 172, 173, 175, 190, 204, 242, 244–47, 282, 290, 310
Coffman, John S., xiv
Coffman, Samuel Frederick, 235, 237, 239
Conner, Jesse, 156

Names Index

Craig, Jim, xiii, 167, 199
Creighton, Luella (Bruce), 13, 14, 158
Cressman, Grace (Good), 185, 239
Cressman, Henry S., 104, 140
Cressman, John G., 8
Cressman, Lloyd Silas, 282, 287, 293, 294
Cressman, Menno C., 95
Cressman, Sarah (Wagner), 30, 37, 189
Cressman, Silas, 59, 69, 76, 79, 81, 119, 132, 159, 170, 204, 220–22, 225, 234, 240, 242, 268, 272, 273, 280, 289, 310, 315
Crouch, Laura Bell Shaw, 149
Cullis, Charles, 278

Dedels, Marjorie, 295
Detwiler, Abraham Z., 27, 98, 102
Detwiler, Amos S., 98
Detwiler, Fanny (Busch), 77
Detwiler, Jacob Bechtel, 95, 136, 139, 142, 143, 148, 282, 290
Detwiler, John Z., 98
Detwiler, Louisa Jane, 56
Detwiler, Noah, 25, 76, 77, 85, 98, 112, 120–22, 127, 128, 139, 149, 165, 290
Devitt, David, 68
Devitt, Melinda, 215
Ditmer, Russell P., 254, 321
Doherty, David, 266
Doner, Archbald Gormley, 123, 127, 135, 167, 179–82, 196, 198, 200
Doner, Dorine (Gooding), 299
Doner, Josephus and Mary (Steckley), 181
Doner, Martha, 282
Doner, Melissa (Moyer), 181
Doner, Samuel Norman, 296
Doty, Thomas K., 85, 134
Douglas, Janet, 42, 66, 198
Dow, Thomas Edward, xiii
Dowie, Alexander, 278
Dresch, Jacob and Caroline (Diefenbacher), 201
Dresch, Mary Ann, 140, 162, 164, 173, 196, 201
Drinkall, Thomas John, 231

Dubs, Rudolf, 65
Dumont, Gabriel, 53
Dunlop, Charles, 174
Dunnington, Ebenezer, 204, 206
Dunnington, James, 206
Dunnington, Mary, 124, 140, 206
Duplessis, David, 22

Eastman, Ethel, 282
Eaton, Matthew, 229
Eby, Amos, 60, 119, 135, 139, 179, 196, 197, 200, 222, 223, 243
Eby, Benjamin, 26
Eby, Blanche, 253
Eby, Daniel C., 138, 143
Eby, Elias, 27, 29, 30, 74
Eby, Esther "Hettie" (Moyer), 166, 179
Eby, Ezra E., 18, 19
Eby, Martin W., 60, 62
Eby, Nathaniel, 189
Eby, Peter, 68
Eby, Solomon, 29–32, 59–61, 64, 66–68, 71, 75, 90, 98, 102, 104, 109, 111, 115, 119, 120, 126, 135, 137, 138, 154, 164, 171, 175–79, 188, 196, 197, 200, 222, 223, 243
Ecker, Levi, 262
Edwardson, Harold, 270
Egle, William, 113
Elliott, Fred, 231
Eltherington, Robert, 114, 118, 139, 150, 174, 282, 285
Epp, Frank H., 4, 229, 238, 239
Epp, Marlene, 75
Erb, Isaac H, 282, 295, 296
Erb, Moses, 27
Erdel, Timothy Paul, 3, 4, 113, 229, 258
Ernest, Joe, 76
Erskine, Anna, 118
Esher, John J., 65, 145
Euler, William D., 239
Evans, Edith M., 140, 209, 224
Evans, William, 294

Fairbairn, Charles V., 83
Fidler, Bertha, 271, 282

Names Index

Fidler, Joshua E., 139, 163, 167, 172, 209, 212, 282
Field, Benjamin, 110
Finlay, John S., 127
Finney, Charles G., 89, 103, 110, 115
Fisher, George E., 111, 128, 192, 194
Fisher, George P., 134, 205
Flatt, Kevin N., 260
Fletcher, John W., 88, 103, 114, 153
Foote, E., 286
Foster, Randolph, 85
Franson, Fredrik, 309
French, W. H., 311
Fretz, David, 123, 140, 179, 196, 202, 203, 207, 209
Fretz, Frank, 101
Fretz, Harvey T., 209
Fretz, Maggie, 202
Fretz, Sylvester H., 107, 138, 181, 282
Frey, Harvey R., 138, 245, 280, 315
Friesen, Abram A., 239
Friesen, Jacob P., 239
Frodsham, Stanley Howard, 166, 175–77
Fuller, Isabel (Oliver), xiv
Fuller, James Clare, 77
Fuller, Lois K., 49

Galletly, Fred, 39, 140, 161, 166
Gardner (Gartner), Katie, 77, 97
Gayman, Christian, 231
Gehman, William George, 58, 174, 199
Geiger, Amos, 138
Geiger, Peter, xi, 25, 27, 49, 139
Geiger, Ulrich, 27
Gerber, Annamaria (Anna Maria), 94, 118
Gerig, Jared F., 205
Gerig, Joseph K., 257–259
Gibson, Glenn A., 10, 49, 200, 304, 305, 317, 318
Gillam, Martha, 59
Gingerich, Charles, 10, 30, 101, 133, 193
Gingerich, Orland, 28
Goertzen, Peter, 140
Good, Andrew, 94, 127, 147
Good, Cyrus Nathaniel, 76, 83, 98, 119, 124, 127, 132, 138, 161, 170, 171, 177, 184, 186, 192, 204, 208, 209, 212, 220–23, 225, 232, 236, 237, 243, 244, 252, 271, 273, 280, 281, 284–87, 295, 310, 311, 319, 321
Good, E. Reginald, 15
Good, Edith Myrtle (Lageer), 250
Good, Emma, 140, 202
Good, Esther (Trefelet), 165
Good, Gordon H., 268
Good, J. Henry, 106, 281, 296
Good, Josiah R., 161, 165
Good, Livy (Hallman), 97, 208, 239
Good, Lovina (Schneider/Snyder), 76
Gooding, Alonzo T., 280, 291, 299
Gooding, Dorine, 299
Gooding, Dorothy, 299
Gooding, Evelyn, 55, 129, 141, 276, 299, 302
Goudie, Abraham, 21, 22, 129, 141, 226, 302, 303
Goudie, Allen "Allie" Howard, 5, 101, 130, 149, 249, 298, 321
Goudie, Arthur R., 21, 302
Goudie, Benjamin, 19, 249
Goudie, David, 14, 15, 17, 20, 36, 37, 78, 116, 220, 317
Goudie, David Wanner, 20, 37, 112, 118, 129, 144, 209, 210
Goudie, Donald "Donnie," 297, 298
Goudie, Eliza Jane, 12, 22, 55, 56, 66, 76, 101, 116, 119, 122, 123, 127, 130, 151, 157, 159, 162, 165, 213, 214, 266, 290, 292, 297, 319, 321
Goudie, Elton, 130, 303
Goudie, Emaline "Emily," 17, 19, 22, 23, 71, 74, 130
Goudie, Ethel, 303
Goudie, Fletcher Smith, 5, 76, 125, 149, 157, 213, 249, 298, 321
Goudie, Helen, 297, 299, 302
Goudie, Henry, 6, 11, 20, 22, 27–31, 37–39, 41, 43, 51–53, 56, 57, 60, 62, 65, 66, 71, 72, 77–79, 82, 90, 98, 108, 119, 129, 135, 136, 139, 141, 146, 147, 182, 187, 225, 247, 249, 250, 282, 289, 290, 302, 303, 310, 318, 319

Names Index

Goudie, Hugh, 16, 19, 30
Goudie, Ida Almina, 144
Goudie, Isaac, 21, 22, 129, 302
Goudie, Ivan, 297, 301
Goudie, Jacob, 21, 22, 35, 116, 129, 142, 302
Goudie, James, 21, 22, 129, 130, 250, 302, 303, 319
Goudie, Jane, 16, 19
Goudie, Pearl, 69, 125, 212–14, 298, 321
Goudie, Tobias, 19, 249
Goudie, Wilford and Mary (Oldford), 302
Graybiel, William, 90, 116, 118, 127
Green, H. C., 66
Grey, Earl Albert, 149
Groh, John, 16
Gross, Jacob (Mennonite bishop), 25
Grove, Leslie, 282
Grove, Levi, 231
Grove, Robert, 274
Gugin, J. F.,138, 147
Guy, Euphemia, 79–81, 100, 107, 140, 167, 180, 183, 190, 196, 200, 213
Guy, Jesse Samuel, 79–81, 90, 100, 111, 190, 191

Hagey, Daniel, 41
Hagey, Joseph, 28, 30, 39
Hagey, Joseph B., 37, 39, 130
Hagopian, Garabed D., 117, 118
Haist, Aaron Y., 113
Hall, George, 183
Hallman, Abraham S., 95
Hallman, Harvey S., 280, 292, 231
Hallman, Henry Schlichter, 38, 41, 56, 63, 66, 79, 81, 90, 92–95, 97, 112, 113, 117–19, 126, 127, 132, 140, 144, 149, 156, 162, 168, 170, 174, 178, 196, 204, 206, 210, 218, 222, 223, 233, 235, 242, 244, 254, 262
Hallman, Livy, 91, 97, 208
Hallman, Maria, 166
Hallman, Simeon Schlichter, 125, 222
Hallman, Wendell, 41
Haney, Milton L., 85
Harris, Elmore, 117, 126

Harrow, John M. L., 167, 191
Hartin, David, 49, 140
Hartin, Rebecca, 49
Hartley, Leslie Poles, 4
Harvey, Ernest, 282
Hastings, Thomas, 183
Haug, Michael, 64, 143
Haug, Solomon Leander, 98, 138
Hawkins, Albert, 185
Hebden, Ellen and James, 122, 161, 163, 167, 202
Heise, David W., 231, 236
Hembling, Rebecca, 21, 302
Hembling, William and Mary, 21, 27
Hershey, Eusebius, 95, 133
Hespeler, Jacob, 36
Hessenaur, Marjorie Priscilla (Blakeney), 201
Hilts, Joseph, 62
Hilts, William John, 53–55, 62, 108, 292
Hisey, John and Frances, 191
Hisey, Martha, 191
Hisey, Martha M., 162, 164, 180, 191–93, 196, 200
Hobbs, Helen G., 4, 231
Hoch, Daniel, 20, 25–28, 31, 42, 57–59, 137
Hogue, T. Wilson, 85
Holm, Maria, 20, 74
Holmes, L., 193, 194
Holmes, Letitia Ann, 63, 193, 194, 196, 200
Holmes, W. John, 193, 281
Homuth, Charles T., 187, 281, 287
Hood, Martha, 244, 282
Hoover, Doris, 182–84
Hoover, Lloyd, 280
Horner, Ralph Cecil, 84, 312
Horsch, John, 205
Horst, Isaac R., 29, 40, 62, 109
Hossler, Bill, 247
Hostetler, Daniel and Lydia (Shantz), 76, 166, 178, 179, 189, 192, 197
Hostetler, Ella Mae, 176, 192
Hostetler, Emma, 127, 140, 148, 151, 152, 162, 167, 192, 194
Hostetler, Rebecca, 140, 192, 282

Names Index

Hottel, W. S., 216
Howland, William, 126
Huber, Christian S., 27
Huber, Henry Albert, 74
Huber, Herbert Detwiler, 233, 296
Huber, Jacob, 27
Huffman, Jasper Abraham, 1, 47, 93, 97, 110, 132, 155, 166, 168, 205, 216–21, 226, 241, 242, 250, 251, 257, 258, 260, 266, 267, 277, 293, 294
Huffman, Lambert, 217, 221
Hunking, Leamon, 69
Hunsberger, Jacob (of New Dundee), 41, 42
Hunsberger, Jacob (of Vineland), 123
Huson, Frank and Catherine, 288, 299, 321
Hutchings, Charles and Ida (Goudie), 143, 144, 148
Hygema, Jacob, 219, 220, 294

Irish, Webster, 139, 175
Irvine, Reva J. (Ball), 167

Jackson, Edith, 249
James, Mildred, 214
Jesske, Theodore E., 145

Kaatz, C. G., 146
King, William Lyon Mackenzie, 237, 239
Kitching, John Norman, 74, 127, 132, 152, 162, 163, 173, 175, 190, 196, 202, 204, 222, 225, 231, 286
Kitching, Thomas, 212, 287
Kleinstauber, R. Wayne, 33, 34
Knapp, Martin Wells, 85
Knechtel, Samuel R., 113
Knowles, Olive N., 302
Kratz, Barbara, 123
Krauth, Charles F., 64, 75, 79, 80, 100, 101, 138, 164, 173, 179, 190, 244
Krauth, Fannie (Schroen), 64
Krauth, Gottlieb, 64
Krauth, Johanna, 179
Krauth, Lavina E., 64
Krauth, Susanna "Susan" (Sommer), 64

Kreutziger, Bernhard, 54
Krupp, John, 32
Kulbeck, Gloria Grace, 182, 183

Lageer, Audrey, 302
Lageer, E. Eileen, 3, 97, 154, 173, 295, 308
Lageer, Edith Myrtle, 250
Lageer, Ellis, 11, 185
Lageer, Kevin, 316
Lageer, Peter John, 250
Lageer, Russell G., 250
Lageer, Susannah (Doner), 250
Lageer, Wilmot E., 250
Lamb, Bertha, 287
Lambert, David U., 54
Lambert, George, 93, 94
Lambert, Norah, 257
Lambert, Rose, 93, 94, 253, 257
Lambert, Sidney, 94, 257
Lapp, John, 29
Laurier, Wilfrid, 2, 149
Lehman, Annie Alice (Heise), 252
Lehman, Arthur D., 281
Lehman, Flavius J., 282
Lehman, Isaac O., 252–53
Lehman, Lewis J., 140, 141, 219, 220
Lehman, Percy G., 234, 281, 294, 295, 299, 319, 321
Lehman, Violet, 299
Liele, George, 133
Litt, J. G., 128
Little, Jennie, 140, 282
Loop, Carrie, 140
Lucas, Ernest, 48, 87, 281
Luther, Martin, 48, 87, 275

Macdonald, Norman, 31
Mackey, Lloyd, 4
Mahan, Asa, 153
Mains, Lura (Laura), 42
Mann, W. E., 1
Markle, Mary, 140, 148, 152, 162–64, 172–74, 177, 180, 194–96
Martin, Jesse B. and Noah M. Bearinger, 232
Matheson, Frances, 140, 252, 282

McAlister, Robert E., 166, 176, 194
McClelland, Maud, 140, 162, 191, 209
McDonald, John A., 2
McDowell, James, 10, 144, 183, 196
McGavran, Donald, 2, 306
McHardy, Robert, 111
McLaren, R. J., 138, 213
McNally, Angus H., 114
McNally, John, 27, 114, 140, 277
McNally brothers (John and Angus), 2, 137
McQuarrie, Sarah, 140, 193
Mendell, Wilhelm Oscar, 74
Menno Simons, 28, 103
Mertens, Ina Dorcas, 249, 297
Meuser, August, 64
Miller, Barbara, 145
Miller, Christian R., 96, 105–7, 139, 150, 159, 166, 171, 180, 188–90, 196, 200
Miller, Elmina, 107, 188, 189, 190
Miller, Mary and Jacob, 77
Miller, Phoebe D., 56
Miller, Ruth, 189
Miller, Thomas W., 4, 161, 176, 192
Milsted, Charles, 281
Milsted, Evelyn (Gooding), 55, 299
Montgomery, Lucy Maud, 72
Morgan, Laura, 147
Morgan, Raymond G., 224, 225
Moss, John, 265
Motherwell, William, 239
Motz, Arnell, 2
Mowat, Oliver, 127
Moyer, Ada, 118, 174
Moyer, David H., 66
Moyer, Elmer B., 245, 281
Moyer, Esther "Hettie," 119, 179
Moyer, Franklin Wismer, 100, 123, 134
Moyer, Laura, 104
Moyer, Lizzie, 97
Moyer, Melissa, 182
Moyer, Menno, 101, 107
Moyer, Samuel A., 100, 101, 123, 127, 140, 181
Moyer, Samuel S., 40, 41
Moyer, William B., 137, 295

Moyles, Russell Gordon, 111
Murray, George A., 111, 192
Musselman, Harvey B., 174
Musselman, William B., 67, 68

Neill, Margaret "Maggie," 282, 286
Neill, Stephen, 48
Newell, William R, 276
Nienkirchen, Charles, 153

Oberholtzer, Jacob, 26, 27, 58
Oke, Edward, 85, 124
Olsen, Roger, 259, 275
Overhulser, Josephine (Ummel), 307

Palmer, Phoebe, 153
Panabaker, Cornelius Arthur, 17
Pannabecker, Anna, 29
Pannabecker, Cornelia Winnifred, 224, 306
Pannabecker, David, 17, 18, 29, 129, 321
Pannabecker, Earl Ray, 238
Pannabecker, Harold Ross, 224
Pannabecker, Jacob Nelson, 219, 220
Pannabecker, Lloyd, 220
Pannabecker, Oliver R., 125
Pannabecker, Ray P., 220, 321
Pannabecker, S. Floyd, 20, 109, 220
Pannabecker, Samuel and Martha (Cober), 38, 220
Perkins, John M. and Miriam, 191
Peterson, Eugene, 313
Phair, Robert, 149
Philpott, Peter W., 111, 112, 120, 128
Pike, Isaac, xii, 172, 201, 204, 225, 265
Pike, Russell J., 88, 281, 285
Pike, William Raymer, 172, 196, 201, 202
Pipher, Lewis Raymer, 280, 296
Pipher, Luella Mary, 128, 129
Pitts, Roy, 292
Pool, Sarah, 81, 96, 100, 124, 127, 140, 160, 167, 185, 187
Porter, David K., 171
Powers, George Maxwell, 282, 287, 311, 312
Powers, John, 52
Pritchett, Elizabeth A., 56, 116, 117

Names Index

Pritchett, Thomas, 117
Pugh, Albert, 157
Purdy, Margaret (Kercher) and William J., 271

Ramer, Lewis Peter, 139, 210
Ramseyer, Joseph Eicher, 53, 113
Rawlyk, George, 195
Raymer, Abraham, 26, 31, 52, 242
Raymer, Christian "Chris," 108, 100, 115, 135, 138, 142, 165, 166, 179, 190, 209
Raymer, Christina (Stouffer), 108
Raymer, Dan W., 156, 208
Raymer, Edith, 282, 311
Raymer, John and Sarah, 52
Raymer, Joseph, 242
Raymer, Levi and Fannie (Raymer), xii, 52, 130, 150, 268, 270
Raymer, Phoebe Ann (Moyer), 182
Raymer, Wilmot, 183
Redinger, Lauren K., 111
Rees, Seth Cook, 85
Reesor, Adah, 298
Reesor, Jacob "Jake," 214, 298
Reesor, Martha (Pike), 20, 74
Reesor, Ben, 185
Reesor, Peter, 158
Reesor, Thomas, 231, 236
Reeve, Ruby, 140, 192, 224
Reichard, Josiah H., 59, 116
Reichard, N. H., 129
Reimer, Jacob W., 239–40
Reimer, James, 317
Remington, Albert, 139
Remington, Blanche, 253
Rennie, Ian, xiii, 313, 318
Reynolds, Hiram F., 309
Rich, Nicholas W., 210, 258
Rickert, John, 27
Riel, Louis, 53
Rikoto brothers, Sakaba Tom and Zomi, 307
Ritchie, T. H., 292
Roberts, Benjamin T., 85
Roberts, Charles G. D., 211
Robinson, Margaret "Maggie," 182

Robinson, R., 122
Robson, Frank, 144
Roffe, Alfred W., 11, 128
Roth, David, 258
Rudd, Douglas, 167, 183
Rudy, Cora Mae, 119, 140, 156, 233
Rudy, Ella N., 156
Ruth, Christian Wismer, 112, 262, 291

Sage, Charles H., 26, 33
Salmon, John, 111, 153, 167, 170
Sanderson, S., 262
Sangster, William E., 87
Sapelak Fonds, David, 11, 219, 243, 254, 316
Sarkar, Pronoy, 308
Sauer, A. W., 146
Schaaf, Charlie, 166
Schantz, Nancy, 25, 26
Scheifele, Minerva, 180
Schell, Joshua, 79, 80, 108
Schlichter, Jacob, 54, 55
Schlichter, Samuel, 27, 42, 74, 242
Schlichter, Wesley, 54, 55, 116
Schlimm, Edgar, 186
Schneider, David B., 25
Schneider, Jacob "Yock," 16
Schroeder, William, 63, 67
Schroen, Eva Elizabeth, 64
Schwalm, Nicholas Hilton, 193, 281
Scott, Clifford I., 225, 250, 251, 257, 260, 288
Scott, R. J., 148
Sell, Henry T., 187, 205
Seymour, William, 164, 170, 199
Shantz, Ben, 61, 62
Shantz, Catherine (Hipple), xii
Shantz, Christian Martin, 74, 75, 140
Shantz, David Stauffer, 57, 59, 97, 139, 142
Shantz, Diana, 140
Shantz, Elias, 38
Shantz, Elmina, 188
Shantz, Harriet, 148
Shantz, Henry (MBiC minister), 151
Shantz, Henry (Mennonite Bishop), 74
Shantz, Herbert, 280

Names Index

Shantz, Isaac, 188
Shantz, Jacob B., xii, 204, 225
Shantz, Jacob Y., xii, 2, 143
Shantz, Lydia, 143
Shantz, Mary (Davidson), xi, 282, 310
Shantz, Abe, 143
Shantz, Joseph S., 239
Shantz, Norah, 224, 225, 271, 293
Shantz, Sidney Shupe, 237, 280, 295
Shantz, V. Clarence, 282
Shantz, Ward Montford, 109, 110, 172, 177, 185, 195, 197, 239, 295, 296
Shantz, William Albert, 96, 133, 282
Shaw, S. B., 85
Sheilds, Thomas Todhunter, 259
Shell, Joseph, 63
Sherk, Arthur F., 120
Sherk, Benjamin A., 132, 258
Sherk, Eldon T., 156
Sherk, Emma Lillian (Shelley), 201
Sherk, Ira Washington, 209, 224, 306
Sherk, J. Harold, 234, 237, 238, 281, 293–296
Sherk, J. Hubert, 265
Sherk, Jesse Ramer, 172, 196, 201
Sherk, Samuel (Michigan), 54
Sherk, Samuel (Sherkston), 57
Sherk, Sarah, xii
Sherk, Titus, 124, 210
Shisler, J., 124
Shoemaker, Aaron S., 166, 172, 189, 196
Shuert, Ernie D., 293
Shupe, Hattie, 156
Shupe, Peter, 95, 146, 165, 232
Sider, Cora May, 107
Sider, John Abram, 57, 98, 100, 122, 139, 175, 182
Sievenpiper, Ephraim, 79, 80, 138, 165, 174, 184, 204, 222, 225, 231, 234, 236, 244, 280, 310, 311
Sigsworth, John Wilkins, 83
Simmons, Mary Ann (Hallman), 81, 98
Simpson, Albert Benjamin, 3, 105, 134, 153, 276–78, 309
Sims, Albert, 85, 256, 262
Sinden, C. Isaac, 139, 223, 282
Slagle, Emanuel, 257–59

Smith, C. Henry, 32
Smith, Campbell B., 194
Smith, Clara Amelia, 56, 59, 116, 302
Smith, Orrin, 56, 116
Smith, Oswald J., 309
Smith, William and Mary, 56
Smith, William Edwin "Edd," 56, 59, 116
Snyder, Calvin F., 96
Snyder, Caroline Helena, 21, 250, 303, 319
Snyder, Jacob, 257
Snyder, Joseph B., 18
Snyder, L. C., 142
Snyder, Lydia, 21, 129, 276
Snyder, Oliver Bricker, 59, 90, 131, 132, 142, 156, 174, 210, 219
Sorenson, Faith (Lehman) and Thomas, 253
Spaetzel, Roy C., 166, 188
Spaetzel, Viola (Chambers), 188
Sprott, Henry and Jane, 105
Sprunger, John A., 94, 113
Srigley, Anna Melissa "Annie," 140
Stackhouse, John G., 4
Stadelbauer, W., 98
Stauffer, Harvey, 138
Stauffer, Isaac, 75, 76
Stauffer, Samuel Shelley, 55, 77, 139, 147, 148
Steckley, John Hoover, 60, 68, 102, 108, 111, 115, 183
Steckley, Mary, 181
Steinacher, C. Mark, xiii, 34
Steiner, Samuel J., xii, xiii, 9, 14, 15, 29, 30, 35, 84, 102, 109, 229, 231, 235, 238, 239, 267, 270, 271, 315, 316, 317
Stephenson, John G., 4
Sternall, Alvin, 186
Sternall, Irvin, 199
Sternall, Reuben Eby, 65, 176, 185, 186, 196, 199, 203
Steuernagle, Conrad and Magdalena, 65, 185
Stewart, Charles, 239
Stewart, William, 126

Stoltz, August Fried, 79, 81, 82, 90, 93, 94, 113
Stoltz, Caroline, 94
Storms, Dorwin J., 106, 202
Storms, Everek Richard, 10, 61, 70, 92, 93, 97, 147, 154, 203, 267, 274, 277, 305, 308
Storms, Franklin Webster, 106
Storms, Paul L., 106, 156
Storms, Richard and Fanny, 106
Stouffer, Abraham, 158
Stouffer, Abraham S., III, 225
Stouffer, Abram S., IV, 225
Stouffer, Allen Phillip, 160, 249, 319
Stouffer, Louie, 213, 298
Stouffer, Noah, 156
Strycker, Arnold, 18
Strycker, Catharine, 18
Strycker, Henry and Frances "Fanny" (Wanner), 19
Swalm, Ernest J "Ernie," 79, 237
Swalm, Luella, 140, 147

Taylor, Donald, 124
Taylor, Hudson, 309
Taylor, William, 95, 309
Thede, Dora, 268
Thompson, Hattie, 174, 262
Thompson, Sister, 174, 262
Thomson, Mildred (Reesor), 214
Traub, Alvin, 85, 199, 272–75, 315
Traub, George, 124
Troupe, James, 100, 192
Troxel, John, 119
Troxell, Ida, 268
Troyer, Christian, 26, 31, 52, 102, 242

Ummel, Joseph, 132, 229, 307
Upper, Peter, 55
Urquhart, Thomas, 126

Vance, Archibald, 16

Wagner, Louis Henry, 128
Wambold, Isaac, 231
Wanner, Catharine, 17, 74, 231
Wanner, George M., 19

Wanner, Henry, Jr, 19
Wanner, Henry, Sr, 18, 23
Wanner, John, 17
Wanner, Nancy Strycker, 17, 18, 22, 74, 116, 30, 142, 321
Wanner, Tobias W., 17–19, 23
Wanner, Veronica "Fanny," 19
Ward, Alfred George, 162–66, 169, 170–74, 176–78, 180, 193, 194, 196, 199, 200, 211
Ward, C. Morse, 176, 195
Warder, Alfred George, 106, 162, 244
Warner, Daniel, 110–11
Warner, George, 19
Warner, Samuel, 19
Warren, Max, 48
Watson, George Douglas, 73, 85, 122, 123, 288
Weaver, Katie (Bredemus), 253
Weaver, Margaret E., 56, 116
Weaver, Peter Nelson and Phoebe (Miller), 56
Webb, George, 107, 111, 112, 127
Weber, Andrew, 146
Weber, Christina "Tina" (Sherk), 168, 185
Weber, Eldon D., 18
Weber, Ephraim, 146
Weber, Moses, 98, 137, 139, 168, 183, 185
Wesley, Charles, 72, 85
Wesley, John, 3, 44, 46, 48, 72, 85–89, 99, 102, 103, 110, 153
White, Mary Ann/Anne, 127, 140
Wickware, C. B., 27
Wideman, Caspar, 102
Wideman, Kenneth, 60
Wideman, Tobias, 168
Wildfong, Elijah and Nancy, 29
Wildfong, Sarah, 20, 29, 249, 319
Williams, Elizabeth, 148
Williamson, Jonathan S., 113
Wilson, Henry, 276
Wilson, Mary Ann, xi, 25, 49
Wilson, Woodrow, 257
Winger, Dorothy (Gooding), 299
Winter, Ralph D., 248

Wiseman, Peter, 295
Wismer, Arthur J., 106
Wismer, Daniel, 20, 27–30, 32, 41, 74, 75, 109
Wismer, Henry S., 75, 90, 109, 111, 114, 134, 135
Wismer, Lucinda (Miller), 114
Witmer, Joseph, 21
Witmer, Susannah, 21, 302
Wood, James Smith, 291
Wood, John A., 85
Wood, Walter E. and Mary (Dayhoff), 252
Woodsworth, James S., 144
Wyant, Isaiah, 140

Yates, William H., 273, 281, 291, 295, 296

Yeager, W. J., 106
Yoder, Abraham Bixler, 132, 210, 219, 226, 251, 254, 257, 258, 260, 291
Young, Daisy, 107

Zavitz, Elman, 124
Zavitz, John, 25
Zeller, Amanda, 156
Ziegler, Daniel G., 95
Zimmerman, Reuben J., 111
Zook, Abraham F. and Eunice F. (Lehman), 253
Zook, John Roel, 118
Zook, Menno P., 118
Zyner, M. A., 27

Subject Index

Africa, 112, 224, 253, 320
Alberta, 38, 136, 142, 149, 197, 198, 247, 310, 315, 318, 320
alcohol (drink, liquor), 2, 31, 117, 129, 247
altar (mourner's bench, penitent's bench), viii, 69, 80, 81, 115, 123, 149, 176, 246
Altona, ON, 60, 159, 160, 297, 298
American Civil War, 84, 228
anoint with oil, 63
apostasy, 221, 277
Apostles' Creed, 275, 278
Arkansas, US, 32
Armenia (Turkish Armenia), 94, 95, 117, 270
Arminian theology, 5, 73, 84, 85, 88, 103, 273, 277, 313
Arran Township, Bruce County, ON, 63, 193
Articles of Faith (MBiC), 46, 85, 105, 108, 177, 179, 199, 200, 204, 225, 227, 246, 247, 274
Assiniboia, District of, NWT, 143, 148
assurance of salvation, 5, 26, 61, 86, 115, 314
assurance of sanctification, 40
Aurora, ON, 150
Ayrshire, Scotland, 16, 31

backsliders reclaimed, 69, 80, 90, 105, 115, 126
Baden, Germany, 201
Baden, Wilmot Township, Waterloo County, ON, 188

Balarampur, West Bengal, India, 252
Ballantrae, Ayrshire, Scotland, 15
ban (shunning), 28, 277
baptism, 28–30, 43, 44, 46, 63, 82, 90, 148, 162, 163, 291
baptism, believer's, 163, 165
baptism, immersion, 160, 246, 277
baptism, trine, 277
Baptism and Fullness (Stott), 88
baptism of fire, 80, 170
baptism (with, in, of) the Holy Spirit, 88, 153, 154, 164, 165, 168–71, 173, 177, 181, 195, 199, 206, 210, 211, 216, 320
Beamsville, ON, 213
Beeton, ON, 158
Belleville, ON, 158
Bentinck Township, Grey County, ON, 61, 182
Berlin/ Kitchener, Waterloo County, ON, 2, 18, 21, 27, 32, 36, 38, 51, 59, 67, 74, 76, 83, 94, 95, 108–110, 115–19, 127–30, 140, 143, 146, 152, 156, 162, 164, 165, 167, 174, 188, 197, 202, 206, 254
Berne, IN, 53, 94, 113
Bethlehem, PA, 207
Bible readings, 149, 210, 216, 233, 279
Bible schools/colleges, vii, 47, 103, 104, 205, 221, 233, 245, 293–95
Bihar, India, 252
binational church, 1, 3, 5, 9, 10, 32, 262, 323
bishop(s), 29, 32, 44, 59, 65, 102, 133, 134, 155, 156, 171, 204

361

Subject Index

Black Creek, Niagara Region, ON, 25
Blair (now part of Cambridge), ON, 2, 27, 114, 140, 303
Blair Memorial Cemetery, Waterloo County, ON, 303
Blenheim Township, Oxford County, ON, 27, 41, 156, 188
Bloomingdale, Woolwich Township, ON, 16, 19, 25
Bosanquet Township, Lambton County, ON, 27
Box Grove, Markham Township, ON, 250
Brandon, MB, 162
Brazil, 9
Breslau, ON, 21, 22, 28, 36, 37, 41, 43, 70, 78, 96, 116, 130, 142, 156, 161, 165, 201, 264, 274
Bridgeburg, NY, 107
Bridgeport, ON, 188, 265
Britain/ British Empire, 14, 84, 121, 158, 223, 230
British Columbia, 201, 319, 320
British North America, 23
Brockville, ON, 295
Brown City, MI, 66, 74, 98, 116, 204, 302
Bruce County, ON, 26, 62, 68, 193, 194
Bruce Peninsula, 63, 98
Buffalo, NY, 101, 107

Caistor, Lincoln County, ON, 62
Calcutta/ Kolkata, India, 252
Calgary, AB, 142, 148
Cambridge, ON, xiii, 18, 35
Campbell River, BC, 201
Campbellford, Northumberland County, ON, 158
camp meetings, vii, viii, 39, 67, 78, 81–85, 104, 106, 169, 170, 264–266, 268, 314
Canada West (Ontario), 9, 14, 52, 56, 145, 158
Cape Chin, Bruce County, ON, 63
Carlock, IL, 257
Caro, Tuscola County, MI, 302
Carrick Township, Bruce County, ON, 61

Cashtown, Simcoe Township, Simcoe County, 193
catechism(s), 200, 205, 264, 272–79, 286, 312
Cayuga, Haldimand County, ON, 17
Cedar Grove, Markham Township, ON, 302
Center Valley, PA, 272
Centreville, Waterloo Township, ON, 265
charismatic gifts, 137, 153, 163, 205, 217–18, 311
Chicago, IL, 194
Chicopee, Waterloo Township, ON, 21
Chile, 118
China, 96, 236
Chippawa Hill, Bruce County, ON, 63, 65
church growth, 8, 24, 144, 154, 155, 197–99, 304, 305, 317, 318
church history, xiii, 44, 163, 187, 205, 313, 318
church planting, 48, 49, 120, 144, 152, 163, 190, 316
circle (ring) fellowship, 66, 68, 69, 82
city mission movement, 3, 121, 122, 269
city mission work, viii, 11, 121, 124, 126, 127, 227, 318
Clarence Center, NY, 29
class (college, school, Sunday School), 35, 114, 159, 205, 266, 267, 295, 313, 318
class (Methodist structure), 45, 46, 49, 58, 63, 66, 86, 102, 141, 170, 227, 247, 253, 314
class (social), 89, 126
clergy, xi, 50, 262
Cleveland, OH, 94, 207
Clinton Township, Lincoln County, ON, 26
Colbourne Township, Huron County, ON, 19
Collingwood, ON, 105
colonies, colonization, 14, 15, 23, 158, 238, 239
Columbus, OH, 178
comity, 252

Subject Index

conditional/unconditional, 44, 46–50, 137, 141, 207, 226, 282, 284, 285, 290, 310
Conestoga River, 76
conference (polity), 44, 45, 47–49, 93, 104, 112, 119, 130–132, 141, 155, 170, 173, 174, 204, 221, 227
congregationalism, 7, 8, 26, 44, 104, 268, 317
connectional theology, 8, 44, 47, 104, 160, 317
conversion, 5, 22, 27–29, 39, 40, 61, 72, 74, 79–82, 90, 169, 243, 292, 307, 312, 318
Coopersburg, PA, 90, 96
creeds (articles of faith, confessions), 89, 177, 199, 200, 233, 234, 246, 275, 278
Creemore, ON, 191
Cressman Mennonite Cemetery, 303
culture, 4, 5, 8, 42, 44, 81, 104, 131, 144, 229, 238, 248, 285, 313, 316, 317
culture, theology of, 81, 131, 317
Cumberland, County, PA, 18

Dayton, OH, 168, 217
deacon/deaconess, 28, 44–46, 91, 92, 94, 102, 151, 210, 269
Deansville (Brown City), MI, 54
decrees of God, 277
Deeper Life (Keswick) movement, 3, 86, 91, 93, 134, 153, 163, 167, 168, 170, 199, 206, 216, 294
denomination-building, 101, 102, 133, 157
depression (economic), 31, 254, 263, 279, 286, 298, 308, 309, 311, 321
Dickson Hill, Markham Township, York County, 60, 265
Didsbury, AB, 1, 80, 127, 142, 143, 146–148
disciplines, 37, 39, 42, 44, 45, 48, 90, 91, 102, 109, 120, 137, 168, 171, 173–175, 177, 179, 180, 199, 204, 227, 231, 247, 248, 284, 295, 305, 312

district superintendent (UMC official), 10, 31, 44, 160, 234, 321
districts (in a Conference), 8, 44, 83, 90, 137–39, 141–143, 149, 265, 273, 280, 281, 310
Doon, Waterloo County, ON, 20, 27, 98, 102
Dordrecht Confession (1632), 28, 91, 103, 238, 278
Dundalk, ON, 142
Dundas Junction, Toronto, 121, 122, 209, 304
Durham Region (formerly Ontario County), ON, 60, 159

East Gwillimbury Township, York County, ON, 59
Eastern Transvaal, 253
Eastwood, Renfrewshire, Scotland, 16
Edmonton, AB, 81, 124, 147, 149, 318
Egremont Township, Grey County, 142
elder, eldership, 4, 10, 39, 44–46, 50, 279
elder, presiding, 5, 10, 39, 44, 46, 50, 59, 78, 108, 119, 137, 142, 172, 222, 265
Elkhart, IN, 9, 92, 251, 258
Elkland, PA, 187
Elkton, MI, 53
Elmira, ON, 11, 189
Elmwood, ON, 62, 64, 162, 163, 194, 272
EMCC studies/ further studies, xiv, 3, 4, 8, 82, 90, 156, 179, 196, 244, 253, 260, 273
England, 40, 88, 269
English (language), 20, 22, 24–26, 30, 47, 70, 92, 103, 114, 115, 144, 230, 238
Erie, Lake, 57, 58, 100
Europe, 224, 228, 239
Evangelicalism, 3, 85, 317
evangelism, evangelistic work, 8, 26, 39, 42, 43, 48–50, 52, 63, 102, 107, 111, 112, 114, 115, 120, 139, 140, 143, 154, 186, 199, 200, 230, 244, 264, 288, 291, 292, 305, 311, 312, 317, 318

Subject Index

Evangelist(s), viii, 42, 77, 81, 82, 140, 141, 190, 195, 261, 266, 291
excommunicated/ disfellowshipped, silenced, turned out, 26, 32, 57, 109, 177, 223
Executive Committee (MBiC), 5, 92, 93, 168, 206, 207, 226, 227, 241, 242, 251, 254, 272, 274, 286, 294

faith, divine healing, 44, 63, 105, 123, 161, 196, 199, 213, 276, 278, 319
fellowship meeting(s), 79–81, 247
Ferndale, Bruce County, ON, 63
field/circuit, 38, 45, 46, 82, 141, 151, 181, 187, 214, 268, 309
First Mennonite Cemetery (East End Mennonite, Kitchener), 64, 129, 189
Fisher's Mill, Waterloo Township, ON, 17
Floradale, Woolwich Township, ON, 27
Florida, US, 190, 200, 320
foreign country analogy, 4, 10, 44, 48, 71, 83, 93, 97, 121, 127, 195, 233, 267, 275, 292, 313
Forget, District of Assiniboia, NWT, 148
Freeport, Waterloo Township, ON, 25
Frontenac County, ON, 83
fundamentalism, 42, 43, 47, 111, 221, 229, 260, 273, 279, 294

Galt (now part of Cambridge), ON, 16, 18, 39, 140, 161
General Assembly (EMCC), 131
General Conferences, 9, 44
General Conference Forward Movement, 241, 242
General Superintendent (UMC), 93
generational change, 49, 50, 121, 137, 155, 171, 184, 195, 196, 207, 267
Geneva, Gladwin Township, Gladwin County, MI, 54
Georgian Bay, 51, 62, 84, 261
German (language), 9, 14, 17, 20, 24, 25, 47, 56, 61, 70, 75, 76, 80, 91, 103, 109, 114, 115, 144, 145, 230, 239, 240
Germany, 64, 65, 201

Glenallen (Glen Allen) Peel Township, Wellington County, 75, 76
Gormley, Whitchurch Township, York County, ON, 180, 182, 225, 263, 265, 296, 299
Goshen, IN, 251, 258
grace, 5, 55, 72, 80, 84, 289, 313
Grand Rapids, MI, 53
Grand River, 20, 40, 41, 188, 277
Grange Hall, Nottawasaga Township, Simcoe County, 52
Greenwood, St. Clair County, MI, 54–56, 59, 74
Guelph, ON, 16, 18
Guelph Township, Wellington County, ON, 16
Gwillimbury. *See* East Gwillimbury.

Haldimand County, ON, 15, 17
Hamilton, ON, xi, 112, 120, 123, 179, 213
handicaps on growth, 6
Hanover, ON, 152
harvest theology, 2, 306
Hay Township, Huron County, ON, 25, 27
Heise Hill Cemetery, Whitchurch Township, York County, ON, 182
helper(s) (MBiC officials), 11, 38, 41, 46, 49
Hespeler (now part of Cambridge), ON, 16–18, 20–22, 27, 29, 35, 36
higher criticism, 217, 218, 221
holiness conventions, 89, 97, 98, 112
holiness movement, 3, 73, 84, 86, 164, 171, 199, 201, 203, 215, 314
holiness theology, 85–90, 134, 168, 169, 196, 206, 258, 260, 277
Holland, 28
Holmes Settlement, Bruce County, ON, 63, 193
Home Council (UMS), 306
Howick Township, Huron County, ON, 61
Huron County, ON, 26
Huron, Lake, 53, 60, 67
hymnbooks, 90, 92, 110, 156, 300, 312

Subject Index

Idaho, US, 294
Igbeti (formerly Igbetti), Oyo State, Nigeria, 307
Illinois, US, 219, 220, 258
India, 94, 127, 192, 224, 252, 282, 309
Indiana, US, 29, 32, 54, 103, 104, 130, 132, 219
infant and maternal mortality, 17, 19, 106
Ingersoll, Middlesex County, ON, 158
International Sunday School Lessons, 70
interpretation of history, xiii, xiv, 4, 8, 85
Inverness, Scotland, 25

Jamaica, 9, 133
Japan, 269
Jebba, Kwara State, Nigeria, 307
Johannesburg, South Africa, 253
Jordan Cemetery, Lincoln County, ON, 58
Jordan Station, Lincoln County, ON, 298
just war theology, 233, 315

Kent County, MI, 53
Kettle Point Reserve, ON, 271
Kilsyth, Sullivan Township, ON, 66, 197, 206
Kingston, ON, 85
Kinsail (fictional town), 13
Kitchener (formerly Berlin), ON, 16, 21, 192, 201, 250, 265, 296, 302, 319
Kurtzville, Wellington County, ON, 75

laity, xi, 132, 273, 289
Lancaster County, PA, 18
law of God, 86, 87, 313
leakage, 6, 104
legalism, 7, 28, 81, 114, 247, 275, 313
Lexington, Waterloo County, ON, 25
Liberia, 95, 167, 191–93, 200
Lincoln County, ON, 25, 26, 305
Lincolnville, Whitchurch Township, York County, ON, 60
Liverpool, England, 118
local help (MBiC official), 38, 41, 60, 137, 141, 182, 231, 280

local memory, histories, xiii, xiv, 5, 6, 12, 55, 185, 192, 214, 265, 270
Lord's Prayer, 275, 277, 278
Lord's Supper (communion), 29, 32, 46, 58, 80, 115, 124, 141, 148, 164
Los Angeles, CA, 136, 148, 170
Louisville, KS, 149
Louisville, KT, 127
Lower Canada (Quebec), 14, 23
lower criticism, 217

Manitoba, 144, 145, 162, 238
Manitoulin Island, ON, 2, 67, 214
Mannheim, Wilmot Township, Waterloo County, ON, 27, 98
Mapleton Township, Wellington County, ON, 75
Marcham, Berkshire, England, 15
Mariposa (fictional town), 158
Markham (town), ON, 20, 158, 183, 184, 190, 194, 201, 202, 226
Markham Township, York County, ON, 20, 51, 52, 74, 79, 83, 102, 140, 157, 167
Maryborough Township, Wellington County, ON, 75
Meaford, ON, 62
membership (church), 2, 6, 7, 28, 43, 44, 63, 159
membership, statistics, 10, 91, 109, 138–40, 197, 198, 221, 227, 287, 292, 303, 304, 316
mergers, unions, 112, 260–62
Michigan, US, 22, 38, 53–56, 58, 59, 98, 116, 119, 129, 134, 143, 204, 220, 302
Miller Lake, Bruce County, ON, 63
ministerial conventions, 11, 69, 70, 72, 96, 98, 108, 114, 160, 232, 233, 243–49, 272, 275, 288, 293, 295, 314, 315
mission of the church, 48, 93, 95, 131, 199, 245, 314
missionary newsletters, reports, 117, 253, 254, 308
missionary strategy, 95, 121, 133, 265, 308

modernism, liberalism (theology), 32, 44, 47, 217, 221, 259–61, 273, 274, 294
Mount Forest, ON, 184, 186
Mount Joy, Markham Township, York County, ON, 140, 208
Mozambique (formerly Portuguese East Africa), 253

Nappanee, IN, 130
Natal, South Africa, 201
Nebraska, US, 252, 294
New Brunswick, 23, 84, 211
New Carlisle, OH, 225
New Dundee, ON, 27, 54, 199, 265, 296
New France, 14
New Hamburg, ON, 53, 74
New York (city), 96, 178, 189
New York (state), 33, 56
Newfoundland, 42
Niagara Escarpment, 101
Niagara Peninsula, 25, 26, 57, 202, 277, 290
Niagara Regional Municipality, 158
Niagara River, 57
Nigeria, 9, 14, 49, 70, 118, 127, 131, 141, 167, 169, 192, 246
Nipissing, Lake, 298
Nith River, 43, 265
Niverville, MB, 143
nonconformity (to the world), 5, 70, 87, 216, 229, 246, 247, 313, 315, 317
non-resistant, 5, 11, 197, 229–33, 236, 237, 245, 249, 257, 277, 312, 315
Norfolk County, ON, 26
North America, vii, 23, 28, 42, 44, 84, 94, 104, 111, 121, 164, 193, 255, 307
North Bay, ON, 127
North Dumfries Township, Waterloo County, ON, 27
North Norwich, Oxford County, ON, 56
North West Territories, 143, 145, 148, 150
Norwich, Oxford County, ON, 56
Nottawasaga Township, Simcoe County, ON, 105, 191, 201
Nova Scotia, 23, 73, 84

Nyack, NY, 186, 199

oaths, 32, 246, 247, 277
Ohio, US, 45, 147, 225, 227, 254, 321
Oklahoma, US, 201
Ontario County (Durham Region), ON, 159
Ontario Lake, 57, 101, 123
open communion, 32, 58
order of salvation (*ordo salutis*), 277
organized religion, 2, 133
orphanages, orphans, 94, 95, 106, 113, 117, 149, 189, 219, 270, 286
Oshawa, ON, 182
Ottawa, ON, 231, 235, 239
Owen Sound, ON, 31, 148, 184–86, 191, 197, 220
Oxford County, ON, 26
Oxford, England, 85

Parkdale, Toronto, 189
Patigi, Kwara State, Nigeria, 118
Pembroke, ON, 186
Pennsylvania, US, 14, 18, 23, 26, 58, 112, 158, 239, 253, 257
Pentecostal movement, 4, 149, 153–55, 161, 166, 169, 195, 197–200, 203, 228, 323
Perth County, ON, 26
Perth East Township, Perth County, ON, 188
Philippines, 229
Pike Bay, Bruce County, ON, 63
Pine Tree Harbour, Bruce County, ON, 63, 193
Pittsburgh, PA, 129
Port Colborne, Welland County (now Regional Municipality of Niagara), ON, 57
Port Elgin, ON, 2, 19, 29, 60, 62, 63, 66–68, 101, 127, 201
Port Huron, MI, 59, 116, 302
post-modernism, 310
prayer, 55, 80, 89, 97, 115, 123, 157, 168, 187, 193, 196, 213, 215, 230, 246, 249, 254, 278, 287, 288, 291, 298, 308, 314, 319–21

Subject Index

prayer meetings, 25, 28, 43, 45–47, 62, 64, 65, 76, 122, 124, 126–28, 164, 166, 167, 178, 194, 202, 208, 267, 288
probationers' reading course, 74, 85, 90, 91, 101–4, 110, 133, 134, 187, 191, 196, 204, 205, 226, 241, 245, 272, 294, 295
Preston (now part of Cambridge), ON, 18, 19, 22
Proton Township, Grey County, ON, 142
protracted meetings, viii, 10, 39, 89, 207, 314
Purulia, West Bengal, India, 252
Puslinch Township, Wellington County, ON, 17, 20, 38, 224

quarterly conference, 41, 45–47, 80, 119, 123, 142, 149, 151, 165, 168, 170, 204, 212–14, 242, 264, 268, 288, 300, 314
Quebec (Lower Canada), 14
Queen's Park (Ontario Provincial Legislature), 127

reference committee (Ontario MBiC), 170, 174, 175, 206, 222, 225, 227, 236, 261, 263, 265, 266, 273, 286, 288, 289
Reformed/ Calvinist theology, 42, 43, 47, 73, 86–88, 93, 103, 134, 160, 276, 316, 317
regeneration, 86, 245, 246, 277, 291
Regina, SK, 149
Renfrewshire, Scotland, 16
rescue missions, 167, 187, 286, 287
respectability, 33
revival, 10, 24, 32, 73, 75, 76, 83, 84, 89, 97, 104, 154, 159, 164, 209, 291, 311
revivalism, xiii, 8, 24–26, 39, 57, 58, 72, 102, 104, 106, 195, 199, 202, 215, 247, 267, 291, 292, 317
Riverdale Cemetery, Toronto, 127
Riverdale Park, Toronto, 127
Rochester, NY, 186

Rosebank, Wilmot Township, Waterloo County, ON, 20
Rosebud River, 147
Roseville, North Dumfries Township, Waterloo County, ON, 27
Rosthern, District of Saskatchewan, NWT, 146
rural areas, 2, 33, 35, 36, 52, 112, 125, 130, 158, 197, 304
rural churches, vii, 2, 31, 47, 108, 121, 124, 158, 239, 294, 305, 318
Russia, 143, 228, 236, 238, 239

Saddler's Settlement, Bruce County, ON, 63
St. Clair County, MI, 53, 292
St. Thomas, ON, 77
Salka, Niger State, Nigeria, 307
salvation, 52, 70, 73, 74, 80, 82, 86, 89, 90, 106, 115, 128, 161, 202, 219, 275, 291, 313
salvation, assurance of, 5, 26, 61, 86, 115, 314
sanctification, 52, 70, 80, 82, 85, 86, 89, 90, 93, 103, 115, 162, 168–71, 174, 178, 195, 204, 206, 215, 216, 245, 246, 277, 288, 314
Sanctuary Park Cemetery, Port Elgin, ON, 64
Saskatchewan, 53, 144, 148, 149, 239
Saugeen Reserve, 62
Saugeen Shores, ON, 60
Saugeen Township, Bruce County, ON, 60, 62, 185
Sault Ste. Marie, ON, 189
Schneider Creek, 277
schools, 37, 47, 102, 129, 158, 201, 213, 219, 220, 245
Scotland, 14, 16
Scott Township, Ontario County (Durham Region), 142
Scriptures (Bible), 3, 5, 22, 68, 74, 82, 86, 103, 110, 117, 119, 131, 168, 171, 182, 210, 215–17, 233, 234, 245, 267, 275, 276, 279, 285, 291, 298
Second Line Cemetery, Nottawasaga Township, Simcoe County, 52

Subject Index

secret societies/lodges, 32, 70, 80, 110, 114, 247
Sherkston, Welland County, ON, 57, 58, 123
shouting (religious practice), viii, 60, 79, 80, 97, 124, 137, 155, 185
Simcoe County, ON, 24, 26, 51, 59
Simcoe, Lake, 158
sinless perfection, 277
South Cayuga Cemetery, Haldimand County, ON, 17
South Cayuga, Haldimand County, ON, 58
South Norwich, Oxford County, ON, 56, 223
Southampton, Bruce County, ON, 60, 186
Spain, 237
Speed River, 17, 18, 35
splits, divisions, 4, 24, 26, 30, 32, 33, 62, 75, 84, 109, 113, 156, 168, 169, 183, 184, 187, 205, 211, 258, 261, 316
stationing committee, 11, 39, 49, 50, 59, 63, 120, 142, 183, 184, 187, 188, 190, 290
Stayner, ON, 140, 167, 182, 186, 250
steward(s) (MBiC official), 45, 46, 141, 151, 210
Stoney Point Reserve, ON, 271
Stouffville, ON, 5, 13–15, 55, 79, 83, 108, 150, 157–59, 168, 212, 213, 225, 287, 290, 293, 296, 297, 301, 302
Stouffville Municipal Cemetery, 212, 214, 321
Stratford, ON, 274
Sullivan Township, Grey County, ON, 42
Sunday school(s), 8, 30, 32, 37, 50, 68, 70, 114, 159, 214, 242, 266, 267, 286, 287, 291, 300, 304–6, 312
Sunday School Conventions, 70, 160, 212
Sunday School Superintendent (MBiC official), 46, 68, 141, 151
Sunnidale Township, Simcoe County, ON, 52, 130, 268
superintendent of youth, 268
Syria, 309

tabernacle/tent meetings, viii, 43, 66, 107, 139, 146–148, 162, 188, 264, 265
Tantramar Marsh, NB, 211
temperance, 31, 70, 117, 235
testimony, 3, 7, 55, 57, 73, 74, 81, 87, 89, 95, 105, 122, 124, 168, 169, 187, 191, 202, 210, 218, 319
testimony meetings, 26–28, 30, 55, 57, 74, 184, 314
theological education, 7, 8, 102, 110, 134, 199, 205, 218, 244, 262, 267, 293
Thorold, Welland County, 158
tobacco, 2, 31, 70, 81, 94, 247
tongues-speaking, 44, 155, 161–163, 165–172, 176, 178, 181, 183, 186, 194–96, 199, 201, 202, 207
Toronto, ON, 13, 20–22, 74, 107, 111, 112, 118, 120, 121, 123, 126–29, 139, 141–43, 149–51, 157, 161, 162, 165, 174, 197, 231, 237, 249, 256, 302, 303
tradition(s)/custom(s), 3, 8, 33, 89, 210, 233, 246, 247, 274, 275, 317, 321
Tsonga (formerly Shonga), Kwara State, Nigeria, 224
Tuberculosis (TB), 56, 80, 190, 214
Tuckersmith Township, Huron County, ON, 303
Tungan Magajiya ("TM"), Niger State, Nigeria, 220
Turkey, 94, 95, 106, 117, 223, 224, 252
Twenty Mile Creek, 25, 57

Uhthoff, Severn Township, Simcoe County, ON, 150
Union School, Hespeler, 36
Union Station, Toronto, 143
United States of America, xii, 3, 9, 31, 44, 92, 145, 226, 229, 257, 266, 269
United States census, 56
unity, 9, 69, 109, 206, 227, 243, 251, 256, 257, 314
Upper Canada (Ontario), 9, 14–16, 23, 56

Subject Index

urban populations, 2, 33, 90, 125, 130, 154, 197, 227, 292, 304
uses of the past, 4
Uxbridge, Ontario County (Durham Region), 142

Verona Mills, MI, 21, 303
Vineland, Lincoln County (Niagara Region), ON, 100, 101, 106, 112, 140, 179, 192, 235, 298

Walkerton, ON, 194
Wallace, Wallace Township, Perth County, ON, 75
war(s), 2, 11, 14, 71, 84, 115, 155, 160, 197, 198, 220, 223–26, 228–38, 250, 252, 255, 257, 263, 267, 270, 271, 279, 293, 298, 313, 315,
war relief, humanitarian service, 95, 226, 229, 230, 232, 236, 237, 257, 293
Wasaga Beach, ON, 150
washing the saints' feet (foot washing), 7, 46, 80, 141, 164, 244, 246, 274, 277, 313
Washington, DC, US, 257
Washington, US, 294, 320
Waterloo County (Waterloo Region), ON, 12–18, 22, 25–27, 42, 60, 94, 113, 129, 157, 189, 273, 303
Waterloo Temperance Convention, 117
Waterloo Township, Waterloo County, ON, 14, 16–23
Waterloo (town), ON, 201

Welland, Welland County, ON, 55
Welland County, ON, 26, 33
Wellington County, ON, 15, 220
Wesleyan holiness theology, 3, 5, 84–86, 134, 168, 197, 206, 258, 260, 277, 313, 317
West Africa, 224
Whitchurch Township, York County, ON, 128, 157, 158, 231
Whitchurch-Stouffville, ON, 158
Wichita, KS, 294
Wilmot Township, Waterloo County, ON, 59, 77, 188
Winnipeg, MB, 13, 144, 145, 148, 162, 163, 189, 194, 197, 201, 202, 209
Winterbourne, Woolwich Township, Waterloo County, ON, 25, 40
women preachers, viii, ix, 42, 43, 46, 64, 81, 108, 187, 190, 196, 200, 206, 224, 243, 269, 271, 273, 305, 318
women's reading course, 191
Woodland Cemetery, Kitchener, ON, 201
Woolwich, Township, Waterloo County, ON, 16, 21, 38
Worldliness (cf. non-conformity), 33, 70, 71, 73, 81, 234, 238, 247, 259, 275

Yale, MI, 54, 116
York County (York Region), ON, 25, 26, 33, 305

Zimbabwe (formerly Rhodesia), 253
Zurich, Huron County, ON, 53

www.ingramcontent.com/pod-product-compliance
Lightning Source LLC
Chambersburg PA
CBHW071757300426
44116CB00009B/1107